AF522344

Crimes in Cyber Space-Scams and Frauds

Crimes in Cyber Space-Scams and Frauds

Satish Kumar

Crimes in Cyber Space-Scams and Frauds

ISBN 978-93-5111-913-5

Published in 2016 in India by

RANDOM PUBLICATIONS

4376-A/4B, Gali Murari Lal, Ansari Road
New Delhi-110 002
Phone : +9111-43580356, 011-23289044, 011-43142548
e-mail: sales@randompublications.com,
info@randompublications.com, randomexports@gmail.com

Reprinted 2022

Type Setting by : Friends Media, Delhi-110089
Digitally Printed at : Replika Press Pvt. Ltd.

Preface

The aggregation of Internet, Intranets and the World Wide Web is dubbed as cyberspace. The Internet has opened up a virtual heaven for the people for both good and bad, native to interact with lot of diverse cultures and demographics.

Crime, in modern times this term doesn't have any universally accepted definition, but one can define crime, also called an offence as an act harmful not only to some individual, but also to the community or the state also known as public wrong. Such acts are forbidden and punishable by law. What is a criminal offence is defined by criminal law of each country. While many countries have a crime catalogue known as the criminal code however in some common law countries no such comprehensive statute exists.

Cyber crime is the most recent type of crime, which affects many people. This is the biggest challenge for police, prosecutors and lawmakers. If we do not wake up now, we would be more spectators in cyber world. The criminal provisions deal with offences such as tampering with source code, hacking into computer systems, publishing of obscene information and misuse of licenses and digital signature etc.

Internet is the fastest technique on earth that one can find these days and for everything it is the best solution that people consider looking into. It has all the benefits and advantages like communication, advertisement, online movie and songs downloads, emailing, instant messaging and searching out the concerns and issues there are plenty of things that internet has got wrong as well. There are different kinds of internet scams and frauds that are happening and one needs to be very careful. This is something that has been bothering individuals and organizations ever since internet was introduced and many a time, simple things could make you a victim even when you are unaware of it.

The present book aims to make humble effort to understand the crime onset prevention and management in the digital world.

– ***Author***

Contents

1

Cyber Crime

Most reports, guides or publications on cyber crime begin by defining the term "cyber crime". One common definition describes cyber crime as any activity in which computers or networks are a tool, a target or a place of criminal activity. One example for an international approach is Art. 1.1 of the Draft International Convention to Enhance Protection from Cyber Crime and Terrorism (CISAC) that points out that cyber crime refers to acts in respect to cyber systems.

Some definitions try to take the objectives or intentions into account and define cyber crime more precisely, defining cyber crime as "computer-mediated activities which are either *illegal or considered illicit* by certain parties and which can be conducted *through global electronic networks*". These more refined descriptions exclude cases where physical hardware is used to commit regular crimes, but they risk excluding crimes that are considered as cyber crime in international agreements such as the "Convention on Cyber crime". For example, a person who produces USB -devices containing malicious software that destroy data on computers when the device is connected commits a crime as defined by Art. 4 Council of Europe Convention on Cyber crime.

However, the act of deleting data using a physical device to copy malicious code has not been committed through global electronic networks and would not qualify as cyber crime under the narrow definition.

This act would only qualify as cyber crime under a definition based on a broader description, including acts such as illegal data interference. This demonstrates that there are considerable difficulties in defining the term "cyber crime". The term "cyber crime" is used to describe a range of offences including traditional computer crimes, as well as network crimes.

As these crimes differ in many ways, there is no single criterion that could include all acts mentioned in the Stanford Draft Convention and the Convention on Cyber crime, whilst excluding traditional crimes that are just committed using hardware. The fact that there is no single definition of "cyber crime" need not be important, as long as the term is not used as a legal term.

TYPOLOGY OF CYBER CRIME

The term "cyber crime" includes a wide variety of crime. Recognised crimes cover a broad range of offences, making it difficult to develop a typology or classification system for cyber crime. An interesting system can be found is found in the Council of Europe Convention on Cyber crime.

The Convention on Cyber crime distinguishes between four different types of offences:

- Offences against the confidentiality, integrity and availability of computer data and systems;
- Computer-related offences;
- Content-related offences; and
- Copyright-related offences.

This typology is not wholly consistent, as it is not based on a sole criterion to differentiate between categories. Three categories focus on the object of legal protection: "offences against the confidentiality, integrity and availability of computer data and systems"; content-related offences; and copyright-related offences.

The fourth category of "computer-related offences" does not focus on the object of legal protection, but on the method. This inconsistency leads to some overlap between categories. In addition, some terms that are used to describe criminal acts (such as 'Cyber terrorism' or 'phishing') cover acts that fall within several categories. Nonetheless, the categories provided by the Convention on Cyber crime serve as a useful basis for discussing the phenomena of cyber crime.

ECONOMIC IMPACT OF CYBER CRIME

Without any doubt, the financial damage caused by computer and Internet crimes is significant. Various recent surveys have been published analysing the economic impact of cyber crime, highlighting its significant impact. The same general concerns about crime statistics also apply to estimates of financial damage – it is uncertain to what extent surveys provide accurate figures and statistics, as many victims may not report crimes.

RESULTS OF SELECTED SURVEYS

The Computer Security Institute (CSI) Computer Crime and Security Survey 2007 analysed the economic impact of cyber crime, based on the responses of 494 computer security practitioners in U.S corporations, government agencies and financial institutions. It is mainly relevant for the United States. Taking into account the economic cycle, the survey suggests that, after rising until 2002, the financial impact of cyber crime decreased over the following years. The survey suggests that this finding is controversial, but it is unclear why the number of reported crimes and the average loss of the victims may have decreased. In 2006, the extent of losses climbed again. The survey does not explain the reduced losses in 2002 or the rise in 2006. From 21 categories identified by the survey, the highest dollar losses were associated with financial fraud, viruses, system penetration by outsiders and theft of confidential data. The total losses for 2006 of all respondents amounted to some USD 66.9 million. After a number of years of decreasing average losses per respondent, a turnaround is taking place. In 2006, the average loss was USD 345,000. In 2001, the average loss was nearly ten times higher (USD 3.1 million). The average loss per respondent depends strongly on the composition of respondents - if mainly small and medium sized enterprises (SMEs) respond one year and are replaced by larger companies the next year, the change in participants strongly affects the statistical results.

The FBI Computer Crime Survey 2005 follows an approach similar to the CSI Survey, but with a greater and more extensive coverage. The FBI survey estimates that the cost of security incidents from computer and Internet crimes amounted to USD 21.7 million. The most popular offences that detected by respondents organisations were virus attacks, spyware, port scans and sabotage of data or networks. The FBI Computer Crimes Survey 2005 includes an estimate of the total loss for the United States economy.

Based on average losses and the assumption that some 20 per cent of US organisations are affected by computer crime, a total loss of USD 67 billion was calculated. However, there are concerns as to how representative these estimates are, and the consistency of participants year on year. The 2007 Computer Economics Malware Report focuses on the impact of malware on the worldwide economy by summing up total estimated costs caused by attacks. One of its key findings is the fact that offenders designing malicious software are shifting from vandalism to a focus on financial profits.

The report finds that the financial losses caused by malware attacks peaked in 2000 (USD 17.1 billion) and 2004 (USD 17.5 billion), but have reduced Since, 2004 to USD 13.3 billion in 2006. However, similar to the survey results, there is uncertainty as to whether the statistics on the impact of malware are realistic.

There are large discrepancies between reported losses and proven damages – take the case of the Sasser Worm, for example. Millions of computer systems were reported to be infected. In the civil law suit against the software designer, very few companies and private individuals responded to the request to prove their losses and join the lawsuit. The case ended with a settlement that the designer of the virus should pay compensation of less than ten thousand US dollars.

DIFFICULTIES RELATED TO CYBER CRIME STATISTICS

It is unclear how representative the statistics on the economic impact of cyber crime are and whether they provide reliable information on the extent of losses. It is uncertain to what extent cyber crime is reported, not only in surveys, but also to law enforcement agencies. Authorities engaged in the fight against cyber crime encourage victims of cyber crime to report these crimes.Access to more precise information about the true incidence of cyber crimes would enable law enforcement agencies to better prosecute offenders, deter potential attacks and enact more appropriate and effective legislation. Several public and private sector organizations have tried to quantify the direct and indirect costs of malware. While it is difficult to estimate the cost to businesses, it is even more difficult to assess the financial losses inflicted by malware and the like to individual consumers, although there is scattered evidence that damages can be very large.

However, such costs have different components. They may result in direct damages to hardware and software as well as financial and other damages due to identity theft or other fraudulent schemes. The range of estimates differs, although the emerging overall picture is quite coherent. Businesses on the other hand may avoid reporting cyber crime offences for several reasons: Businesses may fear that negative publicity could damage their reputation.

If a company announces that hackers have accessed their server, customers may lose faith. The full costs and consequences could be greater than the losses caused by the hacking attack. However, if offenders are not reported and prosecuted, they may go on to reoffend. Targets may not believe that law enforcement agencies will be able to identify offenders. Comparing the large number of cyber crimes with the few successful investigations, targets may see little point in reporting offences. Automation also means that cybercriminals follow a strategy of reaping large profits from many attacks targeting small amounts (*e.g.,* as happens with advance fee fraud). For only small amounts, victims may prefer not to go through with time-consuming reporting procedures. Reported cases are often based on extremely high fees. By targeting only small amounts, offenders design scams that will often not be followed up.

THE FUTURE OF CYBER CRIME ACTIVITY

During an eight day period in August of 2003, three separate worms cost the U.S., economy close to two billion dollars in lost production. Later that summer, the east coast of the United States experienced a massive blackout that might have been exacerbated by a worm called Blaster. Robert Cringley believed that same year that "the cost to society of identity theft is in the range of $4-5 billion per year and may be even higher." With the convergence of organised crime and technically savvy cyber criminals, the growing fear of cyberterrorism, the inability to understand security from major software vendors and the slow footedness of the government, the future seems to point to an Internet that is not only vulnerable to major attacks, but also infested with scams, thieves, and ever increasing opportunities for exploitation.

Although inherently difficult to predict trends within the field of technology, there are some eventualities that seem certain, like the growth of extortion and fraud though the Internet. These difficulties will of course result in new responses that better protect customers and force criminals into new realms. Although it is a hackneyed expression, the Internet is still in the Wild West stages. It is important to remember, though, that the Wild West eventually turned into suburbia after successful methods were found to control and police criminals, making their life extremely difficult. An examination of some of the potentialities will help to illustrate how the Internet and cyber crime can be envisioned, at least in the near term future.

FUTURE TRENDS IN CYBER CRIME ACTIVITY

The pace at which cyber crime is growing is one of the most disturbing trends. Valerie McNiven, a U.S., Treasury Advisor, has proclaimed "last year was the first year that proceeds from cyber crime were greater than proceeds from the sale of illegal drugs, and that was, I believe, over $105 billion." She further added that "cyber crime is moving at such a high speed that law enforcement cannot catch up with it." It seems clear that the issue will only become worse in the next few years, now that professionals have realised the potential windfalls if exploited properly. Recently, there has been significant discussion over the amalgamation of organised criminals and cyber crime. Such a pairing indeed forebodes an ill omen for the near term future. With most of the criminal groups operating out of eastern Europe, Russia and Asia, where laws and enforcement are scanty, there seems little hope in containing and neutralising the threat through traditional means.

Phil Williams, a visiting scientist at CERT, summarised the issue succinctly. "The Internet provides both channels and targets for crime and enables them to be exploited for considerable gain with a very low level of risk.

For organised crime it is difficult to ask for more." The result that can then be expected will be an increase in sophisticated phishing attacks and other means for identity theft that may be two pronged. For example, using call centers to notify "customers" ahead of time of some issue, and then following up with e-mails that request personal information. These types of social engineering attacks can be very damaging and have had a long history of success within cyber crime and fraud related transgressions.

The Internet makes it even easier since, a degree of authority can be imparted with official looking e-mails and fraudulent web sites that mimic their legitimate counterparts exactly. In the past, such social engineering relied on interpersonal skills like gaining trust. Now, the same idea has been transferred to technology, which can be done with greater ease by a wider group of people. Another aspect of fraud will result from the aggregation of personal information in many third party data centers, making them valuable targets to infiltrate. It is not hard to imagine criminals using data mining techniques to find the most gullible consumers, or tailoring phishing e-mails for specific people based on their medical, financial or personal history. Identify theft will also move in more automated directions.

For example, botnets will become vehicles not just for denial of service attacks and spam, but also as giant search platforms for finding personal information, like credit cards and social security numbers. Controllers of the botnets will then receive payment to run queries on their "database." With professional criminals managing the money laundering and organisation of such schemes, it begs to ask where will all the technical know-how come from in order to perform cyber crime? Unfortunately, there are growing numbers of intelligent black-hats with university degrees spread around the globe, many of them operating in countries where legal employment does not pay as well and the chances of being caught are slim. But more troublesome is that it has become easier than ever before to be a hacker capable of inflicting great harm on networks and committing cyber crime.The Internet has created a repository of knowledge where anyone is able to learn the fundamentals of subverting computer systems, with numerous tutorials available that spell out in nearly layman's terms how to perform a buffer overflow or a man in the middle attack. Interestingly, the greatest problem is not those who will take the time to learn and find new exploits. In fact this group will probably remain a small, highly intelligent network of researchers and security groups focused solely on finding holes in software. In this, it is preordained, that even if someone is motivated to learn how exploits work, finding a new exploit takes a degree of investigation, skill and diligence that most are not willing to invest.

The real threat comes from the profound ease at which anyone can run a programme like "MetaSploit," a framework for running exploits against targets that allows new modules to be imported and run automatically. The attacker literally needs to know nothing about how computers work, besides how to operate one. In fact, for almost all attacks, the hard work is done by a small group of people, and then released into the public domain, allowing almost anyone to just run the attack.Botnets are no longer handcrafted software made by one group who truly understood the fundamentals, but instead are opensource collaborative efforts that aim to make it as easy as possible to control remote computers, such as BotNET, eggheads and CSharpBot, all available from SourceForge.

Thus, the barrier to entry to the field is so low that it allows almost anyone to experiment and join the swelling ranks of cyber criminals. With the learning curve so low, it should prompt discussion on the need for a new paradigm of thought in how to pre-empt and deal with criminals, in a way that is no longer tied to traditional methods. For example, for someone to break into a house, not only do they need to plan the opportune moment, but they may also have to be aware of lock picking, security system evasion and possess a degree of gumption to overcome moral thresholds.

In opposition, the ease of cyber crime seems inversely proportional to the lucrativeness that it bestows and moreover, these trends show signs of accelerating. Beyond the "who" and the "why" of future cyberattacks, the "how" will also change as operating systems become more secure and harder to exploit. With the damage that comes with each new security hole released, Microsoft, Apple and open source vendors have finally begun to seriously focus on security. Of course that hasn't stemmed the flow of vulnerabilities discovered, but techniques such as address space randomisation to stop buffer overflows, advanced and automatic code reviews and more training will reduce the ability to compromise a machine through operating system protocols over time.

The real danger in the future lies with user applications, which are created by individuals or small groups without the knowledge or training required to implement security correctly. Especially dangerous are web applications that can be installed on web servers. The traditional problem with these types of security vulnerabilities was finding susceptible hosts. But with Google, a programme can automatically search for sites with a specific version of a programme installed and then launch an attack.

If remote code can be executed, the programme may not be able to take over the whole system, but it can run programmes as the user which may be enough to install bots and automatically replicate. The first instance of such an attack occurred in December of 2004 with the Santy worm that attacked a popular bulletin board system by searching through Google to find hosts with a specific file that was vulnerable. Such attacks aim their weapons at the least secure and vetted of software created. Although the installed base of such systems may be small, with "Google Hacking," they can still be quickly located and exploited. Another avenue of attack that will open up will be through embedded systems, such as cell phones, mobile devices and other electronics that may connect to the Internet for the most mundane of purposes. Software is usually recreated for each iteration of a device as it is specifically designed for the hardware.

This allows for security problems to creep back in over time that may have been eliminated before. As these devices start to allow consumers to make purchases, while storing valuable information, they will become more attractive for criminals. The incentives now to do so are low, so security researchers have only seen "proof-of-concept" viruses, like the one that infected cellphones running a version of the Symbian OS that could spread automatically. It appears organised crime has not moved into this area due to the lack of research and understanding of how such attacks can be made profitable. Much as with the Internet, it will take time to exploit successfully.

In the same vein, eventually automobiles, home electronics devices, refrigerators and almost all devices can and will use the Internet in order to perform maintenance, download upgrades or monitor performance. These will present opportunities for maliciousness and blackmail that doesn't equate in the same way as the purely virtual environment of the Internet. If someone enters their car, controlled by a foreign agent that demands a wire transfer or else the car will be crashed at high speeds, a situation arises that people will no longer accept. Whether such a scenario will occur is debatable, but the possibility will certainly exist.

MITIGATING CYBER CRIME ACTIVITY

Although it is inevitable that cyber crime will increase and continue to explore new vectors for undermining privacy, authentication and law enforcement, there will also be valid and useful attempts for mitigating the abilities of criminals, as well as the effects of cyber crime. These solutions will take form in better software, anti-spyware and anti-virus software integrated into operating systems and more user education regarding phishing and identify theft. These solutions will come primarily from software vendors themselves. On the other side, legislators will work with banks to reduce and prevent fraud, putting some of the liability with those most able to prevent it.

Finally, advanced solutions coming out of research and academia will try to inhibit the inherently anonymous and insecure nature of the Internet. With Microsoft's upcoming release of Vista, the latest version of their operating system, they'll have a new chance to focus on not only improving the general security of the system through fundamental changes, but also in providing methods for eliminating common problems, such as botnets, spyware and phishing attacks. In October of 2005, Microsoft began working together with the FTC to educate customers about botnets and the danger of allowing a computer to turn into a zombie. To deal with the problem of phishing, Microsoft released a programme in July of 2005 called the "Microsoft Phishing Filter," which aims to invalidate the ability of phishers to reach Microsoft customers by dynamically notifying them when there is a high chance that what is being viewed is a phishing attack.

Finally, Microsoft released their "AntiSpyware" programme in January of 2005, to be included with Vista as well, that automatically scans your computer for programmes that match spyware signatures or that try to perform suspicious actions, like modifying system functionality or trying to run upon computer start up. If cyber crime continues to grow to epidemic proportions, as all indications seem to point to, legislation will invariably step in, but more importantly, those with the most to lose will become more involved. This includes credit card companies, banks, lending operations and other organisations dealing with monetary transactions.

Paypal.com has quickly come to dominate the online payment industry, while also serving as a bank in many capacities. With only an e-mail address and a password required to send money, this low hanging fruit has been one of the most heavily exploited realms for phishing attacks. In response, Paypal has offered at least a thousand dollars of purchase protection and a supposed one hundred per cent protection against unauthorised payments sent from an account.

A fraud investigation team responds to queries and according to their web site, they have software that automatically monitors every transaction for inconsistencies. This last measure used by Paypal has also become fertile ground for credit cards companies, as their systems have become powerful at identifying fraudulent purchases though the use of neural networks, a type of software emerging out of the field of artificial intelligence. In some cases, this software has been able to reduce fraud by thirty per cent or more. It's important to remember that the systems are not perfect solutions, but do address a large portion of illegal activity. Combined with other efforts, the goal is to reduce the effect of fraud, while making it more difficult to achieve.

Legislation will attempt to do its part as well, even though it has moved notoriously slowly when dealing with cyberthreats. The past few years have seen laws specifically crafted for spam and dealing with attacks that threaten the integrity of the infrastructure of the Internet. If the botnet problem continues to grow, coupled with identify theft, surely more action will be taken. Although, it is still unclear how effective it will be without a significant contribution to cyberforensic development and funding for the various governmental enforcement agencies responsible for handling cyber crime matters.

Another issue discussed in the Legal Policies section is the need for more international cooperation in locating, extraditing and prosecuting foreign criminals when possible, as the current system leaves much to be desired. Finally, as with any dangerous and difficult problem, there will be new and inventive ways to handle security issues coming out of research. One contribution that has limited, but not eliminated many common security flaws that are exploited, is the use of randomisation in dealing with code, data and other programmatic necessities. By introducing a factor of unpredictability, it can make the work of a hacker much more difficult and prone to error, limiting the ability of those who do not posses the skill to effect a novel attack. Other interesting proposals have included trace back systems that can remove the anonymous identity of data traveling through the Internet, devising a system for fast and accurate discovery of the source of even one packet of data.

Stopping distributed denial of service attacks and worm discovery has also been proposed as a method that can be automated and integrated into the backbone of the Internet, high speed routers. By analysing similar patterns coming from separate locations, such detectors can realise an attack while it is in its infancy and isolate infected hosts. There is also still room for ISPs to actively monitor and discourage botnets, spam and DDoS attacks from occurring. As the first link in the chain for many zombie hosts, as well as attackers, they are in a prime position for stopping spam, either by blocking outgoing mail, which most users have no need for, or by identifying when one host is sending out a large amount of data that does not match expected behaviour.

Additionally, if they noticed that a number of hosts were acting in concert, with regards to the data being disseminated from those machines, they may assume with likelihood that they are being controlled remotely. Consequently, the ISPs can examine logs to find who is sending the commands and initiate a complaint with the F.B.I. The problem holding back this kind of proactive approach has not been technical in nature, but rather legalistic, as it can be considered an invasion of privacy. Furthermore, such methods are being used to track down minor copyright violations, instead of focusing on more substantial problems, such as cyber crime and identify theft.

LOOKING AHEAD

The future of the Internet is still up for grabs between criminals and normal users. Fears of a cyber-apocalypse still abound, while the potential extent of damage that can be caused by wide scale fraud is nearly unbounded. These anxieties should be rationally tempered with the knowledge that the problems are being addressed, although perhaps not fast enough. The usefulness of the Internet has proved itself in numerous and myriad ways that will hopefully be enough to ensure it does not become a wasteland of criminal activity and a bastion for the malicious.

The government still has an important role to play, but most of the prevention needs to be done by commercial entities producing software and those with the ability to stop fraud. Relying on consumer education programmes will only affect a percentage of possible victims. The others need to be automatically protected through measures that do not stress and require considerable participation. Security needs to be easy and effective if it is do work. Whether cyber crime is still a pertinent issue ten years from now is unknowable in a sense, but if the Internet will continue to grow, it must be solved so that the realities of cyber crime will be proportional to real-world crimes, if not better.

INTERNATIONAL DIMENSIONS OF CYBER CRIME

Cyber crime often has an international dimension. E-mails with illegal content often pass through a number of countries during the transfer from sender to recipient or illegal content is stored outside the country. Within cyber crime investigations, a close cooperation between the countries involved is very important. The existing mutual legal assistance agreements are based on formal, complex and often time-consuming procedures.

The setting-up of procedures for quick response to incidents, as well as requests for international cooperation, is therefore vital. A number of countries base their mutual legal assistance regime on the principle of "dual criminality". Investigations on a global level are generally limited to those crimes that are criminalised in all participating countries. Although there are a number of offences that can be prosecuted anywhere in the world, regional differences play an important role. One example is illegal content. The criminalisation of illegal content differs in various countries. Material that can lawfully be distributed in one country can easily be illegal in another country. The computer technology currently in use is basically the same around the world.

Apart from language issues and power adapters, there is very little difference between the computer systems and cell phones sold in Asia and those sold in Europe. An analogous situation arises in relation to the Internet. Due to standardisation, the protocols used in countries on the African continent are the same as those used in the United States. Standardisation enables users around the world to access the same services over the Internet. The question is what effect the harmonisation of global technical standards has on the development of the national criminal law. In terms of illegal content, Internet users can access information from around the world, enabling them to access information available legally abroad, that could be illegal in their own country.

Theoretically, developments arising from technical standardisation go far beyond the globalisation of technology and services and could lead to the harmonisation of national laws. However, as shown by the negotiations over the First Protocol to the Council of Europe Convention on Cyber crime, the principles of national law change much more slowly than technical developments.

Although the Internet may not recognise border controls, there are means to restrict access to certain information. The access provider can generally block certain web sites and the service provider that stores a Web site can prevent access to information for those users on the basis of IP-addresses linked to a certain country ("IP-targeting"). Both measures can be circumvented, but are nevertheless instruments that can be used to keep retain territorial differences in a global network. The OpenNet Initiative reports that such kind of censorship is practised by about two dozen countries.

CONSEQUENCES FOR DEVELOPING COUNTRIES

Finding response strategies and solutions to the threat of cyber crime is a major challenge, especially for developing countries. A comprehensive Anti-Cyber crime Strategy generally contains technical protection measures, as well as legal instruments. The development and implementation of these instruments need time. Technical protection measures are especially cost-intensive. Developing countries need to integrate protection measures into the roll-out of the Internet from the beginning, as although this might initially raise the cost of Internet services, the long-term gains in avoiding the costs and damage inflicted by cyber crime are large and far outweigh any initial outlays on technical protection measures and network safeguards. The risks associated with weak protection measures could in fact affect developing countries more intensely, due to their less strict safeguards and protection.The ability to protect customers, as well as firms, is a fundamental requirement not only for regular businesses, but also for online or Internet-based businesses. In the absence of Internet security, developing countries could encounter significant difficulties promoting e-business and participating in online service industries.

The development of technical measures to promote cyber security and proper cyber crime legislation is vital for both developed countries and developing countries. Compared with the costs of grafting safeguards and protection measures onto computer networks at a later date, it is likely that initial measures taken right from the outset will be less expensive. Developing countries need to bring their anti-cyber crime strategies into line with international standards from the outset.

CYBER CRIME VARIANTS

There are a good number of cyber crime variants. A few varieties are discussed for the purpose of completion. This article is not intended to expose all the variants. The readers are directed to other resources.

CYBER STALKING

Cyber stalking is use of the Internet or other electronic means to stalk someone. This term is used interchangeably with online harassment and online abuse. Stalking generally involves harassing or threatening Behaviour that an individual engages in repeatedly, such as following a person, appearing at a person's home or place of business, making harassing phone calls, leaving written messages or objects, or vandalizing a person's property.

HACKING

"Hacking" is a crime, which entails cracking systems and gaining unauthorised access to the data stored in them. Hacking had witnessed a 37 per cent increase this year.

PHISHING

Phishing is just one of the many frauds on the Internet, trying to fool people into parting with their money. Phishing refers to the receipt of unsolicited e-mails by customers of financial institutions, requesting them to enter their username, password or other personal information to access their account for some reason. Customers are directed to a fraudulent replica of the original institution's Web site when they click on the links on the e-mail to enter their information, and so they remain unaware that the fraud has occurred. The fraudster then has access to the customer's online bank account and to the funds contained in that account. F-Secure Corporation's summary of 'data security' threats during the first half of 2007 has revealed that the study found the banking industry as soft target for phishing scams in India.

CROSS-SITE SCRIPTING

Cross-site scripting (XSS) is a type of computer security vulnerability typically found in web applications which allow code injection by malicious web users into the web pages viewed by other users. Examples of such code include HTML code and client-side scripts. An exploited cross-site scripting vulnerability can be used by attackers to bypass access controls.

VISHING

Vishing is the criminal practice of using social engineering and Voice over IP (VoIP) to gain access to private personal and financial information from the public for the purpose of financial reward. The term is a combination of "voice" and phishing. Vishing exploits the public's trust in landline telephone services, which have traditionally terminated in physical locations which are known to the telephone company, and associated with a bill-payer. The victim is often unaware that VoIP allows for caller ID spoofing, inexpensive, complex automated systems and anonymity for the bill payer. Vishing is typically used to steal credit card numbers or other information used in identity theft schemes from individuals.

CYBER SQUATTING

Cyber squatting is the act of registering a famous domain name and then selling it for a fortune. This is an issue that has not been tackled in IT act 2000. Bot Networks A cyber crime called 'Bot Networks', wherein spamsters and other perpetrators of cyber crimes remotely take control of computers without the users realising it, is increasing at an alarming rate. Computers get linked to Bot Networks when users unknowingly download malicious codes such as Trojan horse sent as e-mail attachments. Such affected computers, known as zombies, can work together whenever the malicious code within them get activated, and those who are behind the Bot Neworks attacks get the computing powers of thousands of systems at their disposal.Attackers often coordinate large groups of Bot-controlled systems, or Bot networks, to scan for vulnerable systems and use them to increase the speed and breadth of their attacks. Trojan horse provides a backdoor to the computers acquired. A 'backdoor' is a method of bypassing normal authentication, or of securing remote access to a computer, while attempting to remain hidden from casual inspection. The backdoor may take the form of an installed Programme, or could be a modification to a legitimate Programme. Bot networks create unique problems for organisations because they can be remotely upgraded with new exploits very quickly, and this could help attackers pre-empt security efforts.

VULNERABILITY

The Open-Source Vulnerability Database (OSVDB) project maintains a master list of computer - security vulnerabilities, freely available for use by security professionals and projects around the world. Vulnerability information is critical for the protection of information systems everywhere: in enterprises and other organizations, on private networks and intranets, and on the public Internet.

INDIAN CRIME SCENE

The major cyber crimes reported, in India, are denial of services, defacement of web sites, SPAM, computer virus and worms, pornography, cyber squatting, cyber stalking and phishing. Given the fact that nearly $ 120 million worth of mobiles are being lost or stolen in the country every year, the users have to protect information, contact details and telephone numbers as these could be misused. Nearly 69 per cent of information theft is carried out by current and ex-employees and 31 per cent by hackers. India has to go a long way in protecting the vital information. Symantec shares the numbers from its first systematic survey carried out on the Indian Net Security scene: The country has the highest ratio in the world (76 per cent) of outgoing spam or junk mail, to legitimate e-mail traffic. India's home PC owners are the most targeted sector of its 37.7 million Internet users: Over 86 per cent of all attacks, mostly via 'bots' were aimed at lay surfers with Mumbai and Delhi emerging as the top two cities for such vulnerability.

PHISHING

Phishing attacks were more popular among Indian users due to rising Internet penetration and growing online transactions. India has now joined the dubious list of the world's top 15 countries hosting "phishing" sites which aims at stealing confidential information such as passwords and credit card details. A non-resident Malayali, had an account in a nationalised bank in Adoor, lost $ 10,000 when the bank authorities heeded a fake e-mail request to transfer the amount to an account in Ghana.

In Mangalapuram, a person transferred a large sum of money as "processing charge" to a foreign bank account after he received an e-mail, which said he had won a lottery [Kerala: The Hindu Monday Oct 30 2006]. Reports of phishing targeted at customers of banks appear to be on the rise. Web sense Security Labs, in a statement released recently, said it had received reports of such attacks from customers of AXIS Bank.

The Economic Offences Wing (EOW), Crime Branch, Delhi Police, unearthed a major phishing scam involving fake e-mails and web sites of UTI Bank, An analysis of the accounts of the four arrested Nigerian nationals indicated financial transactions of over ₹ 1 crore in an eight-month period till December 2006. Investigations revealed that the scam is multi-layered with pan-India and international characteristics The Lab went on to say that it found a mal ware in the Web site of Syndicate Bank. The users through a spoofed e-mail were asked to renew certain services and claiming that failure to do so would result in suspension or deletion of the account. The e-mail provided a link to a malicious site that attempted to capture the personal and account information. Phishing e-mails have increased by approximately twenty five per cent over the last year but are harder to detect as they increasingly trick unsuspecting people with ordinary scenarios instead of improbable ones such as sudden cash windfalls.

It has been six months since the phishing attack on ICICI bank customers became public, and during that period, two more such attacks were reported on customers of financial institutions in India, one of UTI Bank and the other. State Bank of India. RSA's 24/7 Anti-Fraud Command Centre of AFCC has just uncovered a 'Universal man-in-the middle Phishing Kit' in online forums which helps quickly create the fraudulent web sites, often borrowing code from the original site.

CYBER CAFES—E-MAILS

Cyber cafes have emerged as hot spots for cyber crimes. Even terrorists prefer the anonymity of a cyber cafe to communicate with each other. The mushrooming of cyber cafes in the city, which provide the secrecy through cabins constructed for users, has also made the porn literature easily accessible to the people visiting them. A 23- year-old person from Tiruchi was arrested by the City Cyber Crime police on Thursday on charges of sending an e-mail threat to the Chief Minister and his family. In another case, the police team investigating the e-mail threat on the lives of the President and the Prime Minister has prepared a sketch of the suspect, who had sent the e-mail from a cyber cafe in the city.

The Case of The State of Tamil Nadu vs Suhas Katti is notable for the fact that the conviction was achieved successfully.The case related to posting of obscene, defamatory and annoying message about a divorcee woman in the yahoo message group. E-Mails were also forwarded to the victim for information by the accused through a false e-mail account opened by him in the name of the victim. The posting of the message resulted in annoying phone calls to the lady. A travel agent was arrested for allegedly sending a threatening mail to blow up the National and Bombay stock exchanges in Kolkata.

STALKING

A tenth standard boy from Bangalore got into trouble when a girl much older than him started stalking him. She pasted 'I Love You' slips on his gate and called his On reviewing his Orkut profile, it was realised that he had accepted chat invites from more than 20 people; only two of who were his real-life friends.

HACKING

A case of suspected hacking of certain web portals and obtaining the residential addresses from the e-mail accounts of city residents had recently come to light. After getting the addresses, letters were sent through post mail and the recipients were lured into participating in an international lottery that had Australian $ 23 lakhs at stake. Computer hackers have also got into the Bhaba Atomic Research Centre (BARC) computer and pulled out important data. Some computer professionals who prepared the software for MBBS examination altered the data and gave an upward revision to some students in return for a hefty payment. A key finding of the Economic Crime Survey 2006 of Price water house Coopers (PwC) was that a typical perpetrator of economic crime in India was male (almost 100 per cent), a graduate or undergraduate and 31-50 years of age. Further, over one-third of the frauds in the country were perpetrated by insiders and over 37 per cent of them were in senior managerial positions.

GLOBAL ANTI-MALWARE MARKET

Malware is software designed to infiltrate or damage a computer system without the owner's informed consent. The expression is a general term used by computer professionals to mean a variety of forms of hostile, intrusive, or annoying software or Programme code. The global anti-malware market is driven by cyber criminal threats. The commercialisation of cyber crime is spurring malware-writing activity and leading to more threats of this nature. In the consumer space, this translates into identity theft and stolen passwords Growth opportunities have led to intensified competition in both consumer and enterprise segments.

On the other hand, loss of intellectual property and customer data coupled with extortion with the threat of taking down Web sites or revealing sensitive information are on the rise in the enterprise space. Organised crime is now employing KGB-style tactics to ensnare the next generation of hackers and malware authors. Cyber-criminals are actively approaching students and graduates of IT technology courses to recruit a fresh wealth of cyber skill to their ranks Today's worms are the handiwork of malcontents for whom cyber crime affords lucrative returns. A flourishing market exists where large blocks of infected machines that can be controlled remotely are for sale.

So big demonstrated the close nexus between malware writers and spammers, machines infected by the Sobig mass mailing worm were offered to spammers for price. The thriving market for subverted PCs has swung the underworld into hyperactivity.

The past ten months have seen several hacker groups and cyber crime syndicates setting up attack networks (botnets) and releasing remote attack tools through increasingly crafty malware such as Blaster, Sinit, MyDoom, Phatbot, Bagle and Netsky. New analysis from Frost and Sullivan, World Anti-Malware Products Markets, finds that the world market for antivirus solutions reached $4,685 million in 2006, up 17.1 per cent from $4,000.7 million in the previous year and expects this market to grow at a 10.9 per cent compound annual growth rate (CAGR) from 2006 to 2013, reaching $9,689.7 million by 2013.

ANTI-CYBER CRIME INITIATIVES

In a first of its kind initiative in India to tackle cyber crime, police have taken the initiative to keep an electronic eye on the users of the various cyber cafes spread over the city. The Kerala State IT Mission has launched a Web portal and a call centre to tackle cyber crime. The Central Bureau of Investigation (CBI) and the Mumbai police have recommended issuance of licenses to cyber cafe owners. Many countries, including India, have established Computer Emergency Response Teams (CERTs) with an objective to coordinate and respond during major security incidents/events.

These organisations identify and address existing and potential threats and vulnerabilities in the system and coordinate with stakeholders to address these threats. Policy initiatives on cyber crime are as yet lethargic because of a general sense that it is nothing more than juvenile hackers out to have fun or impress someone. Prateek Bhargava, cyber law expert says, "There is huge potential for damage to national security through cyber attacks. The Internet is a means for money laundering and funding terrorist attacks in an organised manner. In the words of Pavan Duggal, Supreme Court Lawyer, "Cyber crime is omnipresent and although cyber crime cells have been set up in major cities, most cases remain unreported due to lack of awareness."

TYPES OF COMPUTER CRIME

We begin by providing an overview of cyber-crime and criminal techniques used to penetrate protected computer networks. The CFAA, how it is applied, and how it has changed over the past decade. Then we will look at other laws that are on the books that the federal government uses to control computer crimes. Due to the international nature of cyber-crimes, we discuss briefly some of the international cooperative developments. A computer can be the target of the offence, the tool used in the offence, or may contain evidence of the offence. An understanding of the different uses of a computer will provide the foundation of the application of the criminal statutes.

The computer is an indispensable tool for almost all cyber-crimes. However, as more devices are enabled to communicate with the Internet, the hackers arsenal of tools is likely to multiply.

When a computer is the target of the offence, the criminal's goal is to steal information from, or cause damage to, a computer, computer system, or computer network. Hacking, cracking, espionage, cyber-warfare, and malicious computer code viruses are common forms of crimes that target the computer. The perpetrators range from teenage "cyber-joyriders" to organized crime operations and international terrorists. According to a survey conducted by Michael G. Kessler and Associates Ltd., a New York security firm, computer theft of proprietary information is committed by discontented employees (35 per cent), outside hackers (28 per cent), other U.S. companies (18 per cent), foreign corporations (11 per cent), foreign governments (8 per cent), and miscellaneous (10 per cent).

The computer may also be a tool of the offence. The criminal uses the computer to commit a traditional crime, such as counterfeiting. For example, a counterfeiter that used to engrave plates to create the counterfeit currency can now use sophisticated graphic computers with advanced colour printers. An example of a computer used to perpetrate a traditional crime is the extortion attempt by George Matos Rocha from North Carolina. Mr. Rocha was charged with bombing three home improvement stores and subsequently threatened the retail chain to continue the bombings unless he received $250,000. Using the Internet, Mr. Rocha set up a bank account in Latvia and instructed the company to wire the extortion money to his Latvian account. The FBI was able to identify the account and trace its origin back to the United States with the help of his Internet Service Provider. Mr. Rocha pleaded guilty in December to explosives charges and extortion. He could have faced life in prison.

Computers can also be incidental to the offence, but are nevertheless important because they contain the evidence of a crime. Money launderers, for example, may use a computer to store details of their laundering operation instead of relying on paper accounting records. Child pornographers' computers are often seized as the key evidence that the defendant produced, possessed, received, and/or distributed child pornography.

DENIAL OF SERVICE

A Denial of Service ("DoS") attack is a rather primitive technique that overwhelms the resources of the target computer which results in the denial of server access to other computers. There are several different techniques that hackers use to "bring down" a server. As the network administrators learn how to limit the damage of one technique, hackers often create more powerful and more sophisticated techniques that force system administrators to continually react against assaults. In order to understand how to apply the law to these attacks, a basic understanding of the anatomy of the attacks is necessary.

There are basically three main network exploits that are used to overwhelm a system's server: SYN Flood Attacks, UDP Flood Attacks and ICMP Flood Attacks. Each technique exploits a weakness in the way computers communicate amongst each other over the Internet. A basic understanding of the TCP/IP Internet protocols is helpful to differentiate between the techniques.

Internet Protocols

The Internet is a network of computers that are connected so they can exchange information amongst each other. The computer that is asking for information from another computer is the "client" and the computer that is receiving the request is the "server." When the client wants to receive information that is located on the server, it sends a request for the information. However, the computers must establish a connection before data can be exchanged. The server needs to know who it is going to send the information to and needs to make sure the client computer is ready to receive the information. This is considered a "3-way handshake." The first part of the handshake occurs when the client computer sends a message to the server with a "SYN flag" that tells the server how to identify it. Second, upon receiving the request, the server will send out its own identification number, called an Initial Sequence Number ("ISN") in a SYN for this request and an acknowledgement ("ACK") of the client's request.

In the third part of this "handshake," the client computer receives the SYN and ACK from the server and sends back the ACK with the server's numbers, like a secret code the two of them share so the server can keep track of multiple clients. Now the data transfer can take place. In summary, the client sends a message to the server, the server sends back a message to the client that the server is "awake" and ready to process the requests, then the client sends back an acknowledgement that they are ready. This may seem redundant, but the need to establish the connection on both sides is very important because the data is broken up into small pieces by the server and sent out over the Internet to the client. The client needs to know how to organize the data puzzle as the packets arrive and the client also needs to know if any packets are missing. As each piece of the puzzle arrives, the client lets the server know the piece has been received, so the server knows if it has to re-send it.

TCP/IP stands for Transmission Control Protocol and Internet Protocol. Basically, the TCP is the workhorse of the communication on both sides. If a file is requested by the client, the server locates the file on its computer and breaks the file into tiny pieces. The tiny pieces are called datagrams. Each datagram is "wrapped" in a bundle of instructions that tells it where to go. These little bundles are called "packets." The TCP assigns a sequence number to every byte transferred so it can track what it has sent and eliminate the need to duplicate sending the same piece twice unless the piece is lost somewhere along the line to the client. The "packet header," contains the sequence numbers that also tells the client the next sequence number to expect after each packet, so the client can start arranging the packets and conduct a rolling inventory. The TCP acts as a digital shipping and receiving department.

The job of the Internet Protocol ("IP") is easier. The IP's job is to route the packets across the Internet to the client. Each computer on the Internet has an IP address that tells the computers where the other is located.

The IP address is very similar to a zip code. For example, a zip code that begins with a 9, belongs to an address located on the west coast of the United States.

If the next number is a 4, the location is in the San Francisco area, and so on until the precise region is located. However, to parallel the IP addresses, each house in the zip code area would be assigned a number, instead of an address. So when a client or server sends a packet out over the Internet, the packet is "routed" through many other servers to reach its final destination. The IP tacks on the numerical address and ships it out, hoping the packet arrives where it is supposed to go. If the server does not receive a response that the packet was received on the other end, the IP can send an error message to the client, called an Internet Control Message Protocol, or ICMP, letting the client know that the packet did not get there. It is this system of trust and cooperation between the computers that is exploited by a denial of service attack.

SYN Flood Attacks

One of the weaknesses in the system is the amount of SYN requests the TCP can handle. When the TCP receives more requests than it is programmed to handle, it puts the other incoming SYN requests in a queue. When the queue is filled to capacity, there is no more room to put the other incoming SYN requests and they are turned back. Hence, they are "denied service."

Another technique is to slow down the TCP process by making the TCP wait for all of the ACKs it sent out to be acknowledged by the client. When the attacker sends a message to the server requesting data, the server sends out a SYN and an ACK and waits to hear back from the attacker's client, as part of the third part of the 3-way handshaking. However, the attacker has "spoofed" his return address so that the server sends a "self-addressed and stamped" envelope to an address that is either false or belongs to a computer that is not responding. If enough of these "spoofed" SYN messages are sent, the server is paralyzed by its wait for non-existent confirmations. "SYNK" is a common SYN flood programme that is widely downloadable on the Internet.

UDP Flood Attacks

User Datagram Protocol ("UDP") flood attacks work in very much the same manner as the SYN Flood attacks. In a server, the UDP provides information about the server to other computers, such as the server's local time, echo, chargen, etc. When the server is hit with multiple requests for information about itself, the server can be quickly overwhelmed by its inability to process so many UDP packets.

The result is total consumption of the server's processing power and bandwidth, thereby "denying service" to others who are trying to access the server. The problem is multiplied when a hacker connects one computer's chargen port with another's echo port. The result is the generation of a massive amount of packets that overwhelm the system and render it useless.

ICMP Flood Attack

The Internet Control Message Protocol ("ICMP") flood attack is also similar to the above flood attacks. The ICMP is used to handle errors and "pings."

Pings are small "feelers" that are sent out to other computers to see if they are turned on and connected to the same network. Ping is also used to determine if there is network congestion and other network transport problems. When a ping packet is sent to an IP broadcast address from a computer outside of the remote computer's network, it is broadcast to all machines on the target network.

The ICMP attack begins when a large number of forged ping requests are sent to a broadcast address on a third-party's server. These packets contain the return address of the intended victim. The flood of ping requests causes the targeted server to answer with a flood of responses which can cause both the target site and third-party sites to crash.

A variation on the ICMP attack is the "Ping of Death." The Ping of Death is a large ICMP packet that is sent to the target server. The target receives the ping in fragments and starts to re-assemble the packets as they arrive. However, the completed size of the packet is larger than the buffer, or than the room the computer has allocated to such packets, and the computer is overwhelmed, often resulting in the server shutting down or freezing up.

2

Internet Related Scams and Frauds

INTERNET FRAUD

The best source of information concerning the growing incidence of fraud committed on the Internet is the Internet Fraud Complaint Center (IFCC), a partnership between the National White Collar Crime Center (NW3C) and the Federal Bureau of Investigation (FBI).

The following findings are taken from the IFCC's 2001 Internet Fraud Report:

- From January 1, 2001 – December 31, 2001 the IFCC's Web site received 49,711 complaints. This total includes many different fraud types and non-fraudulent complaints, such as computer intrusions, SPAM/unsolicited e-mail, and child pornography. During this same time period, the IFCC referred 16,775 complaints of fraud, the majority of which was committed over the Internet or similar online service. The total dollar loss from all referred cases of fraud was $17.8 million, with a median dollar loss of $435 per complaint.
- Internet auction fraud was by far the most reported Offence, comprising 42.8 per cent of referred complaints. Non-deliverable merchandise and payment account for 20.3 per cent of complaints, and Nigerian Letter fraud made up 15.5 per cent of complaints. Credit/debit Card fraud and Confidence fraud (such as home improvement scams and multi-level marketing) round out the top five categories of complaints referred to law enforcement during the year. Among those individuals who reported a dollar loss, the highest median dollar losses were found among Nigerian Letter Scam ($5,575), Identity Theft ($3,000), and Investment fraud ($1,000) complainants.
  - The Nigerian Letter Scam is defined as a correspondence outlining an opportunity to receive non-existent government funds from alleged dignitaries that is designed to collect advance fees from the victims. This sometimes requires payoff money to bribe government officials. While other countries may be mentioned,

the correspondence typically indicates "The Government of Nigeria" as the nation of origin. This scam has run since the early 1980's and is also referred to as "419 Fraud" after the relevant section of the Criminal Code of Nigeria, as well as "Advance Fee Fraud." Because of the scam, the country of Nigeria ranks 2nd for total complaints reported at the IFCC on businesses by country.

- Nearly 76 per cent of alleged fraud perpetrators are individuals (as opposed to businesses), 81 per cent are male, and half reside in one of the following states: California, Florida, New York, Texas, and Illinois. While most are from the United States, perpetrators have a representation in Canada, Nigeria, Romania and the United Kingdom.
- The amount loss by complainants tends to be related to a number of factors. Business victims tend to lose more than individuals and males tend to lose more than females. This may be a function of both online purchasing differences by gender, and the type of fraud the individual finds themselves involved in. While there isn't a strong relationship between age and loss, proportion of individuals losing at least $5,000 is higher for those 60 years and older than it is for any other age category.
- Electronic mail (E-mail) and web pages are the two primary mechanisms by which the fraudulent contact took place. Nearly 70 per cent of complainants reported they had e-mail contact with the perpetrator.

The primary federal statute used to prosecute Internet fraud is 18 U.S.C. § 1343, which provides that:

Whoever, having devised or intending to devise any scheme or artifice to defraud, or for obtaining money or property by means of false or fraudulent pretenses, representations, or promises, transmits or causes to be transmitted by means of wire, radio, or television communication in interstate or foreign commerce, any writings, signs, signals, pictures, or sounds for the purpose of executing such scheme or artifice, shall be fined under this title or imprisoned not more than five years, or both. If the violation affects a financial institution, such person shall be fined not more than $1,000,000 or imprisoned not more than 30 years, or both.

The following essay by Jonathan Rusch, Special Counsel for Fraud Prevention in the Fraud Section of the Criminal Division at the U.S. Department of Justice, describes in more detail the types of fraud frequently perpetrated through the Internet and the Justice Department's efforts – relying on section 1343 and other statutes – to stop them.

INTERNET HACKING AND SURVEILLANCE

As technology continues to advance, social and ethical issues arise in regards to privacy and security of personal information. Many people are aware of widespread issues in computer technology, such as surveillances and attacks. One major form of infringement on privacy and security is hacking, an unauthorised access into a system in order to gain information. Hacking includes a wide range of activities such as monitoring, thievery, exploitation, altering, vandalism, and destruction of computer systems, all of which endanger individuals' rights to privacy and security. Although this intrusion is frequently associated with negativity, some aspects of hacking can be useful and beneficial towards society. Businesses can benefit from ethical hacking, and law enforcement officials can benefit from the skills and knowledge of convicted hackers.

The subtopic of this chapter describes how the U.S., government can benefit from a form of passive hacking called "Carnivore" or "DCS 1000", an Internet surveillance system that eavesdrops on the public's electronic transmissions. Finally, the rest of the chapter discusses how this dynamic nature of technology challenges individuals, businesses, and the government to consider new social and ethical standards regarding personal privacy and security.

PRACTICAL USES AND CONSIDERATIONS

Computer hacking is performed to monitor, modify, and/or use the informational content for one's own gain, whether for fun or fraudulent purposes. A hacker can gain access to a wide range of personally identifiable information that endanger and damage the privacy of individuals, businesses, and government. Information that can be hacked into includes: personal health, financial, and inter-banking information; social security numbers; driver's license data; utility grids; emergency information systems; controls for dams and locks; military communications; and other sensitive information that travels on communication networks such as the Internet. Although not every attack results in theft or security loss, hackers often cost companies a great deal of time and money.

The hacking process is performed by a hacker, a person that uses programming skills to gain illegal access to a computer, a network or a file. This hacker is classified according to his/her primary intentions and level of damage done to individuals and/or businesses. He or she may be benign and has the intention to simply monitor or learn more about the system, without planning to destroy, change, or leave anything behind. Another type of hacker, the information thief, causes more damage because he/she gains access to company or customer information systems, retrieves individuals' personal information, and puts them to his/her own use.

This type of hacker provides or sells the stolen information to others for many purposes, including credit card and financial theft, corporate blackmail, or espionage. Lastly, the intention of the functionality thief is to gain knowledge from the interception of web services, then to proceed to alter, wreck, or crash the systems' operation. This type of hacking ranges from basic fun pranks to more serious crimes with the intent of revenge, damage, or the achievement of political and defence corruption. A hacker uses various methods of penetrating through systems to monitor and retrieve personal information, or to crash a system itself.

Different methods are briefly discussed here. First, a denial of service attack (DOS) overloads a network with such a great amount of traffic that it crashes, denying users access to the service. An example of a DOS attack would be the loss of service to a web mail service provider.

Second, a hacker may also use Internet Protocol (IP) spoofing as a way of disguising his/her real identity. This method allows a hacker to gain unauthorised access to computers by sending a message to a computer with an IP address showing that the message is from a trusted host. To accomplish this, a hacker must use different tools to find an IP address of a trusted host, and then alter the packet headers so it appears that the packets are coming from the host.

Third, another technique called Google hacking finds easily exploitable targets and sensitive data on the web by using Google, a powerful search engine used by many people. Google has gained popularity and offers many features, including "language and document translation; web, image, newsgroups, catalogue, and news searches". These features also come with a price, as many hackers use the value of this search engine for bad intentions.Fourth, one of the more common methods of hacking, phishing, imitates the e-mails of legitimate companies. It links recipients to fraudulent web sites that were designed to trick people into sharing their personal information. This may include "personal financial data such as credit cards numbers, account usernames and passwords, and social security numbers." Phishers are usually able to convince up to 5 per cent of targets. Some big name companies that a hacker may imitate are Citibank, eBay, Visa, Washington Mutual, Wells Fargo, AOL, and Yahoo.

Both Google hacking and phishing can often be used simultaneously. Lastly, the phishing method is a form of social engineering. With social engineering, a hacker can gain unauthorised access to a computer by deception, tricking the user into providing passwords and other needed information. One popular form of this is the use of deceptive mass e-mails, such as pretending to be a system administrator who needs people's passwords for important network access. The widespread fraud and privacy abuses trigger people's concerns about their own security and the use and control of their personal information. If an identify theft impersonates an authorised user, he or she can inflict damage to the real user's personal records, credit history, and reputation.

Moreover, there exists the fear of political or national threat in which an intruder can break into, damage, steal, and/or act on private information from computer systems worldwide. From a business perspective, hacking causes financial loss when an intruder accesses a company's web site and web service, linking to sensitive records containing customers' credit card information, address, and phone numbers. A hacker may be able to alter or damage the data, or use the information to sell to other people or companies. Competitors may also hack a company's web service to gain reports about potential clients, further using the list of leads for their own business benefit. Hacking also negatively impacts E-commerce, as consumers lose their trust in the Internet as a reliable and secure commerce medium.

The result is a loss of sales opportunities for businesses due to the reduction of online transactions. Additional consequences of hacking include time, money, and human miscommunication costs. A loss of time and money occurs in order to discover, test, apply, and train employees with technology needed to keep computer and network systems secured. The security processes used to ensure privacy include the continuous assessment of systems' security to identify risks, the evaluation of policies and protection, and the implementation of detection systems such as technology encryptions and firewalls. These processes not only contribute to money costs, but also take away valuable time and may slow down regular businesses.

A human miscommunication crisis can also occur and lead to erroneous proceedings. When the victim does not acknowledge that the wrongful incident is a result of hacking, he or she may blame the incorrect person or company that did not actually commit the crime. From another perspective, hacking may be considered ethical and beneficial to society if it is proven legitimate. Increasingly, businesses and authorities are willing to work with hackers to prevent online attacks and make improvements in computer securities. This type of hacking can be justifiable as long as the hacker has good intentions and commits no theft, vandalism, or breach of confidentiality. The exploration of systems by the benign hacker can be useful because it allows new findings and learning of others' capabilities.

Some hackers can avoid prosecution and criminal charges by trading in their abilities to help the government protect sensitive computer systems against other hackers, thieves and terrorists. Furthermore, in some cases the government may be willing to pay hackers to search the Internet for vulnerable computer systems, track criminals' online activities, and help make sensitive government networks more secure.

Another positive aspect of hacking is called ethical hacking, a method used to determine the strength, reliability, and vulnerability of Internet security measures. Ethical hackers use simulations to purposely attack, exploit, or expose the systems to hackers in order to test the security of networks, servers, and applications. This type of hacking is useful in finding and fixing unknown security leaks.

Ethical hacking makes it possible for businesses to be better prepared in the case that a real hacking incident occurs. It allows businesses to reduce or prevent the time and costs used to fix damages. It also puts pressure on companies to frequently update their computer systems in order to create and revise more secured networks. For example, vendors like Microsoft have a separate department that works solely to prevent people from hacking into their programmes. By detecting the methods hackers use, Microsoft has been able to evolve programmes to stop this dilemma.

ANALYSIS OF INTERNET SURVEILLANCE VIA "CARNIVORE" OR DCS 1000"

On July 11, 2000, the U.S., Federal Bureau of Investigation (FBI) announced its use of an Internet surveillance system called "Carnivore", or "DCS (Digital Collection System) 1000." The system is a computerbased application installed with an Internet Service Provider (ISP) to intercept and collect the electronic transmissions of criminal suspects. The FBI uses Carnivore as a form of passive hacking tool to keep track of individuals that execute their criminal plans through cyberspace.

By installing these "black boxes" on the main network, the government can increase law enforcement by connecting directly to the public's Internet traffic. This surveillance has been beneficial since, it has helped secure the convictions of thousands of felons. However, opposing viewpoints exist within the society since, the usage of such a system generates ethical and privacy concerns. From the beginning of Carnivore's invention, the main mechanics have been kept a closely guarded secret. No information about the first version was made to the public, but there were speculations that this first version was in fact a readily available commercial programme called Etherpeek.

In 1997, the second version was created with the name of Omnivore. According to the very little reports given by the FBI, Omnivore's purpose was to "look through e-mail traffic traveling over a specific ISP and capture e-mail from a targeted source, saving it to a tape-backup drive or printing it in real-time". This system was used until 1999, when it was replaced by a more advanced structure called the Dragonware Suite. This structure contained added features, such as the capability to download files and web pages from suspected criminals, and better developed software to search e-mail messages. Dragonware encompasses three parts: Pacleteer, Coolminer, and Carnivore.

Packeteer, on which there has been no official information released, appears to be an application for reassembling packets into cohesive messages or web pages. Coolminer, on which there has also been no official information released, is most likely an application for extrapolating and analysing data found in the messages. Although there has been no official information on Paketeer or Coolminer, the Carnivore feature has been used since, the Cold War, where the U.S., Navy was able to "tap into Soviet undersea fibre optic lines by using special submarines, and gain complete knowledge of that set of communication". Since, then, Carnivore has thrived to become a main form of government Internet surveillance today.

IMPLEMENTATION AND USAGE

Carnivore uses a Windows NT/2000-based system that captures information through a form of packet sniffing. A packet sniffer is a form of technology used by computer administrators to monitor networks, perform diagnostic tests, and troubleshoot problems. Sniffing programmes exist in two forms, either as commercial packet sniffers used to help maintain networks, or as underground packet sniffers used to break into computers. In the case of Carnivore, a packet sniffer is a programme that plugs into computer networks and enables a person to view all traffic information passing through.

Each packet is "sniffed" as the programme carries information to the viewer, without interfering with any of the information. A packet sniffer can be set up in two ways: unfiltered, which captures all the packets, or filtered, which captures only the packets that comprise of specific data. In the case of Carnivore, a filtered system is used to capture only the targeted individuals' transmission. After the intended packet is found, the data is copied and then stored in memory or on a hard drive. The process of setting up the Carnivore system involves four stages: installation, filtration, segregation, and collection.

Before any of the stages, the FBI needs to receive judicial approval. Once approved, they check to see if the suspect's Internet Service Provider has the technology to comply with the court order. If not, the FBI cooperates with the ISP technicians to place Carnivore in the network where the suspect's communication packets can be isolated. Once cooperation with the ISP is achieved, the initial filtering is set up. During this process, Carnivore monitors all the ISP traffic from both targeted and non-targeted individuals, then proceeds to filter the packets at the ISP's designated speed. Carnivore takes a picture each second, searching for the suspect's information.

If the suspect's information does not exist, the packet automatically disappears and is not collected, stored, or saved. If there are traces of information, Carnivore proceeds to the third stage. The third stage consists of segregating the suspect's information. Once detection has been made, the packets containing some traces of the suspect's information are then segregated for additional filtration and storage. This leads ultimately to the last stage of collection, which involves more filtering of the suspect's information. Carnivore then collects and processes the final information that can be used according to the court order, discarding any non-retrievable information. A defence method that individuals can use to protect their privacy is through encryption technology. A personal computer (PC) can encrypt messages with codes that are difficult to break.Officials may monitor a suspect's online communications and sniff up the data, but they are not able to understand this encrypted information. The most popular encryption uses online key systems, known as the public-key encryption. A user issues a public key that others can use to send the user a message, which can be decoded only with the user's private key. To overcome this, law-enforcement officials have advocated the use of different software that use a "back door" feature to read the encrypted e-mail or files of criminals. However, it can be argued that allowing back door software would actually weaken codes used for Internet security, which hackers and criminals could exploit. Nonetheless, the point still stands that if material is encrypted, the individual is protected from the government's intrusion to some extent because it is generally difficult to break the encryption.

THE POSITIVE ASPECTS OF INTERNET SURVEILLANCE

Millions of people around the world use the Internet. With the infinite knowledge and possibilities it provides, the Internet can definitely be utilised to connect people to one another and/or make everyday tasks easier. However, many people are unaware of the prospective perils the Internet has. "The rise of the Internet, with e-mail, instant messages, and more, has opened gigantic pipelines for all to use, including criminals". These criminals view the internet as the perfect way to commit crimes, to con individuals, or to affect millions of people through cyber-terrorism. Criminals also use e-mail to spread information to other criminals since, the process is convenient and fast.

This is where the Carnivore system comes in: it keeps an eye on these hazardous people to put a stop to their evil intentions. That in itself, Carnivore is a form of passive hacking used to detect the "real" illegal hackings and other wrongdoings. Carnivore is used by the FBI in five areas: cyber-terrorism, information warfare, child pornography, fraud, and virus writing. Terrorism is a great threat throughout the world. Particularly in the United States, cyber-terrorism can be devastating because of the society's reliance on computers. Cyber-terrorists have the capability to shut down national infrastructures like energy usage, transportation, water, and telecommunications as a means to intimidate and harm the society.

Carnivore attempts to stop or hinder terrorism by monitoring and supervising the Internet activities of known terrorist groups, with procedures equivalent to tapping phones lines. While testifying on the worldwide threat of terrorism, George Tenet, the Director of Central Intelligence, states that "terrorist groups, including Hizbollah, HAMAS, the Abu Nidal organisation, and Bin Laden's al Qu'ida organisation, are using computerised files, e-mail, and encryption to support their operations". These organisations have yet to succeed terrorising America through cyber terrorism; however, the potential threat is still greatly present. This is the very reason the FBI sees Carnivore as a necessity, because the system makes it possible for officials to monitor activity and prevent any catastrophic tragedies from occurring.

There have already been early signs of promise, such as when the FBI discovered that e-mail was a major method used for communication for a terrorist group. Thus, the FBI was able to stop this group from stealing explosives from National Guard Armories in several southern states. It was also discovered that this same terrorist group used the Internet to download information on Ricin, the 3rd deadliest toxin in the world. In instances like this, Carnivore can follow the steps of terrorists and stop them before they strike. Next, Carnivore is helpful when tracking down those individuals that intend to use information warfare against the United States.

Information warfare is a subcategory of cyber-terrorism. Since, many nations cannot measure up to America's power in terms of military strength, they seek information warfare as retaliation. "This type of war attempts to exploit our 'Achilles heel,' a national dependence on information technology in government, commercial, and private operations." A book published by two Chinese military officials explains that the use of unconventional techniques, such as spreading computer viruses, is the only way to neutralise the United States. Moreover, the Russian government has been known to think along the same lines.

Russian government officials acknowledge that attacking America's computer infrastructure could lead to the same result as using weapons of mass destruction; either way hurts the United States immensely. Another crime that Carnivore prevents is child pornography. Even though this is not a national security threat, it is destructive to communities and society. The offenders may download graphics from child pornography web sites and/or use the Internet as a device to arrange meetings between themselves and young children. This can lead to violent and sometimes deadly consequences. "Between 1995 and 2001, the FBI investigated over 800 cases involving offenders crossing state lines to carry out an illegal sexual relationship and more than 1,800 cases involving the exchange of child pornography over the Internet".

It is vital to track these people because they have the tendency to victimise repeatedly. Studies have shown that a child molester typically abuses approximately 70 children in his or her lifetime. With the help of Carnivore, the FBI devised a plan to capture these sexual predators through processes such as "Innocent Images." This site is intended to capture those who distribute child pornography with the Internet. A FBI agent will go undercover as a child over the internet and lure sex offenders to meet with them, allowing the agent to arrest and prosecute the criminal. Fraud is an issue that countless Americans have encountered. The Internet is ideal for fraud for three reasons.

First, people can be easily targeted with the amount of features that it offers, such as chat rooms, instant messages, e-mails, and forums. A person can look up names, addresses, and e-mail addresses through a directory and start sending out spam e-mails.

Secondly, individuals can remain anonymous. When a person creates a web site selling defective materials that do not actually work, he or she may experience fewer, if any, consequences because his or her real identity is kept secret. It is difficult to trace the real identity of the creators of millions upon millions of web sites that can be found. "The critical difference in fraud committed over the Internet is that the perpetrator can 'virtually' vanish, leaving consumers wondering to whom or where to turn to for help".

Thirdly, those that commit fraud do not face expenses with obtaining a toll-free number, mail, and/or hiring people to maintain the mail. Since, they can sign up for free e-mail with companies like Yahoo and Hotmail and obtain a screen name for instant messages with AIM, these previous expenses are no longer necessary. According to the North American Association, Internet related fraud estimates to be about $10 billion per year. In one meticulous case in 2000, 19 individuals implemented an insider trading scheme, where a person with stock information passed along tips to firms through chat rooms.

These 19 people were accused of fraud and discovered to have pocketed several million dollars worth of illegal money. Had Carnivore been in place at the time of this occurrence, they may have been caught sooner than through traditional methods. Finally, the spreading of computer viruses is becoming increasingly perilous. Viruses can be detrimental to company and government computer systems, hurting individuals who simply open an e-mail. Viruses such as the Melissa Macro Virus and the Explore.Zip worm have destroyed individuals' computer files and programmes around the world. They can entirely shut down e-mail systems and delay communications. For example, in some incidents, Microsoft had to put a halt to all outgoing e-mails throughout the company. A hacker can also spread a virus to a company to destroy its database, which often holds immeasurable valuable information. This can be costly and some of the data lost may never be recovered. All things considered, this new programme will eventually be able to do exactly what it was invented to do: monitor, track, and prevent criminals from breaking the law; protect potential victims from facing harmful consequences, and give society assurance that the world is safer place. Even with the loopholes found in Carnivore currently, the overall benefits this plan offers can outweigh its negative aspects. Since, this programme has recently been revealed and is relatively new, the public will have to wait and see if the FBI and government officials can keep their word on its potentials.

THE NEGATIVE ASPECTS OF INTERNET SURVEILLANCE

Evidence suggests that Carnivore may be powerful, but it still has several shortcomings. At the first glance, the name "Carnivore" alone suggests a negative connotation. The fact that Carnivore is for wiretapping and spying on citizens raises the public's concern. It has drawn significant criticism from civil rights groups. The main critics of Carnivore are the Electronic Privacy Information Center (EPIC) and the American Civil Liberties Union (ACLU), two public interest groups devoted to civil liberties issues.

On July 11, 2000, EPIC sued the FBI under the Freedom of Information Act (FOIA). It pursued the public release of Carnivore's background information, source code, technical details, and the potential privacy issues of the technology. The group was able to obtain some information and records, although the FBI still refused to turn over Carnivore's source code and some of its inner workings. The secrecy surrounding exactly how Carnivore operates causes the public, IT managers, and ISPs to feel ambiguous about its implementation. The public is also generally unclear the activities between the intelligence agencies and law enforcement. Many people have confused the Carnivore system with the "Echelon" system, a global mass surveillance system used by intelligence agencies. Hence, EPIC's general counsel David Sobel argues that "Carnivore's use should be suspended until the questions surrounding it finally can be resolved. There's a great deal about Carnivore that we still don't know". The main privacy concern is that the government and the FBI can misuse Carnivore by examining more data than their court orders permit. In other words, it can do a broad sweep and spy on all individuals' Internet traffic and e-mails. Carnivore's intended function is to track and record E-mail subject headers, URLs, and IP addresses, but not the actual contents of an E-mail. Donald Kerr's statement to the U.S., House of Representatives is that Carnivore "does not search through the contents of every message and collect those that contain certain key words like 'bomb' or 'drugs'".

EPIC's legislative counsel Chris Hoofnagle says that although the government claims to only monitor data traffic's subject headers, the real interceptions often include more substance. The FBI moves beyond the scope of a search warrant because it also has access to other information such as message size, time of transmission, the number of jumps that a message takes to reach its destination, and other valuable data that can be extracted. Although the FBI states that Carnivore does not have the capacity to monitor every single individual's e-mails and that the monitoring is only restricted within the court's terms, the public has no actual way of knowing whether the FBI will misuse their power or exactly what Carnivore is capable of. Carnivore's intended function is to filter the data traffic and only retains the relevant data.

The system should have the ability to distinguish between communications that have or have not been authorised for interception. For instance, Carnivore can be configured to intercept e-mail but not online shopping records. However, the software does not always work correctly. In some circumstances, the system picks up both the authorised and unauthorised interceptions. The reason that the system is not as selective with the data captured as the FBI has claimed is due to several imprecise technical functionalities. The controversy over Carnivore comes from the fact that communications through the Internet and the phone are different.

In phone communications, a direct connection exists between two parties. However, Internet communication is broken up into tiny packets, which mixes together pieces of many different conversations. Consequently, extracting one person's data often involves inspecting the data of many others as well. Overall, there is not enough confidence to ensure that Carnivore will only pick up the intended traffic. The intercepted data may be misinterpreted if a single packet is dropped, repeated, or miscategorised. Dynamic IP addresses also make it difficult to identify which computer the data is coming from.

Additionally, since, ISPs vary in their architecture, the system's components may work in one system's architecture but fail in others. ISPs and IT managers are also concerned that the system may damage the company's technology infrastructure. Lastly, the possibility of hacking exists since, Carnivore is controlled remotely and has open security holes. Since, the Carnivore system also intercepts unnecessary non-targeted content, it may have blocked the actual targeted criminal investigations. The unauthorised interceptions not only violate an individual's privacy, but also disrupt or delay anti-terror investigations.

For example, in March 2000 the system was unable to perform effectively under the FBI's International Terrorism Operations Section (ITOS) called "UBL Unit," which refers to the government's official designation of Osama Bin Laden. The Carnivore system was turned on, but it blocked the actual surveillance of the target by also picking up electronic communications of on non-targeted individuals. By this, critics have argued that the FBI is unable to effectively manage foreign intelligence surveillance activities. Privacy advocates are also concerned that Carnivore violates the Fourth Amendment of the Constitution.

The central purpose of the Fourth Amendment is to protect the public's privacy and security from the government's unreasonable invasion. Law enforcement must obtain warrants of probable cause or suspicion in order to conduct searches and seizures. However, law enforcement is allowed to conduct searches without these warrants under limited circumstances, such as those involving government issues. In other words, the government's interest can outweigh an individual's expectation of privacy.

An example is the pen-trap order, in which a probable cause is not needed to obtain a suspect's information. In criminal cases, a court order allows the interception and collection suspects' Internet transmissions without the suspects' knowledge or consent. However, at the same time, the system is given access to the data of those individuals that are not suspects. In the case that the system does capture the data of someone's illegal activity, to a certain extent that information may still be used as evidence in prosecution. Furthermore, an issue concerning property arises in regards to who has the ultimate control of the system.

Responsibility may be divided between the government that uses the system for surveillance, and the technical agents that install and operate the system. In this case, the technical agents are the ones that must configure the system properly so it does not collect data beyond what is permissible by the laws and court orders. The downside is that Carnivore does not have an auditing function to keep track of individual users' identities.

The system logs all users on as 'administrator' and gives everyone full access to all resources. In other words, if an agent changes the settings of Carnivore, it would be difficult to determine the actual person guilty of violating the restrictions. Whether the deed is intentional or due to error, the result is an over-collection of data instead of just the restricted data. The system still needs improvement with stricter controls and independent monitoring, where individual users can be held responsible for their actions within the system.

ETHICAL ANALYSIS AND THE FUTURE

Internet technology has grown tremendously over the past decade, and the same growth will continue to persist into the future. Cyberspace is accessible to a wide range of members in society, including those with criminal intents. With this growth, the United States government has placed more limits on individuals' privacy and promoted the more extensive use of electronic surveillance. Furthermore, the September 11th terrorist attacks have rapidly increased the pace of security measures all around the world. In the United States, law enforcement officials are given even greater power to conduct communications interceptions. The Patriot Act allows the use of Carnivore Internet surveillance technology without a judicial warrant but only a court order.

The warrant requirements needed for monitoring have been reduced, allowing government officials easier access to individuals' records. In addition, the government is promoting policies that require developing communication technologies to have built in surveillance capabilities, and is also seeking limits on devices that provide encryption. The Carnivore system's primary intention is seemingly a responsible and necessary approach to assist the law enforcement in capturing criminals. However, while it can protect the citizens' security, the government must also consider its ability to invade on the citizens' privacy.

Many people believe that electronic surveillance must be limited to only unusual circumstances, since, they are a highly intrusive form of monitoring. The controversial aspect of this issue is that governmental actions can never be equally supported by all viewpoints. When an investigative method such as Carnivore is used, privacy advocates criticise the government for invading the public's privacy rights. On the other hand, when there is a failure to eliminate a potential criminal threat, crime control advocates criticise that the government for being negligent in its regulation of social welfare. As technology advances, the government can no longer use existing standards to manage the surveillance of communications.

Due to the changing disposition and sensitivity of personal information, it is important to provide protection for individuals' privacy and human rights. Consequently, the government must be able to effectively apply new laws, policies, and standards to keep up with the changing technologies. The government has to decide the most appropriate method to increase the nation's security while maintaining a level of freedom and privacy for individuals. The Electronic Communications Privacy Act (ECPA) clarifies how existing wiretap laws can be applied to Internet surveillance and sets boundaries on how much the government can invade the citizens' online privacy.

As long as the Carnivore system is used within the constraints and guidelines of ECPA, it has the potential to be a useful weapon against criminal and national security threats. Due to the new anti-terrorism and security legislations, the level of Internet monitoring by the government will probably not decrease. Several methods can be used to protect the security and privacy concerns of individuals that are monitored by this Carnivore system surveillance. First, technical changes must be considered to address the problem. Improvement of Carnivore's configuration is needed so that it only extracts the intended data traffic.

This will reduce the system's possibility of invading into non-targeted individuals' privacy, and not jeopardise other important investigations, such as those involving terrorism. Second, specific identifications are needed to distinguish FBI agents operating on the system. This way, agents are responsible for any mishaps, such as the change of control settings to collect more data than the system is intended for. Third, many countries now require the public information reporting about the use of surveillances by the government agencies.

The FBI should disclose more about the systems' internal workings so there is not such a secrecy surrounding exactly how it operates. This way, the public can alleviate their security and privacy concerns once they become more aware about the functions of the Carnivore system.

FRAUD INVOLVING ONLINE AUCTIONS

Online auction fraud typically involves several recurring approaches. The most common approach appears to be the offering of some valuable item, such as computers, high-priced watches, or collectible items, through a known online auction site. The individuals who are informed that they are successful bidders send their money to the seller, but never receive the promised merchandise. In a variation of this approach, the criminals send counterfeit merchandise in place of the promised merchandise. A third approach involves the criminal contacting losing bidders in a particular online auction, informing them that additional units of the item on which they bid have become available, and taking the bidders' money without delivering the items.

Consumers interested in a particular auction sometimes want to learn if other buyers have had favorable experiences with the purported seller in that auction. Major auction sites like eBay and Amazon.com allow legitimate customers to provide feedback on their experiences with particular sellers. Criminals, however, can also use false e-mail identities to provide "shill feedback" — false favorable information about themselves — to make it appear that they are satisfied customers and to give consumers a false sense of security about that auction.

In a recent prosecution, United States v. Denlinger, No. 00CR573IEG (S.D. Cal. filed Feb. 28, 2000), the defendant used online auction sites to offer Beanie Babies for sale, but failed to deliver the products after receiving the victim's money. He used various "screen names" (or aliases) in sending e-mails to prospective victims, and provided them with screen names and e-mail addresses of persons he falsely described as "references." In fact, those screen names were assigned to the defendant, so that when victims e-mailed the "references," the defendant responded with messages that gave victims false and favorable information about his own reliability and trustworthiness as a seller. The defendant also used two techniques to prevent victims from contacting him directly: he gave victims a pager number and falsely told them it was his home telephone number; and he asked them to send their payments to various commercial mail receiving agencies, which he falsely told them was his home address. His scheme defrauded more than 200 victims of nearly $50,000. (The defendant, after pleading guilty to mail and wire fraud, was sentenced to twelve months imprisonment and $46,701 in restitution.)

Fraud Involving Online Retail Sales

One category of fraud that overlaps with auction fraud is fraud in online retail sales of goods and services. The IFCC reports that so-called "non-deliverable" merchandise accounts for 22 per cent of all referred complaints. One approach to retail fraud has involved placing banner advertisements on an auction site that offers the same types of goods being auctioned. Prospective buyers who click on the banner advertisement are taken to a different Web site that is not part of the auction site, and that offers none of the protections that leading auction Web sites have adopted for their members. Another approach involves using unsolicited commercial e-mail ("spam") to lure prospective victims to a Web site which purports to sell items of the same type that are available through well-known online auction sites.

In retail sales of services, some criminals have taken advantage of the complexities of the Internet's operations to compel or mislead consumers into visiting their Web sites. In United States v. Kashpureff, 98CR0218 (E.D.N.Y. filed March 19, 1998), the defendant operated a Web site, AlterNIC, that competed with the InterNIC Web site for domain name registration. He wrote and placed software on that Internet that caused persons who wanted to visit the InterNIC Web site to be involuntarily redirected to his Web site. Ultimately, he pleaded guilty to a violation of the computer fraud statute, 18 U.S.C. § 1030.

In United States v. Lee, No. 99-00560 SOM (D. Haw. filed Dec. 9, 1999), the defendant knew that the Hawaii Marathon Association operated a Web site with the Uniform Resource Locator (URL) "www.hawaiimarathon.org" to provide information about the Marathon and enable runners to register online. Although he had no affiliation with the real Hawaii Marathon, he copied the authorized Marathon Web site, and created his own Web site with the confusingly similar name, "www.hawaiimarathon.com." Runners who came to his Web site thinking that it was the real Hawaii Marathon site were charged a $165 registration fee — $100 more than the real site charged for entry. The defendant also operated another Web site where he sold Viagra over the Internet without a prescription. (The defendant later pleaded guilty to wire fraud and unlawful sale of Viagra, and in February 2001 was given a split sentence of ten months imprisonment.)

Investment Fraud

Another major category of online fraud is investment fraud. The Securities and Exchange Commission (SEC) has reported that it receives between 200 and 300 online complaints each day about possible securities fraud online. While the major types of online securities fraud generally parallel traditional securities fraud schemes, market manipulation schemes are a frequent focus of enforcement actions.

"Pump-and-Dump." The most widely publicized form of online market manipulation is the so-called "pump and dump" scheme. In a "pump and dump," criminals identify one or more companies whose stock is thinly traded or not traded at all, then adopt various means to persuade individual online investors to buy that company's stock. These means can include posting favorable, but false and misleading, representations on financial message boards or Web sites, and making undisclosed payments to people who are ostensibly independent but who will recommend that stock. Once the price has increased sufficiently, the participants in the scheme — who may be company insiders, outsiders, or both, sell their stock, and the stock price eventually declines sharply, leaving uninformed investors with substantial financial losses. While an outsider who merely expresses his opinions about the worth or likely increase or decrease of a particular stock may not be committing criminal fraud, outsiders or insiders whose conduct extends beyond mere advocacy to manipulation of markets for their personal profit by giving the public false and misleading information may violate securities fraud statutes and other criminal statutes.In one pump-and-dump case, United States v. Aziz-Golshani, No. 00-007-GAF (C.D. Cal. filed Jan. 4, 2000), two defendants manipulated the stock of a bankrupt company, NEI Webworld, Inc. They posted messages on several financial message boards, falsely stating that NEI was going to be taken over by a California company, and, with the help of a third individual, bought 130,000 shares of NEI before their manipulations resulted in a dramatic price increase. In an attempt to conceal their identities, the two defendants and their confederates used computers at the UCLA Biomedical Library to post the false reports. An SEC amended complaint charged that the defendants and another individual had also engaged in similar manipulative conduct concerning the securities of eleven other issuers in 1999. (In January, 2001, both defendants were sentenced to fifteen months and ten months imprisonment, respectively).

"Cybersmear." The converse of the "pump and dump" is the "cybersmear." A "cybersmear" scheme is organized in the same basic manner as a "pump-and- dump," with one important difference: the object is to induce a decline in the stock's price, to permit the criminals to realize profits by short-selling. To accomplish a sufficiently rapid decline in the stock's price, the criminal must resort to blatant lies and misrepresentations likely to trigger a substantial sell off by other investors.

In United States v. Moldofsky, No. S100CR388 (RPP) (S.D.N.Y. convicted March 8, 2001), the defendant, a day trader, on the evening of March 22, 2000, and the morning of the next day, posted a message nearly twenty times what was designed to look like a Lucent press release announcing that Lucent would not meet its quarterly earnings projections. For most of those postings, he used an alias designed to resemble a screen name used by a frequent commentator on the Lucent message board who had historically expressed positive views of Lucent stock. He also posted additional messages, using other screen names that commented on the release or on the message poster's conduct. On March 23, Lucent's stock price dropped more than 3.7 per cent before Lucent issued a statement disavowing the false press release, but rose by 8 per cent within ten minutes of Lucent's disavowal.

In United States v. Jakob, No. CR-00-1002-DT (C.D. Cal. indictment filed Sept. 28, 2000; pleaded guilty Dec. 29, 2000), the defendant engaged in even more elaborate fraudulent conduct to effect a "cybersmear." After he tried to short-sell stock in Emulex, but found that the market was bidding up the price, he wrote a press release falsely reporting that Emulex was under investigation by the SEC, that Emulex's Chief Executive Officer was resigning, and that Emulex was reporting a loss in its latest earnings report. He then caused his former employer, a company that distributed online press releases, to send it to major news organizations, which reported the false statements as fact. When Emulex stock rapidly declined, the defendant covered his short-sale position by buying Emulex stock and realizing nearly $55,000 in profits. He also bought more Emulex stock at lower prices, and sold when the stock had recovered most of its value.

One notable feature of online market manipulation schemes is the speed with which the scheme's participants can induce dramatic, though short-term, fluctuations in stock prices, and can realize substantial profits by correctly timing their purchases and sales. In Aziz-Golshani, during the week of November 9, 1999, the defendants bought their NEI stock at prices ranging from 9 cents to 13 cents per share. On November 15, 1999, NEI stock opened at 9:00 a.m. Eastern time at $8 per share, and within 45 minutes had risen to $15 5/16 per share. Less than a half-hour later, NEI stock had dropped to approximately 25 cents per share. By selling when the stock price was still high, the defendants realized profits of more than $360,000. In Jakob, once the false press release was distributed, Emulex's stock price dropped in less than one hour from more than $110 per share to approximately $43 per share, and the trading volume of Emulex stock increased significantly as individual traders sold off the stock at notably lower prices. The defendant realized nearly $55,000 in profits from his short sale, and additional profits of nearly $187,000 as the stock price rebounded.

PAYMENT CARD FRAUD

One of the fastest-growing categories of Internet fraud is payment card (*i.e.*, credit card and debit card) fraud. One Internet research firm, Meridien Research, predicted in January 2001 that online payment-card fraud worldwide will increase from $1.6 billion in 2000 to $15.5 billion by 2005.

Online credit card fraud causes substantial problems for online merchants. Initially, many online merchants were defrauded when people, using others' credit card numbers, ordered merchandise and had it shipped to foreign locations that were clearly different from the addresses of the true credit card holders. Under the policies that major credit card issuers established, merchants must bear the losses for online purchases, which qualify as "card- not-present" transactions. As a number of merchants took defensive measures, such as installing software designed to flag possibly fraudulent online transactions, some criminals changed their methods to request shipment of the goods they ordered with others' credit card numbers to United States addresses. Confederates then sell or ship those goods to another location.

To commit online payment-card fraud, criminals need access to valid payment-card numbers. One means of acquiring them is the unlawful accessing of e-commerce Web sites. Within the past year, several computer intrusions that made possible the downloading of tens of thousands, if not millions, of credit card numbers — such as the exposure of more than 3 million credit cards at Egghead.com — have received worldwide attention in the media.

A number of Internet credit card schemes involve computer hacking as the means of accessing the numbers. For example, in United States v. Bosanac, No. 99CR3387IEG (S.D. Cal. filed Dec. 7, 1999), the defendant was involved in a computer hacking scheme that used home computers for electronic access to several of the largest United States telephone systems and for downloading thousands of calling card numbers (access codes).

The defendant, who pleaded guilty to possession of unauthorized access devices and computer fraud, used his personal computer to access a telephone system computer and to download and transfer thousands of access codes relating to company calling card numbers. In taking these codes, the defendant used a computer Programme he had created to automate the downloading, and instructed his coconspirators on how to use the Programme. The defendant admitted that the loss suffered by the company as a result of his criminal conduct was $955,965. He was sentenced to eighteen months' imprisonment and $10,000 in restitution.

IDENTITY THEFT AND FRAUD

Online payment-card fraud is closely related to the problem of identity theft and fraud. The Federal Trade Commission (FTC) reports that its Consumer Sentinel Web site, which provides law enforcement with access to more than 300,000 complaints about all types of consumer fraud, has received more complaints about identity theft and fraud than any other category of consumer fraud. While identity theft can be committed in furtherance of many types of crime, a number of recent federal prosecutions have combined identity theft and Internet fraud.

In United States v. Christian, No. 00-03-SLR (D. Del. filed Aug. 3, 2000), two defendants obtained the names and Social Security numbers of 325 high-ranking United States military officers from a public Web site, then used those names and identities to apply for instant credit at a leading computer company and to obtain credit cards through two banks. They fenced the items they bought under the victims' names, and accepted orders from others for additional merchandise. The two defendants, after pleading guilty to conspiracy to commit bank fraud were sentenced to thirty-three and forty-one months imprisonment and restitution of more than $100,000 each.

Similarly, in United States v. Wahl, No. CR00-285P (W.D. Wash. sentenced Oct. 16, 2000), the defendant obtained the date of birth and Social Security number of the victim (who shared the defendant's first and last name and middle initial). He then used the victim's identifying information to apply online for credit cards with three companies and to apply online for a $15,000 automobile loan. He actually used the proceeds of the automobile loan to invest in his own business. (The defendant, after pleading guilty to identity theft, was sentenced to seven months' imprisonment and nearly $27,000 in restitution).

Business Opportunity Fraud

Business opportunity or "work-at-home" schemes are also making their way onto the Internet. In United States v. Shklowskiy (C.D. Cal. sentenced June 9, 2000), the defendants used the Internet to harvest e-mail addresses and send more than 50 million unsolicited e-mails ("spam") to offer people a "work-at-home" opportunity that promised tremendous returns in exchange for a $35 "processing fee." Approximately 12,405 individual victims sent money to what they thought were various businesses, but in fact, were postal mailboxes. As part of the scheme, the defendants forged the e-mail headers in their "spam" to make it appear that the e-mails were coming from an Internet service provider, BigBear.Net. As a result of the header forgery, when approximately 100,000 recipients of the spam responded with complaints by e-mail, the unexpected large volume of e-mails caused BigBear.Net's computer file servers to crash or cause disruptions in their service to customers. BigBear.Net had to hire three temporary workers for nearly six months to respond to the large numbers of complaints. (Ultimately, two defendants, after pleading guilty to conspiracy to commit mail and wire fraud, were sentenced to twenty seven months' imprisonment and restitution of $104,000 to fraud victims, including BigBear.Net).

The Response to Internet Fraud

As the case examples above indicate, more and more United States Attorneys' Offices are pursuing significant cases of Internet fraud. The cases being prosecuted tend to show that the criminal statutes that apply to other types of white collar crime — conspiracy, mail and wire fraud, credit card fraud, securities fraud, money laundering, and identity theft — are equally applicable to various forms of Internet fraud. In addition, a variety of existing sentencing guidelines enable federal prosecutors to seek higher sentences in appropriate cases of Internet fraud. These include enhancements for mass-marketing (USSG § 2F1.1(b)(3)), identity theft (USSG § 2F1.1(b)(5)(C)), conducting a substantial part of a scheme from outside the United States (USSG § 2F1.1(b)(6)(B)), large numbers of vulnerable victims (USSG § 3A1.1(b)(2)(B)), and use of a special skill (USSG 3B1.3; compare United States v. Petersen, 98 F.3d 502, 506-08 (9th Cir. 1996), with United States v. Godman, 223 F.3d 320, 322 (6th Cir. 2000)).

IMPACT OF TECHNOLOGY ON ECONOMIC CRIME

The growth of the information age and the globalization of Internet communication and commerce have impacted significantly upon the manner in which economic crimes are committed, the frequency with which those crimes are committed, and the difficulty in apprehending the perpetrators. A recent survey conducted by the Gartner Group of 160 retail companies selling products over the Internet reveals that the amount of credit card fraud is twelve times higher online than in the physical retail world. There is no reason to believe that this figure is unique to the credit card industry. Another recent study indicates that the number of search warrants issued by the federal government for online data has increased 800 per cent over the past few years. Technology has contributed to that increase in four major respects—anonymity, security (or insecurity), privacy (or the lack of it) and globalization. Additionally, technology has provided the medium or opportunity for the commission of traditional crimes.

Criminals continue to make false statements in credit applications submitted over the Internet, bank employees continue to embezzle funds by wire transfer or account takeover, and swindlers continue to misrepresent products at auction sites over the Internet. However, it is the widespread use of technology and the Internet for business transactions and communications, and the confluence of anonymity, security, privacy and globalization that have exposed the public and private sectors to an alarming new array of cyber attacks. In addition to their inability to prevent such attacks, both government and the private sector lack effective enforcement tools and remedies to bring the perpetrators to justice. Technology and the Internet have contributed to the growth of economic crime in each of the identified industries in similar ways.

Anonymity enables the criminal to submit fraudulent online applications for bank loans, credit card accounts, insurance coverage, brokerage accounts, and health care coverage or to construct a counterfeit web site in order to establish an inflated value for publicly traded stock in order to sell the stock at a falsely inflated price ("pump and dump" schemes). Anonymity also enables employees to pilfer corporate assets. For example, bank employees can embezzle money through electronic fund transfers and employees of credit card issuers can capture account numbers and sell them to outsiders, electronically transferring the account numbers to the coconspirators.

Further, anonymity provides enhanced opportunities for two types of perpetrators—the organised crime mobster and the teenage hacker. Security, or the lack of it, enables criminal hackers to disrupt e-commerce in several ways. They can engage in denial of service attacks, compromise payment systems in online banking, penetrate web sites and extract credit card account numbers for resale or as ransom for the extortion of cash from the card issuer, or hijack a web site for the purpose of stealing the identity of the e-commerce merchant, directing the proceeds of sales to the hijacker. Privacy protections enable thieves to take advantage of the benefits of anonymity, while hampering the efforts of law enforcement and private sector fraud investigators to track the thieves. Lastly, the Internet enables communication and commerce to occur beyond or without borders, presenting significant problems in the prevention, investigation and enforcement of those crimes.

BANKING

There is no pending legislation that specifically addresses frauds in connection with online banking. The Internet provides fertile ground for those intending to defraud financial institutions. Because the online customer is anonymous, the risk of fraud is greater. Projected increases in the volume of online transactions and repeal of the Glass-Steagall Act, which has expanded the types of institutions that may provide banking services, could increase the exposure to cyber attack. Congressional focus is currently on cyber laundering, specifically the electronic transfer of funds into U.S. banks from sources outside the country and subsequent transfers by those banks to cyber laundering havens. On the regulatory side, the Federal Trade Commission and other agencies have proposed regulations dealing with the privacy of financial data, the circumstances when disclosure may be made, and the conditions precedent to such disclosures.

Those regulations, which are scheduled to take effect on November 13, 2000, require financial institutions to provide privacy notices to consumers, limit the disclosure of non-public personal information to non-affiliated third parties, and allow consumers to opt-out of certain restrictions. The Electronic Signature in Global and National Commerce Act, which became law on July 1, 2000, is a major effort to facilitate the consummation of contracts, including agreements with banking and financial institutions, electronically. While the Act facilitates e-Commerce, it provides yet another opportunity for the theft of a significant aspect of one's identity—the signature. The Act contains no provision imposing criminal sanctions for the theft or piracy of one's signature. The access device statute should be amended to include electronic and digital signatures as a "means of identification. Additional legislation is essential to reduce the risks presented by anonymity and database insecurity, including prescribed authentication procedures and encryption protections.

CREDIT CARD

The use of credit cards for online retail purchases, as well as for online gambling and to gain access to pornography and child pornography sites, is expected to increase exponentially. Online transactions are not conducted face-to-face; therefore, the merchant cannot identify the customer in the traditional manner. The increased volume of online transactions and the absence of face-to-face interaction provide greater opportunity for fraud, including identity theft for the purpose of conducting an online transaction.While substantive laws provide ample redress for the criminal use of credit cards (and debit cards) in cyberspace, the implementation of new technologies for credit purchases, such as smart cards and electronic wallets, may raise issues regarding the applicability of existing criminal statutes. Those statutes should be amended to prohibit the theft or fraudulent sale, distribution or possession of a counterfeit, stolen or fictitious account number regardless of whether that account number is used in connection with a plastic card, electronic wallet or other form of digital storage.

The amendment should also state that the crime applies to the theft by computer of account numbers or information that could be used to identify an account number. There is currently no pending legislation that would regulate the use of credit cards for online transactions. However, S. 699, the Telemarketing Fraud and Seniors Protection Act, would amend the wire fraud statute to include schemes or artifices to defraud, perpetrated via Internet communications. Because credit card fraud can be prosecuted under this statute, the proposed legislation would enhance significantly the enforcement arsenal for credit card fraud. Further, the proposed Identity Theft Protection Act of 2000 would strengthen protection against fraudulent practices committed with stolen credit cards.

That Act requires the card issuer to confirm any reported change of address and notify the cardholder of any request for additional cards. It also requires credit-reporting agencies to inform the card issuer if the address on the application for a credit card is different than the address shown in the consumer's records. Section 4 of the Act would also add a requirement that, upon the request of the consumer, a consumer reporting agency must include a fraud alert in the consumer's file and notify each person seeking credit information of the existence of that alert. That Act would provide significant protection from the technological identity theft.

HEALTH CARE

Currently, there is no pending legislation designed to address health care frauds committed in cyberspace. Future legislative attention should focus on the attributes of the Internet and e-commerce that promote fraudulent activity in the provision of health care products and services.

INSURANCE

There currently are no pending federal laws or regulations that address insurance fraud committed in cyberspace. Historically, regulation of the insurance business has been the province of the states. The 1999 Gramm-Leach-Bliley Act, which repealed the Glass-Steagall Act, enabled financial institutions to provide a variety of services, including insurance. The federal government should establish broad legislation designed to regulate and secure the online sale of insurance products. Arguably, the only effective weapon at the disposal of federal prosecutors is the wire fraud statute. Additional legislation that requires secure connections and seeks to prevent fraudulent activity regarding online insurance applications and claims should be a priority.Moreover, because the Internet is an instrument of interstate commerce, Congress should rethink that portion of the Gramm-Leach-Bliley Act which leaves the regulation of issues such as the use of non-public information by insurance companies to the state regulators. Federal involvement in this area would provide uniform regulation and would not subject financial institutions that provide banking, securities and insurance products to a different regulatory scheme for the offering of insurance products.

SECURITIES

The Internet is an instrument of interstate commerce. Thus, section 10(b) of the Securities Exchange Act of 1934 and Rule 10b-5 provide criminal sanctions for fraudulent acts committed in cyberspace involving the purchase or sale of securities. Also, the mail fraud and wire fraud statutes provide an additional weapon for the prosecution of frauds and swindles involving securities.

Again, substantive criminal laws provide ample sanction for fraudulent conduct impacting upon the securities industry. The Securities Exchange Commission is, however, faced with the difficult task of detecting and investigating securities frauds committed in the online venue. It has created a new enforcement unit to deal specifically with online trading and frauds committed with respect to securities, but legislation is required to assist investigators in the detection and investigation of such frauds. The Online Investor Protection Act of 1999, S. 1015, would be a start in that direction.

TELECOMMUNICATIONS

Section 699, The Telemarketing Fraud and Senior Protection Act would amend the wire fraud statute to prohibit fraudulent telemarketing practices over the Internet. That statute should be further amended to prohibit fraudulent conduct over the Internet transacted in part through a wireless connection.

INTELLECTUAL PROPERTY AND COMPUTER CRIME

Although existing criminal laws will continue to provide effective weapons to combat cyber crimes committed upon the traditional service industries that offer their services and products through e-commerce, Congress and the global community must move swiftly to provide an effective array of substantive laws designed specifically for Internet transactions. That array should include laws and treaties to provide law enforcement and the private sector with the tools essential for the detection and investigation of cyber crime. Some Congressional attention has focused on peripheral issues such as privacy and encryption, and there are signs that Congress is beginning to address Internet-specific issues. Five pending Congressional bills suggest that Congress is aware that law enforcement must be equipped with adequate resources and remedies to combat cyber crime. A High Tech Crime Bill was introduced on February 24, 2000 by senators Charles Schumer and John Kyl.

This bill proposes amendments to the computer fraud statute that would include fraudulent acts committed upon "protected computers" in the United States, by persons in foreign countries and would include damage done to computers and computer systems irrespective of property damage losses. That amendment would encompass damage caused by, for example, denial of service attacks.The proposed bill also would amend 18 U.S.C. § 3123 (c), enabling law enforcement to employ trap and trace devices to assist in the investigation of computer attacks. The Internet Security Act of 2000, introduced in April 2000 by Senator Leahy, would expand the jurisdictional scope of the computer fraud statute to include international hacking. It would amend section 3123 to enable law enforcement to employ trap and trace devices, impose encryption standards, and authorise the prosecution of juvenile hackers. It would also appropriate $25 million for each of the next four fiscal years for law enforcement training Programmes in computer fraud investigations. Both bills seek to react to recent attacks upon e-Commerce sites, including the denial of service attacks. The Internet Integrity and Critical Infrastructure Protection Act of 2000, introduced on April 13, 2000 by Senator Hatch, co-sponsored by Senator Schumer, would impose criminal penalties for cyber hacking committed by persons under 18 years old, create a National Cyber Crime Technical Support Center to serve as a resource center for federal, state and local law enforcement and assist them in the investigation of computer-related crimes, and provide the implementation of computer crime mutual assistance agreements in order to enable reciprocal assistance for foreign authorities.

Also on April 13, 2000, Senator Hutchinson introduced S. 2451 that would increase the criminal penalties for computer fraud committed in violation of 18 U.S.C. § 1030 and establish a National Commission on Cyber security to study incidents of computer crimes and the need for enhanced methods of combating such crimes. Finally, on May 9, 2000, Congressman Boehlert introduced the Law Enforcement Science and Technology Act of 2000, co-sponsored by Congressman Stupak. This bill would establish an Office of Science and Technology in the Office of Justice Programmes of the Department of Justice.

The mission of that office would be:

- To serve as the national focal point for work on law enforcement technology; and
- To carry out Programmes to improve the safety and effectiveness of, and access to, technology to assist Federal, State and local law enforcement agencies.

The bill would direct the appropriation of $40 million for regional National Law Enforcement and Corrections Technology Centers, $60 million for research and development of forensic technologies and methods to improve crime laboratories, and $20 million for the testing and evaluation of technologies. Additional governmental attention must be focused on extradition and mutual assistance treaties that will enable the United States to prosecute cyber crimes committed by international terrorists and hackers.

INTERNET ARCHITECTURE AND VULNERABLE SECURITY ASPECTS

Fear of security breaches on the Internet is causing organizations to use protected private networks or intranets. The Internet Engineering Task Force (IETF) has introduced security mechanisms at various layers of the Internet Protocol Suite. These security mechanisms allow for the logical protection of data units that are transferred across the network.

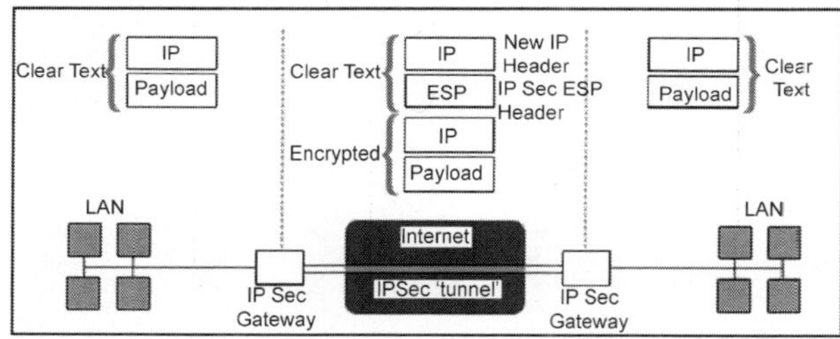

Fig. IPsec Contains a Gateway and a Tunnel in order to Secure Communications.

The current version and new version of the Internet Protocol are analysed to determine the security implications. Although security may exist within the protocol, certain attacks cannot be guarded against. These attacks are analysed to determine other security mechanisms that may be necessary.

The security architecture of the internet protocol, known as IP Security, is a standardization of internet security. IP security, IPsec, covers the new generation of IP (IPv6) as well as the current version (IPv4). Although new techniques, such as IPsec, have been developed to overcome internet's best-known deficiencies, they seem to be insufficient.

IPSec is a point-to-point protocol, one side encrypts, the other decrypts and both sides share key or keys. IPSec can be used in two modes, namely transport mode and tunnel modes.

IPV4 AND IPV6 ARCHITECTURES

IPv4 was design in 1980 to replace the NCP protocol on the ARPANET. The IPv4 displayed many limitations after two decades. The IPv6 protocol was designed with IPv4's shortcomings in mind. IPv6 is not a superset of the IPv4 protocol; instead it is a new design.

The Internet protocol's design is so vast and cannot be covered fully. The main parts of the architecture relating to security.

IPv4 Architecture

The protocol contains a couple aspects which caused problems with its use. These problems do not all relate to security. They are mentioned to gain a comprehensive understanding of the Internet protocol and its shortcomings.

The causes of problems with the protocol are:

- Address Space
- Routing
- Configuration
- Security
- Quality of Service.

The IPv4 architecture has an address that is 32 bits wide. This limits the maximum number of computers that can be connected to the Internet. The 32 bit address provides for a maximum of two billions computers to be connected to the Internet. The problem of exceeding that number was not foreseen when the protocol was created. The small address space of the IPv4 facilitates malicious code distribution.

Routing is a problem for this protocol because the routing tables are constantly increasing in size. The maximum theoretical size of the global routing tables was 2.1 million entries. Methods have been adopted to reduce the number of entries in the routing table. This is helpful for a short period of time, but drastic change needs to be made to address this problem. The TCP/IP-based networking of IPv4 requires that the user supplies some data in order to configure a network. Some of the information required is the IP address, routing gateway address, subnet mask, and DNS server. The simplicity of configuring the network is not evident in the IPv4 protocol. The user can request appropriate network configuration from a central server. This eases configuration hassles for the user but not the network's administrators.

The lack of embedded security within the IPv4 protocol has led to the many attacks seen today. Mechanisms to secure IPv4 do exist, but there are no requirements for their use. IPsec is a specific mechanism used to secure the protocol. IPsec secures the packet payloads by means of cryptography. IPsec provides the services of confidentiality, integrity, and authentication. This form of protection does not account for the skilled hacker who may be able to break the encryption method and obtain the key.

When Internet was created, the quality of service (QoS) was standardized according to the information that was transferred across the network. The original transfer of information was mostly text-based. As the internet expanded and technology evolved, other forms of communication began to be transmitted across the Internet. The quality of service for streaming videos and music are much different than the standard text. The protocol does not have the functionality of dynamic QoS that changes based on the type of data being communicated.

IPv6 Architecture

When IPv6 was being developed, emphasis was placed on aspects of the IPv4 protocol that needed to be improved.

The development efforts were placed in the following areas:

- Routing and addressing
- Multi-protocol architecture
- Security architecture
- Traffic control.

The IPv6 protocol's address space was extended by supporting 128 bit addresses. With 128 bit addresses, the protocol can support up to $3.4 \times (10)^{38}$ machines. The address bits are used less efficiently in this protocol because it simplifies addressing configuration.

The IPv6 routing system is more efficient and enables smaller global routing tables. The host configuration is also simplified. Hosts can automatically configure themselves. This new design allows ease of configuration for the user as well as network administrator. The security architecture of the IPv6 protocol is of great interest. IPsec is embedded within the IPv6 protocol. IPsec functionality is the same for IPv4 and IPv6. The only difference is that IPv6 can utilize the security mechanism along the entire route. The quality of service problem is handled with IPv6. The Internet protocol allows for special handling of certain packets with a higher quality of service. From a high-level view, the major benefits of IPv6 are its scalability and increased security. IPv6 also offers other interesting features that are beyond the scope of this chapter.

INTERNET SPYING

Beginning with the Antiterrorism and Effective Death Penalty Act of 1996 (AEDPA), which severely limited the rights of prisoners to obtain *habeas corpus* relief from federal courts, 2001's Authorization for Use of Military Force (AUMF) which handed the Executive Branch carte blanche to wage endless, undeclared wars, and now the National Defence Authorization Act of 2012 (NDAA), which empowers the President to order the military to pick up and indefinitely imprison anyone, anywhere in the world declared a "terrorist," including American citizens detained on U.S. soil, without charge or trial, the architecture of a police state is firmly in place.

The Electronic Frontier Foundation's (EFF) Trevor Timm averred, "the formless phrase 'national security' has invaded many arenas of government action, and has been used to justify much activity that did not involve legitimate terrorist threats. The most obvious (and odious) example is the unfortunately named USA-PATRIOT Act, a law that was sold to the American public as essential to combating terrorism, but which has overwhelmingly been applied to ordinary American citizens never even suspected of terrorism."

Citing the example of the FBI, Timm pointed out that under the rubric of "stopping terrorism" the Bureau "issued more than 192,000 National Security Letters to get Americans' business, phone or Internet records without a warrant. These invasive letters–which come with a gag order on the recipient so they can't even admit they received one–have been used to gather information about untold number of ordinary citizens, including journalists." The "'Information sharing'–CISPA's mantra–has also created privacy nightmares for daily Americans in the name of national security. The federal government routinely shares its massive national security databases with local law enforcement agencies with predictable results."

Amongst CISPA's controversial supplies, the Director of National Intelligence (DNI), the *Obergruppenführer* of America's 16-agency Intelligence Community, "shall issue guidelines providing that the head of an element of the intelligence community may, as the head of such element considers necessary to carry out this subsection: (A) grant a security clearance on a temporary or permanent basis to an employee or officer of a certified entity; (B) grant a security clearance on a temporary or permanent basis to a certified entity and approval to use appropriate facilities; and (C) expedite the security clearance process for a person or entity as the head of such element considers necessary, consistent with the need to protect the national security of the United States."

Under "Definitions," (1) a "certified entity" is described as a "protected entity, self-protected entity, or cyber security provider that–(A) possesses or is eligible to obtain a security clearance, as determined by the Director of National Intelligence; and (B) is able to demonstrate to the Director of National Intelligence that such provider or such entity can appropriately protect classified cyber threat intelligence." "(2) The term 'cyber threat information' means information directly pertaining to a vulnerability of, or threat to, a system or network of a government or private entity, including information pertaining to the protection of a system or network from–(A) efforts to degrade, disrupt, or destroy such system or network; or (B) theft or misappropriation of private or government information, intellectual property, or personally identifiable information. (3) Cyber threat intelligence.–The term 'cyber threat intelligence' means information in the possession of an element of the intelligence community directly pertaining to a vulnerability of, or threat to, a system or network of a government or private entity, including information pertaining to the protection of a system or network from–(A) efforts to degrade, disrupt, or destroy such system or network; or (B) theft or misappropriation of private or government information, intellectual property, or personally identifiable information."

A "certified entity" is any one of the thousands of Fibre-secretive "cyber security firms" with their stable of "cleared" employees who hold top secret and above security clearances who rely upon and do the bidding of their masters–corporate shareholders and the federal government. The bill's draconian words would in essence transform investigative journalism and whistleblowing into a crime since "the theft or misappropriation of private or government information, intellectual property, or personally identifiable information" is *precisely* the meat and potatoes used by journalists and outraged citizens to uncover corporate and government lawbreaking.

Indeed under CISPA, the employees of firms such as the ultra-spooky Endgame Systems, SAIC, Lockheed Martin, or General Dynamics, the designers of "boutique cyber weapons" for the government as *BusinessWeek* disclosed last summer, would ply their dirty trade in destructive algorithmic weapons with more than a wink-and-a-nod: they would be empowered to do so and earn big bucks (courtesy of U.S. taxpayers) in the process! To get a sense of some of the surveillance "products" which have transformed private data into weaponized kit for the secret state, readers are well-advised to peruse The Spyfiles published last December by the whistleblowing web site WikiLeaks."In the last ten years," WikiLeaks informed us, "systems for indiscriminate, mass surveillance have become the norm. Intelligence companies such as VASTech secretly sell equipment to permanently record the phone calls of entire nations. Others record the location of every mobile phone in a city, down to 50 meters. Systems to infect every Facebook user, or smart-phone owner of an entire population group are on the intelligence market."To cite but one example culled from The Spyfiles, NICE Systems, founded by "retired" members of Israel's equivalent of the National Security Agency, Unit 8200, has become a key player in the global Surveillance-Industrial Complex. With decades of experience surveilling, tracking and repressing Palestinian and left-wing activists at home and abroad, the NiceTrack Mass Detection Centre is a perfect tool that provides "nationwide interception, monitoring and analysis" to enterprising securocrats who need a leg-up on home-grown "subversive elements."

The Mass Detection Centre "helps intelligence organizations and national security agencies fight terrorism and reduce national threat levels. It supports both mass and target monitoring workflows and helps operators and analysts find new suspects, generate new leads and monitor existing targets." Indeed, the software suite "stores and analyses all types of telephony and Internet content." We're informed that "collecting and storing nationwide data enables broadening the scope of target information and performing on-going and post-event investigations." NiceTrack Target 360° according to brochures published by WikiLeaks "is the leading communication intercept system for tracking, monitoring, and investigating targets' activities, securing 1.5 billion people worldwide." Indeed, "the system is designed to provide Law Enforcement Agencies (LEAs), intelligence organizations and SIGINT agencies with hermetic 360° target monitoring by collecting, processing, retaining and analysing any type of communication activity." Amongst the product's "Key Benefits" we learn that Target 360° can "help" law enforcement "reduce crime, prevent terrorism" and "identify other security threats" by providing "persistent situation awareness" of a "target" through "advanced IP monitoring," "open source intelligence" and "lawful hacking."

Additionally, Target 360° can "manage and efficiently structure millions of internet activities and unstructured data into a simple and meaningful intelligence picture." Target 360° "is designed to handle all types of Web 2.0 internet applications, including Facebook, Twitter and other social networks, forums, chats, and e-mails, and is scalable to support new services" and can "be integrated with legacy systems for telephony and mobile interception and provide a comprehensive solution for all types of communication interception." As numerous critics and journalists have pointed out, the privatization of the government's intelligence and security functions, theoretically transparent under provisions of the Freedom of Information Act (FOIA), would, under CISPA, fall under the purview of the Department of Homeland Security (DHS) and the National Security Agency (NSA) where "disclosure" is little more than a euphemism for "down the memory hole."

In all likelihood, privatized spooks would be exempt from revealing the state's blanket surveillance of its citizens under any number of provisions built into the Freedom of Information Act. For example under section (b)(1), the secret state can prevent "disclosure [of] national security information concerning the national defence or foreign policy, provided that it has been properly classified in accordance with the substantive and procedural requirements of an executive order." Since, an "an employee or officer of a certified entity," *i.e.*, a private contractor, telecom or ISP will be empowered by Congress to share user information with NSA and other departments of the federal government, such information "shall be considered proprietary information and shall not be disclosed to an entity outside of the Federal Government except as authorized by the entity sharing such information." Under CISPA it will be virtually impossible for the average citizen to learn whether they have been spied upon since Section (b)(4) of FOIA specifically protects "trade secrets and commercial or financial information obtained from a person [that is] privileged or confidential.

This exemption is intended to protect the interest of both the government and submitter of information." And once an "employee or officer of a certified entity" has been "read into" a CIA, FBI, DHS or NSA black programme, they are automatically exempt from disclosing such information to a lawful court since CISPA "prohibits a civil or criminal cause of action against a protected entity, a self-protected entity (an entity that provides goods or services for cyber security purposes to itself), or a cyber security provider acting in good faith under the above circumstances."

With CISPA, official lawbreaking is automatically precluded from review by a lawful court and the average citizen, who may have lost their job because of malicious or flawed data collected by a "certified entity" will be stripped of their ability to obtain compensation from deputized cyber snoops "acting in good faith." Most controversially perhaps, the statute reads: "notwithstanding any other provision of law," companies can share information "with any other entity, including the federal government."As CNET News analyst Declan McCullagh pointed out, "By including the word 'notwithstanding,' House Intelligence Committee Chairman Mike Rogers (R-Mich.) and ranking member Dutch Ruppersberger (D-Md.) intended to make CISPA trump all existing federal and state civil and criminal laws." Indeed, by inserting the word "notwithstanding" into the legislation, it "would trump wiretap laws, Web companies' privacy policies, gun laws, educational record laws, census data, medical records, and other statutes that protect information," McCullagh wrote.

"CISPA's authorization for information sharing extends far beyond Web companies and social networks. It would also apply to Internet service providers, including ones that already have an intimate relationship with Washington officialdom," CNET reported. "Large companies including AT&T and Verizon handed billions of customer records to the NSA; only Qwest refused to participate," McCullagh reminded us. "Verizon turned over customer data to the FBI without court orders. An AT&T whistleblower accused the company of illegally opening its network to the NSA, a practice that the U.S. Congress retroactively made legal in 2008."

What's to prevent firms such as Google, Facebook or Twitter from turning over our private data to the government, after all, they have their customers' best interests at heart as part of their business model, right? Better think again!*The New York Times* reported Sunday that "Google's harvesting of e-mails, passwords and other sensitive personal information from unsuspecting households in the United States and around the world was neither a mistake nor the work of a rogue engineer, as the company long maintained, but a programme that supervisors knew about, according to new details from the full text of a regulatory report." That report, prepared by the Federal Communications Commission "draws a portrait of a company where an engineer can easily embark on a project to gather personal e-mails and Web searches of potentially hundreds of millions of people as part of his or her unscheduled work time, and where privacy concerns are shrugged off."

"As early as 2007," the Times disclosed, "Street View engineers had 'wide access' to the plan to collect payload data. Five engineers tested the Street View code, a sixth reviewed it line by line, and a seventh also worked on it, the report says." "Google's rogue engineer scenario collapses in light of the fact that others were aware of the project and did not object," Marc Rotenberg, the executive director of the Electronic Privacy Information Centre told the Times.

"This is what happens in the absence of enforcement and the absence of regulation."Such practices will be infinitely worse under CISPA. Google's harvesting of their customers' private data or Facebook's routine cooperation with law enforcement "requests" for users' information could in fact be turned over whenever an intelligence agency declares that doing so is in the interest of national-or cyber security and we would have no way of ever learning about it since harvested e-mails, web searches and stored profiles could be deemed "proprietary information." With a ginned-up panic over "cyber security" taking its place alongside imperialism's other "wars" on "terror," "drugs" and "crime," the secret state's "unprecedented attacks on democratic rights, in which the entire political establishment and both Democrats and Republicans are participating," as the *World Socialist Web Site* warned, "must be understood as pre-emptive preparations by the political establishment to meet the coming social upheavals with police state measures."

PRIVACY THROUGH INTERNET

An electronic communications network that connects computer networks and organizational computer facilities around the world, the Internet has led to significant changes within our society. An infinite amount of information can be easily obtained and through the development of technology, has become more accessible. The introduction of the Internet into our daily activities has transitioned our society into a technology dependent era. The Internet has become an increasingly popular source for gathering information and a frequent form of communication. Privacy focuses on the control over information about oneself, and is argued vital for human dignity and intimacy. The Internet increased the availability of personal information that can be tracked, recorded, and accessed. The personal invasion of privacy due to Internet monitoring has become more of an ethical concern and looking at aspects from the business world we can better determine how the evolution of the Internet has shaped our lives.

THESIS: ISSUE OF PRIVACY

The issue of privacy and ones right to privacy while at work or on the Internet has become increasingly an important issue companys deal with everyday. Companies have to spend time and money to write policies to cover these issues to protect themselves as well as the well being of their employees. They need to monitor their employees to ensure productivity and to make sure they are not doing anything illegal at work that could hurt the company. How far these companies can go to protect these things is what makes such an interesting issue. A person has a right to privacy and what they do on their break or outside of the office should be their business, but more and more companies are tapping into this to monitor them. A company can only go as far as to monitor them while they are working or doing work related activities anything outside of this realm in their private lives and e-mails should not be exploited.

Utilitarianism

Ethics has become a major concern within our society, especially within the business world. It is important to conduct business in an appropriate manner, monitoring productivity, and profit, while maintaining employee satisfaction. There are two fundamental ideas that underlie utilitarianism; *first*, that the results of our actions are the key to their moral evaluation, and *second*, that the one should assess and compare those results in terms of the happiness or unhappiness they cause "or, more broadly, in terms of their impact on peoples wellbeing." It is important to install morals into all aspects of business, including competitors, customers and employees. It is important to keep a sense of well being in order to provide a trustworthy service. Utilitarianisms guiding impulse is simple and transparent, and many people have found it attractive: human well-being or happiness is what really matters and, accordingly the promotion of well being is what morality is, or ought to be, all about. From a utilitarian perspective employees should be provided with a well being that satisfies each ones personal goals.

The Right of Privacy

The right of privacy has become a controversial issue. While there is no fundamental law or amendment that states ones right to privacy; however it has been implied by the Supreme Court in the United States Amendments and is considered ethically correct in our society. There is no specific law that governs ones right to privacy and this has resulted in a fine line between what is deemed acceptable and what information can be revealed to the public. This has resulted in various court cases in which citizens have tried to determine their own right to privacy. There have been numerous cases over the past century where the Supreme Court has had to determine whether a citizens privacy rights have been violated. This dates back to May 25, 1891 in the Union Pacific Railway Co. v. Botsfold, where it was decided that the plaintiff did not have to submit to physical examination as "no right is held more sacred, or is more carefully guarded, by the common law, than the right of every individual to the possession and control of his own person, free from all restraint or interference of others".

THE EVOLUTION OF THE INTERNET IN THE WORKPLACE

The evolution of the Internet has shaped the way that companies conduct business. This has led to a dramatic change within the workplace and the responsibilities of employees. It is an employers responsibility to monitor employees and assess the quality and quantity of work that is being achieved. In the past, employers have done this by monitoring punch cards, productivity reports, profits and consumer satisfaction. The increase in technology and development of computers and the Internet has changed the security and supervision of daily business activities. Companies have a variety of reasons to maintain surveillance within the workplace. There are concerns for employees well being, competitors obstruction, and the productivity and profits of the business. These concerns are all relevant; however, the use of technology has made it easier for employers to snoop on their employees.

Employers have the ability to intercept electronic communication and access the information that has been stored on the companys computers. The easy access that employers have to this information raises the question of whether employers can ethically monitor employees. It has become Employees are expected to conduct business productively and to complete their job under the expectations that they were hired for. The Internet has made it easier for employees to be distracted from their tasks. Personal e-mailing and browsing the Internet has become a major concern within corporations, leading to the increase in electronic monitoring.

Right of Employers to Keep Workplace Efficient

Employers use electronic monitoring for two basic functions: providing feedback and implementing control. Providing feedback is an essential aspect in conducting business. Employees are monitored in order to provide performance-related feedback and suggestions for improvement, such as with recording a receptionists typing speed or accuracy of data entry clerks. This form of monitoring is understandable and an efficient way to conduct business. The type of monitoring that implements control is more harming to the business environment and calls into question the ethics of the company. The competitiveness of industries in todays business society has led to an increase in security and the need to monitor efficiency within the workplace. This has increased the level of acceptance of employee monitoring, especially through electronic measures. The increase of use of the Internet and its ease, has led to a dependency of many businesses using this form of a communication for all their business transactions. The security that each business requires, also involves the monitoring of their employees online activity in order to ensure there are no security breaches. This form of monitoring is vital in order to maintain the success of the business; however there is a fine line between monitoring electronic activity for the security of the business and monitoring to spy on employees.

Right of Employees Privacy

It is customary for every business to install a code of ethics, setting the standards for employee behaviour, standard of practice and it can also be used as a benchmark of evaluation. "The need for special ethical principles in a scientific society is the same as the need for ethical principles in society as a whole. They are mutually beneficial. They help make our relationships mutually pleasant and productive. A professional society is a voluntary, cooperative organization, and those who must conform to its rules are also those who benefit from the conformity of others. Each has a stake in maintaining general compliance."

It is important for both employers and employees to follow these ethical guidelines. Employers create codes in order to provide standards to which employees should obey; however employers also have to maintain an ethical stance, ensuring the well being and utilitarian rights of their employees. Employees are often unaware of the control that their supervisors have and the intrusion that this can have on their personal life. In the historic case Smyth vs. The Pillsbury Company, Smyth sent inappropriate e-mails from his home computer to the Pillsbury system. At a later date the company intercepted these e-mail messages and terminated Smyths employment based upon their content. There had been a prior promise of confidentiality within the company; however, this did not protect Smyths rights to privacy.

Employees should be able to work in a trusting environment where they are respected. The Fourth Amendment states the public has the constitutional right to privacy. This is a fundamental right that is upheld within the United States; however, the increase in technology and the ability to observe others has weakened this imperative right. "The computers eye is unblinking and ever present. Sophisticated software allows every minute of every day to be recorded and evaluated." The introduction of the Internet to the workplace has made it easier for employers to observe what employees are doing at every moment. It is an employees utilitarian ethical right to receive privacy and to be treated in a manner that will result in happiness for the entire staff. They have the ethical right to dutiful respect and the right of common good, which contributes most to the achievement of quality of life. It is under these ethics that employees should be made aware of the surveillance within their workplace and the duties that are expected of them.

Right of Employers to Keep the Workplace Safe

The Internet has led to an increase in pornography, racist jokes, and inappropriate forms of electronic communication. The government has condoned the use of electronic monitoring to ensure the safety of employees and uphold civil rights. Under Title VII of the Civil Rights Act, an employers inefficient monitoring of the Internet and e-mail use and abuse may allow racial offensive or sexually explicit material to pervade the work environment and create or contribute to a hostile environment. Employers are expected to monitor their employees activities online to ensure civil rights are not violated and that employees receive the fundamental rights they are entitled to. This has been an effective form of detection within the workplace. In Strauss vs. Microsoft Corporation, the court held that among other remarks several jokes and parodies of a sexual nature e-mailed by a supervisor to employees were administered and relevant evidence of sexual harassment. The government has approved online regulation however no standards have been introduced that respect the well being of the employees or considers the effects that these actions cause. The ethical values of employees have been discarded.

3

Intelligence for Cyber Space

Although many of the intelligence methodologies and principles remain the same, new ways of thinking appropriate to the cyber-domain are essential. The lack of borders in cyber-space is a critical difference from the more familiar domains of intelligence. Indeed, geography and political borders often aided traditional military intelligence analysis-it is a simple thing to develop threat scenarios if the potential enemy can only use certain terrain or sea lines of communication and then, only at certain times of the year-while simple factors of physics such as time and distance also provided opportunities for warning. Within the Internet, however, these limiting factors are absent, (although other limiting factors, such as geometry of network connectivity, might exist in a form useful to be incorporated into intelligence analysis), contributing to what can appear to be "instantaneous threats".

Assessment of cyber-space threats requires not only a merger of old methodologies and new modes of thinking but also analysts willing and able to approach the art of threat assessment and warning from new perspectives. Only with a distinctive blend of the traditional and the new will it be possible to obtain real understanding of threats and vulnerabilities, to differentiate among types of intrusions and to forecast or anticipate specific incidents or clusters of incidents in ways that lengthen warning time. Enhancing the ability to identify perpetrators is also highly desirable: removing the cloak of anonymity would make perpetrators more concerned about the potential costs and risks of their actions and could have an important deterrent effect. In short, there are several fundamental questions at the heart of the intelligence process. They consist of variations on the who, what, when, where, why and how questions that are familiar parts of most research and analysis.

SECURITY CHALLENGING

Efforts to identify intruders are critical both to the assessment of the challenge and the nature of the response. Potential intruders run the gamut from young hobbyists engaged in the equivalent of joy riding to terrorist organizations and nations that are intent on maximizing damage to the target.

The problem of identification is particularly difficult in a domain where maintaining anonymity is easy and there are sometimes time lapses between the intruder action, the intrusion itself, and the actual disruptive effects. Moreover, the consequences are not always commensurate with the objectives, in some cases falling short of what the intruders hoped to achieve, and in others going well beyond what they had envisaged.

There is a broad spectrum of potential intruders on the Internet and an almost equal number of motives for intrusions against organizations. Not surprisingly, this includes perpetrators conducting operations against other perpetrators. As enticing as this prospect is, it does not mitigate the effects of such internecine rivalry. New and more sophisticated tools are often the result of such interplay. This sort of jousting can also provide valuable insights to analysts once it is recognized, but does not simplify the analytic task and puts an incredible strain on limited analytic/warning resources. With the continuing proliferation of sophisticated computer technologies into the mainstream population, attribution for an intrusion becomes more difficult by the day.

The dynamism of the intruder population is itself a problem. On the one hand, success breeds imitation and the sophistication of readily available tools means that even those with limited skills can become intruders.

On the one hand, there is a certain degree of attrition in the intruder community. Indeed, there are many reasons why intruders might cease their activity, including increased maturity, a need to find gainful employment, and a perception of the rewards of working to increase network security rather than attack it. The implication, of course, is that the mix of agents threatening network security is changing as the nature of the Internet changes.

The vast majority of the intrusions are probably being conducted by nuisance hackers or "ankle-biters" who have limited objectives and are usually satisfied with the actual penetration of the system or conduct relatively harmless cyber-vandalism such as the defacement or alteration of web-sites. While aggravating to the target, no significant or lasting damage occurs. The more serious problem occurs when an intrusion is carried out by a more sophisticated intruder (either an individual or a group) whose objective is better defined and involves malicious intent. Motives for these sorts of intrusions are also as varied as the persons carrying them out. They range from greed to defined military strategy and doctrine, and all that falls in between.

Four of the more dangerous, and less well defined categories of intruder are governments conducting operations against other sovereign states, the organized terrorist group, insurgency or revolutionary groups, and organized crime. All these entities are beginning to appreciate the potential power, anonymity, and effectiveness of the Internet. There are myriad examples of governments instituting programmes for Computer Network Warfare. In the case of Russia, policy-makers consider the security of their information infrastructure so critical that–rhetorically at least-they equate an attack against it with a strategic nuclear strike (and have promised an appropriate response). As a result of the realization of the criticality of information infrastructures, computer warfare is now a part of the formal Russian Military Strategy and Doctrine. The same is true of organized terrorist groups. In fact, "most of the 30 top terrorist organizations identified by the U.S. government have web pages and use e-mail, and are "fairly well developed" at using the Internet."[Casciano] In many cases, dependence on technology is viewed as an Achilles Heel to be exploited by terrorist organizations.

Within the U.S., many of the more militant indigenous groups have discovered the power of the Internet and have well designed and effective Web sites. Indeed, militia and supremacist groups have had significant increases in membership since developing their Web pages. It is a natural progression from using the Internet for propaganda and recruiting to exploiting its potential as a weapon. There is also growing evidence that some of the active insurgency groups around the world are discovering the potential of the computer. It is just a matter of time until they discover the effect of a computer-generated attack against the infrastructure of the government they are fighting. Once that realization is made, cyber-attacks will likely become a weapon of choice for organizations intent on overthrowing an existing government. Disturbingly, Aum Shinrikyo, the group responsible for the Sarin gas attack on the Japanese subway, has increasingly been involved in the Japanese software industry!

Organized crime probably was the first of the sophisticated intruder threats to realize the power and value of the computer. In 1995, it was discovered that the Cali cartel had sophisticated state-of-the-art equipment for electronic eavesdropping, while smaller drug trafficking organizations in Colombia are using the Internet to pressure the Colombian government to change the policy of extraditing traffickers to the United States. Furthermore, the use of computers by organized crime organizations to garner illicit profits is well documented. However, some criminal efforts have gone beyond simple siphoning of funds and money laundering. Extortion of money from financial institutions by threatening to destroy or modify their computer databases is also evident. It is probable that at least some of these extortion operations are conducted by transnational criminal groups. Some of the extortion efforts go wrong–as did the effort to extort Bloomberg. In other cases, however, large payoffs are almost certainly made to the extortionist. It seems likely, therefore, that larger and potentially more dangerous operations should be anticipated.

The obvious challenge is to develop a capacity to identify and track the activities of these potential intruders with the goal of being able to provide predictive analysis and warning of intrusions. Some of the traditional intelligence techniques should apply to these threats, but new methodologies and the ability to contemplate new and complex concepts have to be developed concurrently.

This will become even more important (and difficult) as perpetrators of increasing sophistication operate on the Internet. As motivations vary, so will the efforts of the individuals behind malicious operations to either conceal or reveal their responsibility. All of this complicates efforts to track responsible parties determine attribution. Nations and transnational criminal organizations, by their nature, will be diligent in their efforts to maintain anonymity. In some of these cases, identifying the intended victim may give valuable insight into tracking the intruder. Sometimes the target of an intrusion allows the analyst to rule out certain possible perpetrators. A multi-million dollar extortion plot against a major financial institution is probably not the work of a 13-year-old hacker working out of his bedroom. At the same time, however, many victims, especially within government or sensitive industries such as banking or insurance, often complicate the effort to track intruders because of their reluctance to report the incident. In other cases, such as politically motivated attacks, the perpetrators may want their identity known, but not their location. As such operations become more sophisticated, tracking the attack back to its point of origin will be a major challenge to the intelligence analysts involved. What is clear from all of this is that tracking intruders and gaining attribution is much more than just a technical challenge.

One difficulty, of course, is that there are legal constraints on intelligence collection, especially by the military and the national security establishment. Traditionally the focus of intelligence has been on foreign threats, and there are restrictions on intelligence activities directed against individuals or groups that are domestic in nature. Insofar as these groups are the focus of government attention, it is from the law enforcement community. This points to yet another problem: that of coordination and information sharing between the traditional national security agencies and the law enforcement community. Generally law enforcement focuses on individual cases and wants evidence that stands up in court; intelligence agencies in contrast are concerned with protecting the sources of their information so that they can continue to use them. The problem with cyber-threats is that they fall in the gray area where crime and national security merge into one another.

FORMS OF INTRUSION ARE OCCURRING

It is tempting to see intrusions in terms of a pyramid that goes from transient vulnerability probing and defacing web-sites at the base to large scale efforts to undermine the critical missions of an organization or the critical functions of a nation at the top-and to suggest that there is an inverse relationship between frequency and significance, with many trivial incidents and comparatively few of the more serious incidents. There are several difficulties with this however. The first is that probes that appear relatively insignificant could be a harbinger of more serious intrusions. The second is that there is sometimes a gap between intent and consequences–the effects and impact of an incident can either fall far short of what was intended, or far exceed what the perpetrator initially envisaged. This lack of congruence between limited intent and far-reaching consequences stems from the capacity of worms and viruses for infinite replication and multiplication combined with the seamless inter-connectivity of systems. Incidents such as the Love Bug cross the public-private divide and have an indiscriminate impact on corporations, governments, and private individuals irrespective of the initial target. In cases such as this, the consequences have less to do with targeting than with the ubiquity of a particular programme such as Microsoft Outlook that is used as the vector of transmission. In effect, the incident takes on its own momentum.

When the consequences are widespread, of course, the incident becomes very public and is the subject of much media and official commentary. In many other cases, however, there is far greater reticence about the scale, type and targets of attack. The analytic effort must successfully build a trust relationship for the collection of data across a broad variety of organizations. This trust relationship allows for observation of incidents from early probing and experimentation through widespread deployment of automated forms of intrusion. For example, in recent months (June and July 2000) CERTÒ/CC has received reports of intrusions involving a wide variety of automated tools, ranging from simple viruses and system corruption toolkits through complex viruses designed to attack relatively hardened sites with low probability of detection and distributed tools designed to crash network infrastructure. Roughly 10 per cent-25 per cent of the CERT/CC reports involve viruses. Roughly 20 per cent-40 per cent are intrusions where the victim site cannot discern the type of the intrusion from available data. The remaining intrusions are a large number of other forms of intrusion, including compromise of system administration accounts, web defacements, reconnaissance attempts and misuse of computing resources.

Being Intruded Upon

Determining who are the victims of intrusions is, in some respects, an enormously significant part of the intelligence process. It is important-at least in those cases where attacks are not indiscriminate-to differentiate between public and private targets, to distinguish infrastructure targets from individual targets, to distinguish between intrusions that focus on targets of convenience and those that are much more precise and calculated. For example, existing analysis has shown a link between port scanning and certain types of later intrusions, but this needs to be more fully explored to provide for effective warnings. Profiling victims can sometimes play a critical role in determining the nature of the intrusion and the nature of the intruders. For this to be done, understanding is needed of the level of "background noise", probes and intrusion attempts occurring across the Internet. Once understood, it may be possible to isolate this activity from the more significant activity directed at a particular victim.

Victim profiles will be just as important, in terms of strategic intelligence analysis of the Internet, as profiling potential intruders. The more serious the intrusion, the more critical this sort of profiling will be. One of the potential hurdles to this effort, however, will be the natural tendency of the victim, whether private or public, to withhold sensitive or proprietary information. A few examples of this kind of reticence would be financial institutions withholding information about loses due to intrusions; companies failing to divulge the nature of an intrusion due to proprietary corporate data; or a government agency protecting information that is sensitive or even classified. Beyond simply protecting proprietary or sensitive data, there are also serious legal questions that have not yet been resolved in the courts or in the legislature. These include constitutional guarantees of privacy; contradictory national laws (or lack of laws) as perpetrators use the global network; laws limiting various governmental agency's efforts to track down the source of an intrusion, and the need to determine what is domestic and what is foreign.

If these barriers can be overcome, critical information will become available. Details of the victim's infrastructure, the nature of the intrusion, identity clues left by the intruder, network traffic flow as observed by the victim site, and intrusion tools left as artifacts on the victim hosts can all provide indispensable clues. Without such information, motivation becomes more difficult to define and profiling efforts will be seriously flawed. Some work has already been accomplished in this area by organizations involved in incident monitoring, including the members of the Forum of Incident Response and Security Teams (FIRST) community.

Much more remains to be accomplished, however, as new cooperative agreements are forged and additional analytic efforts and methodologies are developed. Furthermore, while it is true that some of the legal restrictions are avoided by the voluntary nature of the cooperative relationships, they are by no means completely overcome. The keys to success seem to be twofold. First, the analytic organization has to prove itself to be a highly secure confidant, never disclosing victim identities while working to assist victims in recovering from intrusions. Second, it must return information that is of value to the victims, including information that might place the intrusion in a larger context as well as providing assistance in dealing with vendors or other sites. More simply put, the exchange of information must be in both directions. Experience with other organizations has shown that neither trustworthiness nor returned value alone is sufficient, but both appear to be required for effective information gathering with victims.

Beyond their reticence, victim organizations are often unaware of critical parts of their security stance. Available data suggests that victims are often not aware that their networks have been intruded upon. The effectiveness of installed security measures is often overestimated. Levels of trust given to users by computing practices are often unwarranted. All of this hampers both analysis and defence.

One of the reasons that profiling the victims is so critical is that it provides insights in to motivations that can greatly assist analysts in predicting future intrusions under similar circumstances. This insight will need to incorporate identification of circumstances that facilitate or hamper intrusion. For example, K-12 educational institutions might offer a significant opportunity for intruders to stage their attacks, since many such institutions lack knowledgeable system administrators. However, such hosts may be removed from the network during summer break and other times when school is not in session. During the Year 2000 rollover, conditions for system intrusion were relatively poor not only because of the active presence of a large number of system administrators, carefully monitoring their systems, but also the significant number of alternative activities available to potential intruders. These examples serve to identify that there exist time-varying circumstances; further analysis is required to delineate these factors more fully.

Intrusions being Implemented Taking Place

This is both the most technical aspect of the problem and, for specialists in the area, the easiest question to answer. Methods of intrusion are the on-line equivalent of military tactics. And just as in the military world there has historically been a dialectic between defence and offence so on the Internet, there is a similar dialectic between protection and intrusion. One difference lies in the ability of intruders to obfuscate their methods of intrusion by manipulation of the sources of intrusion and of the on-line records of activity. The sources of intrusion are manipulated either by staging intrusions through a series of already-intruded and corrupted hosts, or by falsification of source information found in network traffic. Both of these methods are common in intrusions. The on-line records of activity are commonly falsified either by direct modification of the records themselves or by replacement of the monitoring software that produces these records. While there are analogies to these activities in the physical world, the ease, rate, and invisibility of these activities on the Internet especially complicates the analysis task.

The timing of intrusions might or might not be significant. It is possible, for example, that an intrusion on a particular company could have been precipitated by a particular action of the company, whether in the marketplace or in relation to one or more of its employees. Similarly, an intrusion on a country's infrastructure could come about in an international crisis, as part of an adversary's effort to prevent or disrupt military intervention in a specific region or country. A particular sequence of intrusions might also be important in determining whether probing activities are taking place as a preliminary to a more serious assault. Another important component is whether or not the intrusions are accompanied by any other actions–such as the demand for payment that would be an essential ingredient in any extortion contingency.

The timing of an intrusion, especially one that is more serious in nature will often have significance with regard to the motive for the intrusion, hence the importance of victim profiling. Given the global nature of business today and the amount of political upheaval throughout the world, myriad events must be examined on a daily basis for clues to possible impending intrusions. Awareness of upcoming political events, corporate announcements or openings of new industrial facilities will be essential to the analytic process. This sort of situational awareness, combined with the historical perspective provided by profiling, will have a major impact on the ability to provide predictive analysis and warning. There is a need for care here in distinguishing significant from background activity. Experience at the CERT/CC with informal measures of significance, as are used in generation of advisories, may be useful in facilitating this distinction.

Although the virtual world is borderless, the points at which it connects to the real world are geographic locations. Indeed, the simple question of "where?" has to be broken down into point(s) of origin, digital routing, and point(s) of attack. Indeed, it is physical actions at a particular location that start the attack process–even if there is sometimes a time lag prior to the implementation of the attack itself. This becomes particularly significant when the actions initiated at this location go beyond web defacement and involve more serious criminal, terrorist, and war-like actions. Tracing the attack back to source, therefore, becomes particularly important in determining both the responsibility for the action and the appropriate target for counter-measures or reprisals. Where the attacker is determined to be another nation then this has particularly important implications. Even in less extreme situations, however, location is critical–and because of law as well as geography. In some jurisdictions, for example, there are no laws against computer intrusions. This was why the Filipino perpetrator of the love bug was not placed on trial in the Philippines itself. In other jurisdictions, of course, the laws are quite severe.

For criminals and terrorists, these divergences offer opportunities to launch attacks at minimal risk–even if the source of the attack is somehow discovered. This suggests that there might be a form of jurisdictional arbitrage with potential attackers seeking out low risk jurisdictions from which to launch their attacks. Over the longer term, of course, the opportunities for arbitrage of this kind can be diminished through more inclusive laws criminalizing this kind of activity, through the harmonization of laws among states, and through the extension of extradition treaties and mutual legal assistance treaties. As well as using jurisdictional arbitrage computer intruders also seek to cover their tracks by going through multiple jurisdictions. In some cases, this makes it impossible to track the activity back to source by complicating the digital trail. In others, it adds significant legal obstacles as some states are simply unwilling to cooperate in investigations There is also the potential for mischief with the possibility that skilful intruders might lay a false trail that lead to unwarranted but damaging accusations against innocent parties (whether individuals, groups or nations).

With respect to victim location, physical location can also provide key insights. Local threats might arise through local activism (such as the Sierra Club opposition to military exercises in California; this did not involve cyber threats, but analogous activities in the future might well do so). Beyond physical location, there is logical location. A site might come under attack because either its Internet service provider or a subsidiary site is vulnerable. This logical location could be entirely unrelated to physical location: a site in New York might be on a network logically associated with one in Florida. This could occur due to mergers and acquisitions, but more typically takes place due to the difficulties in securing Internet addresses. Whatever the cause, however, it adds yet another complication to the location issue.

Using either physical or logical locations, there are several sorts of victims that might be of interest. One is the intended target of the incident. Another is an intermediate site used as a means of access or interference to the intended target, which might be termed the vector for the incident. In some circumstances this can involve substantial collateral damage to the vector site (or sites) even though it is not the intended victim. Intruders on a vector might extract information, reconfigure computers and hamper desirable operation, all for the purpose of striking the intended target.

Actions Taking Place

From a predictive intelligence analysis perspective, threat is most simply defined as capability plus intent. Capabilities, in terms of more powerful computers and more malicious covert software, are expanding rapidly. Attacks that required deep technical expertise in the recent past are within the reach of casual users today. Malicious intent is less easy to pin down, but can be assumed to be widespread and varied. History alone teaches us that much. Determining those two factors is the foundation of strategic intelligence analysis. Categorization of the nature of attacks and of the victims is critical to the success of any analytic effort. Historically, the more serious attacks will often have a specific catalyst: a corporation builds a production facility in a third world country that is viewed as an exploitive action by one or more activist groups; a government sponsors a peace conference that is viewed as an attempt to subvert the political viability of a disaffected part of the population; a repressive regime massacres a band of rebels near the capital; an organized crime syndicate reacts to crack downs by law enforcement. These are just a handful of examples of motivations for more serious incidents. Just as importantly, a more serious incident, while probably more sophisticated, also has a greater potential for an unintended cascading effect.

Objectives can range from revenge (a disgruntled employee) to political statements (terrorism) to a full-scale attack on infrastructure as an act of warfare or at the very least part of "coercive diplomacy". Although the inference of intent is sometimes problematic (particularly where the damage or disruption is either less or more than the intruder intended), the effort is an essential component of the intelligence process. In many cases, intrusions that are politically motivated will be relatively easy to interpret. The effect of the intrusion will be muted if the underlying political intent is not publicized. Depending on the nature of the goal, this publication of intent may be quite localized and covert–*e.g.*, to gain power within the intruder organization. Nonetheless, such publication might be identifiable and could provide a historical perspective that will greatly assist in predicting possible future intrusions. On the other hand, activities by governments and criminal elements are, almost by definition, covert in nature. Intrusions of those types will provide a much greater challenge to the goal of providing predictive assessments and warnings. It also has to be recognized that in some incidents, there are no clear objectives. The lack of motive can be truly confounding.

In this connection, it is essential to acknowledge the limits of intelligence. No one has articulated these more effectively than Sherman Kent, formerly the Director of the Office of National Intelligence Estimates, who noted that intelligence consists of three kinds of information: "The first is easily disposed of; it is the statement of indisputable fact... The second and third kinds do not carry any such certainty; each rests upon a varying degree of uncertainty. They relate respectively (a) to things which are knowable but happen to be unknown to us, and (b) to things which are not known to anyone at all." In effect, much of the analysis process involves what Kent also called the "speculative-evaluative" component of intelligence–especially when it involves efforts to anticipate future behaviour and future threats, and when the targets of intelligence collection and analysis are engaging in systematic concealment or deception designed to thwart these efforts.

Such limits notwithstanding, the ultimate goal of intelligence analysis is predictive, strategic intelligence, disseminated to a consumer, based on the fusion of technical assessments, global analysis of incident data, and analysis of intruders and victims. It fuses three kinds of knowledge: that rooted in monitoring technology to obtain assessments about tools and weapons of disruption; that obtained from analysis of incident data; and that obtained from monitoring of possible intruders–individuals, terrorist and criminal groups and nations. Accordingly, Table below summarizes the three kinds of activity to be monitored and identifies the components of the collection and analysis processes in each activity area.

Table: An Intelligence Model for Cyber-Threats

	Technical	***Incident***	***Intruder/Victim***
Methods of Analysis	Technical assessment of the threat and what can be done to exploit vulnerabilities	Analysis of Patterns of Incidents and how they might develop in the future.	Traditional threat analysis of Intruders/Victims
Methods of Collection	Monitoring of new technologies that are developed independently of the actors who use them. Sensor grid (equivalent of DEW line) Equivalents of Sigint	Indicators of incidents: Significance Intruders Targets Extensiveness	Traditional collection methods: Humint: Informants Infiltration Interrogation Sigint: Electronic surveillance Non-traditional: Cyberint
Activities and Threats relevant to security in cyber-space	Weapons capabilities Technologies that are developed and shared (from civil to military applications)	Incidents Use of these technologies for certain kinds of disruptive purposes	Development of organizations that have the capabilities and the will to initiate attacks on the Internet.

The critical task for intelligence is to fuse the three kinds of knowledge obtained in the top row. In one sense this follows the classic intelligence pattern in which fused intelligence is the ultimate goal. In the context of cyber-threats, however, the fusion of these different methods of analysis is an aspiration rather than an achievement. Success in this area would provide the kinds of strategic intelligence that makes possible the creation of an indicators and warning system. The difficulties of the task, however, go beyond the intellectual complexities. They include organizational and legal dilemmas that are still far from being resolved.

In addition to supporting attribution, operational analysis should lead to sparking defensive coordinated efforts. What is needed is to connect these efforts into some form of cohesive goal that can promote a measurably effective response to on-line threats.

THE NATURE AND LEVELS OF INTELLIGENCE ANALYSIS

Intelligence analysis requires many of the same analytical methods and techniques, irrespective of domain. From this perspective, intelligence analysis for Internet security is no different from the intelligence task in any other area of national and international security. The commonality is the concern with those who want to inflict harm and the vulnerabilities they can exploit to do this. Threats can come from many sources: the military activities of hostile nations; inimical economic strategies pursued by adversarial or even allied states; the activities of terrorist groups intent on inflicting harm on society in order to achieve political objectives; transnational criminal organizations pursuing the acquisition of large profits through illegal activities, violence, and corruption; and groups (including any of those just mentioned) and individuals with the ability and desire to distort, disrupt, degrade or destroy information and communications systems. Whatever their source, threats are inextricably linked to vulnerabilities. Indeed, absolute security could only be achieved if there were no vulnerabilities to be exploited. It is crucial, therefore, not only to identify vulnerabilities but also to understand how hostile groups or individuals might exploit them. Strictly speaking, real security threats only come from those with a combination of hostile intent (*i.e.* a desire to do us harm) and the capacity to inflict harm (*i.e.* exploit vulnerabilities in ways that transform intent into reality).

In the realm of cyber-space, vulnerabilities are inescapable. There are many reasons for this, ranging from the inherent weaknesses in complex systems to specific problems in the creation of software code. Even if protective security measures were an integral part of information systems rather than being subsequently grafted onto them, problems would remain. Some vulnerabilities stem from the underlying protocols used to communicate on the Internet, which were formulated when the Internet was a relatively small community of trusted systems, with connectivity determined by government contract. Other vulnerabilities stem from development practices, which may ignore validation of input (or even length checking) and avoid controlling the environment in which programmes execute. Finally, vulnerabilities stem from the rapidly evolving use of software, in which programmes meant for a limited purpose are applied in ways not anticipated by their developers. The intruder community is constantly seeking to find interesting (and, from their point of view, profitable) ways to discover and exploit vulnerabilities. This behaviour tends to be quite trend-driven. A newly discovered interesting vulnerability exploit in an application will spawn both intensive interest in other vulnerabilities in that application and an intensive search for similar vulnerabilities in other applications. This results in waves of discovered vulnerabilities that impact both specific vendors and the community in general. At the same time, the recognition that there are measurable trends in vulnerability exploitation are at least a temporary advantage to intelligence analysis efforts. From a tactical perspective, the recognition of a trend in intrusion tools and their applications may well allow for at least short-term predictive analysis and the potential for limited warning.

One of the greatest challenges to system owners and administrator is determining how much security is enough. Managing risks inherent in information systems is problem that changes as fast as new technologies are brought online. Intelligence analysis of the threats to information systems should, by definition, be a major component of the risk management process. Without application, intelligence analysis efforts are merely an intellectual exercise and have no value. It is only when the results of that analysis, the assessments derived from the analytic process, are provided to operators that they begin to have value.

Obtaining prior knowledge of both threats and vulnerabilities–as well as sensitivity to possible opportunities to exploit the vulnerabilities-is essential. Intelligence analysis, of course, operates at different levels, ranging from the specific to the general, and from short-term incidents and operations to long term patterns and challenges. Each form or level of analysis is crucial, and complements and supplements the others. Nevertheless, it is important to distinguish them from one another and to be clear at which level the activities are taking place. It is also important to recognize that the most critical insights will be obtained from fusion efforts that combine these different levels. The several complementary levels of intelligence analysis are strategic analysis, tactical analysis and operational analysis. In practice, these categories shade into each other and are not always sharply differentiated, and differing definitions for these terms exist in the intelligence community. Nevertheless, they offer a useful framework within which intelligence tasks and requirements can initially be delineated.

STRATEGIC INTELLIGENCE ANALYSIS

Strategic analysis is perhaps the most important form of intelligence. It provides a framework within which other forms of intelligence collection and analysis take place, offers an overall assessment from the top down rather than from the bottom up, and helps to provide a basis for policy formulation, strategic planning, and resource allocation. Its weakness is its focus on macro-level issues rather than the more detailed levels of analysis. On the Internet, such analysis is even more problematic, due to the rapidly evolving nature of Internet usage. Prior to 1994, for example, Internet commerce was illegal. Today it is a multi-billion dollar economic force. New methods of organizational and economic cooperation are constantly evolving, with greater or less security. Maintaining continuity on this constantly shifting environment is one of the greatest challenges to conducting effective strategic analysis of cyber-threats. Furthermore, for many consumers, strategic intelligence is irrelevant to day-to-day tasks and needs. At the end of the day, however, the importance of strategic intelligence analysis is undeniable. Such an effort helps to discern and make sense of trends, to identify and extract patterns that would otherwise not be visible, and to provide an overall picture of the evolving threat environment and the level of damage that might be occurred in certain specified contingencies.

Analytical initiatives that would fall under the rubric of strategic intelligence analysis include:

- *Overall threat assessments*. These include in the analysis the vulnerabilities of critical missions (including levels of dependence), the kind of disruption and damage that could be caused to the implementation of these missions, the kinds of weapons/instruments that could be used to cause such disruptions, and the likelihood of such attacks and intrusions taking place.
- *Sector threat assessments*. Such analyses focus on vulnerabilities and threats either in particular areas such as national infrastructure, or in particular sectors of the economy such as banking or e-commerce. In effect, a strategic analysis of this kind has to take account of changes in what can be a very dynamic environment.
- *Trend Analysis to highlight changing threats and vulnerabilities*. These might include base-line assessments so as to better recognize departures from the baseline. Alternatively, they might focus on future threats and vulnerabilities in an effort to determine in what ways the problem is evolving–and what can be done to anticipate and contain future challenges. The way in which e-commerce has become a major issue suggests that the pace of change in the cyber-space environment is posing novel challenges that can best be understood through strategic intelligence analysis that is very forward looking. Indeed, trend analysis is likely to be most effective when it is linked with careful attention to drivers, *i.e.* fundamental trends in the political, economic, social and technological sectors that will shape the future threat and vulnerability environment of the future.
- *Potential Damage Assessments*. Because of the macro-level view taken by strategic analysis, it also offers the best approach for assessing

potential cascade effects of intrusions. The specific target of a an intrusion might be a regional electric power grid, but the effects of a failure to that system can cascade to include telecommunications, public emergency services, water systems, etc. The potential for such wide-spread effects will be recognized most readily as a result of in-depth strategic analysis–which in turn would offer opportunities to develop both defensive and mitigation strategies. Crisis management, contingency planning, mitigation strategies, and disaster management would all be enhanced by strategic analysis of potential damage assessment. Indeed, the capacity for effective and rapid reconstitution might depend on such analysis.

- *Categorizing and differentiating attacks and attackers*. Intrusions in cyber-space can emanate from individuals, whether insiders or outsiders; from hacker groups intent on displaying their skills and capabilities; activist groups using direct action on the Internet to publicize their political cause; terrorist organizations using intrusions to create massive disruption or other forms of large-scale harm, and seeking to obtain widespread publicity and create a climate of fear; transnational criminal organizations responding to law enforcement pressure with cyber-retaliation, and states using attacks on, or through, information systems as a form of asymmetric warfare. One of the most important tasks of intelligence analysis for the Internet is to discover ways of differentiating among intrusions from these various sources. This will be especially true as groups or individuals develop intrusion strategies that mimic other forms and thereby lessen their chances of identification or, in the case of nation states, provide plausible deniability of their actions. From the perspective of strategic intelligence analysis, this is critical in efforts to determine appropriate responses that might go beyond simply defensive or mitigation strategies. How specific attacks are categorized, of course, will also be an issue at the tactical and operational level. But the differentiating and categorization methodologies, initially at least, are a matter for strategic analysis.
- *Identification of Anomalies*. Searching for anomalies that provide indicators of emerging threats and problems is an important task of strategic intelligence analysis (albeit one that both feeds into and relies on tactical and operational efforts). Anomalies in this context can be understood as developments or events that do not fit typical or known patterns. The detection of anomalies or novel patterns can be a major element in anticipating new methods of intrusion, new targets, or even new classes of intruders. It is a macro-level task that requires careful and systematic "environmental scanning" as well

as the coalescing of tactical and operational intelligence reports that identify and highlight specific aberrations from the norm.

- *Analysis of Future Net Environments*. The greatest constant about the Internet is change. Strategic intelligence analysis must take that into account and attempt to provide assessments of potential future environments on the Net and the potential impact of malicious activity within those environments. Given the dramatic changes in technology within the recent past, and seeing the rapid pace with which innovation continues to grow, it seems a reasonable assumption that the Internet (in one form or another) will become more and more integrated into the fabric of society. As this occurs, intrusions or attacks will have far more wide-ranging consequences. Considerations of social as well as political and economic impacts will have to be factored into intelligence assessments.

It is clear from this discussion that not only does strategic intelligence analysis provide a framework for tactical and operational assessments, but that work done at these levels in turn helps to shape the strategic intelligence focus. As for the strategic assessments themselves they should be useful for consumers, providing forecasting estimates that help to reduce uncertainties in ways that feed into policy processes, providing a basis for more informed decision-making and more effective resource allocation. As strategic analytic methodologies mature, they will also offer the basis for predictive or anticipatory assessments that can serve to provide warning of potential hostile operations. In effect, strategic intelligence assessments provide a basis for the development of high-level policy and strategy and for strategic responses to vulnerabilities, whether actual or potential.

TACTICAL INTELLIGENCE ANALYSIS

Tactical analysis is a necessary and important complement to work done at the strategic level. It is the natural linking element between macro-level analysis and the micro-level focus on individual cases.

Among the kinds of studies that come under the level of tactical analysis would be:

- Cluster and pattern analysis designed to discern temporal patterns, the use of particular intrusion methods, commonalities of targets, and attempts to build profiles of perpetrators, whether hackers or insiders.
- Stimulus-response analysis designed to identify potential actions that could be taken by intruders in response to specific known or predicted events. This analysis could be used both proactively in development of warnings or reactively in lending significance to otherwise-unrecognized activity.
- Network environmental analysis methods will have to be developed.

> It is probable that in-depth analysis of the Internet will reveal patterns similar to those in the physical world. Net weather is already being discussed, and network terrain is a viable concept. Unlike physical environments, however, the Internet environment will probably be subject to much more rapid shifting. That places this sort of analytic effort squarely in the realm of Tactical Analysis.

In physical space, geography helps to differentiate tactical from strategic, but on the Internet this component is lacking, an absence that makes the distinction between strategic and tactical somewhat more tenuous than in other domains. At the same time, the strategic and tactical levels are mutually reinforcing: although strategic intelligence analysis provides the framework for tactical assessments, these assessments in turn help to feed strategic analysis. With a highly dynamic inter-relationship among the various levels of analysis, each level is strengthened by and strengthens the others.

OPERATIONAL INTELLIGENCE ANALYSIS

Operational intelligence analysis overlaps with investigation and is often single-case oriented. It involves technological assessments of the methods used for an intrusion, specific investigations of intruders, and the like. An important component of operational analysis is identifying the particular vulnerability or vulnerabilities that have been exploited and providing guidance on how it or they can be minimized or eliminated. Another component of operational analysis will be the potential ability to provide attribution during, or shortly after an intrusion.

The data collected during an incident, combined with the profiling efforts provided at the tactical level could lead to attribution. While there are significant policy and legal questions associated with such a capability, its importance to the overall analytical process cannot be overstated. Most of the existing analysis of network intrusions has been capability analysis, dealing principally with information privacy, integrity and availability. Selected methodologies to address organizational missions in a network context exist, but have not been widely applied. Intent and effect analysis has not been systematically pursued. In addition to supporting attribution, operational analysis should lead to sparking defensive coordinated efforts. What is needed is to connect these efforts into some form of cohesive goal that can promote a measurably effective response to on-line threats.

THE ROLE OF INTELLIGENCE IN THE CYBER ARENA

As in any form of security, intelligence is a key component of tactical and strategic decision-making. Effective cyber intelligence will enhance our ability to assess the effects of cyber attacks, mitigate risks associated with the threat, and streamline cyber security into an efficient and cost-effective process based on well informed decisions.

THE ROLE OF INTELLIGENCE

The role of intelligence in any capacity is to collect, analyse, and produce information to provide complete, accurate, timely, and relevant threat assessments to inform decision makers who act on the information. It is usually most effective when it is disseminated at the lowest possible classification level for the maximum number of relevant users facing these threats. In performing this mission, the intelligence agencies seek to penetrate actual or potential threat targets consistent with national strategic, operational, and tactical priorities. These agencies then seek to produce intelligence on adversary or threat capabilities and intentions in a manner that "connects" with the maximum number of relevant customers.

Intelligence and threat analysis does not exist for its own purposes. When threat details are suppressed or ignored, national security incurs significant consequences. It is important to sustain a high level of performance in the dynamic cyber arena. This environment is where threats develop rapidly and are fuelled by new concepts for the use of pervasive IT. new waves of innovative capabilities seem to break over users in tsunami fashion, be it the coming cloud architectures or the continuing revolution in personal devices connected to the networks. given this relentless and constantly unfolding environment, intelligence might be successful in keeping pace with technological innovation. Conversely, it might be slow, or even wrong in its assessments of the threat dynamic. It is therefore important to evaluate public and private cyber intelligence activities that support these security missions in a strategic manner.

THE CYBER INTELLIGENCE COMMUNITY

This unique, currently *ad hoc*, community is made up of government, telecommunication and Internet providers, CERTs, and other formal information security entities, specialty companies, and vendors. The members of this community engage in a myriad of activities that could be the potential victim of a cyber threat. This "Cyber Intelligence Community" is currently an informal coalition of the willing that collects and analyses unclassified and classified cyber intelligence data and trends. There is no formal mechanism across industry and government cyber intelligence entities that successfully collects, processes, and analyses all identifiable key cyber threat behaviour and reports it at an unclassified or reasonable classification level to all appropriate customers. An effective connection between intelligence provider and the customer means that the customer has understood and internalized the intelligence resulting in action to work the intelligence and mitigate the threat.

Good intelligence professionals relentlessly pursue interactions with customers to ensure that: the data is collected, analysed, and conveyed; the intelligence serves customers' purposes; and some action is being taken (or deliberately not taken). This cycle can be referred to as a constant process of story-finding, story-telling, story-updating, story-listening, and story-heeding. A concept to institutionalize this *ad hoc* community is currently missing.

Investing in Cyber Intelligence Tradecraft

A substantial and continuing investment in cyber intelligence should be a strategic imperative in the information age. It is also imperative to use that intelligence to safe guard our ability to maintain security. We must ensure that stable domestic and international economies are not jeopardized by possible conflict with rival powers, rogue states, failing or failed states, modern terrorists and thieves, and WMD proliferators.

All formal and informal intelligence disciplines contribute to these imperatives, including Signals Intelligence (SIGINT), Human Intelligence (HUMINT), Open Source Intelligence (OSINT), Geospatial and Measurement Intelligence (GEOINT), and the volumes of unclassified network data and behaviour being watched by global CERTs. Continuous liaison among all related parties is critical so that sharing is seamless. This ensures an evolving, improved level of insight and reporting to an increasingly secure and highly performing cyber environment for all.

This evolving cyber intelligence tradecraft requires deep and powerful technical and analytic expertise at all levels. Such technical talent and related capabilities remain ill-defined and in short supply across government and industry. An institution that has made some headway in this regard is the Information Assurance Directorate (IAD) at the National Security Agency. IAD is the front line of the defensive cyber mission. It commands substantial resources, high performing talent, strong processes, and informed outreach. It also works hand in hand with military, public, and private partners to ensure that our cyber capabilities and intellectual property are defended and that our defence is informing offence and vice versa. IAD is a good start, but we must emulate their good practices and innovativeness in defining professional attributes, associated education, and training goals for the unique career fields associated with the cyber realm.

INTELLIGENCE OR COUNTERINTELLIGENCE

Even though the term counterintelligence is not used nearly as much by the media, it plays a significant role in an overall intelligence programme. Loosely defined, counterintelligence is monitoring and interdicting your adversary's ability to monitor and interdict your operations.

These are the "spy catchers" of national security programmes. The role of counterintelligence is generally separated from intelligence in national security settings, but in the realm of law enforcement and private security any separation would be based on available resources. In some instances this may be not possible at all. The importance of discussing counterintelligence here is the recognition that any techniques of gathering information, legal and illegal, may be used against you and your organization. An extremely well developed counterintelligence programme is capable of "feeding" disinformation directly to an adversary's collection efforts while being aware of what "true" information has been collected. This creates phenomenal dangers to operations, and so the importance of protecting your own collection programme and organization from hostile collection and infiltration should not be understated. The best collection programme in one organization can be undermined by a strong counterintelligence effort in another organization when the analysis process is ultimately contaminated. Remember it is not safe to assume that your adversary will adopt as high an ethical threshold as you and your organization, so appropriate precautions should be taken to guard your organization from hostile collection efforts. This includes Competitive Intelligence in the business realm, which is used by businesses to gain information on their competitor's products and services. That topic is beyond our scope here but should be considered one reason why an adversary would want confidential business information. Typically the programmes and efforts used for preventing information leakage are referred to as Operations Security or OPSEC. As we discuss the role of intelligence within protection programmes and law enforcement also consider the parallel role of counterintelligence.

CRIMINAL INTELLIGENCE AND CRIME ANALYSIS

Within Law Enforcement there are at least two different fields of analysis. The most common are criminal intelligence and crime analysis. Although the two are often grouped together in many settings and discussions, there are subtle differences. Crime analysis consists of the techniques and processes for studying crime patterns and trends, their affect on a jurisdiction, and any law enforcement response. Criminal intelligence, however, is more concerned with people, organizations and any relationships between them (IACA, 2005). Our discussion will continue to focus on the use of intelligence, rather than the specific organizational role of the analyst.

Data Types and Sources

Data, the fundamental building block of intelligence, is collected via "sources" which can be broadly classified into two groups, open source and closed source. Open sources are those generally available to the public and closed sources typically are not available to the public. The concept is simple enough. From this, many may believe that closed source information is what everyone needs, and in some instances that may be true, however the bulk of intelligence is often derived from open sources. It may be hard to believe that a great deal of information is obtained through public sources. Open source information is more readily available, but its limitations are found in tight knit planning groups, criminal operations, and within classified government activities where public releases are not common. This should not indicate that open source information is not useful in these situations. Let's consider this more closely.

It is important to note some of the legal differences in the United States between law enforcement intelligence and intelligence activities in the private sector. As a direct result of abuses over the last several decades, particularly during the Vietnam era, there have been several rulings concerning how law enforcement agencies are allowed to gather intelligence, for what purposes, and how these records must be maintained. In short law enforcement agencies may only collect intelligence on individuals or groups based on a criminal predicate or an articulated belief that future criminal actions will be committed. Agencies may not collect information based on race, ethnicity, political beliefs, religion, or other lawful characteristics.

Protecting civil liberties is an essential government responsibility in a free society, and as such collection efforts must be based on a "criminal predicate." In the private sector, however, information collection is limited only by imagination, and by few legal constraints. These legal restraints most often deal with wiretap/eavesdropping laws, lying to government or financial institutions, and unlawfully acquiring protected credit data. There are other restrictions as well, and involved in collection efforts should be familiar with all state and local laws. Private investigators often have greater leeway in what information they may collect and how they may collect it. Whereas Law enforcement, in collecting information, takes the risk that its efforts may be attacked by civil libertarians when, for example, attempting to gain access to library circulation records. A private investigator, on the other hand, may be able to gain information through a phone call depending on local legal constraints and their personality.

Data Quality

Sources of information come in all shapes and sizes, but they are not necessarily of the same quality. Information is valuable, but not all information has the same value to us. What affects the value of information? Timeliness, reliability and applicability. If the information we receive is old or outdated, its value is reduced in the context of forecasting a specific future event. Information that cannot be trusted, or is unreliable, is less valuable to us because we must take extra effort to make sure it is accurate. Finally, if the information we collect does not apply to our goals then it will be of little use.

To ensure that the intelligence we provide is accurate, we must first be certain of the data we are using. If we consider data as the fundamental building block of intelligence and information as consisting of smaller components of data, it becomes easier to recognize that poor data makes for poor information and thus flawed intelligence. As a result of poor intelligence, the wrong people may get hurt or killed, and the credibility of future efforts will not be held in high regard.

The timeliness of Information is relatively self explanatory in the context of its value. If you are told that you will receive something the day after it arrives, it's not intelligence it's history. It is easy to become a historian if there is not a constant drive to develop predictive information. It is easier to be a historian but the value of your work is far less. What should be noted about timeliness is that collection efforts occur over time. In some instances, the collection timeline causes earlier data to expire. To avoid this it is sometimes necessary to divulge this information in an interim report or statement to preserve its usefulness. The different types of intelligence products. It is, however, important to recognize that the "Time value of information" causes the value of information to dissipate over time. It may be one hour, one day, or one decade, but the value of that particular piece of information is generally reduced.

The importance of accuracy cannot be understated. Inaccurate data will ultimately lead to inaccurate intelligence, not accounting for luck or acts of nature. Accurate information ensures that our organization's actions are proportional. If a retailer is told to expect an enormous theft at their distribution centre their response may be equally enormous, however it may be a little disheartening if that attempted theft turned out to be just a few items of moderate value.

Resources will be mobilized, causing unnecessary expenditures based, in part, on the intelligence assessment. The intelligence analyst must also be cognizant of the fine line between being an alarmist and being a historian. The alarmist indicates that every future event will be enormous and most of the time they will be incorrect. This is an indicator of either lazy analytical work or an analyst that is out of touch with reality. Regardless of the cause, either will result in poor intelligence products. On the other hand, the historian fails to forecast anything but is more than capable of describing the incident, and its shortcomings, in the past tense. Although past incidents may at times help predict future activities; that should be part of the analysis as a whole, and not the whole analysis. It is important that an analyst avoid being either an alarmist or a historian. Data accuracy must also be examined from the standpoint that the data collected may be disinformation, or information that is specifically released and is intentionally wrong.

This is a useful counterintelligence tool and one to be wary of if your adversary possesses this capability. While disinformation is used to deliberately mislead adversaries, misinformation is the term used when identifying unintentional errors in presented information. Consider an informant that deliberately releases false and misleading information about someone they have become angered with. The result could be devastating to that person in the short term, and embarrassing to law enforcement if they rely to heavily on the informant's information. Be aware that information obtained by motivated sources, especially that which is unsolicited, should be weighed carefully before conclusions are drawn. Not only should the data be reviewed for accuracy but the final analyst report should be logically supportable as well. It is not always possible to ensure the accuracy of collected data. It is obtained from many different types of sources, and all of these sources have different motivations and idiosyncrasies.

To account for potentially inaccurate data, it is necessary to assess the reliability of the source. A source becomes known for reliability over time as data obtained from this source is consistently accurate. One way to determine the reliability of any data is corroboration. Corroborating data is nothing more than obtaining the same information from another unrelated source. In the world of the Internet it is common for persons to claim that they are corroborating information from multiple locations, however upon closer examination it is usually the case that each of these sources obtained their information from the same original source. "Sourcing" data, or tracing it back to the earliest known existence is one way to avoid incorrectly believing that data has been corroborated. Corroborating data allows us to neutralize the "spin" that different sources may put on the same information. To further evaluate why a source "spins" a specific way consider their motivation for generating the data. In those instances for which the data may not be corroborated the reliability of the source becomes even more important. Why was the source motivated in the past, if they provided information previously and why is he or she motivated now? The reason for any changes may indicate a significant change in their reliability.

Data should be challenged to ensure its accuracy, timeliness and validity. Failing to do so may result in unnecessary injuries, expenditures, and embarrassment. The goal is to provide a reliable product to assist in formulating an effective and economical response to a particular issue. Reviewing data from several perspectives allows us to increase our certainty that our analysis will be built on a solid foundation.

COUNTERING THREATS THROUGH CYBERSPACE

In the United States, surveillance has been at the heart of changes in traditional defence, as well as attempts to counter so-called "asymmetric" security threats. Guided by the principle that "what can be seen can be hit," battlefield surveillance was at the heart of the U.S., "revolution in military affairs" during the 1970s, 1980s, and 1990s. Two asymmetric threats in particular have caught the imaginations of those within the United States who have worked consistently to increase government surveillance capabilities: the threats of terrorism and cyber attack.

The idea that information-age conflict in general, and the fight against terrorism in particular, constitute a global "battle for hearts and minds" has been popular among U.S., defence and security professionals for at least a decade. Various observers have worried about terrorist use of the Internet as a tool for fundraising, organising, recruiting, and propaganda. It is in this spirit that Arquilla has urged the U.S., government to remove terrorist web sites from the Internet. Likewise, it is in this spirit that groups of self-organised, online volunteers engage in various types of online activities in support of the U.S., "war on terrorism," including intelligence gathering and counter-propaganda activities.

The work of Shannen Rossmiller and her group Phoenix Global Information Systems is the most notable example of intelligence-focused, volunteer cyber-counterterrorism. In response to the terrorist attacks of September 11, 2001, Rossmiller, a municipal judge from a small town in Montana, began trolling jihadist web sites to learn more about those who had attacked the United States and what they might be planning next. In January 2003, Rossmiller joined forces with at least six other individuals whom she met in the online discussion forum. They created a web site and began calling themselves 7-Seas Global Intelligence.

Members of 7-Seas live in the United States, Canada, Australia, and Singapore and include an economist, a physicist, a computer systems engineer, a corporate security consultant, and a private investigator. Rossmiller and members of 7-Seas have used a number of techniques to gather intelligence about terrorists online. These have included creating multiple false personas complete with pictures and detailed life histories. To appear as convincing as possible to her targets, Rossmiller has learned Arabic, studied the Quran, and read Arabic literature. They also employ translation software, tools to map the IP addresses of the online jihadists with whom they interact, software to mask their own IP addresses and make it appear that they are located in the Middle East or South Asia, and even spyware that is remotely installed on the computers of some of those that they investigate.

While their initial goal was to predict future terrorist attacks, they soon shifted to gathering and analysing information from terrorist web sites, forums, and chat rooms, and then turning that information over to authorities. Rossmiller's efforts in particular have contributed to two high-profile arrests of would-be terrorists, including the 2004 case of Specialist Ryan Anderson, a Washington state National Guardsman who attempted to sell classified information about vulnerabilities of U.S., weapons systems to an al-Qa'ida member that he met online.

That al-Qa'ida member was actually Rossmiller. Anderson is now in prison serving five consecutive life sentences, the harshest penalty yet dealt to an American in the war on terrorism. In another case, and again posing online as a member of al- Qa'ida, Rossmiller uncovered a plot by Pennsylvania resident and al-Qa'ida sympathiser, Michael Reynolds, to blow up several gas pipelines and oil refineries in the United States. Reynolds was convicted and is now serving fifty seven years in prison. Rossmiller is reported to have provided information to U.S., law enforcement or intelligence in as many as 240 other cases, leading to the detention of dozens of suspects worldwide and even some arrests and deportations of terrorism suspects from the United States.

For all the success that Rossmiller and 7-Seas has had, there remains a great deal of ambivalence, ambiguity, and tension in their relationship with authorities. On the one hand, the volunteers are motivated in part by calls by authorities to be vigilant. They believe authorities' claims about the seriousness of the threat of terrorism and want to help. One the other hand, they are also motivated by feelings that the government is either unable or unwilling to counter extremists' use of the Internet. Similarly, while Rossmiller has received a great deal of praise and assistance from authorities—the FBI has compensated her for her expenses, provided her with Arabic translation services, and provided her with security, a former Secretary of Commerce has said that she deserves a medal, she has been consulted by the Defence Intelligence Agency, and she has been an invited speaker at an FBI cyber security conference—these agencies have also sometimes expressed concern or doubt about her work and the work of others like her.

For her part, Rossmiller has at times complained that her work is being undervalued by authorities and has been clear to assert her independence from the state. But for all the tensions between authorities and volunteers, and for all that Rossmiller and 7-Seas have tried to distance themselves from the authorities, they nonetheless seek both approval and profit from the authorities. Both 7-Seas and later Phoenix Global Intelligence Systems have sought government contracts and intelligence and security consulting work for government clients.

In 2009, Rossmiller announced at an FBI-sponsored cyber security conference that she had formed a company and was seeking a partnership with a defence contractor to offer cyber-intelligence training and services to the government. She has been encouraged to do so by former CIA Director, James Woolsey. In the end, there are real reasons for tension and for concern. Both sides are right. The authorities likely cannot monitor and analyse that much Web content, making the work of the volunteers indispensable.

However, the volunteers do not have the ability to physically arrest suspects or materially disrupt terrorist planning or operations in any significant way, making the capabilities of the state indispensable in achieving their goals. Additionally, there are clear difficulties in making the relationship work. Sometimes authorities and volunteers can work at cross purposes. If authorities rely too much on volunteers, or if the role of volunteers becomes formally institutionalised, then their main value can be compromised. Finally, Michael Reynolds' defence strategy—*i.e.*, claiming that he too was just trying to catch terrorists online like Rossmiller—also points to some of the potential difficulties in this new relationship between producers and consumers of security online.

COUNTERING THREATS TO CYBER SPACE

Other groups have worked to counter threats to cyber space. This includes efforts to investigate and analyse cyber attack incidents such as denial of service attacks and targeted use of malware. Founded in August 2008 by former intelligence analyst Jeffrey Carr, Project Grey Goose was an experiment in online, volunteer, open source intelligence (OSINT) aimed at investigating possible Russian government involvement in the large-scale cyber attacks that hit the country of Georgia during the Russian military invasion earlier that month. On August 22, 2008, Carr used his blog to announce the project and to put out a call for volunteers.

The final cadre of twelve that was listed in the group's October 2008 report was comprised primarily of current and former members of the intelligence community, academic researchers, and defence and security professionals. Contributors to a second Grey Goose report released in early 2009 largely fit the same demographic profile. The group has described their OSINT methodology as relying on "data mining" and "machine translation" of "foreign language forums and social media sites," technical analysis of "serverlevel data," "an examination of geopolitical events occurring around the time of the cyber attacks," and "a review of the Nation State's military doctrine related to Information Warfare." They believe that the open source nature of their work is a distinct advantage, allowing them to work more quickly and with greater participation from international volunteers.

The two Grey Goose reports have had a substantial impact on shaping perceptions of Russia's involvement in the 2008 Georgia cyber attacks, as well as shaping public debate about the threat of cyber war. Members and supporters of Project Grey Goose even believe that data that they turned over to authorities may have prevented some cyber attacks, as well caused the Kremlin "to reduce its support of various [hacker] groups". Jeffrey Carr has become a sought-after expert on issues of cyber war, resulting in his publication of the book *Inside Cyber Warfare* for O'Reilly Media in 2009. Carr's book is now on the Commander's recommended reading list for members of U.S., Strategic Command, the parent organisation of the newly-formed U.S., Cyber Command.

Once again, the case of Project Grey Goose indicates the ambivalence and ambiguities that often exist between producers and consumers of security. Like Rossmiller and others, Carr has argued that bureaucratic inefficiencies often prevent government from effectively countering "terrorism in cyber space". One of those limitations, he argues, is that state actors do not yet understand the power of either the Internet, open sources of information, or collaborative processes of knowledge production.

Thus, governments have proven ill-equipped for countering terrorists online or meeting the challenge of cyber attacks. He sees Project Grey Goose as exemplary of the value of applying the open source software development model to intelligence work and hopes that "it will prove that we do not have to wait for official channels to adopt innovative solutions". Carr and his supporters identify Project Grey Goose as an example of what they call a "security trust network" (STN). Michael Sinkowitch, an executive at Fujitsu Australia who specialises in national security and intelligence, has defined STNs as "expert affiliations of interested organisations and individuals that can investigate and mitigate cyber crime threats".

Alexander Klimburg, a fellow at the Austrian Institute for International Affairs and a contributor to Carr's 2009 book, defines them as the liberal, democratic, Western antithesis to Russian and Chinese "patriotic hackers." Where "patriotic hackers" are seen as beholden to or controlled by the state and composed of malicious actors with a dubious moral code, STNs are defined as free to "choose when and if" to support a government, as trustworthy and credible partners for government, and as "shar[ing] a common moral code" based in "doing the right thing" and "operating within the remits of the law". Carr, Sinkowitsch, and Klimburg all see STNs like Project Grey Goose as examples of the security-producing "informal groups and volunteer networks" that Klimburg speaks about in the epigraph to this chapter.

In the realm of cyber security in particular, Klimburg has claimed that most work is already being done by STNs and business with "government bringing up the rear". He has claimed that STNs are particularly good at addressing the "attribution problem" in cyber security—*i.e.*, figuring out the origin of a cyber attack, which is "a notoriously difficult task". Sinkowitsch has gone so far as to claim that cyber security STNs are able to "defeat, or at the very least limit the damage of, these adversaries [*i.e.*, cyber attackers of various sorts]". But like the other cases of convergence security examined here, STNs too are ultimately dependent upon their relationship to the state.

Even Sinkowitsch admits that "There is not much they [STNs] can do about stopping the threats". Though STNs are theoretically free to choose when and if they work with the state, in practice having an impact requires working with the state. Since, the original call for volunteers for Project Grey Goose, Carr has solicited volunteers for a project he calls "Grey Balloons," which is an open-ended project to create a standing pool of volunteers that are ready and able to help the U.S., intelligence community with whatever challenges it might face. Grey Balloons is a reflection of Carr's "hope that a bridge could be established connecting intelligence community professionals with independent volunteers with the necessary expertise". Finally, as in the case of Rossmiller and cyber-counterterrorism, there is profit to be made in assisting the state.

In 2009, Project Grey Goose became Grey Logic, "a consultancy and information services provider to governments". It is perhaps unsurprising then that Sinkowitsch and Klimburg have encouraged Western governments to promote and support the formation of STNs as a necessary component of their national cyber security strategies. Finally, there are real reasons for concern when it comes to STNs. When questioned about the legal status of STNs and whether their work borders on vigilantism, Sinkowitsch claimed that there is no legal problem with what STNs do because they rely on information that is freely available on the Web; they are merely collecting and analysing it in a different, more effective way.

But recent scandals over advertiser use of social media content, as well as the case of a defence contractor mining and analysing social media content to smear supporters of WikiLeaks and political opponents of the U.S., Chamber of Commerce, indicate that there are legitimate privacy and legal concerns when volunteers begin doing their own online intelligence work on behalf of the state or powerful corporate interests.

PATROLLING NATIONAL BORDERS IN CYBERSPACE

Online, volunteer cyber-surveillance efforts have also been used to aid in the production of more traditional forms of security, such as defending territorial integrity by patrolling national borders. Since, 9/11, the debate over immigration from the global South has been increasingly linked to the "War on Terror." Part of this linkage can be found in the actions and discourse of what are collectively called "Minutemen" groups. Minutemen groups are most known for their use of physical presence on the U.S.-Mexico border, especially in 2005, a presence spurred by organisers who wanted to draw attention to what they perceived to be the government's lack of intervention in illegal immigration.

Although the Minutemen are not a government agency, their border-watching efforts were meant to supplement—and not replace —the physical intervention of the U.S., Border Patrol; thus the Minutemen appropriated part of the state's power of surveillance without impinging on the state's monopoly on the use of force. In addition, Minutemen groups have also deployed "Cyber Minutemen," extending surveillance onto the Web. Using a mix of fibre-optic fencing, Web cameras, motion detectors, infrared sensors, and even aircraft, various Minutemen groups have posted images and live streams to a variety of Web sites.

This use of relatively inexpensive surveillance and Web technology is touted by Cyber Minutemen as a viable, high-tech, modern way for citizens to succeed where the state has ostensibly failed in stemming the flow of immigrants across the Mexican border. Jim Wood, founder of the nowdefunct Border Fence Project, argues that citizen groups are more efficient and cost-effective than state efforts to secure the border. "The bottom line is this," he argues in a letter to supporters, "Despite bureaucratic refusals, delays and boondoggles, we civilians on the border can build a national Border Fence without them, repairing the old and erecting the new... Therefore, we as American citizens and patriots must stand up and do this ourselves."

Part of the efficiency arises from the use of distributed volunteers across the Web; volunteers from as far away as Australia have reportedly spotted illegal border crossings. In this case, the convergence of state aims and privately deployed technologies echoes previous, new media "crowdsourcing" efforts such as Wikipedia and the NASA Clickworkers project. As in the other convergence security cases, Cyber Minutemen have enjoyed some support from the state, as well as from Internet entrepreneurs. Texas governor Rick Perry, the Texas Border Sheriff's Coalition, and private landowners joined Internet company BlueServo in a "publicprivate partnership" to distribute live feeds of the border to Web volunteers. This public-private partnership is a for-profit endeavor. BlueServo claims, "Because www.BlueServo.net is an internet social network, in the future, BlueServo anticipates that high volume of traffic to its web site will generate advertising revenue to defray the operations cost of the Virtual Community Watch to the Texas Border Sheriff's Coalition." Thus, in keeping with convergence media business practices, BlueServo intends to meld the Cyber Minutemen desire to secure the border with the political economy of attention found in other Web 2.0 sites such as Facebook and YouTube. This entrepreneurial form of convergence border security has also been proposed by the Heritage Foundation.

However, as with other convergence security groups, the Minutemen have had ambivalent, ambiguous, and tense relationships with the state. Although Texas Governor Perry and California Governor Arnold Schwarzenegger publicly endorsed the movement, George W. Bush referred to them as "vigilantes". The Department of Homeland Security rejected a proposal to formally integrate volunteer citizen patrols into the Border Patrol.

For their part, the Minutemen groups have not sought integration with the state. Rather, they have largely called for an increased police or military presence at the border; they tend to frame their activity as drawing attention to the perceived problem of illegal immigration, drug trafficking, and terrorism. In the main, the Minuteman movement has been strict with members about the use of violence; thus the Minutemen have been careful not to infringe on the state's monopoly on violence for fear of political and legal repercussions.

A large Minuteman group, the Minutemen Civil Defence Corps (MCDC), disbanded in 2010 not long after a leader in that organisation called for a "locked and loaded"—*i.e.*, publicly armed—patrol of the border. The "locked and loaded" muster was intended as a show of arms rather than an explicit call to violence. However, the proposed muster led to an enthusiastic response among members that the MCDC leadership interpreted as potentially violent, stoking fears within the organisation that the MCDC would not be able to prevent members from using weapons on alleged illegal border crossers, thus echoing Bush's earlier fears of vigilantism. The leaders of the MCDC did not want to cross the border between civil society groups and state-sponsored military groups.

Ultimately, in the case of the Minutemen, their proposed virtual surveillance of the border was accepted by the state far easier than their proposed, *embodied* patrol of the border. While the MCDC disbanded in light of the potential use of force by members, BlueServo and its Web camera network remains active to this day. State officials who decry potential vigilantism at the border tend to ignore or tolerate the use of Web-based surveillance. Most state officials who want increased border security eschew Minutemen-style groups and opt instead for state-sanctioned groups such as the U.S., Border Patrol, the National Guard, or new bureaucratic formations such as the Department of Homeland Security.

4

Criminal and Legal Aspects of Fighting Computer Crime

Nowadays, intensive use of computer technologies in various spheres of human activity has significantly changed an idea of a place and a role of information in present-day society. National information resources have appeared as a new economic category. They became one of the most important factors of post industrial world development. Society is getting features of an information society. This happens owing to development of computer technologies processing information.

Unfortunately, new kinds of crime as "computer crime", "cyber terrorism" and "information war" appeared. Special anxiety is related to crimes in sphere of computers. Number of computers in developed countries is constantly growing. Trend of increase in such crimes is extending. We have a number of cases illustrating computer technologies use for criminal purposes. Serious problems of information security constantly arise as homeland is integrating in the Internet.

A united policy is realized at the state level on purpose of national interests security maintenance from threats in information sphere; a balance of need for free information exchange and admissible restrictions for its distribution are established; the legislation is being improved; activity of state authorities on safety in the information environment is being coordinated; state information resources are being protected at defence enterprises; native telecommunication and information means are being developed; information structure of IT development is being improved; means of search, collecting, storage, processing and the analysis of information are being unified on purpose of entering global information infrastructure.

The urgency of research in this issue is caused also by a problem of increase in efficiency of fighting computer criminality on the part of law enforcement. Creating of the corresponding legal base in law enforcement agencies is of high priority. In process of studying the legislative experience in foreign countries, some separate scientists drafted recommendations and offers on criminal legal regulation of this field in native legislation. According to D. Azarov "regulations in the new Criminal Code concerning responsibility for crimes in sphere of computers and computer systems demand a careful analysis. We consider that it is necessary to take into account experience of other European countries in this sphere. Issues of criminalization and, probably, decriminalization of certain actions in sphere of computers, systems and networks demand a further studying. The international experience shows a presence of certain actions that belong to a category of computer crimes, and crimes of some other character, rather than those which attributes are determined in the Criminal Code".

Especially, European Council experts in criminal law suggest to criminalize such socially dangerous acts in sphere of computer information:

- Computer fraud;
- Computer forgery;
- Damage of computer information or software;
- Computer sabotage;
- Unauthorized access;
- Unauthorized interception.

The analysis of law that regulates public information relations in Ukraine, allows to assert that our government takes measures of stimulating the infrastructure development on the basis of the newest technologies, along with necessary measures of containment and counteraction to negative events in sphere of computer technologies.

Among top-priority steps of state policy in sphere of counteraction to computer criminality is an appearance of new Section 16 in the Criminal Code of Ukraine- "Crimes in Sphere of Computers, Systems and Networks". Having recognized information as a subject of theft, assignment, extortion and other criminal acts, criminal law has confirmed status of information as an object of the property right that is coordinated with substantive regulations of information legislation. Till recently, criminal legal doctrine unreasonably unfilled information from the list of possible subjects of theft or other property crimes.

In this connection, appearance of the mentioned section in the Code is natural and objective necessity of legal means in process of solving problems related to fundamental modification of technology, world outlook of people, international relationship under conditions of a wide scope computerization of information sphere.As is well-known, "Illegal interference with operation of computers, systems and networks", that is an illegal interference with operation of automated computers, systems or networks resulted in distortion or erasing of computer information or destroying its carriers, and also to spreading of computer viruses by using software and hardware designed for illegal penetration into these machines, systems or networks and capable of distortion or erasing computer information or destroying its carriers";

"Theft, misappropriation, extortion of computer information or its capture by swindling or abusing official position" and the "Violation of automated electronic computer operating rules": violation of operating rules of automated computers, systems or networks on the part of a person responsible for their operation, if it has entailed theft, distortion or erasing of computer information, security means, or illegal copying of computer information, or essential infringement of such facilities, systems or networks operation.

The components of crimes defined in the mentioned section are correlated with existing needs of public legal actuality. Also, they are aimed at protection maintenance of the corresponding rights, liberties and legitimate interests of individuals and legal entities. Unfortunately, these legal norms have some weaknesses at the same time.

The owner of automated system is any person that legally uses services of information processing as the proprietor of such system (computer, systems or networks) or as the person that has the right to use such system.

It always has a character of fulfilment of certain actions, and it can be a penetration into computer system by use of special technical means or software, allowing to overcome installed systems of protection from illegal application of obtained passwords or masking under a kind of a legal user with purpose of penetration into computer system.

So, "illegal interference with operation of automated computers, systems and networks that has led to distortion or destruction of computer information or carriers of such information" as penal action. This component of crime is of material character. Consequences are obligatory element of the crime. The person who has performed the specified actions in forms, not defined in the Article 361, is not subject to criminal liability.

The Criminal Code has established the responsibility for distribution of computer viruses. But an obligatory element of the objective side of this crime lies in the way of its commitment, namely: by application a software and/or other means with intent of illegal penetration into automated machines, systems and networks and capable to cause distortion or destruction of computer information or carriers of such information. If the person distributes a computer virus in a different way or by application of other instruments and means which are not bearing the above-stated attributes in aggregate, such person is not subject to the responsibility according to the Criminal Code.

Direct object of a crime is the information property right, that is the broken right of the proprietor's ownership, use or control over information. Interpretation of this term in a context of automated systems is placed in the Article 1 of the Automated Systems Information Security Law "... information in automated systems is a set of all data and Programmes used in automated systems, irrespectively of means of their physical and logic representation... ".Displays of the objective side of crime components are: actions like distortion or destruction of computer information or carriers of such information, and also distribution of... carriers of such information, and also distribution of computer virus.

As used here, destruction of information is its loss, when information in sphere of computers, systems and networks ceases to exist for individuals and legal entities that have full or limited property right to it. Termination of access to information should be considered as blocking of information. Such actions can be performed, for example, with the help of electromagnetic, laser and other effect on data carriers in which info is materialized or with the help of which it is transferred; by forming of signals of means and blocks of Programmes effecting information, its carriers and means of technical protection that causes violation of integrity of information, its distortion or destruction.

Distortion of information is a modification of its contents, violation of its integrity, including partial destruction. Establishing of a mode of access to information is regulated by the Information Law. It defines the order of reception, use, distribution and retention of information. Depending on a mode of access, information is divided into open information and information with restricted access (confidential and secret). According to the Article 30 of the mentioned law, confidential information is data which is in ownership, use or order of separate individuals or legal entities and is distributed, at their will, according to the terms provided for by them.

Citizens and legal entities that own information of professional, business, industrial, commercial and other character, having obtained it due to own means, or such which is a subject of their professional, business, industrial, commercial and other interest and does not break secret provided for by law, have the right to define independently a mode of access to it, including its belonging to the confidential category, and establish a system (ways) of its protection.

Secret information is information containing data, making state and others secret defined by the law, disclosure of which cause damage to the person, society and the state.

We offer to understand the damage caused by criminal acts (direct and indirect losses) which size is equal or exceeds 100 minimal free incomes of citizen as heavy consequences.

The components of this crime are characterized by presence of the general subject. Commitment of such actions by the person which professional duties include preservation or processing of such information should be admitted as the attribute that burdens the responsibility.Material components structure of the crime is chosen for developing of the first part of this norm. The structure establishes the necessity of criminal consequences approach, like distortion or destruction of computer information or carriers of such information.

The Article directly defines mental attitude of the person to own actions, therefore the guilt form of such person is intention only. Unfortunately, the Criminal Code does not adjust a situation when interference with operation of automated computers, systems or networks is performed owing to careless actions.

Thus, the significant amount of possible infringements and even actions which are really performed with intent, as it is hard to prove the intent of the computer criminal during investigation of circumstances of intervention (*e.g.* a person that usually uses e-mail in the Internet, probably not deliberately but also owing to carelessness, may distribute computer viruses).

Theft, assignment, extortion of computer information or its abstraction by swindle or official position abusing (referring to the Article 362) concerns only "computer" crimes. They make the majority among files of offences in sphere of computers, systems and networks.The definition of "computer information", introduced by the legislation, is very important. In our opinion, it is necessary to understand it as an aggregate of all identified and owned date, used in computers, systems and networks. The identified information is information fixed in the machine carrier with essential properties allowing to identify it. The given norm of the Criminal Code, naturally, does not contain concrete technical requirements. It refers to departmental instructions and the rules establishing the operating procedure and which should be set specially by the authorized person and be brought to users. Application of the specified Article to the Internet is impossible; its effect applies only to local networks of organizations.

An investigatory relation should be established between the fact of violation of operation rules of automated computers and the fact of caused essential harm. It should be completely proved, that consequences come exactly from violations of operation rules.

Determining of essential harm provided for by the Article 361 is an evaluating process. The harm is determined by court in each concrete case, in view of all circumstances, however it is obvious, that essential harm should be less significant, rather than essential consequences. A criminal realizes that he is breaking operation rules; he foresees an opportunity and inevitability of illegal influence on information and causing essential harm or meaningly wishes causing such harm. Such action is punished by deprivation of the right to occupy certain positions or by engaging in certain work for the term up to five years or correctional work for the term up to two years.

Part 1 of the Article 363 of the Criminal Code is complicated for interpretation of the contents. Grammatical, logical and system structural analysis of all the Article allows to say that illegal copying of computer information and essential infringement of operation of automated computers, systems and networks are not forms of crime provided for by this Article, and make up only a set of possible consequences which can arise as a result of its commitment. Part 2 of the Article 363 has a blanket reference to described in the Part 1 illegal action.One more feature of crime is provided for by the Article 363 of the Criminal Code. Only a special subject accounts for its commitment, it is the person responsible for operation of automated computers, systems and networks.

LEGAL POLICIES ON CYBER CRIME

In its nascent stages, cyber crime enjoyed a special legal status that belied common practice used in adjudicating crimes. Hacking was commonly perceived as a prank perpetrated by teenagers. Later, the lone, highly skilled attacker working against a high value target was mythologised and revered in some ways. The media and movie industry continued to foster the notion, so that when Kevin Mitnick was arrested in 1995, there was a relative groundswell of support for his release, despite having broken into systems, stolen millions of dollars in proprietary software, "altered information, corrupted system software, and eavesdropped on users, sometimes prevented or impeded legitimate use."

The idea that cyber crime was "different" from regular crime persisted into the dawn of the Internet age, helped along by an unwillingness among police to get involved in patrolling and investigating cyberspace. Such reluctance may have been due to lack of reference points in law, low rates of successful prosecutions and international resistance to help track cross-border crimes. The perception that cyber criminals are different entities has now been thoroughly discouraged. Indeed, "prosecutors are starting to make aggressive use of the Computer Fraud and Abuse Act, which carries penalties of up to 20 years in prison. The lengthiest sentence so far has been nine years, issued in December." There is no longer any calls to be lenient on a those who use computers to exploit, steal and abuse privileges, such as the Californian software executive who conspired to steal trade secrets from a competitor by illegally accessing network and computer systems.

The change in these commonly held notions happened gradually, but importantly, there is now a strong sense of civic empowerment given to the government to apprehend cyber criminals, which when coupled with the renewed diligence attributed to preventing terrorism, has allowed legislation to evolve rapidly in the past few years. As computers have become more integral to daily life, allowing users to conduct higher value operations, they have naturally become targets for those imbued with the criminal tendency.

Most users have recognised the threat and the need for protection, even if they ignore certain precautions, like maintaining the secrecy of passwords. If users notice that they can no longer effectively use their workstations, legislation has usually been proposed, albeit after a lengthy period of discussion.

For example, a few years ago, spam was threatening to overwhelm the usefulness of e-mail. Subsequently, congress passed the CAN-SPAM Act of 2003, which made certain practices, like harvesting e-mail addresses, illegal, while imposing maximum fines of up to one million dollars.

Despite flaws that some detractors have brought up, such as continuing to allow e-mail addresses to be sold to third parties, the act has provided a legal threshold to base decisions upon and brought notoriously flagrant spammers to justice. In a broader sense, the government has reacted to the demand for better enforcement and the need to extend legal jurisdiction over crimes that may have not been crimes before. The Cyber Security Enchancement Act of 2002, which fell under the Homeland Security Act, and the USA PATRIOT Act both instituted changes to deal with cyber crime. Other, more comprehensive laws, like the Fraud and Related Activity in Connection with Computers, located in the the US Criminal Code and Unlawful Access to Store Communications have been codified for a longer period of time.

The increase in awareness of cyber criminality has begun to manifest itself with the passage of laws, creation of organisations and advisory committees and powers granted to enforcement agencies. Their application to current cyber crime has found varying degrees of success. What needs to then be examined and discussed with the aforementioned issues in mind are the crafting of laws, enforcement and effectiveness. These have to be multiplexed across national and international settings, while being interpreted within a framework of technology and trends that are rapidly evolving. Only then can a broad understanding of the legal policies surrounding cyber crime be achieved.

INTERNATIONAL CYBER CRIME

A significant problem that arises when working with cyber crime is that most crimes transit data through a multititude of international borders before reaching the final, intended target. Such circuitousness has a deleterious effect on investigating cyber crimes as well as the application of laws. An illustrative example of the legal hurdles faced with international incidents comes from the "Searching and Seizing Computers and Obtaining Electronic Evidence in Criminal Investigations" manual for the United State Department of Justice. The manual reports that when seeking assistance from ISPs overseas, officers must work "with the consent of that country," which means certain formalities need to be resolved before proceeding.

First, prior permission of the foreign government must be obtained. Next, approval from the Justice Department's Office of International Affairs, and finally a clear indication that the actions would not be objectionable in the foreign country. The process is long and unwieldy, especially since, by the time the necessary paper work is filed, ISPs may have already deleted the information. Or in a worse case, after the information is obtained, it will then be discovered that the attacker went through another country, forcing the process to be repeated. Many developing countries are short on the resources and technical knowledge needed to expedite this process, causing the investigation to fail.

By 1997, the problem was being recognised internationally and the G-8 Justice and Interior Ministers noted that to be "consistent with the principles of sovereignty and the protection of human rights, nations must be able to collect and exchange information internationally, especially within the short time frame so often required when investigating international high-tech crimes." To aid this process they created a Point of Contact network which required participating countries to specify a specific group that could assist 24 hours a day, 7 days a week. By 2002, twenty countries were participating. These types of mutual legal assistance treaties (MLATs) have been effective where in the past law enforcement has been stymied.

For example, in 1992, the US government required assistance from Switzerland regarding an attack in the U.S., but since, Switzerland had no such laws regarding hacking on the books, they refused to help. In devising MLATs, a country can either create bilateral or multilateral relationships, each having its own benefits and drawbacks. Traditionally, sovereign nations have entered bilateral agreements with countries that they trust and are willing to accept each other's legal characteristics. They are quicker to negotiate, produce more detailed documents, are easier to change and allow nations to feel more comfortable sharing sensitive information. In fact, after the 2001 terrorist attacks, the US was eager to more quickly establish such ties and has concluded over 45 such agreements.

The drawbacks of course are that separate, and perhaps unequal, agreements must be reached, resulting in varying interpretations of crime and legal precedent. Multilateral pacts seem more suited to issues that are global in scale, much like cyber crime. Thus, it was with great fanfare that in November of 2001, thirty countries signed the Council of Europe's Convention on Cyber crime. The convention had been five years in the making and represents the first truly multinational attempt at defining, regulating and providing a framework for the legal issues in relation to cyber crime.

Briefly, it established conduct that is prohibited, identified required national legal processes and addressed international cooperation. At the U.S., Senate hearings on ratifying the treaty, Swartz noted "in the past, if an electronic transmission's trail led to another country, the chances were slim of successfully tracking the communication to its source or securing the evidence before deletion. With the tools provided for under the Convention, however, the ability of U.S., law enforcement to obtain international cooperation in identifying major offenders and securing evidence of their crimes so that they can be brought to justice will be significantly enhanced." Although the Senate Foreign Relations Committee approved the treaty, it has stalled in the Senate for nearly two years, as certain groups have opposed it for reasons related to civil liberties. The current state of multinational legislation thus remains a patchwork of bilateral treaties put together piece by piece. Establishing transnational treaties is a difficult task and remains as an open policy debate. What can be agreed upon is that all nations need multilateral assistance in a global sense, not just a limited group, as cyber criminals can route through any country. Treaties, then, need to harmonise laws, while building capabilities. Most importantly, such treaties should not be used to violate human rights, even though to do so may be legal in some countries.

For example, with the current Convention on Cyber crime, China could ask the U.S., to assist in finding political dissidents and supporters of democracy and the U.S., would be obliged, under the terms of the Convention, to provide assistance. More often than not, even if a successful conviction can be obtained, extraditing a criminal is still a tough legal battle. For example, in October of 2001, a Pakistani man was charged with defacing an American-Israeli organisation's web site. The FBI, working with the U.S., Embassy in Pakistan, was able to identify the attacker and get a warrant issued for his arrest in Pakistan, yet three years later he is still at large. Clearly, there is a need for a more comprehensive international plan.

FUTURE TRENDS IN LEGISLATION

The direction of legislation has slowly been proceeding to more severe and serious punishments for cyber crime. November 3 saw the first prosecution for owning and operating a botnet system. It seems probable as legislatures, federal and state, become aware of threat posed by botnets, and as methods become more advanced in discerning botcontrollers, legislation aimed at the problem will follow.

Whether it will become an effective deterrent probably rests with the ability to investigate and prosecute. Another area of concern is identity theft, a process facilitated to a large degree through the Internet. California has been the first to create legislation aimed at companies with lax security regarding the protection of personal information they may store. The California Security Breach Information Act (SB-1386), which went into effect in July of 2003, forces organisations to notify individuals if there is such a security breach.

It has been a powerful method for not only making people aware of the issue, but also applying a force for change in policy within many organisations, lest they be branded as uncaring and incompetent. With more sensitive information being stored by a greater number of third parties, more states will come to the conclusion California has and indirectly apply pressure to organisations to reform. In another example, a recent piece of county legislation in Westchester, New York proposed to make it illegal for companies storing personal information to allow insecure access to their networks. In a sense, it would criminalise using a wireless network with no security measures. Although, many have pointed out specific weaknesses in the bill, the idea has been praised as a step in the right direction and an important conduit for educating the public.

Cyber crime presents a challenging position for lawmakers, as they struggle to keep up with changes in technology and in the methods used to exploit those technologies for maliciousness. Unfortunately, legal wrangling leaves the judicial system in a state that can be behind the times. It should be realised that in the end, laws can only do so much to regulate an activity. Proactive security, user education and vigilance, combined with effective forensics and enforcement remain the best remedies for combating cyber crime. Legislation still needs to enact appropriate punishments and establish frameworks, though and in that sense it has a crucial role to play in the mitigation of cyber crime.

THE MEANING OF COMPUTER SECURITY

We have seen that any computer-related system has both theoretical and real weaknesses. The purpose of computer security is to devise ways to prevent the weaknesses from being exploited. To understand what preventive measures make the most sense, we consider what we mean when we say that a system is "secure."

SECURITY GOALS

We use the term "security" in many ways in our daily lives. A "security system" protects our house, warning the neighbours or the police if an unauthorized intruder tries to get in. "Financialsecurity" involves a set of investments that are adequately funded; we hope the investments will grow in value over time so that we have enough money to survive later in life. And we speak of children's "physical security," hoping they are safe from potential harm. Just as each of these terms has a very specific meaning in the context of its use, so too does the phrase "computer security."When we talk about computer security, we mean that we are addressing three important aspects of any computer-related system: confidentiality, integrity, and availability.

- Confidentiality ensures that computer-related assets are accessed only by authorized parties. That is, only those who should have access to something will actually get that access. By "access," we mean not only reading but also viewing, printing, or simply knowing that a particular asset exists. Confidentiality is sometimes called secrecy or privacy.
- Integrity means that assets can be modified only by authorized parties or only in authorized ways. In this context, modification includes writing, changing, changing status, deleting, and creating.
- Availability means that assets are accessible to authorized parties at

appropriate times. In other words, if some person or system has legitimate access to a particular set of objects, that access should not be prevented. For this reason, availability is sometimes known by its opposite, denial of service.

Security in computing addresses these three goals. One of the challenges in building a secure system is finding the right balance among the goals, which often conflict. For example, it is easy to preserve a particular object's confidentiality in a secure system simply by preventing everyone from reading that object. However, this system is not secure, because it does not meet the requirement of availability for proper access. That is, there must be a balance between confidentiality and availability. But balance is not all. In fact, these three characteristics can be independent, can overlap and can even be mutually exclusive. For example, we have seen that strong protection of confidentiality can severely restrict availability. Let us examine each of the three qualities in depth.

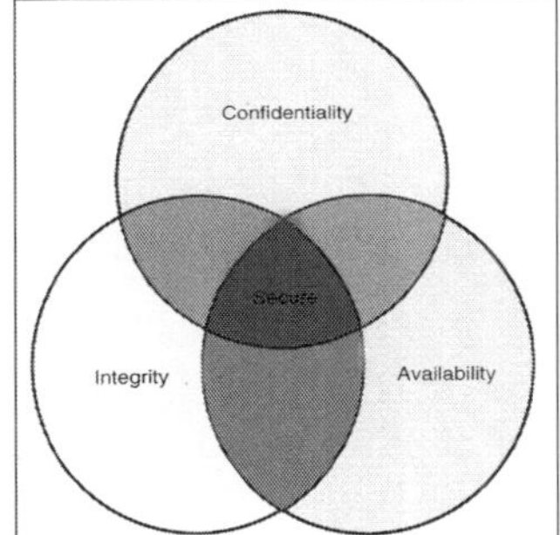

Fig. Relationship between Confidentiality, Integrity, and Availability.

Confidentiality

You may find the notion of confidentiality to be straightforward: Only authorized people or systems can access protected data. However, as we see in later chapters, ensuring confidentiality can be difficult. For example, who determines which people or systems are authorized to access the current system? By "accessing" data, do we mean that an authorized party can access a single bit? the whole collection? pieces of data out of context? Can someone who is authorized disclose those data to other parties? Confidentiality is the security property we understand best because its meaning is narrower than the other two. We also understand confidentiality well because we can relate computing examples to those of preserving confidentiality in the real world.

Integrity

Integrity is much harder to pin down. As Welke and Mayfield point out, integrity means different things in different contexts. When we survey the way some people use the term, we find several different meanings.

For example, if we say that we have preserved the integrity of an item, we may mean that the item is:

- Precise
- Accurate
- Unmodified
- Modified only in acceptable ways
- Modified only by authorized people
- Modified only by authorized processes
- Consistent
- Internally consistent
- Meaningful and usable.

Integrity can also mean two or more of these properties. Welke and Mayfield recognize three particular aspects of integrity authorized actions, separation and protection of resources, and error detection and correction. Integrity can be enforced in much the same way as can confidentiality: by rigorous control of who or what can access which resources in what ways. Some forms of integrity are well represented in the real world, and those precise representations can be implemented in a computerized environment. But not all interpretations of integrity are well reflected by computer implementations.

Availability

Availability applies both to data and to services (that is, to information and to information processing), and it is similarly complex. As with the notion of confidentiality, different people expect availability to mean different things.

For example, an object or service is thought to be available if:

- It is present in a usable form.
- It has capacity enough to meet the service's needs.
- It is making clear progress, and, if in wait mode, it has a bounded waiting time.
- The service is completed in an acceptable period of time.

We can construct an overall description of availability by combining these goals. We say a data item, service, or system is available if:

- There is a timely response to our request.
- Resources are allocated fairly so that some requesters are not favoured over others.
- The service or system involved follows a philosophy of fault tolerance, whereby hardware or software faults lead to graceful cessation of service or to work-arounds rather than to crashes and abrupt loss of information.
- The service or system can be used easily and in the way it was intended to be used.
- Concurrency is controlled; that is, simultaneous access, deadlock management, and exclusive access are supported as required.

The expectations of availability are far-reaching. Indeed, the security community is just beginning to understand what availability implies and how to ensure it. A small, centralized control of access is fundamental to preserving confidentiality and integrity, but it is not clear that a single access control point can enforce availability. Much of computer security's past success has focused on confidentiality and integrity; full implementation of availability is security's next great challenge.

VULNERABILITIES

When we prepare to test a system, we usually try to imagine how the system can fail; we then look for ways in which the requirements, design, or code can enable such failures. In the same way, when we prepare to specify, design, code, or test a secure system, we try to imagine the vulnerabilities that would prevent us from reaching one or more of our three security goals.

It is sometimes easier to consider vulnerabilities as they apply to all three broad categories of system resources (hardware, software, and data), rather than to start with the security goals themselves. The types of vulnerabilities we might find as they apply to the assets of hardware, software, and data. These three assets and the connections among them are all potential security weak points. Let us look in turn at the vulnerabilities of each asset

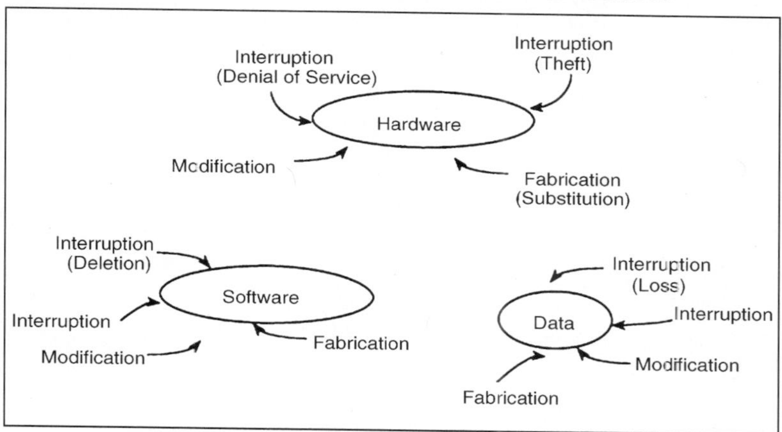

Fig. Vulnerabilities of Computing Systems.

Hardware Vulnerabilities

Hardware is more visible than software, largely because it is composed of physical objects. Because we can see what devices are hooked to the system, it is rather simple to attack by adding devices, changing them, removing them, intercepting the traffic to them, or flooding them with traffic until they can no longer function. However, designers can usually put safeguards in place. But there are other ways that computer hardware can be attacked physically. Computers have been drenched with water, burned, frozen, gassed, and electrocuted with power surges. People have spilled soft drinks, corn chips, ketchup, beer, and many other kinds of food on computing devices. Mice have chewed through cables. Particles of dust, and especially ash in cigarette smoke, have threatened precisely engineered moving parts. Computers have been kicked, slapped, bumped, jarred, and punched. Although such attacks might be intentional, most are not; this abuse might be considered "involuntary machine slaughter": accidental acts not intended to do serious damage to the hardware involved.

A more serious attack, "voluntary machine slaughter" or "machinicide," usually involves someone who actually wishes to harm the computer hardware or software. Machines have been shot with guns, stabbed with knives, and smashed with all kinds of things. Bombs, fires, and collisions have destroyed computer rooms. Ordinary keys, pens, and screwdrivers have been used to short-out circuit boards and other components. Devices and whole systems have been carried off by thieves. The list of the kinds of human attacks perpetrated on computers is almost endless.

In particular, deliberate attacks on equipment, intending to limit availability, usually involve theft or destruction. Managers of major computing centres long ago recognized these vulnerabilities and installed physical security systems to protect their machines. However, the proliferation of PCs, especially laptops, as office equipment has resulted in several thousands of dollars' worth of equipment sitting unattended on desks outside the carefully protected computer room. (Curiously, the supply cabinet, containing only a few hundred dollars' worth of pens, stationery, and paper clips, is often locked.) Sometimes the security of hardware components can be enhanced greatly by simple physical measures such as locks and guards.

Laptop computers are especially vulnerable because they are designed to be easy to carry. Safe ware Insurance reported 600,000 laptops stolen in 2003. Credent Technologies reported that 29 per cent were stolen from the office, 25 per cent from a car, and 14 per cent in an airport. Stolen laptops are almost never recovered: The FBI reports 97 per cent were not returned.

Software Vulnerabilities

Computing equipment is of little use without the software (operating system, controllers, utility programmes, and application programmes) that users expect. Software can be replaced, changed, or destroyed maliciously, or it can be modified, deleted, or misplaced accidentally. Whether intentional or not, these attacks exploit the software's vulnerabilities. Sometimes, the attacks are obvious, as when the software no longer runs. More subtle are attacks in which the software has been altered but seems to run normally. Whereas physical equipment usually shows some mark of inflicted injury when its boundary has been breached, the loss of a line of source or object code may not leave an obvious mark in a programme. Furthermore, it is possible to change a programme so that it does all it did before, and then some. That is, a malicious intruder can "enhance" the software to enable it to perform functions you may not find desirable. In this case, it may be very hard to detect that the software has been changed, let alone to determine the extent of the change.

A classic example of exploiting software vulnerability is the case in which a bank worker realised that software truncates the fractional interest on each account. In other words, if the monthly interest on an account is calculated to be.5467, the software credits only.54 and ignores the $.0067. The worker amended the software so that the throwaway interest (the $.0067) was placed into his own account. Since the accounting practices ensured only that all accounts balanced, he built up a large amount of money from the thousands of account throw-aways without detection. It was only when he bragged to a colleague of his cleverness that the scheme was discovered.

Software Deletion

Software is surprisingly easy to delete. Each of us has, at some point in our careers, accidentally erased a file or saved a bad copy of a programme, destroying a good previous copy. Because of software's high value to a commercial computing centre, access to software is usually carefully controlled through a process called configuration management so that software cannot be deleted, destroyed, or replaced accidentally. Configuration management uses several techniques to ensure that each version or release retains its integrity. When configuration management is used, an old version or release can be replaced with a newer version only when it has been thoroughly tested to verify that the improvements work correctly without degrading the functionality and performance of other functions and services.

Software Modification

Software is vulnerable to modifications that either cause it to fail or cause it to perform an unintended task. Indeed, because software is so susceptible to "off by one" errors, it is quite easy to modify. Changing a bit or two can convert a working programme into a failing one. Depending on which bit was changed, the programme may crash when it begins or it may execute for some time before it falters.

With a little more work, the change can be much more subtle: The programme works well most of the time but fails in specialized circumstances. For instance, the programme may be maliciously modified to fail when certain conditions are met or when a certain date or time is reached. Because of this delayed effect, such a programme is known as a logic bomb. For example, a disgruntled employee may modify a crucial programme so that it accesses the system date and halts abruptly after July 1. The employee might quit on May 1 and plan to be at a new job miles away by July. Another type of change can extend the functioning of a programme so that an innocuous programme has a hidden side effect. For example, a programme that ostensibly structures a listing of files belonging to a user may also modify the protection of all those files to permit access by another user.

Other categories of software modification include:

- Trojan horse: a programme that overtly does one thing while covertly doing another
- Virus: a specific type of Trojan horse that can be used to spread its "infection" from one computer to another
- Trapdoor: a programme that has a secret entry point
- Information leaks in a programme: code that makes information accessible to unauthorized people or programmes.

Of course, it is possible to invent a completely new programme and install it on a computing system. Inadequate control over the programmes that are installed and run on a computing system permits this kind of software security breach.

Software Theft

This attack includes unauthorized copying of software. Software authors and distributors are entitled to fair compensation for use of their product, as are musicians and book authors. Unauthorized copying of software has not been stopped satisfactorily. The legal system is still grappling with the difficulties of interpreting paper-based copyright laws for electronic media.

Data Vulnerabilities

Hardware security is usually the concern of a relatively small staff of computing centre professionals. Software security is a larger problem, extending to all programmers and analysts who create or modify programmes. Computer programmes are written in a dialect intelligible primarily to computer professionals, so a "leaked" source listing of a programme might very well be meaningless to the general public.

Printed data, however, can be readily interpreted by the general public. Because of its visible nature, a data attack is a more widespread and serious problem than either a hardware or software attack. Thus, data items have greater public value than hardware and software because more people know how to use or interpret data. By themselves, out of context, pieces of data have essentially no intrinsic value. For example, if you are shown the value "42," it has no meaning for you unless you know what the number represents. Likewise, "326 Old Norwalk Road" is of little use unless you know the city, state, and country for the address. For this reason, it is hard to measure the value of a given data item.

On the other hand, data items in context do relate to cost, perhaps measurable by the cost to reconstruct or redevelop damaged or lost data. For example, confidential data leaked to a competitor may narrow a competitive edge. Data incorrectly modified can cost human lives. To see how, consider the flight coordinate data used by an airplane that is guided partly or fully by software, as many now are. Finally, inadequate security may lead to financial liability if certain personal data are made public. Thus, data have a definite value, even though that value is often difficult to measure.

Typically, both hardware and software have a relatively long life. No matter how they are valued initially, their value usually declines gradually over time. By contrast, the value of data over time is far less predictable or consistent. Initially, data may be valued highly. However, some data items are of interest for only a short period of time, after which their value declines precipitously.

To see why, consider the following example. In many countries, government analysts periodically generate data to describe the state of the national economy. The results are scheduled to be released to the public at a predetermined time and date. Before that time, access to the data could allow someone to profit from advance knowledge of the probable effect of the data on the stock market. For instance, suppose an analyst develops the data 24 hours before their release and then wishes to communicate the results to other analysts for independent verification before release. The data vulnerability here is clear, and, to the right people, the data are worth more before the scheduled release than Afterwards. However, we can protect the data and control the threat in simple ways. For example, we could devise a scheme that would take an outsider more than 24 hours to break; even though the scheme may be eminently breakable (that is, an intruder could eventually reveal the data), it is adequate for those data because confidentiality is not needed beyond the 24-hour period.

COMPUTER FRAUD

Computer fraud is any dishonest misrepresentation of fact intended to induce another to do or refrain from doing something which causes loss. In this context, the fraud will result in obtaining a benefit by:

- Altering computer input in an unauthorized way. This requires little technical expertise and is not an uncommon form of theft by employees altering the data before entry or entering false data, or by entering unauthorized instructions or using unauthorized processes;
- Altering, destroying, suppressing, or stealing output, usually to conceal unauthorized transactions: this is difficult to detect;
- Altering or deleting stored data; or
- Altering or misusing existing system tools or software packages, or altering or writing code for fraudulent purposes. This requires real programming skills and is not common.

Manipulating banking systems to make unauthorized identity theft with reference to ATM fraud.

OFFENSIVE CONTENT

The content of web sites and other electronic communications may be harmful, distasteful or offensive for a variety of reasons. Most countries have enacted law that place some limits on the freedom of speech and ban racist, blasphemous, politically subversive, seditious or inflammatory material that tends to incite hate crimes.

This is a sensitive area in which the courts can become involved in arbitrating between groups with entrenched beliefs, each convinced that their point of view has been unreasonably attacked.

In England, s28 Crime and Disorder Act 1998 defines a racial group, following Mandla v Dowell-Lee (1983) 2 AC 548 (in which a requirement to wear a cap as part of a school uniform had the effect of excluding Sikh boys whose religion required them to wear a turban), as a group of persons defined by reference to race, colour, nationality (including citizenship) or ethnic or national origin; and a religious group as a group of persons defined by reference to religious belief or lack of religious belief.

Therefore, it is equally an offence to show hostility to a person who practices a particular faith as to a person who has no religious belief or faith.

HARASSMENT

Whereas content may be offensive in a non-specific way, harassment directs obscenities and derogatory comments at specific individuals focusing for example on gender, race, religion, nationality, sexual orientation. This often occurs in chat rooms, through newsgroups, and by sending hate e-mail to interested parties (see cyber bullying, harassment by computer, stalking, and cyberstalking). In England, in a broader form than s43 Telecommunications Act 1984, s1 Malicious Communications Act 1988 makes it an offence to send an indecent, offensive or threatening letter, electronic communication or other article to another person. Now, s2 Protection from Harassment Act 1997 criminalizes a course of conduct amounting to harassment which the defendant knows, or ought to know, amounts to harassment of another. If a reasonable person in possession of the same information would think the course of conduct amounted to harassment of the other, the knowledge will be imputed to the defendant. Although harassment is not defined, s7 states that it includes causing alarm or distress, and conduct is defined as including speech in all its forms.

In DPP v Collins (2006) 1 WLR 308 the defendant repeatedly telephoned the offices of his MP on a wide range of political matters. In conversations with employees at the office and on messages left on the telephone answering machine, he used racist terms to show the frustration he felt at the way in which his affairs were being handled. No-one was personally offended, but the staff became depressed. Charged under s127(1) Communications Act 2003, the magistrates found that the terms were offensive but that a reasonable person would not find them grossly offensive. To determine whether any message content is merely offensive or grossly offensive depended on their particular circumstances and context, *i.e.* in the wider society which is an open and just multi-racial society, the test of offensiveness was objective.

More problematic are deliberate attacks which amount to defamation although, in March 2006, Michael Keith-Smith became the first person to win damages from an individual internet user after she accused him of being a 'sex offender' and 'racist blogger' on a Yahoo! discussion site. She also claimed that his wife was a prostitute. The High Court judge decided that Tracy Williams, of Oldham, was "particularly abusive" and "her statements demonstrated that... she had no intention of stopping her libellous and defamatory behaviour". She was ordered to pay £10,000 in damages, plus £7,200 costs. In general, libel is not treated as a criminal matter except when it may provoke the person defamed into retaliatory violence (see cybersmearing as it affects business. All forms of unsolicited e-mail and advertisements can also be considered to be forms of Internet harassment where the content is offensive or of an explicit sexual nature. Now termed spam, it has been criminalized in various countries.

DRUG TRAFFICKING

Drug traffickers are increasingly taking advantage of the Internet to sell their illegal substances through encrypted e-mail and other Internet Technology. Some drug traffickers arrange deals at internet cafes, use courier Web sites to track illegal packages of pills, and swap recipes for amphetamines in restricted-access chat rooms.

The Internet's easy-to-learn, fast-paced character, global impact, and fairly reliable privacy features facilitate the marketing of illicit drugs. Detecting money laundering of cash earned by drug traffickers is very difficult, because dealers are now able to use electronic commerce and Internet banking facilities. Also, traffickers have been using online package tracking services offered by courier companies to keep tabs on the progress of their shipments. If there happened to be some sort of undue delay, this could signal authority interception of the drugs, which would still allow the dealers time to cover their tracks. Law enforcement is also more deficient because illicit drug deals are arranged instantaneously, over short distances, making interception by authorities much more difficult.

The rise in Internet drug trades could also be attributed to the lack of face-to-face communication. These virtual exchanges allow more intimidated individuals to more comfortably purchase illegal drugs. The sketchy effects that are often associated with drug trades are severely minimized and the filtering process that comes with physical interaction fades away. Furthermore, traditional drug recipes were carefully kept secrets. But with modern computer technology, this information is now being made available to anyone with computer access.

COMPUTER INSECURITY

SECURITY AND SYSTEMS DESIGN

Most current real-world computer security efforts focus on external threats, and generally treat the computer system itself as a trusted system. Some knowledgeable observers consider this to be a disastrous mistake, and point out that this distinction is the cause of much of the insecurity of current computer systems - once an attacker has subverted one part of a system without fine-grained security, he or she usually has access to most or all of the features of that system. [citation needed] Because computer systems can be very complex, and cannot be guaranteed to be free of defects, this security stance tends to produce insecure systems.

The 'trusted systems' approach has been predominant in the design of many Microsoft software products, due to the long-standing Microsoft policy of emphasizing functionality and 'ease of use' over security. Since Microsoft products currently dominate the desktop and home computing markets, this has led to unfortunate effects.

However, the problems described here derive from the security stance taken by software and hardware vendors generally, rather than the failing of a single vendor. Microsoft is not out of line in this respect, just far more prominent with respect to its consumer marketshare.

It should be noted that the Windows NT line of operating systems from Microsoft contained mechanisms to limit this, such as services that ran under dedicated user accounts, and Role-Based Access Control (RBAC) with user/group rights, but the Windows 95 line of products lacked most of these functions. Before the release of Windows 2003 Microsoft has changed their official stance, taking a more locked down approach.

On 15 January 2002, Bill Gates sent out a memo on Trustworthy Computing, marking the official change in company stance. Regardless, Microsoft's operating system Windows XP is still plagued by complaints about lack of local security and inability to use the fine-grained user access controls together with certain software (esp. certain popular computer games).

FINANCIAL COST

Serious financial damage has been caused by computer security breaches, but reliably estimating costs is quite difficult. Figures in the billions of dollars have been quoted in relation to the damage caused by malware such as computer worms like the Code Red worm, but such estimates may be exaggerated.

However, other losses, such as those caused by the compromise of credit card information, can be more easily determined, and they have been substantial, as measured by millions of individual victims of identity theft each year in each of several nations, and the severe hardship imposed on each victim, that can wipe out all of their finances, prevent them from getting a job, plus be treated as if they were the criminal. Volumes of victims of phishing and other scams may not be known.

Individuals who have been infected with spyware or malware likely go through a costly and time-consuming process of having their computer cleaned. Spyware and malware is considered to be a problem specific to the various Microsoft Windows operating systems, however this can be explained somewhat by the fact that Microsoft controls a major share of the PC market and thus represent the most prominent target.

REASONS

There are many similarities (yet many fundamental differences) between computer and physical security. Just like real-world security, the motivations for breaches of computer security vary between attackers, sometimes called hackers or crackers. Some are teenage thrill-seekers or vandals (the kind often responsible for defacing web sites); similarly, some web site defacements are done to make political statements.

However, some attackers are highly skilled and motivated with the goal of compromising computers for financial gain or espionage. An example of the latter is Markus Hess who spied for the KGB and was ultimately caught because of the efforts of Clifford Stoll, who wrote an amusing and accurate book, The Cuckoo's Egg, about his experiences. For those seeking to prevent security breaches, the first step is usually to attempt to identify what might motivate an attack on the system, how much the continued operation and information security of the system are worth, and who might be motivated to breach it. The precautions required for a home PC are very different for those of banks' Internet banking system, and different again for a classified military network. Other computer security writers suggest that, since an attacker using a network need know nothing about you or what you have on your computer, attacker motivation is inherently impossible to determine beyond guessing. If true, blocking all possible attacks is the only plausible action to take.

VULNERABILITIES

To understand the techniques for securing a computer system, it is important to first understand the various types of "attacks" that can be made against it. These threats can typically be classified into one of these seven categories:

EXPLOITS

Software flaws, especially buffer overflows, are often exploited to gain control of a computer, or to cause it to operate in an unexpected manner. Many development methodologies rely on testing to ensure the quality of any code released; this process often fails to discover extremely unusual potential exploits. The term "exploit" generally refers to small programmes designed to take advantage of a software flaw that has been discovered, either remote or local. The code from the exploit programme is frequently reused in trojan horses and computer viruses. In some cases, a vulnerability can lie in certain programs' processing of a specific file type, such as a non-executable media file.

EAVESDROPPING

Any data that is transmitted over a network is at some risk of being eavesdropped, or even modified by a malicious person. Even machines that operate as a closed system (ie, with no contact to the outside world) can be eavesdropped upon via monitoring the faint electro-magnetic transmissions generated by the hardware such as TEMPEST.

The FBI's proposed Carnivore programme was intended to act as a system of eavesdropping protocols built into the systems of internet service providers.

SPYWARE

Spyware, is a computer software programme or hardware device that enables an unauthorized person (such as an abuser) to secretly monitor and gather information about your computer use. There are many types of computer software programmes and hardware devices that can be installed to monitor your computer activities. They can be installed on your computer without your knowledge, and the person installing them doesn't even need to have physical access to your computer. Whether computer monitoring is legal or illegal depends on the state you live in, and the context in which it is installed and used. Regardless of the legality, Spyware is invasive, intrusive, and may put victims in grave danger.

Spyware programmes are sometimes marketed as ways to monitor your children or your employees. As an employer, it is always best to have your employees read and sign a "Technology Use Policy." This policy should explain allowable uses of company property, expectations of online behaviour, and TELL employees if their computer will be monitored. Additionally, choose a software package that displays an icon to remind your employees that they're being monitored.

There are some similarities and differences between Spyware and its close relatives. For example:

- *Adware*: These are hidden marketing programmes that deliver advertising to consumers, and might also profile users' Internet surfing and shopping habits. Adware is often bundled or hidden in something else a user downloads. Most average computer users are infected with adware fairly regularly, and common symptoms include a sluggish system and lots of advertising pop-ups.
- *Malware*: This is any programme that tries to install itself or damage a computer system without the owner's consent. Malware includes viruses, worms, spyware and adware.

SPYWARE WORK

Spyware can keep track of every keystroke you type, every software application you use, every web site you visit, every chat or instant message you send, every document you open, and everything you print. Some spyware gives the abuser the ability to freeze, shutdown or restart your computer. Some versions even allow the abuser to remotely turn on your webcam or make your computer talk.

Once Spyware is installed, it can run in stealth mode and is difficult to detect or uninstall. If the person who installed it has physical access to your computer, he or she can use a special key combination that will cause a log-in screen to pop-up. After entering the password, an options screen will pop up that allows the installer to view all of the computer activity since their last login, including e-mails you sent, documents printed, web sites visited, and more. Perpetrators without physical access to your computer can set the spyware to take pictures of the computer screen (screen shots) every few seconds and have these pictures sent to them over the Internet without a victim's knowledge.

How Does It Get On My Computer?

Abusers can install Spyware on your computer if they have physical or Internet access to your computer or handheld device. Some abusers might hack into your computer from another location via the Internet. Some might send spyware to you as an attached file that automatically installs itself when you open the e-mail or when you initially view it in a preview window. Others may e-mail or instant message a greeting card, computer game, or other ruse in order to entice you or your children to open an attachment or click on a link. Once opened, the programme automatically installs spyware on the victim's computer, in stealth mode without notification or consent, and can then send electronic reports to the perpetrator via the Internet. While most spyware is software based (a programme that can be installed on your computer), there are also some hardware-based spyware devices called keystroke loggers. These tiny keylogging devices may appear to be a normal computer part. However, once the keylogger is plugged into your computer, it can record every key typed, capturing all passwords, personal identification numbers (PIN), web sites visited, and any e-mails sent onto its small hard drive. Additionally, there are keyboards with keystroke logging capabilities built-in.

OVERVIEW OF SPYWARE

Spyware is one type of malicious software (malware) that collects information from a computing system without your consent. Spyware can capture keystrokes, screenshots, authentication credentials, personal e-mail addresses, web form data, Internet usage habits, and other personal information. The data is often delivered to online attackers who sell it to others or use it themselves for marketing or spam or to execute financial crimes or identity theft.

Software installed after the user has read and agreed to a clear privacy policy or to an End-User License Agreement (EULA) that describes the software's data collection activities does not meet the definition of spyware. It is your responsibility to carefully read such polices and agreements to make sure you understand and agree with their terms.

ONLINE ATTACKERS

Online attackers' primary interest in spyware is using it to steal personal information for financial crimes such as carding (illicit trafficking in stolen credit card and credit card information) and identity theft, or to sell that information to someone else who then executes more traditional financial crimes.

Marketing Organizations

Marketing organizations are interested in personal information such as e-mail addresses, online shopping and browsing habits, keywords in search queries, and other personal and trend-related information that can be used to execute marketing campaigns like spam, spim (unsolicited messages received via instant messaging systems), browser popups, home page hijacking (changing the default web address for a user's browser), and more.

Spying by a Trusted Insider Trusted insiders include those who have physical access to computer systems for legitimate purposes. Some examples are employees, contractors, temporary workers, and cleaning crews. A trusted insider might be, for example, an employee who uses spyware to collect corporate information that can be sold in the underground economy, used for blackmail, or used to gain access to more valuable information at some later time. Another example of the trusted insider group includes family members or close relations such as spouses or significant others trying to catch inappropriate behaviour or infidelity.

Data Gathered by Spyware

Spyware can monitor nearly any activity or data related to your computing environment. This is not limited to files on your hard drives but can also include temporary data such as screen shots, keystrokes, and data packets on connected networks.

HOW SPYWARE OPERATES

Spyware tracks online activity looking for web sites visited, financial data or identity data such as credit card numbers on screen or entered into form fields, browsing and online purchasing habits, and authentication credentials. When keywords of interest like names of banks, online payment systems, or pornographic web sites are observed, the spyware starts its data collection process.

E-mail Addresses

E-mail addresses can be harvested from an infected user's computer and marketed for use in spam mailing lists. Common techniques for harvesting e-mail addresses and other contact information includes enumerating e-mail applications' address books, monitoring incoming and outgoing network packets related to e-mail, and scanning files on the system's disks for strings that match the format of an e-mail address. Windows Protected Store Windows contains a service called the Protected Store. Its purpose is to provide encrypted storage for sensitive data.

The following are some examples of data that might be in the PStore:

- Outlook passwords
- Passwords for web sites
- MSN Explorer passwords
- IE AutoComplete passwords
- IE AutoComplete fields
- Digital certificates.

Even though the PStore is encrypted, access to it is indirectly controlled by the data owner's login credentials. Since most spyware runs under the security profile of the user who is logged on, spyware can harvest this information.

Clipboard Content

The system clipboard often contains sensitive information. Some common examples include product registration codes and user credentials that are copied and pasted into login forms. Other information that might be found in the system clipboard buffer includes sections of potentially sensitive data from recently modified documents or personal information about you or your associates that could be used in crimes related to identity theft.

The Keys You Press

Key logging is one of the first spyware techniques used to capture sensitive data from a system. Both hardware and software key loggers exist. Hardware devices usually slip inline between the keyboard cable and computer. Modern key logging hardware is small and unobtrusive and has even been hidden inside the physical keyboard casing, making it almost impossible to detect. One limitation of hardware-based keylogger units is the need for physical access to install and retrieve the device and its data. A more common alternative, and the type present in spyware, is the software key logger. Software key loggers capture keyboard events and record the keystroke data before it is sent to the intended application for processing. Like most other spyware capture technologies, software based keyloggers can turn their capture on or off based on keywords or events. For example, many keyloggers target instant messaging clients, e-mail applications, and web browsers but might ignore other applications that don't provide the kind of data the attacker is targeting for harvest.

Network Traffic

Network traffic is another valuable source of data. Data commonly extracted from network captures includes user names, passwords, e-mail messages, and web content. In some cases, entire files can be extracted and reconstructed from the captured streams.

IMPACT OF SPYWARE

Spyware can cause people to lose trust in the reliability of online business transactions. Similar to the problem of counterfeit currency in the physical world, spyware undermines confidence in online economic activity. Consumers' willingness to participate in online monetary transactions decreases for fear of personal financial loss. Vendors lose confidence that the person making the purchase is who they say they are and not actually a criminal using a stolen identity or illicit funds. In efforts to manage the risk, vendors and financial institutions often implement additional verification and other loss prevention programmes at increased operational cost. Even when financial organizations cover an individual's loss from online fraud, these costs plus the overhead required to administer loss prevention programmes are eventually passed back to consumers in the form of higher service fees, interest rates, or other price increases on the goods and services consumed. As a result, growth rates in commerce are slowed, costs increase, and demand shrinks.

Impact to Computers

By monitoring and reporting user activity, spyware consumes system resources as well as network bandwidth. Depending on the number of spyware components loaded on a system and their functionality, users may experience significant performance degradation. Because spyware is not always carefully written and tested, systems infected by it are often found to have reliability problems. Affected applications may crash more frequently or the entire system may become unstable, resulting in potential productivity and data loss. Often, spyware is difficult to remove without detailed knowledge of how it works or by taking drastic measures such as wiping the system clean and starting over. In many cases, verifying the integrity of the system requires the operating system, patches, and applications to be reinstalled. These difficulties, combined with the efforts necessary to recover user data, can take a lot of time.

Risk of Future Security Incidents

The sensitive information collected by spyware often includes authentication credentials that may be used for future access to the infected system. People often use the same username and password for many different systems, so these stolen credentials may be used to access other systems not yet infected. Once access is gained, additional information theft or malware installation can take place. Another way spyware puts systems at future risk is by installing backdoor access mechanisms. These backdoors give the malware operator access to control the system or to command the system to download and run arbitrary applications. Attackers can build vast collections of compromised systems without originally compromising a single system.

COMMON SPYWARE FORMS

There are thousands of instances of malware. Many forms of malware act primarily as spyware, while other malware programmes contain spyware features.

Browser Session Hijacking

This class of spyware attempts to modify the user's browser settings. Hijacking spyware can be installed in various ways, but the intent is to modify the behaviour of the browser so the user is directed to sites of the malware author's choice instead of sites the user might have reached normally. These redirects often lead users to advertisements that earn the hijackers commissions when they are visited.

Browser Helper Objects

Browser Helper Objects (BHOs) are a feature of Internet Explorer that can be exploited by spyware. They are not always easy to detect. BHOs can access files, network resources, and anything else the user who launched Internet Explorer can access.

Malicious BHOs can be installed via stand-alone dropper malware but are also often installed using the "drive-by install" technique, in which code is installed or requested to be installed simply by the action of a user visiting a malicious or compromised web site. One technology often used in this type of installation is the ActiveX functionality present in Internet Explorer. Depending on system and browser configuration, the installation may take place automatically and be carried out without prompting the user. In cases where there is prompting, information necessary to make an informed decision can be covered with popup windows or other obfuscation techniques such as naming the control "Click yes to download ringtone."

Another effective social engineering technique is inundating the user with repeated popup requests to install the software that only end when the user leaves the site or finally agrees and installs the component. Once the component is installed, it can operate independently, download and install further malware, and even modify browser settings that allow malware to be downloaded with no user notification or interaction.

Cookies and Web Bugs

Cookies are small pieces of information stored on a user's system by a web server. During subsequent visits, the web server can retrieve these cookies. Often, cookies are used for storing user authentication, preferences, and other types of user state information. They can be used to track a user across multiple web sites. Using correlation and techniques such as "web bugs," over time they can be used to build profiles of individual users. Web bugs are HTML elements, often in the form of image tags, that retrieve information from a remote web site. While the image may not be visible to the user, the act of making the request can provide information about the user. Web bugs are often embedded in web pages and HTMLenabled e-mail messages. Links are used to track access using previously set cookies or with unique strings embedded in the URL. A typical use of this is to log the successful delivery of messages to a unique e-mail address (a common technique for spammers). Once a user has accessed the image, a cookie can also be set and associated with their e-mail address as the beginning of a profile. The cookies can then be used to track portions of the user's browsing habits.

False Antispyware Tools

Applications available on some Internet sites advertise themselves as spyware detection or removal tools when in fact they themselves are spyware.

Autonomous Spyware

As a class, autonomous spyware operates as a separate process or injects itself into other processes running on your system. This type of spyware often starts up when you log onto your computer and can frequently access anything on your system. Because autonomous spyware is simply a malicious application, it can be designed to perform almost any type of spying function. Spyware in this class often includes keyloggers, bots, e-mail and web monitoring tools, packet sniffers, and mechanisms that permit the intruder to remotely access and control an infected system.

Bots

A special class of malware known as a bot or zombie is one of the largest malware problems. Bots are remote control agents installed on your system. Bots are often controlled remotely via Internet Relay Chat (IRC). Once a system is infected with a bot, it becomes part of a bot network (botnet) and is used in conjunction with other botnet members to carry out the wishes of the bot owner or bot herder. Bots can scan networks for vulnerabilities, install various distributed denial of service (DDoS) tools, capture network packets, or download and execute arbitrary programmes. Often bots will contain additional spyware or install it. Computers or systems infected with bots can be used to distribute spam to make it harder to track and prosecute the spammers.

ANTIVIRUS AND ANTISPYWARE TOOLS

Installing trusted antivirus and antispyware tools and keeping them and their signatures current is an important part of defensive computer security.

Browser Settings

Configuring your browser to block active content like ActiveX, Java, scripting, pop-ups, images, and other potentially harmful content can increase online security. While disabling active content features can stop many threats, it also has a tendency to break many modern web sites and applications. At the very least, the richness of the browsing experience will be reduced. One browser configuration strategy to manage the risk associated with active content while still enabling trusted sites is the use of Internet Explorer security zones. Using security zones, you can choose preset levels of security.

E-mail Configuration

If you use an e-mail programme, you can configure it to send and display e-mail using plain text instead of HTML. This can eliminate most of the risks from embedded script, web bugs, and other HTML-enabled techniques used by attackers. But just as disabling active content in web browsers reduces the functionality of some features, using plain text can reduce the usability of some features. Also, many e-mail clients are now offering the ability to disable scripting and block images until a user takes some action to display them.

Starting your Computer Safely

Almost all spyware needs a way to start itself when you are using your computer. Spyware often starts in conjunction with system startup, user login, or when certain applications like an internet browser or other software is launched. Not all applications that automatically start are malicious, but it is good to know which software is legitimate. One good method to find and disable spyware on your system is to examine the software installed on your computer and determine whether it starts up automatically or not. You can find this out by looking in the system registry, startup folder, and services control panel.

NEW COMPUTER CRIME LEGISLATION

Senators Charles Schumer and Jon Kyl have introduced new legislation, S 2092, aimed at addressing some of the perceived weaknesses in the CFAA. The three main provisions addressed by this new legislation propose the following: trap and trace orders, federal jurisdiction requirements, and sentencing.

First, the new legislation would make it easier for cyber-investigators to obtain "trap and trace" orders. "Trap and trace" devices are used to capture incoming IP packets to identify the packet's origins. Due to the ease with which hackers are able to "spoof" their true origin, the most effective way to reconstruct the path of a virus, DoS or hacking assault is to follow a chain of trapping devices that logged the original malicious packets as they arrived at each individual router or server. In the case of a single telephone company, it has been relatively easy for investigators to obtain trap and trace orders. According to Congresswoman Scott of Virginia, "one communication is being carried by several different [ISPs], by a telephone company or 2, local or long distance, by a cell company or 2, and soon enough by a satellite company or 2." Once the segment of the route goes beyond the court's jurisdiction, investigators must then go to the next jurisdiction and file a request for a trap and trace order for the next segment. The new legislation would authorize the issuance of a single order to completely trace an on-line communication from start to finish.

The second provision would lower the monetary barrier for federal jurisdiction. Currently, the CFAA requires a damage threshold in excess of $5,000. However, the $5,000 is often difficult to establish when there is no fixed monetary value to the information. For example, how do you put a price on the value of medical records? Also, investigators must currently wait for a damage assessment before they can initiate an investigation, which can cause expensive delays. The new legislation would permit federal jurisdiction at the outset of an attack. Crimes that exceed $5,000 will still be treated as felonies. However, attacks that cause less than $5,000 in damage would be defined as misdemeanors. Finally, the legislation clarifies what is included in the calculation of "damage," making it easy to reach the $5,000 threshold. It provides for the costs of responding to the offence, the damage assessment costs, restoration costs, and any lost revenue or costs incurred from the interruption of service.

The third provision would modify the strict sentence directives contained in the Antiterrorism and Effective Death Penalty Act of 1999 which required a mandatory incarceration for a minimum of six months for any violation of 18 U.S.C. § 1030(a). Some hacking crimes have gone unprosecuted because the six month sentence was considered excessive. The new legislation would provide lesser sentences for lesser crimes, helping to ensure that all levels of hacking cases will be prosecuted.

Finally, the proposed legislation would make juvenile perpetrators fifteen years of age and older eligible for federal prosecution in serious computer crime cases at the Attorney General's discretion.

However, the proposed changes have raised privacy concerns. A report written by the President's Working Group on Unlawful Conduct on the Internet entitled "The Electronic Frontier: the Challenge of Unlawful Conduct Involving the Use of the Internet" has raised the concerns of privacy advocates. The groups are particularly concerned about the potential for trap and trace abuse by authorities. The American Civil Liberties Union ("ACLU"), would like to raise the standards for trap and trace devices, rather than lower them. According to the ACLU, law enforcement currently only needs to overcome "minimum obstacles" to obtain trap and trace devices. The ACLU is concerned that an expansion of the government's power to obtain trap and trace orders will enhance the government's power to "surreptitiously intercept even more personal electronic communications." The current standard for a trap and trace order is that the investigator must assert in writing to the court that the information is "relevant" to an ongoing investigation. According to the ACLU, the "judge to whom the application is made *must* approve the application, *even if he disagrees* with the assertions of law enforcement."

Additionally, the ACLU is concerned that an expansion of the substance of the orders will erode privacy. The ACLU speculates that an expansion of the powers "might allow law enforcement agents to access a variety of data, including dial-up numbers, Internet Protocol ("IP") addresses, electronic mail logs, uploaded files, and so on.... without a court order."

The CFAA is broad enough to cover most computer crimes. The Act protects government and private computers against inside and outside threats to information, fraud, and damage. Continued pro-active legislative changes to keep the Act up to date in the escalating cyber-war between secure web sites and hackers will be critical to maintaining the integrity of our increasingly inter-networked society.

One challenge in the near future will be the expansion of devices that are able to access the Internet. For example, as televisions become "web-enabled," allowing users to access the Internet from their televisions, will televisions be considered "high-speed data processing devices" as defined under the Act's "computer" definition? Would passwords taken from the television's cookie storage be protected under the Act? As Wireless Application Protocol ("WAP") brings the Internet to hand-held devices and mobile telephones, will the devices and telephones be considered "protected computers"? Will refrigerators that are wired to the Internet be covered? Cyber-crime prosecutors are also facing the difficulty of attacks that originate overseas beyond their jurisdiction. If part of a hacking trail is routed overseas, unless the U.S has an agreement with the foreign jurisdiction, that trail could lead to a dead end if investigators do not have access to the server's logs. The world of individual national jurisdictions will need to address the increasingly borderless crimes committed in cyberspace. However, the CFAA provides a solid foundation upon which we can develop new cyber-crime laws for the coming century.

MALICIOUS COMPUTER ATTACKS

MAFIABOY: DENIAL-OF-SERVICE ATTACKS OUTSIDE THE POLITICAL ARENA

On February 2000, news reports indicated that that Yahoo, Cable News Network, eBay, Amazon.com, E Trade, and Buy.com, (among other sites) experienced distributed denial of service ("DDOS") attacks. The challenges to apprehending the suspects proved substantial. In many cases, the attackers used "spoofed" IP addresses, so that the address that appeared on the target's log was not the true address of the system that sent the messages.

The FBI was able to identify a 16-year old Canadian teenager, known as "Mafiaboy" as a suspect by reviewing Internet chat room logs that showed Mafiaboy asking others what sites he should take down - before the sites were attacked. For example, there was discussion of a possible denial of service attack on CNN before CNN's site was taken down. Mafiaboy was arrested in April 2000.

In January of 2001, Mafiaboy pleaded guilty to 56 counts of "mischief to data" in relation to the DDOS attacks from February 2000. He was charged with "a DDOS attack that brought down CNN.com, Amazon.com, eBay, Dell Computer and others between February 8 and 14, 2000. The teenager eventually received a sentence of eight months in detention followed by a year of probation for his actions. The judge also required him to donate $250 to charity. Mafiaboy allegedly caused more than US $1.5 billion in damage in connection with the various DDOS attacks.

Worms and Viruses

Both worms and viruses are malicious programmes which propagate uncontrollably over the Internet. A worm programme is to designed to invade a computer and replicate itself by sending the worm to other computers on a network or in the user's address book. Worms cause damage by clogging up computer networks, slowing down or even crippling individual computers and shared servers.

Unlike worms, which do nothing but replicate themselves, viruses both replicate themselves and carry a malicious payload. This malicious payload may be a programme which immediately corrupts or deletes data on the infected machine. Or the virus may unleash a "logic bomb" which lies dormant on the machine and destroys data when the infected computer's clock reaches a certain date.

In the past, viruses and worms were spread through floppy disks and infected macro attachments to common files like Microsoft Word documents. Today, many viruses and worms are spread through e-mail and activated when the user opens an e-mail attachment. A "Trojan horse" is an e-mail attachment that appears benign. When the user opens the Trojan horse, however, a hidden worm or virus is activated that can damage the user's computer and send itself to other computers on the user's network.

In May of 2000, companies and individuals around the world were stricken by the "Love Bug," a virus (or, technically, a "worm") that traveled as an attachment to an e-mail message and propagated itself extremely rapidly through the address books of Microsoft Outlook users. According to the General Accounting Office, "The [Love Bug] virus reportedly hit large corporations such as AT&T, TWA, and Ford Motor Company; media outlets such as the Washington Post and ABC news; international organizations such as the International Monetary Fund, the British Parliament, and Belgium's banking system; state governments; school systems; and credit unions, among many others, forcing them to take their networks off-line for hours." Further the virus/worm also reportedly penetrated at least 14 federal agencies—including the Department of Defence (DOD), the Social Security Administration, the Central Intelligence Agency, the Immigration and Naturalization Service, the Department of Energy, the Department of Agriculture, the Department of Education, the National Aeronautics and Space Administration (NASA), along with the House and Senate. Damage estimates from the virus range upwards of $10 billion.

Investigative work by the FBI's New York Field Office, with assistance from the NIPC, traced the source of the virus to the Philippines within 24 hours. The FBI then worked, through the LEGAT in Manila, with the Philippines' National Bureau of Investigation, to identify the perpetrator. The speed with which the virus was traced back to its source is unprecedented. The investigation in the Philippines was hampered by the lack of a specific computer crime statute. Nevertheless, Onel de Guzman was charged on June 29, 2000 with fraud, theft, malicious mischief, and violation of the Devices Regulation Act. However, those charges were dismissed in August 2000 by Philippine authorities upon determining that traditional laws did not apply to these newer high-tech cybercrimes. As a postscript, it is important to note that the Philippine government on June 14, 2000 approved the E-Commerce Act, which now specifically criminalizes computer hacking and virus propagation.

Hacking

Hacking involves penetrating a secure area by subverting its security measures. Hackers might accomplish this by setting up programmes like "war dialers" that try thousands of common passwords until one is accepted. A hacker may set up "packet sniffers," programmes that scan data from the target system's network ports to find out more about a network and penetrate it more easily.

Once hackers penetrate the servers that host their target's computer systems, they can alter or remove files, steal information and erase the evidence of those activities. While many hackers break security systems just out of curiosity, other hackers, however, have attempted to use their skills for illegal personal financial gain.

Hacking for Financial Gain

Zezov and Yarimaka are both charged in a four-count Superseding Indictment with one count of unauthorized computer intrusion; one count of conspiracy; one count of interfering with commerce by using extortion; and one count of extortion of a corporation using threatening communications.

According to the Complaints filed in this case, Zezov gained unauthorized access to the internal Bloomberg Computer System from computers located in Almaty, Kazakhstan. In the Spring of 1999, Bloomberg provided database services, via a system known as the "Open Bloomberg," to Kazkommerts Securities ("Kazkommerts") located in Almaty, Kazakhstan. Zezov is employed by Kazkommerts and is one of four individuals at Kazkommerts associated with Kazkommerts' contract with Bloomberg.

In addition, according to the Complaints, Zezov sent a number of e-mails to Michael Bloomberg, the company's founder, under the name "Alex," demanding that Bloomberg pay him $200,000 in exchange for Zezov's telling Bloomberg how he was able to infiltrate Bloomberg's computer system.

According to the Complaints, in e-mail communications to Michael Bloomberg, Zezov demanded that $200,000 be deposited into an offshore account, and Bloomberg opened an account at Deutsche Bank in London and deposited $200,000 into the account.

As described in the Complaint against Yarimaka, Yarimaka and Zezov flew from Kazakhstan to London, and on August 10, 2000, Yarimaka and Zezov met with Bloomberg L.P. officials, including Michael Bloomberg, and two London Metropolitan police officers, one posing as a Bloomberg L.P. executive and the other serving as a translator. At the meeting, Yarimaka allegedly claimed that he was a former Kazakhstan prosecutor and explained that he represented "Alex" and would handle the terms of payment. According to the Complaint, Yarimaka and Zezov reiterated their demands at the meeting. Shortly after the meeting Yarimaka and Zezov were arrested in London. The United States sought their extradition from England and, after being extradited, Yarimaka and Zezov arrived in the United States on May 17, 2002.

If convicted, Yarimaka and Zezov each face up to 5 years in prison on the conspiracy charge, up to 20 years in prison on the interference with commerce by using extortion charge; 2 years in prison for the extortion of a corporation using threatening communications charge; and 1 year in prison for the unauthorized computer intrusion charge. Each defendant faces a maximum fine of $250,000, twice the gross gain or loss resulting from the crime for each count.

Hacking into the Department of Defence

On February 23, 2000, Ikenna Iffih, age 28, of Boston, Massachusetts, was charged with using his home computer to illegally gain access to a number of computers, including those controlled by NASA and an agency of the U.S. Department of Defence, where, among other things, he allegedly intercepted login names and passwords, and intentionally caused delays and damage in communications.

In April 1999, Iffih obtained unauthorized access to a corporate internet account which he then used to illegally access a computer controlled and operated by the U.S. Defence Logistics Agency. Iffih then concealed his actual computer address through a service known as "telnet proxy" which created the appearance that his address was that of the government's computer. Once "hidden", Iffih accessed, without authorization, the web site of internet service provider, ZMOS, and recklessly caused damage to the ZMOS computer located in the State of Washington. As a result, ZMOS, which hosts corporate web pages and provides internet service for corporate customers, suffered a significant loss of business.

Beginning in May 1999 and continuing until August, 1999, Iffih obtained unauthorized access to the same corporate internet account this time using it to access the NASA computer research project web server located in Maryland. Iffih seized control of the NASA computer, allowing him to read, delete or modify any files on the system. He then installed a "sniffer" programme onto the system to intercept and save login names and passwords of users that were transferred over the NASA system for his own later use. The compromised NASA web server did not contain classified or sensitive information and was not involved in any way with satellite command or control.

Iffih also used the NASA computer as a platform to launch attacks on other computer systems, such as an attack on the U.S. Department of the Interior's web server where he defaced its web page with hacker graphics. Iffih accessed various computers operated by Northeastern University from which he illegally copied a file containing the names, dates of birth, addresses and social security numbers of numerous men and women affiliated with the University, either as students, faculty, administration or alumni. Investigators are not aware of any use or dissemination of this information. Northeastern University cooperated fully with investigators on this matter.

On June 29, 2000, Iffih pleaded guilty in federal court to three felony counts. Count one pertained to intentionally intercepting and endeavoring to intercept login names and passwords transmitted to and through a National Aeronautics and Space Administration ("NASA") computer. Count two was intentionally and without authorization accessing a web site, used for interstate and foreign commerce, owned by Zebra Marketing Online Services ("ZMOS"), causing significant damage. Count three was willful and malicious interference with a U.S. Government communication system, that of the Defence Logistics Agency, and obstructing, hindering and delaying the transmission of communications over such system.

On November 17, 2000, he was sentenced to 6 months home detention, placed on supervised release for 48 months, and ordered to pay $5,000 in restitution to victim ZMOS.

Legalizing Hacking by Hollywood?

The growth of peer-to-peer (P2P) networks has been staggering, even by Internet standards. From non-existence a few years ago, today nearly a dozen P2P networks have been deployed, a half-dozen have gained widespread acceptance, and one P2P network alone is responsible for 1.8 billion downloads each month. The steady growth in broadband access, which exponentially increases the speed, breadth, and usage of these P2P networks, indicates that P2P penetration and related downloading will continue to increase at a breakneck pace.

Unfortunately, the primary current application of P2P networks is unbridled copyright piracy. P2P downloads today consist largely of copyrighted music, and as download speeds improve, there has been a marked increase in P2P downloads of copyrighted software, games, photographs, karaoke tapes, and movies. Books, graphic designs, newspaper articles, needlepoint designs, and architectural drawings cannot be far behind. The owners and creators of these copyrighted works have not authorized their distribution through these P2P networks, and P2P distribution of this scale does not fit into any conception of fair use. Thus, there is no question that the vast majority of P2P downloads constitute copyright infringements for which the works' creators and owners receive no compensation. The massive scale of P2P piracy and its growing breadth represents a direct threat to the livelihoods of U.S. copyright creators, including songwriters, recording artists, musicians, directors, photographers, graphic artists, journalists, novelists, and software programmers. It also threatens the survival of the industries in which these creators work, and the seamstresses, actors, Foley artists, carpenters, cameramen, administrative assistants, and sound engineers these industries employ. As these creators and their industries contribute greatly both to the cultural and economic vitality of the U.S., their livelihoods and survival must be protected.

While pursuit of many of these components to the P2P piracy solution requires no new legislation, I believe legislation is necessary to promote the usefulness of at least one such component. Specifically, enactment of the legislation I introduce today is necessary to enable responsible usage of technological self-help measures to stop copyright infringements on P2P networks.

One approach that has not been adequately explored is to allow technological solutions to address technological problems. Technological innovation, as represented by the creation of P2P networks and their subsequent decentralization, has been harnessed to facilitate massive P2P piracy. It is worth exploring, therefore, whether other technological innovations could be harnessed to combat this massive P2P piracy problem. Copyright owners could, at least conceptually, employ a variety of technological tools to prevent the illegal distribution of copyrighted works over a P2P network. Using interdiction, decoys, redirection, file-blocking, spoofs, or other technological tools, technology can help prevent P2P piracy.

There is nothing revolutionary about property owners using self-help — technological or otherwise — to secure or repossess their property. Satellite companies periodically use electronic countermeasures to stop the theft of their signals and programming. Car dealers repossess cars when the payments go unpaid. Software companies employ a variety of technologies to make software non-functional if license terms are violated. However, in the context of P2P networks, technological self-help measures may not be legal due to a variety of state and federal statutes, including the Computer Fraud and Abuse Act of 1986. In other words, while P2P technology is free to innovate new, more efficient methods of P2P distribution that further exacerbate the piracy problem, copyright owners are not equally free to craft technological responses to P2P piracy.

Through the legislation I introduce today, Congress can free copyright creators and owners to develop technological tools to protect themselves against P2P piracy. The proposed legislation creates a safe harbour from liability so that copyright owners may use technological means to prevent the unauthorized distribution of that owner's copyrighted works via a P2P network.

This legislation is narrowly crafted, with strict bounds on acceptable behaviour by the copyright owner. For instance, the legislation would not allow a copyright owner to plant a virus on a P2P user's computer, or otherwise remove, corrupt, or alter any files or data on the P2P user's computer.

The legislation provides a variety of remedies if the self-help measures taken by a copyright owner exceed the limits of the safe harbour. If such actions would have been illegal in the absence of the safe harbour, the copyright owner remains subject to the full range of liability that existed under prior law. If a copyright owner has engaged in abusive interdiction activities, an affected P2P user can file suit for economic costs and attorney's fees under a new cause of action. Finally, the U.S. Attorney General can seek an injunction prohibiting a copyright owner from utilizing the safe harbour if there is a pattern of abusive interdiction activities.

This legislation does not impact in any way a person who is making a fair use of a copyrighted work, or who is otherwise using, storing, and copying copyrighted works in a lawful fashion. Because its scope is limited to unauthorized distribution, display, performance or reproduction of copyrighted works on publicly accessible P2P systems, the legislation only authorizes self-help measures taken to deal with clear copyright infringements. Thus, the legislation does not authorize any interdiction actions to stop fair or authorized uses of copyrighted works on decentralized, peer-to-peer systems, or any interdiction of public domain works. Further, the legislation doesn't even authorize self-help measures taken to address copyright infringements outside of the decentralized, P2P environment.

This proposed legislation has a neutral, if not positive, net effect on privacy rights. First, a P2P user does not have an expectation of privacy in computer files that she makes publicly accessible through a P2P file-sharing network - just as a person who places an advertisement in a newspaper cannot expect to keep that information confidential. It is important to emphasize that a P2P user must first actively decide to make a copyrighted work available to the world, or to send a worldwide request for a file, before any P2P interdiction would be countenanced by the legislation. Most importantly, unlike in a copyright infringement lawsuit, interdiction technologies do not require the copyright owner to know who is infringing the copyright. Interdiction technologies only require that the copyright owner know where the file is located or between which computers a transmission is occurring.

No legislation can eradicate the problem of peer-to-peer piracy. However, enabling copyright creators to take action to prevent an infringing file from being shared via P2P is an important first step towards a solution. Through this legislation, Congress can help the marketplace more effectively manage the problems associated with P2P file trading without interfering with the system itself.

5

Network Security

HISTORY OF NETWORK SECURITY

Recent interest in security was fuelled by the crime committed by Kevin Mitnick. Kevin Mitnick committed the largest computer-related crime in U.S. history. The losses were eighty million dollars in U.S. intellectual property and source code from a variety of companies. Since then, information security came into the spotlight. Public networks are being relied upon to deliver financial and personal information. Due to the evolution of information that is made available through the Internet, information security is also required to evolve. Due to Kevin Mitnick's offence, companies are emphasizing security for the intellectual property. Internet has been a driving force for data security improvement.

Internet protocols in the past were not developed to secure themselves. Within the TCP/IP communication stack, security protocols are not implemented. This leaves the Internet open to attacks. Modern developments in the internet architecture have made communication more secure.

BRIEF HISTORY OF INTERNET

The birth of the Internet takes place in 1969 when Advanced Research Projects Agency Network (ARPANET) is commissioned by the department of defence (DOD) for research in networking.

The ARPANET is a success from the very beginning. Although originally designed to allow scientists to share data and access remote computers, e-mail quickly becomes the most popular application. The ARPANET becomes a high-speed digital post office as people use it to collaborate on research projects and discuss topics of various interests. The InterNetworking Working Group becomes the first of several standards-setting entities to govern the growing network. Vinton Cerf is elected the first chairman of the INWG, and later becomes known as a "Father of the Internet."

In the 1980s, Bob Kahn and Vinton Cerf are key members of a team that create TCP/IP, the common language of all Internet computers. For the first time the loose collection of networks which made up the ARPANET is seen as an "Internet", and the Internet as we know it today is born. The mid-80s marks a boom in the personal computer and super-minicomputer industries. The combination of inexpensive desktop machines and powerful, network-ready servers allows many companies to join the Internet for the first time. Corporations begin to use the Internet to communicate with each other and with their customers.

In the 1990s, the Internet began to become available to the public. The World Wide Web was born. Netscape and Microsoft were both competing on developing a browser for the Internet. Internet continues to grow and surfing the internet has become equivalent to TV viewing for many users.

SECURITY TIMELINE

Several key events contributed to the birth and evolution of computer and network security. The timeline can be started as far back as the 1930s. Polish cryptographers created an enigma machine in 1918 that converted plain messages to encrypted text. In 1930, Alan Turing, a brilliant mathematician broke the code for the Enigma. Securing communications was essential in World War II.

In the 1960s, the term "hacker" is coined by a couple of Massachusetts Institute of Technology (MIT) students. The Department of Defence began the ARPANET, which gains popularity as a conduit for the electronic exchange of data and information. This paves the way for the creation of the carrier network known today as the Internet. During the 1970s, the Telnet protocol was developed. This opened the door for public use of data networks that were originally restricted to government contractors and academic researchers.

During the 1980s, the hackers and crimes relating to computers were beginning to emerge. The 414 gang are raided by authorities after a nine-day cracking spree where they break into top-secret systems. The Computer Fraud and Abuse Act of 1986 was created because of Ian Murphy's crime of stealing information from military computers. A graduate student, Robert Morris, was convicted for unleashing the Morris Worm to over 6,000 vulnerable computers connected to the Internet. Based on concerns that the Morris Worm ordeal could be replicated, the Computer Emergency Response Team (CERT) was created to alert computer users of network security issues.

In the 1990s, Internet became public and the security concerns increased tremendously. Approximately 950 million people use the internet today worldwide. On any day, there are approximately 225 major incidences of a security breach. These security breaches could also result in monetary losses of a large degree. Investment in proper security should be a priority for large organizations as well as common users.

NETWORK INTRUSION DETECTION (NID)

Network intrusion detection deals with information passing on the wire between hosts. Typically referred to as "packet-sniffers," network intrusion detection devices intercept packets traveling along various communication mediums and protocols, usually TCP/IP. Once captured, the packets are analysed in a number of different ways. Some NID devices will simply compare the packet to a signature database consisting of known attacks and malicious packet "fingerprints", while others will look for anomalous packet activity that might indicate malicious behaviour. In either case, network intrusion detection should be regarded primarily as a perimeter defence.

NID has historically been incapable of operating in the following environments:

- Switched networks
- Encrypted networks
- High-speed networks (anything over 100 Mbps).

Recently, however, Cisco released a module for their Catalyst 6000 switch that incorporates network intrusion detection directly in the switch, overcoming the first of these flaws. Additionally, ISS/Network ICE indicated that they are now capable of "packet-sniffing" at gigabit speeds.

HOST-BASED INTRUSION DETECTION (HID)

Host-based intrusion detection systems are designed to monitor, detect, and respond to user and system activity and attacks on a given host. Some more robust tools also offer audit policy management and centralization, supply data forensics, statistical analysis and evidentiary support, and in certain instances provide some measure of access control. The difference between host-based and network-based intrusion detection is that NID deals with data transmitted from host to host while HID is concerned with what occurs on the hosts themselves. Host-based intrusion detection is best suited to combat internal threats because of its ability to monitor and respond to specific user actions and file accesses on the host. The majority of computer threats come from within organizations, from many different sources; disgruntled employees and corporate spies are just two examples. In fact, intrusion detection expert Richard Power states, "each year, we've asked the respondents [of the CSI/FBI survey] to rate the likely sources of [a network] attack. Invariably, disgruntled and dishonest employees have topped the list, with over 80 per cent of respondents citing them as a likely source."

Hybrid Intrusion Detection

Hybrid intrusion detection systems offer management of and alert notification from both network and host-based intrusion detection devices. Hybrid solutions provide the logical complement to NID and HID-central intrusion detection management.

Network-Node Intrusion Detection (NNID)

Network-node intrusion detection was developed to work around the inherent flaws in traditional NID. Network-node pulls the packet-intercepting technology off of the wire and puts it on the host. With NNID, the "packet-sniffer" is positioned in such a way that it captures packets after they reach their final target, the destination host. The packet is then analysed just as if it were travelling along the network through a conventional "packet-sniffer". This scheme came from a HID-centric assumption that each critical host would already be taking advantage of host-based technology. In this approach, network-node is simply another module that can attach to the HID agent. Network node's major disadvantage is that it only evaluates packets addressed to the host on which it resides. Traditional network intrusion detection, on the other hand, can monitor packets on an entire subnet. Even so, "packet-sniffers" are equally incapable of viewing a complete subnet when the network uses high-speed communications, encryption, or switches since they are essentially "without a sense of smell". The advantage to NNID is its ability to defend specific hosts against packet-based attacks in these complex environments where conventional NID is ineffective.

INTRUSION DETECTION SYSTEMS: A BRIEF HISTORY

The goal of intrusion detection is to monitor network assets to detect anomalous behaviour and misuse. This concept has been around for nearly twenty years but only recently has it seen a dramatic rise in popularity and incorporation into the overall information security infrastructure. Beginning in 1980, with James Anderson's paper, Computer Security Threat Monitoring and Surveillance, the notion of intrusion detection was born. Since then, several pivotal events in IDS technology have advanced intrusion detection to its current state. Let's focus on how IDS has progressed since its inception.

James Anderson's seminal paper, written for a government organization, introduced the notion that audit trails contained vital information that could be valuable in tracking misuse and understanding user behaviour. With the release of this chapter, the concept of "detecting" misuse and specific user events emerged. His insight into audit data and its importance led to tremendous improvements in the auditing subsystems of virtually every operating system. Anderson's conjecture also provided the foundation for future intrusion detection system design and development. His work was the start of host-based intrusion detection and IDS in general.

In 1983, SRI International, and specifically Dr. Dorothy Denning, began working on a government project that launched a new effort into intrusion detection development. Their goal was to analyse audit trails from government mainframe computers and create profiles of users based upon their activities. One year later, Dr. Denning helped to develop the first model for intrusion detection, the Intrusion Detection Expert System (IDES), which provided the foundation for the IDS technology development that was soon to follow.

In 1984, SRI also developed a means of tracking and analysing audit data containing authentication information of users on ARPANET, the original Internet. Soon after, SRI completed a Navy SPAWAR contract with the realization of the first functional intrusion detection system, IDES. Using her research and development work at SRI, Dr. Denning published the decisive work, An Intrusion Detection Model, which revealed the necessary information for commercial intrusion detection system development. Her paper is the basis for most of the work in IDS that followed.

Meanwhile, there were other significant advances occurring at University of California Davis' Lawrence Livermore Laboratories. In 1988, the Haystack project at Lawrence Livermore Labs released another version of intrusion detection for the US Air Force. This project produced an IDS that analysed audit data by comparing it with defined patterns. In a telephone interview with the author, Crosby Marks, a former Haystack Project team member and Haystack Labs employee said that, "searching through this large amount of data for one specific misuse was equivalent to looking for a needle in a haystack."

The subsequent iteration of this tool was called the Distributed Intrusion Detection System (DIDS). DIDS augmented the existing solution by tracking client machines as well as the servers it originally monitored. Finally in 1989, the developers from the Haystack project formed the commercial company, Haystack Labs, and released the last generation of the technology, Stalker. Crosby Marks says that "Stalker was a host-based, pattern matching system that included robust search capabilities to manually and automatically query the audit data." The Haystack advances, coupled with the work of SRI and Denning, greatly advanced the development of host-based intrusion detection technologies.

To kick off the '90s, UC Davis's Todd Heberlein introduced the idea of network intrusion detection. In 1990, Heberlein was the primary author and developer of Network Security Monitor (NSM), the first network intrusion detection system. NSM was deployed at major government installations where network traffic analysis provided massive amounts of information. This new awareness generated more interest in the field of intrusion detection and investments in that market increased significantly. Heberlein's contributions also extended to the DIDS project where, along with the Haystack team, he introduced the first idea of hybrid intrusion detection. The work of the Haystack project and the introduction of the Network Security Monitor revolutionized the IDS field and brought it into the commercial world.

Commercial development of intrusion detection technologies began in the early 1990s. Haystack Labs was the first commercial vendor of IDS tools, with its Stalker line of host-based products. SAIC was also developing a form of host-based intrusion detection, called Computer Misuse Detection System (CMDS). Simultaneously, the Air Force's Cryptologic Support Centre developed the Automated Security Measurement System (ASIM) to monitor network traffic on the US Air Force's network. ASIM made considerable progress in overcoming scalability and portability issues that previously plagued NID products. Additionally, ASIM was the first solution to incorporate both a hardware and software solution to network intrusion detection. ASIM is still currently in use and managed by the Air Force's Computer Emergency Response Team (AFCERT) at locations all over the world. As often happened, the development group on the ASIM project formed a commercial company in 1994, the Wheel Group. Their product, NetRanger, was the first commercially viable network intrusion detection device. Nonetheless, commercial intrusion detection systems developed slowly during these years and only truly blossomed towards the latter half of the decade.

The intrusion detection market began to gain in popularity and truly generate revenues around 1997. In that year, the security market leader, ISS, developed a network intrusion detection system called RealSecure. A year later, Cisco recognized the importance of network intrusion detection and purchased the Wheel Group, attaining a security solution they could provide to their customers. Similarly, the first visible host-based intrusion detection company, Centrax Corporation, emerged as a result of a merger of the development staff from Haystack Labs and the departure of the CMDS team from SAIC. From there, the commercial IDS world expanded its market-base and a roller coaster ride of start-up companies, mergers, and acquisitions ensued.

Currently, market statistics show that IDS is amidst the top selling security vendor technologies and should continue to rise. Furthermore, government initiatives, such as the Federal Intrusion Detection Network, (FIDNet) created under Presidential Decision Directive 63, are also adding impetus to the evolution of IDS. Advancements in IDS will ultimately push security technology into a whole new arena of automated security intelligence. So what's next? Well, there's application intrusion detection, heuristics and rules-based intrusion detection, incorporation of artificial intelligence, and who knows what else.Regardless of how intrusion detection technology evolves, one thing is for sure-it is now an important and integral component of information security.

Players

The IDS market appears to grow and shrink with the stock market. In the February 2000 timeframe there seemed to be a gaggle of IDS vendors, but there are now only a few serious ones remaining. Most have faded away or been gobbled up by the bigger fish. It is important to note how different intrusion detection vendors' technologies came to be. So, let's review the current players in the market and discuss how they got here.

Cisco

Cisco currently provides both host-based and network-based intrusion detection products. They first entered the IDS market in 1997 by acquiring the Wheel Group and their NetRanger technology for $124 million. Their IDS 4230 and 4210 series provide typical NID solutions while the Catalyst 6000 module is the first switched-integrated NID offering on the market. On the host-based intrusion detection side, they use Entercept's technology instead of having developed their own.

INTERNET SECURITY SYSTEMS (ISS)

ISS provides both a proprietary hybrid intrusion detection solution and an additional NID system that functions independently of their hybrid offering. ISS ventured into NID with the release of RealSecure, virtually at the same time that CISCO purchased NetRanger. Only two years later, they introduced a host-based component that made their hybrid IDS offering complete. ISS recently made another move towards conquest of the IDS market with the acquisition of Network ICE and their highly respected NID solutions, including their new gigabit NID system.

Symantec

Symantec recently acquired Axent and thus gained their Intruder Alert and NetProwler technologies, bringing them into the IDS market. Symantec offers both NID and HID solutions and a method of providing hybrid integration as well.

Enterasys

Like Cisco, Enterasys/Cabletron realized that providing bridges and routers was a viable means of subsequently offering intrusion detection. Consequently, Enterasys purchased Network Security Wizards and their Dragon NID solution and Squire HID system.

The Rest

Now, let's discuss the rest of the IDS field. Okay, ready, take a deep breath, and here we go.

We start with the merger of the CMDS development staff from SAIC who went on to start Centrax Corporation along with the people from Haystack Labs. Incidentally, the remainder of Haystack was purchased by Trusted Information Systems, which was then acquired by Network Associates. Centrax Corporation was purchased by CyberSafe Corporation and changed the host-based product, Entrax, into Centrax. Centrax then became the first commercially viable host-based intrusion detection product. CyberSafe later introduced NID followed by NNID technologies into their Centrax product; they even partnered with Network ICE to round out the solution-until ISS bought Network ICE and ended that relationship. Meanwhile, CMDS moved to its new home when SAIC sold it to ODS, who renamed it to Kane Security Enterprise and then spun off Intrusion.com to better market the product. Intrusion.com then purchased MimeStar, and its SecureNet Pro NID solution, to provide its customers with a total IDS offering.

Okay, you can let it out now-the long and short of this series of spin-offs, acquisitions, mergers, and failures is that the strong seem to get stronger and the number of IDS competitors continue to decrease.

IMPORTANCE OF INTRUSION DETECTION SYSTEM (IDS)

Security is an important issue for all the networks of companies and institutions at the present time and all the intrusions are trying in ways that successful access to the data network of these companies and Web services and despite the development of multiple ways to ensure that the infiltration of intrusion to the infrastructure of the network via the Internet, through the use of firewalls, encryption, etc.

But IDS is a relatively new technology of the techniques for intrusion detection methods that have emerged in recent years. Intrusion detection system's main role in a network is to help computer systems to prepare and deal with the network attacks.

Intrusion detection functions include:

- Monitoring and analysing both user and system activities
- Analysing system configurations and vulnerabilities
- Assessing system and file integrity
- Ability to recognize patterns typical of attacks
- Analysis of abnormal activity patterns
- Tracking user policy violations.

The purpose of IDS is to help computer systems on how to deal with attacks, and that IDS is collecting information from several different sources within the computer systems and networks and compares this information with pre-existing patterns of discrimination as to whether there are attacks or weaknesses.

6

Evolving Property Rights in Cyberspace

The internet originated in the 1960s with ARPANet, a decentralized computer-based communications network set up by the United States Department of Defence and the National Science Foundation. It has developed into a global technological system of networked computer networks with an estimated 900 million users. In addition, the types of communication that flow over the internet have exploded as new applications have been developed (*e.g.*, Telnet, FTP, Gopher, LISTSERV, Usenet, EDI, E-mail, and so on). One of the most influential developments, the World Wide Web, is only 15 years old (it was created in 1990 by Tim Bernesers-Lee at CERN). Thus, many uses of the internet are relatively recent, and are clearly evolving. For instance, Lucking-Riley and Spulber (2001: 55) report various estimates and projections of the magnitude of business-to-business (B2B) e-commerce. A 1999 estimate by the Gartner group put the level of B2B e-transactions at $90 billion, while a 2000 estimate by Jupiter Communications concluded that these transactions amounted to $336 billion (out of a total of $11.5 trillion).

The accuracy of such estimates are suspect, of course, because e-commerce is a global phenomenon and much of it probably is not reported to any government authority. Nonetheless, they do reveal that B2B e-commerce is substantial, and probably growing. Business-to-consumer (B2C) trading is much more visible, and this component of e-commerce has attracted much more attention from governments and the media (and probably from academia).

Yet, the Gartner Group estimate of B2C e-transactions was $16.7 billion in 1999, including both retail sales and brokerage fees for on-line financial transactions, compared to the $90 billion in B2B transactions. Growth is also evident in B2C e-trading, of course, as Bakos (2001: 69) reports that such trade reached $45 billion for 2000, for instance, and Tedeschi (2004a) cites a Shop.org report that estimated 2003 retail sales for U.S. retailers (not including sales of travel services) on line to be $72 billion (5.4 per cent of total U.S. retail receipts for the year). Nonetheless, B2B e-commerce is likely to continue to be larger and less apparent than B2C e-commerce for institutional reasons. Before turning to such developments, and more importantly, their institutional underpinnings, however, cyberspace itself must be briefly described. After all, as Crews (2003: 1) notes, "the Internet wasn't originally designed to be a mass commercial and consumer medium that it is today. If one were to design a commercial network today from the bottom up, it would probably" look very different. The technological configuration of the internet has raised the cost of some forms of institutional development, but it does not preclude all such innovations.

The internet is not simply a technological system. It also is an implicit agreement, or perhaps more accurately, "a loosely-organized international collaboration of autonomous, interconnected networks" (Internet Engineering Taskforce, RFC 2026) that allows bits to flow among computers using a particular language or "protocol." In may be useful consider the result in terms of layers.

At the bottom there is a physical infrastructure (*e.g.*, cable, satellites, routers, DSL, WiFi). The next layer up consists of applications (*e.g.*, browsers, e-mail, VoIP), and at the top there is a content layer (text, music, speech, images). The bottom two layers separate mechanical transportation of bits from the protocol.

The protocol divides the bits into packages that can be reassembled after transport. Internet hosts (computers that store data that is included in the internet) have domain names that are translated into IP addresses. The TCP/IP protocol allows very heterogeneous infrastructure networks to transport data from one IP address to another. Routers are computers that link the component networks. They contain routing tables, and they mechanically look up parts of the address in a data package in order to send the package on to another router that is closer to the final destination. Thus, the technical part of data transmission is very mechanical.

The "free access" characteristic of the internet applies to the two lower levels. For instance, the logical layer is allowed to run across all (or at least enough of) of the infrastructure layer to reach any IP address in the network of networks. That is, the installers of cables and wireless connections and routers are expected to mechanically and indiscriminately allow TCP/IP to work. Furthermore, the logical layer presumably does not discriminate between applications, so anyone can send any kind of information over the internet. The early tradition of free access to the internet also presumed that, like the infrastructure and the logical layers, the applications layer would not discriminate against particular kinds of content. Thus, free access also presumably extended to that layer in that anyone could send anything to everyone else. Importantly, however, the top two layers are not actually global at all.

They are developed and installed by individuals and organizations such as firms and governments, in order to use the lower layers. If developers of an application choose not to freely allow any and all content to be deposited into an address or addresses in their part of the network cf networks, the internet can still function as a global communications system. Everyone is still free to send whatever content they want to send, but some individuals or organizations might refuse to accept delivery of some kinds of content. Therefore, even though the internet does require free access to the bottom two layers to function as a global communications system, given its current technological configuration, it does not require free access intc all IP addresses by all types of applications of all types of content.

EXTERNALITIES IN CYBERSPACE AND THE EVOLUTION OF PROPERTY RIGHTS

Recall that externalities arise when two or more parties want to use the same scarce resource for conflicting purposes. Externalities are an inevitable result of common access to the internet, a system comprised of scarce resources. Indeed, s more and more uses of this resources are discovered, and more and more people enter the commons, it is not at all surprising to find increasingly costly externality problems arising. People want to use this resource to lower their costs of buying and/or selling goods and services, to transmit and store data, to communicate with friends and colleagues, and for entertainment, but some people also get pleasure from causing harm to others. The net is sufficiently large to support tremendous numbers of activities, but crowding (*i.e.*, conflicting uses) is becoming an increasingly significant problem.

An obvious example is spam. The "bulk-mailing" of large numbers of e-mails advertising viagra and other prescription drugs, pornography sites, and the huge array of other goods and services, crowd the internet, slowing traffic, and more importantly at this point, they crowd e-mail inboxes, raising the cost to recipients who do not want to deal with such "junk mail." As Stross (2005: 1) puts it, recipients of e-mail bear the costs: "It is nominally free, of course but it arrives in polluted form. Cleaning out the stuff once it reaches our in-box, or our Internet service provider's, is irritating beyond words... This muck ... is a bane of modern life."

A December 2004 survey suggested that internet users were spending an average of 10 working days per year dealing with spam, and at least some industry analysts estimate that the 2005 cost of spam to business due to lost productivity and additional network maintenance costs will be around $50 billion for the year. This is not surprising since spam accounts for an estimated 80 per cent of all e-mail traffic. Spammers go beyond just filling in-boxes, and slowing internet traffic, however.

They also "commandeer personal computers as zombie spam transmitters," by using a virus to install Programmes on other people's computers so they will unknowingly act as free relays while simultaneously making it more difficult for others to break through the "cloak of anonymity" to find out the true source of the spam. Some estimates suggest that 50 per cent or more of the spam flowing through the internet is handled by "hijacked machines". As a consequence, "The overlapping and truly global netowrks of spam-friendly merchants, e-mail list resellers, virus-writers and bulk e-mailing services have made identifying targets for prosecution a daunting process. Merchants whose links actually appear in junk e-mail are often dozens of steps and numerous deals removed from the spammers, Mr. Jennings said, and providing culpability 'is just insanely difficult.'"

Most spam involves efforts to convince consumers to purchase various products or services. While spammers probably consider such bulk mailings to be legitimate business practice, as an effective and low cost form of advertising which clearly results in enough sales to cover their costs, they obviously do not consider the external costs they generate for other web users, and especially for recipients who do not want to receive the spam. After all, despite laws passed by various governments that make some of these activities illegal, they are not likely to be held liable for these costs,which, are becoming very high.

Not all spam consists of annoying advertising, however. Phishing was a hacker-coined term which originally referred to the act of stealing AOL accounts, but phishers are expanding their targets. June of 2004 saw 492 different mass e-mailings attempting to convince customers of Citibank that they should provide confidential financial information to them (*e.g.*, account numbers), along with 285 mass mailings to eBay users. Since then, similar mailings have falsely represented themselves as coming from many other financial institutions. Spam of this kind does more than simply crowd e-mail inboxes. It is an intentional effort to harm (impose costs on) others. Viruses and worms are similar in this regard.

A 2002 survey conducted by the FBI and the Computer Security Institute reports that virus attacks caused losses of $49.97 million over a twelve month period during 2001 and 2002, and other surveys put the cost much higher, ranging up to $12 billion. Estimates suggest that the "love bug" virus of 2000 cost the global economy $2.62 billion alone, after all, and the Coordination Center of the Software Engineering Institute reports that attacks on business and government computers doubled in 2001 over the 2000 level, with an addition 26,829 attacks during the first quarter of 2002 (another doubling over the previous year).

Under reporting of such attacks is likely since many businesses and government agencies do not want to reveal their vulnerability. 2003 has been called "the year of the worm" by some computer experts. The year started with the Slammer worm infecting almost 75,000 servers in just ten minutes in January. Among the most spectacular of the infestations that followed was the Blaster worm which infected hundreds of thousands of computers, and Sobig.F, which, at one point, resulted in one out of every 17 e-mail messages being transmitted carrying a copy of Sobig.F. One estimate put the global cost to business of 2003's computer viruses at $55 billion.

Mydoom.A followed in January of 2004, however, and spread even faster than Sobig.F (at its peak, one in five e-mail messages contained a copy of Mydoom.A). The worldwide cost of these worms, for cleanup and lost productivity, clearly is many billions of dollars. The people who intentionally create such attacks obviously do not consider the tremendous costs they are imposing on others, or perhaps more accurately, they do not consider these consequences to be costs at all, since they apparently get personal pleasure from their actions. In fact, such attacks often have a specific target that the programmer apparently has a personal grudge against, but they impose tremendous costs of millions of innocent bystanders in the process. The Blaster worm was developed to attack Microsoft, for instance (it exploited flaws in Windows and attempted to bombard a Microsoft web site with data), while Mydoom.A reprogrammed computers to attack the Web site of another software firm, SCO.

Like viruses, Adware and Spyware are Programmes that are actually installed on a person's computer by someone else, but their purpose is not to disrupt or destroy. Those who deploy these Programmes want users to continue their internet activities, as they are secretly monitored. These Programmes create very real external costs, however. For one thing, they tend to overburden PC's, making them operate slower as they respond to the processes prompted by hidden Programmes. In addition, Adware monitors online activity in order to display pop-up ads to users who show interest in particular kinds of services or products. Large numbers of popup ads create considerable cost themselves, as they typically must be deleted before the user can continue whatever he or she is doing. The extent of the spread of Adware is difficult to determine, because users generally do not know that it has been installed. In all likelihood, however, such Programmes are becoming ubiquitous.

For instance, one Adware vendor, Claria, reportedly had 29 million users running its Adware products on their computers in 2004, up from 1.5 million in 2000. The company's 2003 revenues from firms using popup ads were 90.5 million, which produced a profit of $35 million.Spyware is even more "parasitic." These Programmes are installed on computer hard drives by piggybacking on software Programmes that people intentionally download, or by being sent through security gaps in Web browsers when users visit certain Web sites. Spyware automatically records and discloses everything the person does on line. It can be used to learn passwords, as well as information facilitating identity theft, such as account and credit card numbers, social security numbers, and other information a user keys into his or her computer. Indeed, identity theft has become an issue of considerable concern, whether the thefts are accomplished through low tech activities like phishing, or high tech activities such as distributing spyware and intentionally hacking into targeted databases containing information such as credit card and social security numbers. The Federal Trade Commission reports that an estimated 27.3 million Americans suffered the theft of their identities over the 5-year period from April 1998 to April 2003, and that over a third of these thefts occurred during the final 12 months of the period (O'Brien 2004: 2). A substantial portion of these identity thefts was perpetrated over the internet, and the costs of these thefts was tremendous.

The final 12 month period referred to above saw an estimated $48 billion in losses for financial institutions and businesses as a result of these identity thefts, for instance, on top of the uncountable costs to the direct victims of the thefts (an estimated $5 billion in out-of-pocket expenses were born by victims in order to reestablish their financial identities, but the psychological and time costs were probably much higher). Clearly, the internet has made property rights to many non-cyber assets (*e.g.*, assets other than IP addresses and computers) relatively insecure as well, because those assets (*e.g.*, individual credit and payment arrangements) are used in on-line transactions.

FACTORS INFLUENCING THE EVOLUTION OF PROPERTY RIGHTS IN CYBERSPACE

The economic model of property rights suggests that as a consequence of the rising external costs that we are witnessing in cyberspace, we should be seeing increasing investments in the creation and security of private property rights, and this is clearly occurring. One way of establishing property rights is through laws that threaten punishment for trespassers, thieves and others who violate claims. This deterrence approach requires that the threats of punishment be credible, however, and it is clear that while such threats are being made by some governments (*e.g.*, the U.S. Can Spam Act), the abilities of violators to locate outside those governments' jurisdictions and to cloak their identities make this an ineffective method for creating anything close to secure rights.The alternative is to protect individual pieces of property through watching, walling, and wariness. Much as the invention of barbed wire lowered the cost of defining property boundaries and excluding other people's cattle from land in the American West, new technological developments are lowering the cost of sorting (watching) and excluding (walling) unwanted data from IP addresses and personal computers, and for requiring authentication from senders (wariness).

Other factors are also important, such as innovations in the methods of establishing reputations in cyber commerce, as well as in contractual arrangements and other organizational methods of institutionalizing incentives, including developments in dispute resolution techniques. This sub-subsection will focus on technological innovations which are facilitating the ability of individuals to exclude others from using their addresses and computers, while most of the institutional changes.

Access to a person's computer and/or IP address can be limited if the benefits of doing so in the minds of the computer owner exceed the benefits. Indeed, there are growing numbers of technological innovations available for screening and filtering content in order to prevent entry of unwanted data. One area of considerable development in this regard involves efforts by parents to monitor and restrict children's access to content. For instance, consider the growing use of instant messaging and online chat that allow internet users to communicate virtually instantaneously.

Some parents are increasingly concerned about who their children are communicating with, but physical methods of monitoring such activities are very costly and often ineffective. Technological methods of monitoring are increasingly available, however. Instant messaging and chat rooms are offered as part of many paid online services such as AOL and MSN, for instance, and these services offer control tools to parents that can constrain children's use of these options (they can also limit access to Web sites that are considered by parents to be inappropriate).

AOL subscribers are able to create restricted accounts, for instance, that limit chat and instant messaging opportunities as well as web browsing and e-mail opportunities. The AOL "Kids Only" default category blocks all instant messaging, for example, while the "Young Teen" category does not allow the exchange of images, files, voice, or videos. A "Mature Teen" category is also available that limits chat and Web browsing but not instant messaging. All of these categories can also be customized by individual parents, who can even control how long children can use AOL and when they can do so. Similarly, MSN parental control categories include Teen, Preteen, and Young Child with varying degrees of limitations as well as the ability of parents to customize settings.

Parents can block all use of Microsoft Messenger, or restrict access to people on a specified contact list approved by the parents. MSN also allows parents to block file downloads, and will e-mail reports to parents about their children's online activities.Many other internet access providers (ISPs) have similar options for parents. Of course, children can use browsers not provided by their ISP to circumvent such controls, and even though AOL and other providers offer some options for controlling these activities as well, there is more that parents can do as individuals if they remain concerned. In particular, there are a number of parental control software packages that can be purchased and installed. CyberPatrol can block instant messaging, for instance, and its

Chat Guard feature filters specified strings of characters such as objectionable words, phone numbers, and names. Cybersitter fulfills similar functions, and also allows parents to record the text of instant messaging exchanges. It also cannot be disabled without a password (unlike recording features in Yahoo and MSN messaging software, for instance). Spectorsoft records all e-mail, instant-messaging, and chat conversations and keeps parents informed of their children's online activities by e-mail. Of course, children can always find ways around constraints if they try hard enough, whether the constraints are imposed in geographic or cyber space. However, the fact that access to a child's computer address can be significantly limited, even for children who do not want such limits, suggests that individuals who do not want to receive certain kinds of content themselves can also dramatically limit access to their addresses.

Software to filter incoming messages is developing rapidly, and it is being applied both by individuals (.e.g, Anti-Virus Programmes purchased from Norton, McAfee, and other firms) and through contractual arrangements. Indeed, the same ISPs that offer parents methods for controlling access to their children's computers, offer various methods for preventing access by spammers, Adware popups, viruses, and so on. AOL reported blocking 500 billion spam e-mails intended for their subscribers during 2003, for instance, or roughly 15,000 spams per AOL member. Casual observation of television advertising by such ISPs suggests that these filtering features are very attractive to consumers, and therefore, that they are becoming an increasing important focus of competition.

E-mail services like Yahoo Mail, Hotmail, Eudora, and Outlook also are providing spam filters. Hotmail reports catching 3.2 billion spam messages per day, while Eudora version 6.0's filter is said to have stop 97 per cent of the spam directed at its users after it was released in September of 2003. Such filters are not perfect, of course.

As Barzel (1989: 5) stesses, porperty rights are never likely to be completely and perfectly delineated, given the costs of doing so relative to the benefits. Indeed, the Eudora filter is less accurate than it was when it was first released because spammers have altered their messages to avoid detection. This filter, probably one of the most effective, uses a method called Bayesian scoring. It looks at words in an e-mail message and assigns each word a probability of being part of a spam.

It then calculates a cumulative probability to estimate the total likelihood that the message is spam. The user can set the level of probability that he or she is comfortable with, and the Programme will divert all messages that have a higher probability than the one chosen. Like other filters, the Bayesian scoring method does not filter all spam, and it can divert messages that are not spam. Furthermore, over time, spammers have adjusted by filling messages with words that the filter does not place high probabilities on.

A spam message may have a large number of what appear to be random words at the bottom, for instance, or the ad might be surrounded by poetry. As a result, the number of words recognized as likely to be in spam are swamped by large numbers of words that the Programme does not consider to be likely spam content.

Thus, the filters have to change over time as the spam does. One way that this happens is that the individual users of the filters can adjust the filter. If spam gets through, the user can designate it as such and future messages of that kind will be diverted. Diverted messages can also be sent to a "junk" mailbox that the user can then check occasionally to make sure that desired messages are not being diverted. If they are, the user can tag such messages as valid, so they will not be diverted in the future. In addition, of course, filter providers continue to experiment in an effort to refine the filtering process, just as spammers experiment to undermine it. In the process, such filtering software has become very effective at catching a huge majority of the spam being sent before it ever gets into e-mailboxes.

Others ways to exclude unwanted e-mail are also available. "Challenge-response" systems are used by some e-mail account providers, for instance, including Earthlink and Mailblocks. This technology sends an automatic challenge from an e-mail recipient to the sender, asking for a response of some sort (*e.g.*, supply a generated password, or answer some question) in order to verification that the sender is a real person. Since most spam is sent in bulk by computers, spam mail is not verified by responding to the challenge, and therefore excluded. These systems have proven to be very effective at eliminating spam. Thus, Microsoft reported, in 2004, that it was experimenting with this technology as a possible added protection for the more than 100,000 million users of its Hotmail and MSN mail servers. Indeed, Microsoft has purchased a number of other software firms specializing in security software and is reportedly spending about $2 billion per year on computer security research and development, no doubt in part at least because of growing consumer demands for security and the increasing level of competition offering more secure e-mail and browsing systems. The increasing use of the Firefox browser apparently induced Microsoft to rush Explorer 7.0, with its new anti-spyware technology and improved anti-virus features, onto the market, for instance.

E-mail checking services are also being offered. A user of PermitMail provides the service with a list of permitted addresses for senders, and if an incoming e-mail is not on the list, it is held. The sender receives a message indicating that the mail is being held, and that he or she can fill out a form asking to be put on the user's permit list. The sender must provide a name, and can write a message explaining why he or she should be added to the list. Other kinds of identification and authentication processes are also developing rapidly.

For instance, businesses like banks, brokerage firms, travel sites, and other on-line merchants, have started requiring authentication in an effort to distinguish between their legitimate customers and spam, and to protect their transactions from potential identity theft. One way to do this is by issuing customers a "hardware token," a small device (small enough to attach to a key chain) that displays a six digit number which changes once a minute. When customers access their accounts they type in their user names and passwords, but they also enter the numbers displayed on their tokens.

Several banks in Europe and Australia are already using tokens, and mandating that their online customers have one. A number of U.S. banks have issued tokens to their corporate customers and to their own employees. These banks are all considering the technology for their retail banking services, and U.S. Bancorp is planning an experimental test of the system, while E Trade Financial is offering this type of devise to its customers as an option this year. In fact, virtually every bank in the U.S. apparently is seriously considering the technology.

A number of other technologies are also being developed that can provide similar authentication, such as smart cards (plastic cards with embedded microprocessor chips), biometrics (identification of people by their voice, physical characteristics, or fingerprints), and shared secrets (customers must answer a question that, at least in theory, only they know the answer to). In a similar vein, several ISPs have begun to "stamp" messages leaving their customers' addresses with a "digital signature" of the customers' domain names, using strong cryptography to prevent alteration or counterfeiting of the signature. Recipients can then look for such a signature on incoming mail using DomainKeys software. This identification process is being supported by an organization of ISPs who have agreed to prevent spammers from operating through their ISPs.

Yet another option that is being considered involves pricing of e-mail. An Australian firm, CashRamSpam.com already is offering a payment system. Customers of the service can set a fee for incoming e-mail from unknown sources, and the firm will collect the fee, keep 10 per cent and pass the rest to the customer. Refusal to pay means that the e-mail will be deleted, so a high fee is expected to eliminate all unwanted e-mail, while a lower fee might be paid by some advertisers, providing the customer with a source of income. Whether this system will catch on is unclear, but Microsoft Research is considering an alternative involving payment in time rather than money. The system forces a sender to use the sending computer's resources to solve a computational puzzle devised for each message in order for the message to be "stamped": "The puzzle uses an intricate design involving the way a computer gains access to memory and resists a quick solution by speedy processors, requiring about ten seconds. It is not so long that you'd notice it for the occasional outgoing message, but if you have eight million Viagra messages queued up, good luck in getting each one stamped." An individual can then set his or her e-mail Programme to filter all incoming messages from unfamiliar senders by examining them for their digital stamp (proof of having completed an assigned problem).

Exclusion of non-payers is an issue with another kind of property as well. The free and easy sharing of files can significantly reduce the value of so-called intellectual property rights, particularly to music and films, resulting in substantial pressure by firms in these industries for governments to protect such rights. Legislatures are being lobbied and court cases are being pursued.

Yet, the solution to these intellectual property rights issues also is apparently coming through technological innovations rather than through government. This should not be surprising. After all, as Cox and Crews (2005: 2) explain, "The online intellectual property problems faced by copyright owners do not exist in isolation. They are rooted in the Internet's (perceived) anonymity [and free access] - but so are spam, cybersecurity, spyware, and authentication of transactions.

Indeed, to a large extent, we don't have an intellectual property problem; we have an anonymity/authentication[/free-access] problem." In this context, "digital rights management" (DRM) technology now provides a method of protecting copyrights to digital content distributed on line. A DRM system involves a technological container format for "packaging" the product. Thus, for instance, a music album will contain the music and tract titles, along with a set of rules that the software and hardware music players must follow in order to play the material. This can include paying a price for each play of a song, or for a set number of plays. Alternatively, a consumer might subscribe to a service, perhaps for rentals or demos, and chosen song titles can be valid as long as the subscription is maintained. More significantly, DRM address issues of redistribution, as encrypted controls can limit how users make and distribute copies of the digital files. As with the pricing arrangements, DRM is capable of a tremendous number of options regarding copying. For instance, a different price can be charged for a movie or music album that can be downloaded and/or copied than for the same film or music that cannot be reproduced. Thus, sellers can contract with consumers to meet whatever preferences they may have regarding transferability, but consumers will pay for the ability to reproduce. Formats supporting DRM include Windows Media and Advanced Audio Coding (AAC).

Apple Computer introduced its Internet Music Store in April, 2003 using AAC compression technology and a "light-handed" DRM system called FairPlay (Einhorm and Rosenblatt 2005: 4), for instance. Buyers of music can transfer songs to Apple iPod players, and burn unlimited numbers of CDs, but they can only transmit downloads to three other hard drives. The next version of Music

Store will have a number of additional features. RealNetwork's Rhapsody allows "all-you-can-eat" streaming for a $9.95 per month fee, but charges 79 cents for individual burns. There are several other copyright-respecting music services, including MusicMatch, with 99 cent downloads as well as a subscription service that permits on-demand steaming and playlist sharing with friends (non-subscriber friends can play the first 20 tracks on each playlist they receive, but only up to three times before paying for individual downloads or subscribing), and the re-launched Napster which charges 99 cents per track to download and burn individual songs and along with other subscription services.

DRM provides a way of contracting between suppliers of digital music and film products and their consumers, to give consumers specific use rights while preventing uncompensated redistribution. Norms regarding "fair use" (*i.e.*, "reasonable usage") of downloading and transferring are evolving through the competitive market process, as different firms are offering various alternatives: those that survive and prosper will be the firms that meet the expectations of sufficient groups of consumers while compensating the producers of music and movies for their products.

CUSTOMARY LAW IN CYBERSPACE

As they implemented the mediation programme they instituted for eBay, Katsh, et al. (2000: 728) report discovering that: "As we encountered disputants and observed them as they participated in our process, we began to see eBay not from eBay's perspective, which assumes that eBay is the equivalent of a landlord with little power over how a transaction is finalized, but form the user's perspective. The more we saw of this, the more we became persuaded that disputants were, indeed, participating as if they wee 'in the shadow of the law.' The law whose shadow was affecting them, however, was eBay's law rather than the shadow of any other law." That is, eBay is not just a marketing arrangement. It also is a legal jurisdiction. Parties agreed to participate in mediation "at a very high rate" because of eBay law. Their primary concern was in maintaining their eBay reputations. As Katsh, et al. (2000: 729) explain,

Ebay's response to this public safety problem was not to install a police force to deal with problems after they occurred but to use an information process to try to prevent disputes from occurring. Since the public safety problem largely focused on unknown and perhaps untrustworthy sellers and buyers, eBay put in place a process for sellers and buyers to acquire reputations as trustworthy parties.... Protecting one's feedback rating looms large in any eBay user's mind. As one guidebook to eBay points out, "on eBay, all you have is your reputation."

.... While online auctions try to limit potential liability by creating distance between the auction site and those doing business in the auction site, the site owners are the designers and administrators of the process of creating identities and establishing reputations. This is a formidable power and, while it might appear that the auction site owners are merely making a process available and then letting users employ it, there are terms and conditions governing these data collection and data distribution processes, and these rules are made and administered by eBay and other proprietors of auction sites.

Ebay's rules are not simply created at the arbitrary prerogative of eBay management, of course. Many of the rules develop as a consequence of interactions with users. Recall the response to customer complaints about fraud by sellers in travel auctions, for instance. As a result of these complaints, a new rule was introduced that required all sellers of travel services to register with SquareTrade, the privately owned seller-verification company. Even the dispute resolution process was experimental, intended to see how eBay users reacted to its availability. If users find the arrangement to be unattractive, it will not last in its initial form. Indeed, Ebay law is not, and cannot be, imposed through coercion. After all, there are many other auction service providers that eBay customers could choose. As Post (1996: 167) notes, "Mobility - our ability to move unhindered into and out of these individual networks with their distinct rule-sets - is a powerful guarantee that the resulting distribution of rules is a just one." Ebay dominates the market because its rules and procedures produce a legal environment that is conducive to trust building and voluntary exchange.

POLYCENTRIC CYBER GOVERNANCE

Ebay law, or more generally the alternative legal arrangements of auction sites, is far from unique in cyberspace. As Gibbons, et al. (2002: 41) note, "many traditional businesses have learned that existing institutions such as contract law (private law making) and its corollary alternative non-judicial dispute resolution (private adjudication or ADR) may be used in new and creative ways. Both traditional and ebusiness synergistically couple the efficiency and flexibility of private law and private adjudication with the technological and communicative nature of cyberspace, achieving, in many instances, an economically optimal result." But the same is true of non-commercial groups. The fact is that numerous "online legal cultures containing what might be considered to be legal doctrine and legal processes already are emerging in many online 'places'".

When AOL decides to filter e-mail in order to reject mail arriving from a blacklisted address it has promulgated a rule about spam. Subscribers who believe it is a good rule remain in the AOL community, subject to AOL law, while those who believe it is a bad rule, perhaps because it infringes on the spammer's freedom of speech, or the right of individuals to receive the spammer's advertising, are free to leave the community and enter another

ISP's jurisdiction. If AOL survives in this market with this rule, the implication is that its subscribers prefer the rule (or more accurately, the set of rules that characterize AOL law) over alternatives. As Post (1996: 169) suggests, in cyberspace, users are free to "vote with their electrons." Furthermore, "Cyberspace is not a homogeneous place; groups and activities found at various on-line locations possess their own unique characteristics and distinctions, and each area will likely develop its own set of distinct rules".

Cyberspace has many boundaries, even though they do not correspond to the political boundaries of geographic space. These boundaries can slow or block the flow of information. As Johnson and Post (1996: 1395) note, these boundaries are marked by distinct names and addresses, required passwords, entry fees, and various visual cues created by software that distinguish one part of cyberspace from another: "The Usenet newsgroup 'alt.religion.scientology' is distinct from alt.misc.legal,' each of which is distinct from a chat room on Compuserve or America Online which, in turn, are distinct from the Cyberspace Law Institute listverver or Counsel Connect. Users can only access these different forums through distinct addresses ..., often navigating through login screens, the use of passwords, or the payment of fees." The existence of such borders separating very different kinds of activities allow different internet communities to develop their own distinct sets of rules, and allow those rules to evolve over time. Indeed, rules can change very quickly as online communication and information flows are so rapid. On-line firms and membership clubs can control participation and even prevent outsiders from learning about their activities. The behaviour that may be acceptable in one cyber community need not be tolerated in another community. Rules about who can enter and under what conditions they can copy or redistribute data, can be established and enforced. Violators can be excluded. Indeed, while many of these boundaries can be breached by some hackers, "Securing online systems from unauthorized intruders may prove an easier task than sealing physical borders from unwanted immigration [or smuggling]". Cyber law clearly is polycentric law.

A great deal of internet activity crosses cyber boundaries, of course. E-mail goes for a sender in one ISP to an in box that is served by another ISP. Web searches take individuals all over cyberspace. Individuals download information from distant locations, enter eBay to trade and then leave, perhaps to go to a listserver or a chat room, and so on. The ease with which individuals can move from one jurisdiction to another has important implications. For one thing, individuals can be members of many of the different customary law communities, as long as they behave according to the rules of each community.

For another, "In Cyberspace, ... any given user has more accessible exit option, in terns of moving form one virtual environment's rule set to another's, thus providing a more legitimate 'selection mechanism' by which differing rule sets will evolve over time". Individuals can compare the rules offered by different communities and choose those that best meet their preferences. Competition between different firms and organizations providing similar services will either lead to similar rules if consumers all have similar preferences, or to different rules to accommodate the divergent preferences of different people. Furthermore, technological change that alters the ability ot travel and/or create boundaries may require significant changes in both boundaries and rules.

Finally, inter-jurisdictional arrangements can be expected to develop. Thus, for instance, MAAWG, the organization of ISPs is establishing rules for behaviour that involves communications between their subscribers. This organization is not attempting to "harmonize" the rules that operate within each ISP except to the degree that they might affect inter-ISP transactions. Thus, the polycentric nature of cyber law remains, with the added development of second order clustering, as predicted by Vanberg and Buchanan's (1990) analysis, and illustrated by various real space examples. While this may sound like a very complex and confusing system of rules, it must be recognized that most of these customary communities are very narrowly focused in a functional sense.

Therefore, the set of rules that a community develops only applies to those kinds of interactions that are relevant to the community function. Each community's rules are likely to be quite simple, since their purpose is to facilitate the voluntary interactions of community members and protect those members from harm. One community's rules may be quite different from another community's rules but that does not mean that the two sets of rules are conflict, as they can arise in the context of vary different kinds of interactions. In contrast, a nation state that attempts to monopolize all law will have to have a very large and complex set of rules, these rules often can have conflicting purposes. Thus, polycentric law is not necessary any more complex and difficult to deal with than monocentric law, and it may be much less complex.

7

Integrating Cyber Crime and Law

SUBSTANTIVE CRIMINAL LAW

ILLEGAL ACCESS (HACKING)

Since the development of computer networks, their ability to connect computers and offer users access to other computer systems, computers have been used by hackers for criminal purposes. There is substantial variation in hackers' motivations. Hackers need not be present at the crime scene; they just need to circumvent the protection securing the network.

In many cases of illegal access, the security systems protecting the physical location of network hardware are more sophisticated than the security systems protecting sensitive information on networks, even in the same building. The illegal access to computer systems hinders computer operators from managing, operating and controlling their systems in an undisturbed and uninhibited manner. The aim of protection is to maintain the integrity of computer systems.

It is vital to distinguish between illegal access and subsequent offences (such as data espionage), as legal provisions have a different focus of protection. In most cases, illegal access (where law seeks to protect the integrity of the computer system itself) is not the end-goal, but rather a first step towards further crimes, such as modifying or obtaining stored data (where law seeks to protect the integrity and confidentiality of the data). The question is whether the act of illegal access should be criminalised, in addition to subsequent offences? Analysis of the various approaches to the criminalisation of illegal computer access at the national level shows that enacted provisions sometimes confuse illegal access with subsequent offences, or seek to limit the criminalisation of the illegal access to grave violations only.

Some countries criminalise mere access, while others limit criminalisation to offences only in cases where the accessed system is protected by security measures, or where the perpetrator has harmful intentions, or where data was obtained, modified or damaged. Other countries do not criminalise the access itself, but only subsequent offences. Opponents to the criminalisation of illegal access refer to situations where no dangers were created by mere intrusion, or where acts of "hacking" have led to the detection of loopholes and weaknesses in the security of targeted computer systems.

Convention on Cyber crime

The Convention on Cyber crime includes a provision on illegal access protecting the integrity of the computer systems by criminalising the unauthorised access to a system. Noting inconsistent approaches at the national level, the Convention offers the possibility of limitations that – at least in most cases – enable countries without legislation to retain more liberal laws on illegal access.

The Provision

- Article 2 – Illegal access: Each Party shall adopt such legislative and other measures as may be necessary to establish as criminal offences under its domestic law, when committed intentionally, the access to the whole or any part of a computer system without right. A Party may require that the offence be committed by infringing security measures, with the intent of obtaining computer data or other dishonest intent, or in relation to a computer system that is connected to another computer system.

The Covered Acts

The term "access" does not specify a certain means of communication, but is open-ended and open to further technical developments. It shall include all means of entering another computer system, including Internet attacks, as well as illegal access to wireless networks. Even unauthorised access to computers that are not connected to any network (*e.g.,* by circumventing a password protection) are covered by the provision.

This broad approach means that illegal access not only covers future technical developments, but is also covers secret data accessed by insiders and employees. The second sentence of Article 2 offers the possibility of limiting the criminalisation of illegal access to access over a network. The illegal acts and protected systems are thus defined in a way that remains open to future developments. The Explanatory Report lists hardware, components, stored data, directories, traffic and content-related data as examples of the parts of computer systems that can be accessed.

Mental Element

Like all other offences defined by the Convention on Cyber crime Art. 2 requires that the offender is carrying out the offences intentionally. The Convention does not contain a definition of the term "internationally". In the

Explanatory Report the drafters pointed out that the definition of "intentionally" should happen on a national level.

Without Right

Access to a Computer can only be prosecuted under Article 2 of the Convention, if it should happen "without right". Access to a system permitting free and open access by the public or access to a system with the authorisation of the owner or other rights-holder is not "without right".

In addition to the subject of free access, the legitimacy of security testing procedures is also addressed. Network administrators and security companies that test the protection of computer systems in order to identify potential gaps in the security measures were wary of the possibility of criminalisation under illegal access. Despite the fact that these professionals generally work with the permission of the owner and therefore act legally, the drafters of the Convention emphasised that "testing or protection of the security of a computer system authorised by the owner or operator, are with right". The fact, that the victim of the crime handed out a password or similar access code to the offender does not necessary mean that the offender then acted with right when he accessed the computer system of the victim.

If the offender persuaded the victim to disclose a password or access code due to a successful social engineering approach it is necessary to verify if the authorisation given by the victim does cover the act carried out by the offender. In general this is not the case and the offender therefore acts without right.

Restrictions and Reservations

As an alternative to the broad approach, the Convention offers the possibility of restricting criminalisation with additional elements, listed in the second sentence. The procedure of how to utilise this reservation is laid down in Article 42 of the Convention.

Possible reservations relate to security measures, special intent to obtain computer data, other dishonest intent that justifies criminal culpability, or requirements that the offence be committed against a computer system through a network. A similar approach can be found in the EU Framework Decision on Attacks against Information Systems.

Commonwealth Computer and Computer Related Crimes Model Law

A similar approach can be found in Sec. 5 of the 2002 Commonwealth Model Law:

- Sec. 5.: A person who intentionally, without lawful excuse or justification, accesses the whole or any part of a computer system commits an offence punishable, on conviction, by imprisonment for a period not exceeding, or a fine not exceeding or both.

The main difference to the Convention on Cyber crime is the fact that Sec. 5 of the Commonwealth Model Law does, unlike Art. 2 Convention on Cyber crime, not contain options to make reservations.

Stanford Draft Convention

The informal 1999 Stanford Draft Convention recognises illegal access as one of those offences the signatory states should criminalise.

The Provision

- Art. 3 – Offences:
  - 1. Offences under this Convention are committed if any person unlawfully and intentionally engages in any of the following conduct without legally recognised authority, permission, or consent:
  - (c) enters into a cyber system for which access is restricted in a conspicuous and unambiguous manner;

The Covered Acts

The draft provision shows a number of similarities to Art. 2 of the Convention on Cyber crime. Both require an intentional act that is committed without right/without authority. In this context requirement of the draft provision (*"without legally recognised authority, permission, or consent"*) is more precise than the term "without right" used Convention on Cyber crime and explicitly aims to incorporate the concept of selfdefence. The main difference to the Convention is the fact that the draft provision uses the term "cyber system".

The cyber system is defined in Art. 1, paragraph 3 of the Draft Convention. It covers any computer or network of computers used to relay, transmit, coordinate, or control communications of data or Programmes.

This definition shows many similarities to the definition of the term 'computer system" provided by Art. 1 a) Convention on Cyber crime. Although the Draft Convention refers to acts related to the exchange of data and does therefore primarily focus on network based computer systems both definitions include interconnected computer as well as stand alone machines.

DATA ESPIONAGE

The Convention on Cyber crime as well as the Commonwealth Model Law and the Stanford Draft Convention provide legal solutions for illegal interception only. It is questionable whether Article 3 of the Convention on Cyber crime applies to other cases than those where offences are carried out by intercepting data transfer processes. The question of whether illegal access to information stored on a hard disk is covered by the Convention was discussed with great interest.Since a transfer process is needed, it is likely that Art. 3 of the Convention on Cyber crime does not cover forms of data espionage other than the interception of transfer processes. One issue frequently discussed in this context is the question if the criminalisation of illegal accesses renders the criminalisation of data espionage unnecessary. In those cases where the offender has legitimate access to a computer system (*e.g.* because he is ordered to repair it) and on this occasion (in violation of the limited legitimating) copies files from the system, the act is in general not covered by the provisions criminalising illegal access.Given that much vital data is today stored in computer systems, it is essential to evaluate whether existing mechanisms to protect data are adequate or whether other criminal law provision are necessary to protect the user from data espionage. Today, computer users can use various hardware devices and software tools in order to protect secret information.

They can install firewalls, access control systems or encrypt stored information and by this decrease the risk of data espionage. Although user-friendly devices are available, requiring only limited knowledge by users, truly effective protection of data on a computer system often requires knowledge that few users have. Especially data stored on private computer systems is often not adequately protected against data espionage. Therefore criminal law provisions can offer an additional protection.

Examples

Some countries have decided to extend the protection that is available through technical measures by criminalising data espionage. There are two main approaches. Some countries follow a narrow approach and criminalise data espionage, only where specific secret information is obtained - an example is 18 U.S.C § 1831, that criminalises economic espionage. The provision does not only cover data espionage, but other ways of obtaining secret information as well.

Economic Espionage

- In General — Whoever, intending or knowing that the Offence will benefit any foreign government, foreign instrumentality, or foreign agent, knowingly—
  - Steals, or without authorization appropriates, takes, carries away, or conceals, or by fraud, artifice, or deception obtains a trade secret;
  - Without authorization copies, duplicates, sketches, draws, photographs, downloads, uploads, alters, destroys, photocopies, replicates, transmits, delivers, sends, mails, communicates, or conveys a trade secret;
  - Receives, buys, or possesses a trade secret, knowing the same

to have been stolen or appropriated, obtained, or converted without authorization;

- Attempts to commit any Offence described in any of paragraphs (1) through (3); or
- Conspires with one or more other persons to commit any Offence described in any of paragraphs (1) through (3), and one or more of such persons do any act to effect the object of the conspiracy, shall, except as provided in subsection (b), be fined not more than $500,000 or imprisoned not more than 15 years, or both.

- Organizations — Any organization that commits any Offence described in subsection (a) shall be fined not more than $10,000,000.

Other countries have adopted a broader approach and criminalised the act of obtaining stored computer data, even if they do not contain economic secrets.

Section 202a. Data Espionage

- Any person who obtains without authorization, for himself or for another, data which are not meant for him and which are specially protected against unauthorised access, shall be liable to imprisonment for a term not exceeding three years or to a fine
- Data within the meaning of subsection 1 are only such as are stored or transmitted electronically or magnetically or in any form not directly visible.

This provision not only covers economic secrets, but stored computer data in general. In terms of its objects of protection, this approach is broader compared to § 1831 USC, but the application of the provision is limited as obtaining data is only criminalised where data are specially protected against unauthorised access. The protection of stored computer data under German criminal law is thus limited to persons or businesses that have taken measures to avoid falling victim to such offences.

Relevance of Such Provision

The implementation of such provision is especially relevant with regard to cases, where the offender was authorised to access a computer system (*e.g.* because he was ordered to fix a computer problem) and then abused the authorisation to illegally obtain information stored on the computer system. With regard to the fact that the permission covers the access to the computer system it is in general not possible to cover with provisions criminalising the illegal access.

Without Right

The application of data espionage provisions in general requires that the data was obtained without the consent of the victim. The success of phishing attacks clearly demonstrates the success of scams based on the manipulation of users. Due to the consent of the victim offenders who succeed in manipulating of users to disclose secret information cannot be prosecuted on the basis of the above mentioned provisions.

ILLEGAL INTERCEPTION

The use of ICTs is accompanied by several risks related to the security of information transfer. Unlike classic mail order operations within a country, data transfer processes over the Internet involve numerous providers and different points where the data transfer process could be intercepted. The weakest point for intercept remains the user, especially users of private home computers, who are often inadequately protected against external attacks.

As offenders generally always aim for the weakest point, the risk of attacks against private users is great, all the more so given:

- The development of vulnerable technologies; and
- The rising relevance of personal information for offenders.

New network technologies (such as "wireless LAN") offer several advantages for Internet access. Setting up a wireless network in a private home, for example, allows families to connect to the Internet from anywhere inside a given radius, without the need for cable connections. But the popularity of this technology and resulting comfort is accompanied by serious risks to network security.

If an unprotected wireless network is available perpetrators can log on to this network and use it for criminal purposes without the need to get access to a building. They simply need to get inside the radius of the wireless network to launch an attack. Field tests suggest that in some areas as many as 50 per cent of private wireless networks are not protected against unauthorised interception or access. In most cases, lack of protection arises from a lack of knowledge as to how to configure protection measures. In the past, perpetrators concentrated mainly on business networks for illegal interceptions. Interception of corporate communications was more likely to yield useful information, than data transferred within private networks. The rising number of identity thefts of private personal data suggests that the focus of the perpetrators may have changed. Private data such as credit card numbers, social security numbers, passwords and bank account information are now of great interest to offenders.

The Convention on Cyber crime

The Convention on Cyber crime includes a provision protecting the integrity of non-public transmissions by criminalising their unauthorised interception. This provision aims to equate the protection of electronic transfers with the protection of voice conversations against illegal tapping and/or recording that currently already exists in most legal systems.

The Provision

- Article 3 – Illegal interception: Each Party shall adopt such legislative and other measures as may be necessary to establish as criminal offences under its domestic law, when committed intentionally, the interception without right, made by technical means, of non-public transmissions of computer data to, from or within a computer system, including electromagnetic emissions from a computer system carrying such computer data. A Party may require that the offence be committed with dishonest intent, or in relation to a computer system that is connected to another computer system.

The Covered Acts

The applicability of Article 3 is limited to the interception of transmissions realised by technical measures. Interceptions related to electronic data can be defined as any act of acquiring data during a transfer process. The question if illegal access to information stored on a hard disk is covered by the provision is controversially discussed. In general the provision only applies to the interception of transmissions - access to stored information is not considered as an interception of a transmission.

The fact that the application of the provision is discussed even in cases where the offender physically access a standalone computer system partly arises as a result of the fact, that the Convention on Cyber crime does not contain a provision related to data espionage and the Explanatory Report to the Convention contains two slightly imprecise explanations with regard to the application of Art. 3:

- The Explanatory Report first of all points out that the provision covers communication processes taking place within a computer system. However, this still leaves open the question of whether the provision should only apply in cases where victims send data that are then intercepted by offenders or whether it should apply also when the offender himself operates the computer.
- The guide points out that interception can be committed either indirectly through the use of tapping devices or "through access and use of the computer system". If offenders gain access to a computer system and use it to make unauthorised copies of stored data on an external disc drive, where the act leads to a data transfer (sending data from the internal to the external hard disc), this process is not *intercepted*, but rather *initiated*, by offenders. The missing element of technical interception is a strong argument against the application of the provision in cases of illegal access to stored information.

The term "transmission" covers all data transfers, whether by telephone, fax, e-mail or file transfer. The offence established under Article 3 applies only to non-public transmissions. A transmission is "non-public", if the transmission process is confidential. The vital element to differentiate between public and non-public transmissions is not the nature of the data transmitted, but the nature of the transmission process itself. Even the transfer of publicly available information can be considered criminal, if the parties involved in the transfer intend to keep the content of their communications secret. Use of public networks does not exclude "non-public" communications.

Mental Element

Like all other offences defined by the Convention on Cyber crime, Article 3 requires that the offender is carrying out the offences intentionally. The Convention does not contain a definition of the term "internationally". In the Explanatory Report the drafters pointed out that the definition of "intentionally" should happen on a national level.

Without Right

The interception of communication can only be prosecuted under Article 3 of the Convention, if it should happen "without right".

The drafters of the Convention provided a set of examples for interceptions that are not carried out without right:

- Action on the basis instructions or by authorisation of the participants of the transmission;
- Authorised testing or protection activities agreed to by the participants;
- Lawful interception on the basis of criminal law provisions or in the interests of national security.

Another issue raised within the negotiation of the Convention was the question if the use of cookies would lead to criminal sanctions based on Art. 3. The drafters pointed out that common commercial practices (such as cookies) are not considered to be interceptions without right.

Restrictions and Reservations

Article 3 offers the option of restricting criminalisation by requiring additional elements listed in the second sentence, including a "dishonest intent" or relation to a computer system connected to another computer system.

Commonwealth Computer and Computer Related Crimes Model Law

A similar approach can be found in Sec. 8 of the 2002 Commonwealth Model Law.

- *Sec. 8.:* A person who, intentionally without lawful excuse or justification, intercepts by technical means:
  - Any non-public transmission to, from or within a computer system; or
  - Electromagnetic emissions from a computer system that are

carrying computer data; commits an offence punishable, on conviction, by imprisonment for a period not exceeding, or a fine not exceeding, or both.

Stanford Draft Convention

The informal 1999 Stanford Draft Convention does not explicitly criminalise the interception of computer data.

DATA INTERFERENCE

The protection of tangible, or physical, objects against intentional damage is a classic element of national penal legislation. With continuing digitalisation, more critical business information is stored as data. Attacks or obtaining of this information can result in financial losses. Besides deletion, the alteration of such information could also have major consequences. Previous legislation has in some not completely brought the protection of data in line with the protection of tangible objects. This enabled offenders to design scams that do not lead to criminal sanctions.

Convention on Cyber Crime

In Article 4, the Convention on Cyber crime includes a provision that protects the integrity of data against unauthorised interference. The aim of the provision is to fill existing gaps in some national penal laws and to provide computer data and computer programmes with protections similar to those enjoyed by tangible objects against the intentional infliction of damage.

The Provision

- *Article 4 – Data interference:*
  - Each Party shall adopt such legislative and other measures as may be necessary to establish as criminal offences under its domestic law, when committed intentionally, the damaging, deletion, deterioration, alteration or suppression of computer data without right.
  - A Party may reserve the right to require that the conduct described in paragraph 1 result in serious harm.
- *The covered acts:*
  - The terms "damaging" and "deterioration" mean any act related to the negative alteration of the integrity of information content of data and programmes;
  - "Deleting" covers acts where information is removed from storage media and is considered comparable to the destruction of a tangible object. While providing the definition the the drafters of the Convention did not differentiate between the various ways

data can be deleted. Dropping a file to the virtual trash bin does not remove the file from the hard disk. Even "emptying" the trash bin does not necessary remove the file. It is therefore uncertain if the ability to recover a deleted file hinders the application of the provision.

- "Suppression" of computer data denotes an action that affects the availability of data to the person with access to the medium, where the information is stored in a negative way. The application of the provision is especially discussed with regard to Denial-of-Service attacks.

  During the attack the data provided on the targeted computer system are not available anymore for potential user as well as the owner of the computer system.

- The term "alteration" covers the modification of existing data, without necessarily lowering the serviceability of the data. This act is especially covering the installation of malicious software like spyware, viruses or adware on the victim's computer.

Mental Element

Like all other offences defined by the Convention on Cyber crime Article 4 requires that the offender is carrying out the offences intentionally. The Convention does not contain a definition of the term "internationally". In the Explanatory Report the drafters pointed out that the definition of "intentionally" should happen on a national level.

Without Right

The acts must be committed "without right". The right to alter data was discussed, especially in the context of "re-mailers". Re-mailers are used to modify certain data for the purpose of facilitating anonymous communications. The Explanatory Reports mention that, in principle, these acts are considered a legitimate protection of privacy and can thus be considered as being undertaken with authorisation.

Restrictions and Reservations

Article 4 offers the option of restricting criminalisation by limiting it to cases where serious harm arises, a similar approach to the EU Framework Decision on Attacks against Information Systems, which enables Member States to limit the applicability of the substantive criminal law provision to "cases which are not minor".

Commonwealth Computer and Computer Related Crimes Model Law

An approach in line with Art. 4 Convention on Cyber crime can be found in Sec. 8 of the 2002 Commonwealth Model Law.

Sec. 6

- A person who, intentionally or recklessly, without lawful excuse or justification, does any of the following acts:
  - Destroys or alters data; or
  - Renders data meaningless, useless or ineffective; or
  - Obstructs, interrupts or interferes with the lawful use of data; or
  - Obstructs, interrupts or interferes with any person in the lawful use of data; or
  - Denies access to data to any person entitled to it; commits an offence punishable, on conviction, by imprisonment for a period not exceeding or a fine not exceeding [amount], or both.
- Subsection (1) applies whether the person's act is of temporary or permanent effect.

Stanford Draft Convention

The informal 1999 Stanford Draft Convention contains two provisions that criminalise acts related to interference with computer data.

The Provision

Art. 3:

- Offences under this Convention are committed if any person unlawfully and intentionally engages in any of the following conduct without legally recognised authority, permission, or consent:
  - Creates, stores, alters, deletes, transmits, diverts, misroutes, manipulates, or interferes with data or Programmes in a cyber system with the purpose of causing, or knowing that such activities would cause, said cyber system or another cyber system to cease functioning as intended, or to perform functions or activities not intended by its owner and considered illegal under this Convention;
  - Creates, stores, alters, deletes, transmits, diverts, misroutes, manipulates, or interferes with data in a cyber system for the purpose and with the effect of providing false information in order to cause substantial damage to persons or property;

The Covered Acts

The main difference between the Convention on Cyber crime and the Commonwealth Model Law and the approach of the Draft Convention is the fact, that Draft Convention does only criminalise the interference with data if this interferes with the functioning of a computer system (Art. 3, paragraph 1a) or if the act is committed with the purpose of providing false information in order to causing damage to a person or property (Art. 3, paragraph 1b). Therefore the draft law does not criminalise the deletion of a regular text document of a data storage device as this does neither influence the functioning of a computer nor does it provide false information. The Convention on Cyber crime and the Commonwealth Model Law both follow a broader approach by protecting the integrity of computer data without the mandatory requirement of further effects.

CYBER CRIME LAW IN INDIA

The general laws in India were drafted and enacted in the 19th century. Whilst each of the general laws have undergone modifications and amendments, the broad and underlying provisions have withstood the test of time, including unimaginable advancements in technology, which speaks to the dynamism of the General laws. The general laws referred to in this Article are the Indian Penal Code, 1860 ("IPC"), which is the general penal law of India and the Indian Evidence Act, 1872 ("Evidence Act"), the general law pertaining to admissibility of evidence in civil and criminal trials. The manner in which trial of criminal cases are to be conducted is dealt with under the Criminal Procedure Code, 1973 ("Cr. P. C"). India got its first codified Act in the Information Technology Act, 2000 ("IT Act), which fell far short of the Industry's requirements to meet global standards. The focus if the IT Act was however recognition of electronic records and facilitation of e -commerce. Barely ten sections were incorporated in the IT Act to deal with Cyber Crime. At the time when the IT Act was passed several acts deemed to be illegal in most jurisdictions including virus attacks, data theft, illegal access to data/ accessing and removal of data without the consent of the owner, etc., were listed as civil penalties under the IT Act. The IT Industry continued to rely on self –regulation and contractual undertakings to appease its global clients, as it had done before the passing of the IT Act.

The primary offences under the IT Act were:

- Tampering with source code;
- Deleting, destroying or altering any data on any computer resource with mala fide intent to cause wrongful loss or to diminish its value;
- Publishing or transmitting pornographic material through a computer resource;
- Provisions pertaining to encryption technology, the right of the Government authorities to intercept and decrypt such data and to call upon any entity or individual to decrypt such data were also included in the IT Act. Certain acts affecting the integrity and sovereignty of the nation were classified as offences.

The saving grace of the IT Act were the amendments carried out to the IPC and Evidence Act, which to some extent provided for prosecution of rampant offences like the Nigerian Scams, Phishing and other Banking frauds may be prosecuted. Cyber Crime prosecution was however not resorted to in many instances due to lack of awareness (amongst both the victims and the enforcement authorities) about the applicability of such general Laws to cyber crimes (like Phishing). To add to this, administrative delegation of powers treated offences under the IT Act differently to those falling under general laws! Further, crimes like data theft; illegally accessing/ removal of data; virus attacks etc., could not be prosecuted due to the lack of relevant penal provisions.

S.66 of the Act misleadingly titled "hacking" is one of the most misused and abused provisions in India. Recently *i.e.,* in September 2009, the Delhi High Court has quashed the criminal proceedings initiated in or about July 2005, under S.66 of the IT Act by M/s. Parsec Technologies Ltd., against some of its former employees, who left and started their own Company, holding that the continuation of the proceedings would amount to abuse of process of law.

Likewise the IT Act did not provide sufficient recourse for women and child victims of cyber crimes like Cyber Stalking and paedophilia. Controversy has dogged the IT Act from its inception. The Ministry of Information Technology prepared and posted proposed draft amendments to the IT Act in 2005. In 2006, the IT Bill with substantial changes brought about as a result of the objections to the proposed amendments of 2005 was tabled before the Parliament.

In December 2008 as a knee–jerk reaction to the November 2008 terror attacks in Mumbai, India, the Information Technology (Amendments) Act, 2008 ("ITA, 2008") was hastily tabled before the Parliament and was passed hastily and without any debate whatsoever. Unlike the IT Act of 2000, the focus of the new ITA 2008 is clearly on Cyber Terrorism and to a significant extent, Cyber Crime.

This paper deals with some important provisions of ITA, 2008 relating to data protection, privacy, encryption and cyber crime and to what extent it arms one against emerging trends in Cyber Crime.

DEFINITIONS

The replacement of the word "Digital" with the word "Electronic", which makes the IT Act more technology neutral and expands its applicability beyond just the digital medium.

- Inclusion of cell phones, personal digital assistants and other such devices in the definition of "Communication Devices" broadens the scope of the statute.
- The modified definition of "Intermediary" includes all service providers in respect of electronic records again broadens the applicability while inclusion of Cyber cafes in the definition of Intermediaries removes the need to interpret the statute.

The extensive definition of "cyber security" as including protection of both data and the equipment from unauthorised access, use, disclosure etc., is another vital inclusion that impacts the new Data Protection provisions included under the ITA, 2008. The relevance of these definitions, where applicable are set out below.

DATA PROTECTION

The IT industry has been lobbying for a law to protect Data and the new legislation has addressed the industry's demands to a certain extent particularly since Mphasis Limited, a Pune based Company suffered the notoriety of puncturing the Indian BPO fairy tale in April 2004, when some of its employees stole confidential credit card information of clients and used it to siphon substantial amounts. Apart from highlighting the security lapses within the Company, this case also brought to the limelight the lack of suitable Data Protection Laws in India. Several cases have now been reported where former employees are accused of data theft and misuse of Confidential and proprietary Information and data. In one instance, a BPO Company purportedly closed down due to rampant data theft.

The Indian Legislature's response to the hue and cry raised is the transposition of certain civil penalties into criminal offences and the addition of one section under civil penalties as set out hereunder:

- The only provision under the IT Act for data protection was S.43, which only imposed Civil Penalties in the event of the commission of certain acts without the permission of the owner or person in charge of the computer or computer systems such as:
  - Securing access (without permission);
  - Downloading or copying of data stored in a computer or computer system;
  - Introducing computer viruses;
  - Damaging computers and or data stored therein;
  - Disrupting computers;
  - Denial of access;
  - Abetting such acts; or
  - Illegal charging for services on another's account.

S.43A has now been added under the ITA 2008 to address the data protection requirements of the Industry. S.43A stipulates that any "Body Corporate" possessing, dealing with or handling any "sensitive personal data or information" in a computer resource it owns, controls or operates, is liable for negligence, if it fails to maintain "reasonable security practices and procedures" and thereby causes wrongful loss or wrongful gain to any person. What amounts to reasonable security practices and procedures remains to be finalised by the Central Government.

Apart from the above addition under Civil Penalties, the Civil wrongs set out under S.43 of the IT Act have now been qualified as criminal offences under the ITA 2008 under S. 66. A reverse transposition has further been carried out under the ITA 2008 of two criminal provisions from the IT Act (S.66 and S.65) as civil penalties under S.43 (i) and S.43 (j), respectively. Any act set out under S.43, if committed "dishonestly or fraudulently", would amount to a criminal offence, punishable with punishment of up to three years or fine of a maximum of Rupees Five Lakhs or both, under the ITA 2008.

Though S.66 of the IT Act has purportedly been deleted, the addition of S.43 (i) under the ITA 2008 has in effect resulted in the retention of the contentious S.66 of the IT Act. However retention of S.65 of the IT Act without any modification despite its transposition into S.43 appears to be a tautology, which could be due to oversight. S.66B inserted by the ITA, 2008 is on the lines of similar provisions in the Indian Penal Code ("IPC"), which provides for punishment of the receiver of stolen property. S.66B makes the receipt or retention of a stolen computer resource or communication device punishable with imprisonment up to three years or with fine up to Rupees One Lakh or both.Whilst S.66B may seem to also apply to hardware, which is also covered under the IPC, the term "computer resource" is defined under the IT Act as a "Computer, computer system, computer network, data, computer database or software." The extension of the above provision to the receiver of stolen data, software etc., may prove to be substantially useful when faced with issues of Corporate Espionage.

FURTHER ANALYSIS OF THE DATA PROTECTION LEGISLATION

Although the data protection provisions introduced by the ITA, 2008 may not comprehensively address the industry specific requirements applicable to data providers and handlers; nevertheless this is an important head start towards introduction of specific data protection legislation in India, which is absolutely essential in today's business environment. One of the important outcomes of the ITA, 2008 amendments is the clarity on whether Data theft is considered a criminal offence. Commission of acts provided in S.43 to 66 dishonestly or fraudulently, clearly implies "Data Theft" as an offence in such instances.

However these acts would amount to a punishable offence only if such data is "downloaded, copied or extracted" from a computer resource. Therefore it may be argued that the provisions of S.43 (b) are not inclusive, as they do not provide for removal of data through uploading. Criminal provisions give rise to liability only in cases of unambiguity.

If a provision has to be applied through interpretation, then such interpretation, which favours the Accused, would have to be applied. With the addition of S.43A by the ITA, 2008, the onus of implementing "Reasonable Security Practices" is on the business entity. Whilst this may be a known liability that parties agree upon, unsuspecting companies or firms may get mulcted with liability if duties and obligations are not specified, as the Central Government guidelines will then become applicable. As of now, violations under S.43 A are however not criminal offences.

Confidentiality and Privacy

India was shocked out of its complacent conservatism due to the widespread circulation of a MMS clip shot by a Delhi schoolboy. This case took an unexpected twist when this clip was circulated on Bazee.com and its Chief Executive Officer of American origin was arrested. S.66E has now been introduced under the ITA, 2008 for the protection of physical or personal privacy of an individual.

This section makes intentional capturing of the images of a person's private parts without his or her consent in any medium and publishing or transmitting such images through electronic medium, a violation of such person's privacy punishable with imprisonment of up to three years or with fine up to Rupees Two Lakhs, or both. A case of posting of the personal information and obscene material on a Yahoo! Site was touted as the fastest trial and conviction of a cyber crime case in Chennai. It appears that this conviction has recently been reversed.

S.72 A of the ITA, 2008 now explicitly provides recourse against dissemination of personal information obtained without the individual's consent through an intermediary or under a services contract, with intent to cause wrongful loss or wrongful gain.

The maximum punishment prescribed for this offence is three years imprisonment, or fine up to Rupees Five Lakhs or both. Service providers on the Internet, social networking sites, Companies, firms, individuals and other intermediaries ought to now be careful in the collection, retention and dissemination of personal data. Interactive web sites and P2P site operators also have to be extremely careful to ensure that the provisions of S.66E and S.72 A are not violated.

Other Cyber Crimes Including Cyber Terrorism

Provisions to combat cyber frauds have now been introduced under the ITA 2008. However certain issues relating to protection against banking frauds such as Phishing, money transfers through online hacking, e-mail frauds and cyber squatting (including through wilfully misleading domain names) to name a few have not been addressed separately in the ITA, 2008, even though these are significantly increasing problems. S.66C inserted by the ITA, 2008 makes dishonest or fraudulent use of a person's electronic signature or identity, password or any other unique identification feature punishable as theft with imprisonment of up to three years and fine up to Rupees One Lakh.

S.66D inserted by the ITA, 2008 makes cheating by personating through a computer resource punishable with imprisonment of up to three years and fine up to One Lakh Rupees. It may be noted that S.419 of IPC already provides for punishment for cheating by personating but does not provide for the maximum fine imposable. In addition to S.67 of the IT Act, S.67A and S.67B have been included by the ITA, 2008 *inter alia* to combat child pornography. S.67A makes transmission of a sexually explicit act or conduct punishable and S.67B makes publishing and transmission of child pornography an offence, punishments for which range from five to seven years and fine.

Several exceptions have also been set out to S.67 and S.67A, including for depictions in any book, pamphlet, paper, writing, drawing, painting representation or figure in electronic form. Further, S.67C introduced by the ITA, 2008 imposes liability on Intermediaries for retention and production of information. However the duration, manner and formats of retention of such information are still subject to prescription by the Central Government. This section appears to be directed mainly against Cyber Cafes and has already been subject to dissension. Failure to comply with such requirements is punishable with imprisonment up to three years and also fine.

Observations on the Cyber Crime Provisions under the ITA, 2008

- S.43 was included in the IT Act, 2000 to address certain kinds of illegal acts. However, the Legislature has not looked beyond S.43 to address recent trends in Cyber Crimes and for dealing with such issues.
- S.66 of the IT Act, under the heading "Hacking" which was misleading was criticised for its ambiguity and for the possibility of abuse. However, whilst the proposed amendments sought for its deletion, this section has been transposed to not only being applicable as a civil penalty but is also retained as a criminal offence. With the retention of S.66 of the IT Act, one of the main issues that need to be addressed is the criminality of actions resulting in "diminishing of value" of any information residing in a computer resource. Even if the law – makers thought fit to retain this provision, its use and abuse Since, 2000 ought to have been evaluated when re-defining this provision.
- S.66C only addresses some kinds of cyber frauds and not all such frauds committed without using digital or electronic signatures. Further S.66D may be considered redundant in the light of the amendments made to the IPC after the enactment of the IT Act in 2000, save and except for the maximum fine imposable under the ITA, 2008.
- S.67A is a much – needed introduction to the IT Act and would help

in combating the pernicious offences of child pornography as observed in some recent shocking incidents involving school children. Several new provisions have been introduced under the ITA 2008 to combat Cyber Terrorism. These provisions appear to be a necessary and welcome addition though there are apprehensions about their abuse and whether the Government authorities are well equipped to handle and protect the information, acquired by it in compliance with such provisions.

- S.66A inserted by the ITA, 2008 is an essential provision from the perspective of combating Cyber Terrorism and to address several instances of cyber stalking, cyber harassment, etc. However this provision can also be easily abused. S.66A provides for punishment of three years and fine against any person found guilty of: (i) sending information through a computer resource or devise, which is grossly offensive or of menacing character; (ii) false information intended to annoy, inconvenience, deceive or mislead the addressee or recipient about the origin of such message; or (iii) endanger, obstruct, insult, injure, intimidate or to cause enmity, hatred or ill will. This would not only help the police against anonymous and false messages etc., and harassed individuals, but also corporate bodies, which could rework their internal policies in consonance with this provision.
- S.66F directly addresses the issue of cyber terrorism. Acts intended to: (i) threaten the unity, integrity, security or sovereignty of India; (ii) to strike terror in the people or any section of the people by denial of access, hacking and virus attacks; and (iii) by such means does or may cause death or injuries to persons or damage to property or disrupts supplies or services essential to the life of the community; or (iv) adversely affects the critical information infrastructure; is the commission of Cyber Terrorism, the punishment for which ranges from imprisonment from three years to life and fine depending upon the seriousness of the crime.

Encryption and Data Privacy

Mid 2008, customers in India thought twice about buying Blackberry phones – no reflection on the performance of the phones but due to a sudden conflict between the Department of Telecommunications of the Indian Government ("DoT") and Research in Motion ("RIM") Blackberry Services. DoT requested RIM to share its encryption codes with the department, stating security concerns over data transmitted through e-mail services on Blackberry phones or to set up servers in India and permit DoT to monitor such transmissions. After several rounds of talks the Government of India dropped its request reversing its stand on the issue of a security threat. The Indian Telegraph Act,

1885 vests extensive and absolute power on the DoT *inter alia* to deal with, monitor and regulate transmission of messages within India. These provisions therefore stand automatically extended to transmission of encrypted Data also.

The Guidelines issued by the DoT for transmission of encrypted data and the ISP license requirements permits transmission of encrypted data of 40 bit key length in RSA algorithms or its equivalent in other algorithms without having to obtain permission from the Telecom Authority. However, if encryption equipments higher than this limit are to be deployed (which would be the case for most encrypted data), individuals/groups/organizations require prior written permission of the DoT and may be further called upon to deposit the decryption key, split into two parts, with the DoT. These provisions appear to have prompted the Blackberry case. Now in addition to the above powers vested in the Telecom Authority of India, certain provisions have been added under the ITA 2008 (as set out hereunder), which further strengthens the hands of the Telecom Authority in India.

S.69 of the IT Act, which dealt with encrypted data has been replaced with a new S.69, which empowers the Central Government or a State Government through their authorised officers to intercept, monitor or decrypt any information generated, transmitted, received or stored in any computer resource. These powers may be exercised for reasons set out in S.69 including in the interest of the sovereignty or integrity of India, defence, security of the State, or even for preventing commission of any cognizable offence or for investigation of any offence. The only restraint in exercising such powers is the necessity of maintaining written records of such actions. The additions to S.69 and inclusion of new provisions under S.69A to S.69C under the ITA 2008 may be subject to criticism and concern. S.69A empowers the Central Government or any of its authorised officers to block or cause to be blocked access by public of any information generated, transmitted, received, stored or hosted in any computer resource. Under S.69B, the Central Government may, through its authorised agency, monitor and collect traffic data or information generated, transmitted, received or stored in any computer resource for enhancing cyber security and for identification, analysis and prevention of intrusion or spread of virus in the country. Intermediaries have to provide such data and assistance as sought by the authorised agency and failure to extend such assistance is punishable with imprisonment up to three years and fine.

S.70A and S.70B provides for notification of any Government organization as the national nodal agency for Critical Information Infrastructure Protection and notification of any Government organization as the Indian Computer Emergency Response Team, respectively. S.84A gives extensive powers to the Central Government to prescribe encryption methods to ensure secure use of the electronic medium and for promotion of e-governance and e-commerce.

Other Relevant Provisions

S.77A of the ITA, 2008 provides for compounding of offences under this Act, other than:

- Offences punishable with life or imprisonment for a term exceeding three years;
- In cases of enhanced punishment;
- Those affecting the socio economic conditions of the country; or
- Offences against a child below the age of 18 years or a woman.

Whilst some of these exceptions appear to be precise and appropriate, certain others appear ambiguous *i.e.,* exception on the grounds of socio economic conditions.

S.77B makes all offences punishable with three years and above imprisonment cognizable and bailable, notwithstanding the provisions of the Indian Code of Criminal Procedure, 1973. With the increase in cyber crimes amounting to offences under the ITA, 2008, the power to investigate offences under this Act has been vested with an Inspector instead of the Deputy Superintendent of Police. This may reduce the confusion relating to jurisdiction for registering of offences. Further this would entail commencement of extensive and immediate cyber law awareness measures by the investigation agencies throughout India. There is however anxiety in the minds of the industry about the ability of the police official of such rank being able to handle such additional responsibility.

S.79 has been modified by the ITA, 2008 to restrict the liability of an Intermediary under this section to specific instances, *i.e.,* if he provides access to communication systems for transmission or temporary storage of third party information, data or communication links made available or hosted by him. The Intermediary should however observe due diligence and comply with the prescribed guidelines, while discharging his duties.

S.85 of the IT Act, which imputes vicarious liability in case of offences by companies, has been retained in its original form despite criticism by different industry sectors. As most of the offences under the IT Act have been made cognizable, and with the increase in the number of offences added under the ITA, 2008, this provision may be cause for concern.

ANIMATING CYBER LAW

The following example illustrates the ideal performance of an online community operating with the CyberLaw networking protocol and using the appropriate software platform.

Mr L, a famous photographer, uploads on his platform portal (his webpage) pictures from his upcoming book to "tease" consumers/community participants. The site contains explicit warnings against unauthorised online retrieval. M, a user, intrigued by the images, tries to copy two pictures. Her software asks the hosting platform for authorisation to deliver visual material to M. Since there is no prior relevant input/instructions from the rightful owner, the platform responds negatively to M's demand. Next, the autonomous software inspects M's personal settings for any previous legal relationship that would justify a claim for transferring the pictures; it conducts a quick "legal" search through the full range of the online "allowed" concepts. Failing to discover any valid link between M and L, the shared platform is alerted, informing M's personal browser that there is no authorisation and, thus, the terminal is unable to perform the requested transfer.

M does not give up. She e-mails L asking for permission; L, however, declines until the book is published. Alerted by the e-mail, he "reads" on his software all recent attempts to download his pictures and he instructs it (via his browser's interface) to communicate with corresponding platforms in order to enforce an obligation against deprivation of his property. Furthermore, he institutes the same condition *erga omnes,* in order to prevent further attempts to download the indicated material in the future. His agents travel across the platform and impose the condition on all participants, notifying them against specific contact with L's web site.

M persists and she sends her agents in search of a picture using L's name and an additional description "y" that accompanied the photo on the previous site. The agents discover "L's unofficial fan club" URL, which supports fanatically L's work and has been rewarded with a sneak preview of his new material. Unable to contain their enthusiasm, L's fans have uploaded by chance picture "y", the very same that M desires, without adjusting the necessary restrictions for banning its further transfer.

M's agents converse with the file and they demand acquisition, which, resembling BGB §854, follows the pattern: "NOT<obtain> IF (NOT<consent><other possessor>)". Since there is no restriction from the Fans' URL, M's autonomous agents pick the file without further denial.

However, as the file comes into M's possession, the application identifies import of the marked item "y" and detects direct conflict with L's previous conditional rule, which, alerted in turn, immediately identifies import of the marked item "y". Thereafter, through the application, L is informed about the conducted breach. Under the scope of the "default by debtor" concept another subsequent "compensation for default" concept comes automatically into effect to demand compensation from M. Ultimately, the same procedure would take place simultaneously between L and an infinite number of users/participants.

In terms of community structure and operation, the practical nature of "compensation" would need to be explicitly defined. It might constitute online payment, destruction of a specific file's copy, or a ban from distributing it online. Failure to comply with the "creditor's" notice, possibly within a certain period of time, would cause the software to process and impose "communal" measures against the "debtor". However, a system-placed blockade, for example, could be terminated automatically if M complied with the requested "compensation".

CONCLUSIONS: POTENTIAL AND APPLICABILITY

These simplified examples underline the key element of this distinctive merging of law into technology: the automation of regulating interactivity.

From the lawyer's perspective, within this new system resides inherent potential:

(a) For overcoming legislative ambiguities that emerge from transnational networking communications, and

(b) For shaping global regulatory frameworks.

The CyberLaw protocol's structural logic facilitates the introduction of indirect legal harmonisation for the online community's various participants, regardless of their national origin or status. In this respect, typical conflicts of international private law that emerge from the global online context (*e.g.* jurisdiction) give way to the CyberLaw's main operation of precluding disputes through computer code by keeping behavioural activity in compliance with the law at the precise moment of its execution.

Additionally, as the adopted legal policies are merely a minimalist restatement of the fundamental principles of private law, they are easily understandable across the network community. Exploring the protocol's functionality on this basis, a wide range of areas and issues of law that have required additional legislation for their Internet manifestations (and the institution of further, more complex and ambiguous terminology) revert to familiar legal concepts that outline and prescribe the fundamental proportions of fixed social systems, *e.g.* copyright in CyberLaw is ideally dealt with in the traditional ownership context.

However, the creation of electronic-legal hybrids that would substitute and eventually circumvent the effect of real-world law, is not the intent of the CyberLaw protocol. On the contrary, the protocol provides a practical prevention mechanism against the increasing Internet-related litigiousness that places unsuspecting individual users in costly judicial battles with gigantic international entities.

Moreover, the transparency of the automatically imposed behavioural limits and restrictions over online interactivity is brought under narrow scrutiny. Law enforcement within democratic structures is characterised by clarity and its availability to the public for criticism and debate, a principle social institution, which the "invisible" computer language sequences presumably challenge in practice. However, the protocol does not constitute an administration of justice mechanism but, rather, an interactivity management system which replicates private law methodology. Since CyberLaw acknowledges the community system in a Luhmannian sense the CyberLaw protocol's explicit incorporation of law enhances the respect for the human participant as legal actor, unlike the arbitrarily created software platforms, which currently monopolise the global electronic market. Protection and security through the protocol, though, are provided equally for both the individual and the service provider, reflecting the universality of Law in the electronic environment. Therefore, in assessing the added value for international online transactions, the private sector as well as state authorities are invited to contribute to the development of the CyberLaw protocol, in pursuit of satisfactory regulatory schemes for the Internet.

Referring initially to basic legal modules, the law through the protocol becomes alive: a collective autonomous innovation that, by hosting a series of small cross-operational tasks, ěvolves ultimately only through the initiative of its masters/subjects. In this respect, cyber-democracy, capable of presenting its own tailor-made law, is not just a digital utopia.

Beyond the above-explored option of building local, independent communities, the Internet as a whole is the protocol's ultimate and most ambitious challenge. It is arguable whether the Web has the capacity to integrate globally new socio-legal solutions, especially since a framework of universally shared formal laws was not ab initio cultivated across the users' community. In addition, the commercialisation of the Web has led to the fragmented administration of cyberspace by innumerable, and thus uncontrollable, private operators.

Encouragingly, however, as long as many, and technically more advanced, electronic network constructions are still underway, the CyberLaw protocol proposal offers the promising potential for future interactive systems to construct their operational basis concretely towards human law, predicting and escaping the already encountered ambiguities on the "two-dimensional" Internet.

CYBER LAWS AND LEGAL ISSUES

Cyberlaw is a term that encapsulates the legal issues related to use of communicative, transactional, and distributive aspects of networked information devices and technologies. It is less a distinct field of law in the way that property or contract are, as it is a domain covering many areas of law and regulation. Some leading topics include intellectual property, privacy, freedom of expression, and jurisdiction.

JURISDICTION AND SOVEREIGNTY

Issues of jurisdiction and sovereignty have quickly come to the fore in the era of the Internet. The Internet does not tend to make geographical and jurisdictional boundaries clear, but Internet users remain in physical jurisdictions and are subject to laws independent of their presence on the Internet. As such, a single transaction may involve the laws of at least three jurisdictions: 1) the laws of the state/nation in which the user resides, 2) the laws of the state/ nation that apply where the server hosting the transaction is located, and 3) the laws of the state/nation which apply to the person or business with whom the transaction takes place. So a user in one of the United States conducting a transaction with another user in Britain through a server in Canada could theoretically be subject to the laws of all three countries as they relate to the transaction at hand.

Jurisdiction is an aspect of state sovereignty and it refers to judicial, legislative and administrative competence. Although jurisdiction is an aspect of sovereignty, it is not coextensive with it. The laws of a nation may have extraterritorial impact extending the jurisdiction beyond the sovereign and territorial limits of that nation.

This is particularly problematic as the medium of the Internet does not explicitly recognize sovereignty and territorial limitations. There is no uniform, international jurisdictional law of universal application, and such questions are generally a matter of conflict of laws, particularly private international law. An example would be where the contents of a web site are legal in one country and illegal in another. In the absence of a uniform jurisdictional code, legal practitioners are generally left with a conflict of law issue.

Another major problem of cyberlaw lies in whether to treat the Internet as if it were physical space (and thus subject to a given jurisdiction's laws) or to act as if the Internet is a world unto itself (and therefore free of such restraints). Those who favour the latter view often feel that government should leave the Internet community to self-regulate. John Perry Barlow, for example, has addressed the governments of the world and stated, "Where there are real conflicts, where there are wrongs, we will identify them and address them by our means. We are forming our own Social Contract. This governance will arise according to the conditions of our world, not yours. Our world is different".· A more balanced alternative is the Declaration of Cyber secession: "Human beings possess a mind, which they are absolutely free to inhabit with no legal constraints. Human civilization is developing its own (collective) mind. All we want is to be free to inhabit it with no legal constraints. Since you make sure we cannot harm you, you have no ethical right to intrude our lives. So stop intruding!" Other scholars argue for more of a compromise between the two notions, such as Lawrence Lessig's argument that "The problem for law is to work out how the norms of the two communities are to apply given that the subject to whom they apply may be in both places at once" (Lessig, Code 190).

Though rhetorically attractive, cyber secession initiatives have had little real impact on the Internet or the laws governing it. In practical terms, a user of the Internet is subject to the laws of the state or nation within which he or she goes online. Thus, in the U.S., Jake Baker faced criminal charges for his e-conduct, and numerous users of peer-to-peer file-sharing software were subject to civil lawsuits for copyright infringement. This system runs into conflicts, however, when these suits are international in nature. Simply put, legal conduct in one nation may be decidedly illegal in another. In fact, even different standards concerning the burden of proof in a civil case can cause jurisdictional problems. For example, an American celebrity, claiming to be insulted by an online American magazine, faces a difficult task of winning a lawsuit against that magazine for libel. But if the celebrity has ties, economic or otherwise, to England, he or she can sue for libel in the British court system, where the standard of "libelous speech" is far lower.

NET NEUTRALITY

Another major area of interest is net neutrality, which affects the regulation of the infrastructure of the Internet. Though not obvious to most Internet users, every packet of data sent and received by every user on the Internet passes through routers and transmission infrastructure owned by a collection of private and public entities, including telecommunications companies, universities, and governments, suggesting that the Internet is not as independent as Barlow and others would like to believe. This is turning into one of the most critical aspects of cyberlaw and has immediate jurisdictional implications, as laws in force in one jurisdiction have the potential to have dramatic effects in other jurisdictions when host servers or telecommunications companies are affected.

FREE SPEECH IN CYBERSPACE

In comparison to traditional print-based media, the accessibility and relative anonymity of cyber space has torn down traditional barriers between an individual and his or her ability to publish.

Any person with an internet connection has the potential to reach an audience of millions with little-to-no distribution costs. Yet this new form of highly-accessible authorship in cyber space raises questions and perhaps magnifies legal complexities relating to the freedom and regulation of speech in cyberspace.

Recently, these complexities have taken many forms, three notable examples being the Jake Baker incident, in which the limits of obscene Internet postings were at issue, the controversial distribution of the DeCSS code, and Gutnick v Dow Jones, in which libel laws were considered in the context of online publishing. The last example was particularly significant because it epitomized the complexities inherent to applying one country's laws (nation-specific by definition) to the internet (international by nature). In 2003, Jonathan Zittrain considered this issue in his paper, "Be Careful What You Ask For: Reconciling a Global Internet and Local Law".

In many countries, speech through cyberspace has proven to be another means of communication which has been regulated by the government.

The Open Net Initiative, whose mission statement is "to investigate and challenge state filtration and surveillance practices" in order to "...generate a credible picture of these practices," has released numerous reports documenting the filtration of internet-speech in various countries. While China has thus far proven to be the most rigorous in its attempts to filter unwanted parts of the internet from its citizens, many other countries-including Australia, Singapore, Iran, Saudi Arabia, and Tunisia-have engaged in similar practices of internet censorship. In one of the most vivid examples of information-control, the Chinese government for a short time transparently forwarded requests to the Google search engine to its own, state-controlled search engines.

These examples of filtration bring to light many underlying questions concerning the freedom of speech, namely, does the government have a legitimate role in limiting access to information? And if so, what forms of regulation are acceptable? The recent blocking of "blogspot" and other web sites in India failed to reconcile the conflicting interests of speech and expression on the one hand and legitimate government concerns on the other hand. In the UK the case of Keith-Smith v Williams confirmed that existing libel laws applied to internet discussions.

GOVERNANCE

The unique structure of the Internet has raised several judicial concerns. While grounded in physical computers and other electronic devices, the Internet is independent of any geographic location. While real individuals connect to the Internet and interact with others, it is possible for them to withhold personal information and make their real identities anonymous. If there are laws that could govern the Internet, then it appears that such laws would be fundamentally different from laws that geographic nations use today.

In their essay "Law and Borders — The Rise of Law in Cyberspace", David Johnson and David Post offer a solution to the problem of Internet governance. Given the Internet's unique situation, with respect to geography and identity, Johnson and Post believe that it becomes necessary for the Internet to govern itself.

Instead of obeying the laws of a particular country, Internet citizens will obey the laws of electronic entities like service providers. Instead of identifying as a physical person, Internet citizens will be known by their usernames or e-mail addresses. Since the Internet defies geographical boundaries, national laws will no longer apply. Instead, an entirely new set of laws will be created to address concerns like intellectual property and individual rights. In effect, the Internet will exist as its own sovereign nation.

Even if the Internet represents a legal paradigm shift, Johnson and Post do not make clear exactly how or by whom the law of the Internet will be enforced. Instead, the authors see market mechanisms, like those that Medieval merchants used, guiding Internet citizens' actions like Adam Smith's invisible hand. Yet, as more physical locations go online, the greater the potential for physical manifestation of electronic misdeeds. What do we do when someone electronically turns off the hospital lights?

However, there is also substantial literature and commentary that the internet is not only "regulable," but is already subject to substantial regulation, both public and private, by many parties and at many different levels. Leaving aside the most obvious examples of internet filtering in nations like China or Saudi Arabia or Iran (that monitor content), there are four primary modes of regulation of the internet described by Lawrence Lessig in his book, Code and Other Laws of Cyberspace:

1. Law: Standard East Coast Code, and the most self-evident of the four modes of regulation. As the numerous statutes, evolving case law and precedents make clear, many actions on the internet are already subject to conventional legislation (both with regard to transactions conducted on the internet and images posted). Areas like gambling, child pornography, and fraud are regulated in very similar ways online as off-line. While one of the most controversial and unclear areas of evolving laws is the determination of what forum has subject matter jurisdiction over activity (economic and other) conducted on the internet, particularly as cross border transactions affect local jurisdictions, it is certainly clear that substantial portions of internet activity are subject to traditional regulation, and that conduct that is unlawful off-line is presumptively unlawful online, and subject to similar laws and regulations. Scandals with major corporations led to US legislation rethinking corporate governance regulations such as the Sarbanes-Oxley Act.
2. Architecture: West Coast Code: these mechanisms concern the parameters of how information can and cannot be transmitted across the internet. Everything from internet filtering software (which searches for keywords or specific URLs and blocks them before they can even appear on the computer requesting them), to encryption programmes, to the very basic architecture of TCP/IP protocol, falls within this category of regulation. It is arguable that all other modes of regulation either rely on, or are significantly supported by, regulation via West Coast Code.
3. Norms: As in all other modes of social interaction, conduct is regulated by social norms and conventions in significant ways. While certain activities or kinds of conduct online may not be specifically prohibited

by the code architecture of the internet, or expressly prohibited by applicable law, nevertheless these activities or conduct will be invisibly regulated by the inherent standards of the community, in this case the internet "users." And just as certain patterns of conduct will cause an individual to be ostracised from our real world society, so too certain actions will be censored or self-regulated by the norms of whatever community one chooses to associate with on the internet.

4. Markets: Closely allied with regulation by virtue of social norms, markets also regulate certain patterns of conduct on the internet. While economic markets will have limited influence over non-commercial portions of the internet, the internet also creates a virtual marketplace for information, and such information affects everything from the comparative valuation of services to the traditional valuation of stocks. In addition, the increase in popularity of the internet as a means for transacting all forms of commercial activity, and as a forum for advertisement, has brought the laws of supply and demand in cyberspace.

8

Cyber Crime Attack

HACKING

Hacking means finding out weaknesses in a computer or computer network, though the term can also refer to someone with an advanced understanding of computers and computer networks. Hackers may be motivated by a multitude of reasons, such as profit, protest, or challenge. The subculture that has evolved around hackers is often referred to as the computer underground but it is now an open community. While other uses of the word hacker exist that are not related to computer security, they are rarely used in mainstream context. They are subject to the long standing hacker definition controversy about the true meaning of the term hacker. In this controversy, the term hacker is reclaimed by computer programmers who argue that someone breaking into computers is better called a cracker, not making a difference between computer criminals (black hats) and computer security experts (white hats). Some white hat hackers claim that they also deserve the title hacker, and that only black hats should be called crackers.

CLASSIFICATIONS

Several subgroups of the computer underground with different attitudes use different terms to demarcate themselves from each other, or try to exclude some specific group with which they do not agree. Eric S. Raymond (author of The New Hacker's Dictionary) advocates that members of the computer underground should be called crackers.

Yet, those people see themselves as hackers and even try to include the views of Raymond in what they see as one wider hacker culture, a view harshly rejected by Raymond himself. Instead of a hacker/cracker dichotomy, they give more emphasis to a spectrum of different categories, such as white hat, grey hat, black hat and script kiddie. In contrast to Raymond, they usually reserve the term cracker for more malicious activity. According to a cracker or cracking is to "gain unauthorised access to a computer in order to commit another crime such as destroying information contained in that system". These subgroups may also be defined by the legal status of their activities.

WHITE HAT

A white hat hacker breaks security for non-malicious reasons, perhaps to test their own security system or while working for a security company which makes security software. The term "white hat" in Internet slang refers to an ethical hacker. This classification also includes individuals who perform penetration tests and vulnerability assessments within a contractual agreement. The EC-Council, also known as the International Council of Electronic Commerce Consultants has developed certifications, courseware, classes, and online training covering the diverse arena of Ethical Hacking.

BLACK HAT

A "black hat" hacker is a hacker who "violates computer security for little reason beyond maliciousness or for personal gain". Black hat hackers form the stereotypical, illegal hacking groups often portrayed in popular culture, and are "the epitome of all that the public fears in a computer criminal". Black hat hackers break into secure networks to destroy data or make the network unusable for those who are authorised to use the network. They choose their targets using a two-pronged process known as the "pre-hacking stage".

- *Part 1*: *Targeting*: The hacker determines what network to break into during this phase. The *target* may be of particular interest to the hacker, either politically or personally, or it may be picked at random. Next, they will port scan a network to determine if it is vulnerable to attacks, which is just testing all ports on a host machine for a response. Open ports—those that do respond—will allow a hacker to access the system.
- *Part 2*: *Research and Information Gathering*: It is in this stage that the hacker will visit or contact the target in some way in hopes of finding out vital information that will help them access the system. The main way that hackers get desired results from this stage is from "social engineering", which will be explained below. Aside from social engineering, hackers can also use a technique called "dumpster diving". Dumpster diving is when a hacker will literally search through users' garbage in hopes of finding documents that have been thrown away, which may contain information a hacker can use directly or indirectly, to help them gain access to a network.
- *Part 3*: *Finishing The Attack*: This is the stage when the hacker will invade the preliminary target that he/she was planning to attack or steal. Many "hackers" will be caught after this point, lured in or grabbed by any data also known as a honeypot (a trap set up by computer security personnel).

GREY HAT

A grey hat hacker is a combination of a Black Hat and a White Hat Hacker. A Grey Hat Hacker may surf the Internet and hack into a computer system for the sole purpose of notifying the administrator that their system has been hacked, for example. Then they may offer to repair their system for a small fee.

ELITE HACKER

A social status among hackers, *elite* is used to describe the most skilled. Newly discovered exploits will circulate among these hackers. Elite groups such as Masters of Deception conferred a kind of credibility on their members.

SCRIPT KIDDIE

A script kiddie (or skiddie) is a non-expert who breaks into computer systems by using pre-packaged automated tools written by others, usually with little understanding of the underlying concept—hence the term script (*i.e.* a prearranged plan or set of activities) kiddie (*i.e.* kid, child—an individual lacking knowledge and experience, immature).

NEO-PHYTE

A neo-phyte, "n00b", or "newbie" is someone who is new to hacking or phreaking and has almost no knowledge or experience of the workings of technology, and hacking.

BLUE HAT

A blue hat hacker is someone outside computer security consulting firms who is used to bug test a system prior to its launch, looking for exploits so they can be closed. Microsoft also uses the term BlueHat to represent a series of security briefing events.

HACKTIVIST

A hacktivist is a hacker who utilises technology to announce a social, ideological, religious, or political message. In general, most hacktivism involves Web site defacement or denial-of-service attacks.

ATTACKS

A typical approach in an attack on Internet-connected system is:

- *Network enumeration*: Discovering information about the intended target.
- *Vulnerability analysis*: Identifying potential ways of attack.
- *Exploitation*: Attempting to compromise the system by employing the vulnerabilities found through the vulnerability analysis.

In order to do so, there are several recurring tools of the trade and techniques used by computer criminals and security experts.

SECURITY EXPLOITS

A security exploit is a prepared application that takes advantage of a known weakness. Common examples of security exploits are SQL injection, Cross Site Scripting and Cross Site Request Forgery which abuse security holes that may result from substandard programming practice.

Other exploits would be able to be used through FTP, HTTP, PHP, SSH, Telnet and some web-pages. These are very common in Web site/domain hacking.

TECHNIQUES

- *Vulnerability scanner*: A vulnerability scanner is a tool used to quickly check computers on a network for known weaknesses. Hackers also commonly use port scanners. These check to see which ports on a specified computer are "open" or available to access the computer, and sometimes will detect what Programme or service is listening on that port, and its version number.
- *Password cracking*: Password cracking is the process of recovering passwords from data that has been stored in or transmitted by a computer system. A common approach is to repeatedly try guesses for the password.
- *Packet sniffer*: A packet sniffer is an application that captures data packets, which can be used to capture passwords and other data in transit over the network.
- *Spoofing attack (Phishing)*: A spoofing attack involves one Programme, system, or Web site successfully masquerading as another by falsifying data and thereby being treated as a trusted system by a user or another Programme. The purpose of this is usually to fool Programmes, systems, or users into revealing confidential information, such as user names and passwords, to the attacker.
- *Rootkit*: A rootkit is designed to conceal the compromise of a computer's security, and can represent any of a set of Programmes which work to subvert control of an operating system from its legitimate operators. Usually, a rootkit will obscure its installation and attempt to prevent its removal through a subversion of standard system security. Rootkits may include replacements for system binaries so that it becomes impossible for the legitimate user to detect the presence of the intruder on the system by looking at process tables.
- *Social engineering*: When a Hacker, typically a black hat, is in the second stage of the targeting process, he or she will typically use

some social engineering tactics to get enough information to access the network. A common practice for hackers who use this technique, is to contact the system administrator and play the role of a user who cannot get access to his or her system.

Hackers who use this technique have to be quite savvy and choose the words they use carefully, in order to trick the system administrator into giving them information. In some cases only an employed help desk user will answer the phone and they are generally easy to trick. Another typical hacker approach is for the hacker to act like a very angry supervisor and when the his/her authority is questioned they will threaten the help desk user with their job. Social Engineering is so effective because users are the most vulnerable part of an organization. All the security devices and Programmes in the world won't keep an organization safe if an employee gives away a password. Black Hat Hackers take advantage of this fact. Social Engineering can also be broken down into four sub-groups. These are intimidation, helpfulness, technical, and name-dropping.

- *Intimidation:* With the angry supervisor, the hacker attacks the person who answers the phone with threats to their job. Many people at this point will accept that the hacker is a supervisor and give them the needed information.
- *Helpfulness:* Opposite to intimidation, helpfulness is taking advantage of a person natural instinct to help someone with a problem. The hacker will not get angry instead act very distressed and concerned. The help desk is the most vulnerable to this type of Social Engineering, because they generally have the authority to change or reset passwords which is exactly what the hacker needs.
- *Name-Dropping:* Simply put, the hacker uses the names of advanced users as "key words", and gets the person who answers the phone to believe that they are part of the company because of this. Some information, like web page ownership, can be obtained easily on the web. Other information such as president and vice president names might have to be obtained via dumpster diving.
- *Technical:* Using technology to get information is also a great way to get it. A hacker can send a fax or an e-mail to a legitimate user in hopes to get a response containing vital information. Many times the hacker will act like he/she is involved with law enforcement and needs certain data for record keeping purposes or investigations.

• *Trojan horses*: A Trojan horse is a Programme which seems to be doing one thing, but is actually doing another. A trojan horse can be used to set up a back door in a computer system such that the intruder can gain access later. (The name refers to the horse from the Trojan War, with conceptually similar function of deceiving defenders into bringing an intruder inside.)

- *Viruses*: A virus is a self-replicating Programme that spreads by inserting copies of itself into other executable code or documents. Therefore, a computer virus behaves in a way similar to a biological virus, which spreads by inserting itself into living cells. While some are harmless or mere hoaxes most computer viruses are considered malicious.
- *Worms*: Like a virus, a worm is also a self-replicating Programme. A worm differs from a virus in that it propagates through computer networks without user intervention. Unlike a virus, it does not need to attach itself to an existing Programme. Many people conflate the terms "virus" and "worm", using them both to describe any self-propagating Programme.
- *Keyloggers*: A keylogger is a tool designed to record ('log') every keystroke on an affected machine for later retrieval. Its purpose is usually to allow the user of this tool to gain access to confidential information typed on the affected machine, such as a user's password or other private data. Some keyloggers uses virus-, trojan-, and rootkit-like methods to remain active and hidden. However, some key loggers are used in legitimate ways and sometimes to even enhance computer security. As an example, a business might have a keylogger on a computer used at a point of sale and data collected by the keylogger could be used for catching employee fraud.

HACKING: COMPUTER CRIME

Computer crime often involves illegally accessing and damaging computers. Illegally accessing and damaging computers runs the gamut from the mischievous to the malicious. This section first addresses hacktivism, a relatively benign form of illegal access and damage to computers undertaken for a political purpose. Hacktivism includes web defacement, web sit-ins, and denial-of-service attacks. The discussion then shifts to more malicious denial-of-service attacks; worms and viruses, which propagate destructively through the Internet; and finally systems hacking.

Hacktivism

As Palestinian rioters clashed with Israeli forces in the fall of 2000, Arab and Israeli hackers took to cyberspace to participate in the action. According to the Middle East Intelligence Bulletin, the cyberwar began in October, shortly after the Lebanese Shi'ite Hezbollah movement abducted three Israeli soldiers. Pro-Israeli hackers responded by crippling the guerrilla movement's Web site, which had been displaying videos of Palestinians killed in recent clashes and which had called on Palestinians to kill as many Israelis as possible.

Pro-Palestinian hackers retaliated, shutting down the main Israeli government Web site and the Israeli Foreign Ministry Web site. From there the cyberwar escalated. An Israeli hacker planted the Star of David and some Hebrew text on one of Hezbollah's mirror sites, while pro-Palestinian hackers attacked additional Israeli sites, including those of the Bank of Israel and the Tel Aviv Stock Exchange. Hackers from as far away as North and South America joined the fray, sabotaging over 100 web sites and disrupting Internet service in the Middle East and elsewhere.

The Palestinian-Israeli cyberwar illustrates a growing trend. Cyberspace is increasingly used as a digital battleground for rebels, freedom fighters, terrorists, and others who employ hacking tools to protest and participate in broader conflicts. The term "hacktivism," a fusion of hacking with activism, is often used to describe this activity.

Hacktivists see cyberspace as a means for non-state actors to enter arenas of conflict, and to do so across international borders. They believe that nation-states are not the only actors with the authority to engage in war and aggression. And unlike nation-states, hacker warriors are not constrained by the "law of war" or the Charter of the United Nations. They often initiate the use of aggression and needlessly attack civilian systems. Hacktivism is a relatively recent phenomenon. One early incident took place in October 1989, when anti-nuclear hackers released a computer worm into the US National Aeronautics and Space Administration (NASA) SPAN network. The worm carried the message, "Worms Against Nuclear Killers....Your System Has Been Officically [sic] WANKed....You talk of times of peace for all, and then prepare for war." At the time of the attack, anti-nuclear protesters were trying (unsuccessfully) to stop the launch of the shuttle that carried the plutonium-fueled Galileo probe on its initial leg to Jupiter. The source of the attack was never identified, but some evidence suggested that it might have come from hackers in Australia. In recent years, hacktivism has become a common occurrence worldwide. It accounts for a substantial fraction of all cyberspace attacks, which are also motivated by fun, curiosity, profit, and personal revenge. Hacktivism is likely to become even more popular as the Internet continues to grow and spread throughout the world. It is easy to carry out and offers many advantages over physical forms of protest and attack.

The Attraction to Hacktivism

For activists, hacktivism has several attractive features, not the least of which is global visibility. By altering the content on popular web sites, hacktivists can spread their messages and names to large audiences. Even after the sites are restored, mirrors of the hacked pages are archived on sites such as Attrition.org, where they can be viewed by anyone at any time and from anywhere. Also, the news media are fascinated by cyberattacks and are quick to report them. Once the news stories hit the Internet, they spread quickly around the globe, drawing attention to the hackers as well as to the broader conflict. Activists are also attracted to the low costs of hacktivism. There are few expenses beyond those of a computer and an Internet connection. Hacking tools can be downloaded for free from numerous web sites all over the world. It costs nothing to use them and many require little or no expertise.

Moreover, hacktivism has the benefit of being unconstrained by geography and distance. Unlike street protesters, hackers do not have to be physically present to fight a digital war. In a "sit-in" on the Web site of the Mexican Embassy in the United Kingdom, the Electronic Disturbance Theater (EDT) gathered over 18,000 participants from 46 countries. Hacktivists could join the battle simply by visiting the EDT's Web site.

Hacktivism is thus well-suited to "swarming," a strategy in which hackers attack a given target from many directions at once. Because the Internet is global, it is relatively easy to assemble a large group of digital warriors in a coordinated attack. The United Kingdom-based Electrohippies Collective estimated that 452,000 people participated in their sit-in on the Web site of the World Trade Organization (WTO). The cyberattack was conducted in conjunction with street protests during WTO's Seattle meetings in late 1999.Another attraction of hacktivism is the ability to operate anonymously on the Internet. Cyberwarriors can participate in attacks with little risk of being identified, let alone prosecuted. Further, participating in a cyberbattle is not life-threatening or even dangerous: hacktivists cannot be gunned down in cyberspace.

Many hacktivists, however, reject anonymity. They prefer that their actions be open and attributable. EDT and Electrohippies espouse this philosophy. Their events are announced in advance and the main players use their real names.

Web Defacement and Hijacking

Web defacement is perhaps the most common form of attack. Attrition.org, which collects mirrors and statistics of hacked web sites, recorded over 5,000 defacements in the year 2000 alone, up from about 3,700 in 1999. Although the majority of these may have been motivated more by thrills and bragging rights than by some higher cause, many were also casualties of a digital battle.

Web hacks were common during the Kosovo conflict in 1999. The US hacking group called Team Spl0it broke into government sites and posted statements such as, "Tell your governments to stop the war." The Kosovo

Hackers Group, a coalition of European and Albanian hackers, replaced at least five sites with black and red "Free Kosovo" banners.

In the wake of the accidental bombing of China's Belgrade embassy by the North Atlantic Treaty Organization (NATO), angry Chinese citizens allegedly hacked several US government sites. The slogan "Down with Barbarians" was placed in Chinese on the web page of the US Embassy in Beijing, while the US Department of Interior Web site showed images of the three journalists killed during the bombing and crowds protesting the attack in Beijing. The US Department of Energy's home page read:

"Protest USA's Nazi action!...We are Chinese hackers who take no cares about politics. But we can not stand by seeing our Chinese reporters been killed which you might have know [sic]....NATO led by USA must take absolute responsibility....We won't stop attacking until the war stops!"

Web defacements were also popular in a cyberwar that erupted between hackers in China and Taiwan in August 1999. Chinese hackers defaced several Taiwanese and government web sites with pro-China messages saying Taiwan was and always would be an inseparable part of China. "Only one China exists and only one China is needed," read a message posted on the Web site of Taiwan's highest watchdog agency. Taiwanese hackers retaliated and planted a red and blue Taiwanese national flag and an anti-Communist slogan, "Reconquer, Reconquer, Reconquer the Mainland," on a Chinese high-tech Internet site. The cyberwar followed an angry exchange between China and Taiwan in response to Taiwanese President Lee Teng-hui's statement that China must deal with Taiwan on a "state-to-state" basis.

Many of the attacks during the Palestinian-Israeli cyberwar were web defacements. The hacking group GForce Pakistan, which joined the pro-Palestinian forces, posted heart-wrenching images of badly mutilated children on numerous Israeli web sites. The Borah Torah site also contained the message, "Jews, Israelis, you have crossed your limits, is that what Torah teaches? To kill small innocent children in that manner? You Jews must die!" along with a warning of additional attacks.

Hacktivists have also hijacked web sites by tampering with the Domain Name Service so that the site's domain name resolves to the IP address of some other site. When users point their browsers to the target site, they are redirected to the alternative site.

In what might have been one of the largest mass Web site takeovers, the anti-nuclear Milw0rm hackers joined with the Ashtray Lumberjacks hackers in an attack that affected more than 300 web sites in July 1998. According to reports, the hackers broke into the British Internet service provider (ISP) EasySpace, which hosted the sites. They altered the ISP's database so that users attempting to access the sites were redirected to a Milw0rm site, where they were greeted by a message protesting the nuclear arms race. The message concluded with "Use your power to keep the world in a state of PEACE and put a stop to this nuclear bullshit."

Web Sit-ins

Web sit-ins are another popular form of attack. Thousands of Internet users simultaneously visit a target Web site and attempt to generate sufficient traffic to disrupt normal service. A group calling itself Strano Network conducted what was probably the first such demonstration as a protest against the French government's policies on nuclear and social issues. On December 21, 1995, they launched a one-hour Net'Strike attack against the web sites operated by various government agencies. At the appointed hour, participants from all over the world pointed their browsers to the government web sites. According to reports, at least some of the sites were effectively knocked out for the period.

In 1998, EDT took the concept a step further and automated the attacks. They organized a series of sit-ins, first against Mexican President Ernesto Zedillo's Web site and later against US President Bill Clinton's White House Web site, the Pentagon, the US Army School of the Americas, the Frankfurt Stock Exchange, and the Mexican Stock Exchange. The purpose was to demonstrate solidarity with the Mexican Zapatistas. According to EDT's Brett Stalbaum, the Pentagon was chosen because "we believe that the US military trained the soldiers carrying out the human rights abuses." For a similar reason, the US Army School of the Americas was selected. The Frankfurt Stock Exchange was targeted, Stalbaum said, "Because it represented capitalism's role in globalization utilizing the techniques of genocide and ethnic cleansing, which is at the root of the Chiapas' problems. The people of Chiapas should play a key role in determining their own fate, instead of having it pushed on them through their forced relocation....which is currently financed by Western capital."

To facilitate the strikes, the organizers set up special web sites with automated software. All that was required of would-be participants was to visit one of the FloodNet sites. When they did, their browser would download the software (a Java Applet), which would access the target site every few seconds. In addition, the software let protesters leave a personal statement on the targeted server's error log. For example, if they pointed their browsers to a non-existent file such as "human_rights" on the target server, the server would log the message, "human_rights not found on this server."

When the Pentagon's server sensed the attack from the FloodNet servers, it launched a counter-offensive against the users' browsers, redirecting them to a page with an Applet Programme called "HostileApplet." Once there, the new applet was downloaded to their browsers, where it endlessly tied up their machines trying to reload a document until the machines were rebooted. The

Frankfurt Stock Exchange reported that they were aware of the protest but believed it had not affected their services. Overall, EDT considered the attacks a success. "Our interest is to help the people of Chiapas to keep receiving the international recognition that they need to keep them alive," said Stalbaum.

Since the time of the strikes, FloodNet and similar software have been used in numerous sit-ins sponsored by EDT, the Electrohippies, and others. There were reports of FloodNet activity during the Palestinian-Israeli cyberwar. Pro-Israel hackers created a Web site called Wizel.com, which offered FloodNet software and other tools before it was shut down. Pro-Arab hackers put up similar sites. The Electrohippies have been criticized for denying their targets' right to speech when conducting a sit-in. Their response has been that a sit-in is acceptable if it substitutes the deficit of speech by one group with a broad debate on policy issues and if the event used to justify the sit-in provides a focus for the debate. The Electrohippies also demand broad support for their actions. An operation protesting genetically modified foods was aborted when the majority of visitors to their site did not vote for the operation.

Denial-of-Service Attacks

Whereas a web sit-in requires participation by tens of thousands of people to have even a slight impact, the so-called denial-of-service (DoS) and distributed denial-of-service (DDoS) tools allow lone cyberwarriors to shut down web sites and e-mail servers. With a DoS attack, a hacker uses a software tool that bombards a server with network messages. The messages either crash the server or disrupt service so badly that legitimate traffic slows to a crawl. DDoS is similar except that the hacker first penetrates numerous Internet servers (called "zombies") and installs software on them to conduct the attack. The hacker then uses a tool that directs the zombies to attack the target all at once.

During the Kosovo conflict, Belgrade hackers were credited with DoS attacks against NATO servers. They bombarded NATO's web server with "ping" commands, which test whether a server is running and connected to the Internet. The attacks caused line saturation of the targeted servers.

Similar attacks took place during the Palestinian-Israeli cyberwar. Pro-Palestinian hackers used DoS tools to attack Netvision, Israel's largest ISP. While initial attacks crippled the ISP, Netvision succeeded in fending off later assaults by strengthening its security.

MOBILE PHONES HACKING

Although hacking is generally associated with computers, mobile phones are also at risk from hackers. Mobile phones that use wap use wireless connections to access the Internet and these connections can be easily hacked into. Phone companies have also been hacked before with the hackers gaining access into thousands of mobile phone user records. There are different ways to hack into mobile phones depending on the type of wap connection they use. Bluesnarfing for example is the specific method of hacking into phones that use Bluetooth connections. A hacker would do this in order to copy all of the information on the phone such as the contacts for instance.

People are using their mobile phones to send increasingly private information as technology enables the use of e-mail, etc on mobile phones. Hacking of a mobile phone can cover the hacking that involves tricking the mobile phone company into providing free texts, calls or wap. It can also include the cloning of sims in order to charge calls under another person's name and number or even the use of hacking to gain access to a person's confidential information such as passwords or various account details.

PREPARED FOR CELL PHONE HACKS

Rob Your Money

Other options might use a particular buying feature called SMS. This refers to the fact that money can be taken from your account and transferred into another and a good hacker can sit in one place and access a lot of phones and transfer a lot of money rather quickly - probably in less time than you think!

Give The System A Virus

By using another cell phone hack code, a hacker could kidnap your phone, send it a camouflaged programme or send it a virus. But it does not end there, since, from that point, he can use your phone to retransmit the virus to many other phones almost instantly - potentially disabling the system.

Spy On You

A hacker can also gain access and take over for cell phone spying and remote mobile phone hacking. Literally, once secured, the hacker can have the phone call him, and then be able to listen to all conversations going on around the owner of the phone.

Access Your Voice Mails

Voice mails can also be retrieved by a hacker through a hacking cell phone. After stealing your number, this can easily be done - if your password is disabled. The main thing that needs to be understood here, is that the electronics that give you the modern convenience of interacting with the Internet (getting your voice mails, e-mails, Web surfing, etc.), is also the same technology that allows you to receive the same ills as can befall someone on the Internet.

PREVENTION FORM CELL PHONE HACKERS

It seems that the major cell phone companies, at least at this point, really are not interested in bringing the system up to be able to cope with this threat. Meetings are starting to take place, but for now it is not perceived to be real serious. This could be because it is primarily the older phones that are most susceptible to some types of this mobile hacking.

Until the cell phone manufacturers are able to cope with, or eliminate, the glitches in the system that allows them to overcome these problems, you will largely have to help yourself to cope with these things. Here are a couple of tips that will help you protect your cell phone, its information, and other things.

Use Your Passwords

The cell phone companies tell us that many people have turned off their passwords when they access their voice mail messages, or other things. This little feature, though it may seem to be an annoyance to some, could protect your phone from unauthorized purposes.

Leave The Phone Off

This one is obviously the harder choice, here, simply because most of us who have cell phones like to be reached anytime and anywhere. Others do need to be reachable at all times.

Upgrade Your Phone

While this cannot guarantee that your phone is not hackable, it certainly will help. It should be remembered that the phone companies work hard to deliver the best technology and conveniences - but the cell phone hacks work just as hard to be the first to break the systems designed to defeat them. It is an ongoing battle. Cellular phone hacking, for now, is a fact of life that affects a few of us. Gladly, the numbers are still small, but many feel this problem is just getting started. By being aware of the problems, you can wisely take steps to prevent them from happening to you. Cellphone hacking does not need to catch you unprepared.

CELL PHONES - HACKERS NEXT TARGET

It was bound to happen - they have hacked just about everything else. Now it's the cell phones. Cellphone hacking has just recently surfaced and been made public ever since some one did some cellular phone hacking on Paris Hilton's cell phone.

WHAT DOES IT INVOLVE

The fact of someone hacking cell phone became public knowledge when Paris Hilton's cell phone, along with her information was recently hacked.

Unfortunately for her, all her celebrity friends and their phone numbers were also placed on the Internet - resulting in a barrage of calls to each of them. Cell phone hackers have apparently found a glitch in the way the chips are manufactured.

The good news, though, is that it only applies to the first generation models of cell phones that use the Global System for Mobile communications (GSM). Another requirement is that the hacker must have physical access to the cell phone for at least three minutes - which is a real good reason not to let it out of your sight. Currently, although the problem has been remedied in the second and third generation phones, it seems that about 70 per cent of existing cell phones fall within the first generation category.

Another way that mobile phone hacking can take place is for a hacker to walk around an area with people that have cell phones and a laptop that has cellphone hacker programmes on it. Through an antenna, and a little patience, his computer can literally pick up your cell phone data-if it is turned on. This is more applicable to cell phones that use Bluetooth technology.

What Can A Hacker Do?

Surprisingly, there are quite a number of things that can be accomplished by the hacker. Depending on their intent here are a few of them.

- Steal Your Number

Your phone number can be accessed and obtained by cellphone hacking. This allows them to make calls and have it charged to your account.

- Take Your Information

Mobile hacking allows a hacker to contact your cell phone, without your knowledge, and to download your addresses and other information you might have on your phone. Many hackers are not content to only get your information. Some will even change all your phone numbers! Be sure to keep a backup of your information somewhere. This particular technique is called Bluesnarfing.

BLUETOOTH SECURITY AND HACKS

BLUETOOTH

Bluetooth is a wireless technology for short-range (usually up to a maximum of 100 metres) networking. It is relatively robust, operates on low power, and is a low cost technology. Bluetooth uses a Time-Division Duplex scheme for full duplex transmission.

In other words, Bluetooth technology is simply used to connect an electronic device to another without the physical cable. Bluetooth is intended to be a standard that works at two levels:

- It provides agreement at the physical level (radio-frequency standard).
- It also provides agreement at the next level up, where products have to agree on when bits are sent, how many will be sent at a time and

how the parties in a conversation can be sure that the message received is the same as the message sent.

The Bluetooth protocol uses a combination of circuit and packet switching. To send/receive data Bluetooth uses a frequency-hopping spread spectrum technique which makes it difficult to track or intercept transmissions. The Bluetooth standard uses three transmit power classes. These are 1mW, 2.5mW and 100mW.

Each Bluetooth device has a unique 48 bit hard-wired device address for identity, which allows for 2^48 devices. Bluetooth devices basically form piconets to communicate. Each piconet comprises of up to eight active devices where one is the 'master' and the rest are 'slaves'. The master searches for Bluetooth devices followed by invitations to join the piconet addressed to specific devices.

The 'master' then assigns a member-address to each slave and controls their transmissions. Devices can belong to several piconets. Bluetooth also provides for easy integration of TCP/IP for networking. Bluetooth uses the radio range of 2.45 GHz. This is a globally available bandwidth used worldwide for compatibility.

BLUETOOTH BASICS

Bluetooth operates in the license-free ISM band (Industrial, Scientific and Medical Band) between 2.4 and 2.48 GHz. For prevention of interferences with other devices working within ISM, such as baby phones or microwave ovens, Bluetooth makes use of a technique called *frequency hopping*. Therefore, the base band frequency is switched 1600 times per second to one of 79 frequency steps of 1 MHz band width within the ISM band. Bluetooth is a connection oriented service. In order to connect two Bluetooth devices, one of them, normally the device initiating the connection, elevates to the master, leaving the second device.

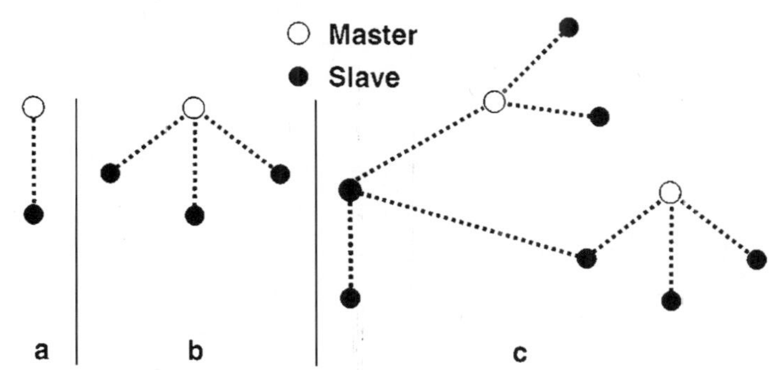

Fig. Piconet of two (a) or more (b) devices, scatternet (c)

In Bluetooth, connections with up to seven devices, which form a *piconet* are possible, where communication is led by the master device. Finally, a device is able to participate simultaneously in several piconets (in only one of them acting as the master). The resulting topology is called *scatternet*. The maximum data rate in Bluetooth connections is 1 MBit/s in Version 1.2, while in the most recent version, 2.0+EDR (*enhanced data rate*) data rates of up to 3 MBit/s are reached. A master may reserve SCO (*synchronous connection oriented*) connections to up to three slaves in his piconet, using certain time slots. Those connections, granting symmetric data rates to both communication partners are used for voice transmission primarily. Unused timeslots may now be used for exchange of point-to-multipoint packets between the master and all slaves in the piconet via ACL (*asynchronous connection less*) packets. These connections grant higher data rates in only one direction. While three different device classes exist, with a rising power consumption from class I to class III in exchange for a larger operating distance, one of Bluetooths greatest advantages is a generally low power consumption.

Power Class	Max. Power Consumption	Max. Operating Range
1	100 mW (20 dBm)	ca. 100 m
2	2,5 mW (4 dBm)	ca. 20 m
3	1 mW (0 dBm)	ca. 10 m

For a secure communication via Bluetooth, the following security targets are defined:

- Confidentiality
- (Device) authentication
- (Device) authorisation
- Integrity

In order to accomplish those security targets, three possible modes of security are defined:

- *Security Mode 1*: No security efforts
- *Security Mode 2*: Service level security, applications have to implement needed cryptographic means
- *Security Mode 3*: Device level security (cryptographic means are implemented in LMP, independent of applications)

Security mode 1 obviously has to be avoided whenever possible. Services make transparent use of a secure channel, which is normally established via the Link Managing Protocol (LMP). Therefore, a pairing process between two devices A and B has to be done, in order to establish a shared cryptographic secret for subsequent encryption or authentication. Beforehand, a rough overview of the most important services and protocols of the Bluetooth protocol stack is given, in order to establish the reader's understanding for the presented vulnerabilities.

BLUETOOTH SERVICES

Bluetooth makes use of a protocol stack, which makes it simple to seperate application logic from physical data connections. In comparison to the *ISO/OSI reference model*, the protocol architecture of Bluetooth allows for straightforward implementation of existing network protocols like HTTP, FTP, etc.

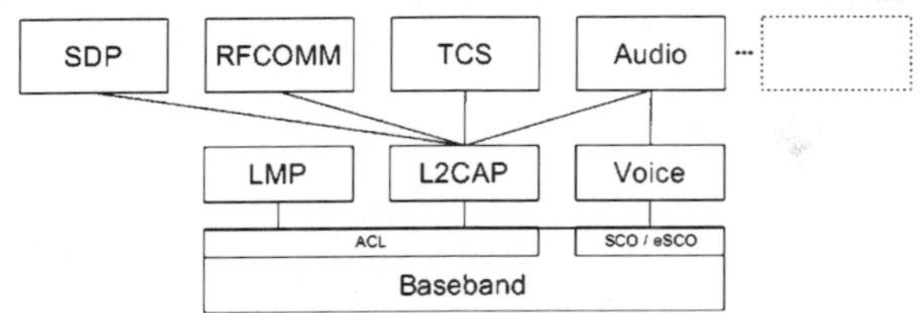

Fig. Bluetooth Protocol Stack

SDP - Service Discovery Protocol

Bluetooth is a technology, which is deployed in a dynamical environment. Devices may get out of range or even switched off, while new devices might become activated. In order to detect services, provided by other devices, a protocol, which detects services makes sense. In Bluetooth, the *Service Discovery Protocol* is responsible for keeping track of services, provided within a device's operating range.

LMP - Link Managing Protocol

Especially interesting for further consideration is the *Link Managing Protocol* (LMP), as one of three possible security modes in Bluetooth is implemented in this layer. Every Bluetooth device contains a Link Manager Unit, which keeps track of connected devices. Those Link Managers communicate via *protocol data units* (PDU), defined in LMP.

New connections are established, using an enquiry routine (detecting device address), followed by a page command (call for a device with known device address), which have to be responded correctly by the opposite device. Subsequently, devices may initiate the pairing process, where a link key, *KAB* is established and the opposite device is stored in the "trusted devices"

L2CAP - Logical Link Control and Adaption Protocol

The *Logical Link Control and Adaption Protocol* (L2CAP) provides connectionoriented and connectionless data services to protocols in upper layers, while making use of ACL (asynchronous connectionless) packets for communication via the Baseband.

RFCOMM - Radio Frequency Communication

The *Radio Frequency Communication* (RFCOMM) provides emulated serial ports and makes use of the lower-level L2CAP protocol. Up to 60 simultaneous connections to other Bluetooth devices are possible, called *RFCOMM channels*.

TCS - Telephony Control Protocol

The *Telephony Control Protocol* provides functionality to control telephony applications and makes use of L2CAP connections.

OBEX - Object Exchange Protocol

The *Object Exchange Protocol* (OBEX) provides services for the exchange of binary data objects. To initiate an OBEX session, an optional OBEX authentication is possible. Therefore, a limited set of commands like PUT, GET or ABORT exist for easy file transfers, comparable to HTTP. In Bluetooth, OBEX is mainly used within the profiles *OBEX Object Push Profile* (OPP) and the *Synchronisation Profile* (SYNCH).

BLUETOOTH PROFILES

In Bluetooth, provided services are composed to a *Bluetooth Profile*. Bluetooth devices communicate via the profiles, that act as "interfaces". For example, a Bluetooth-enabled mobile phone might make use of a Bluetooth headset, which implements the *Headset Profile* (HSP), which means that SCO (synchronous connection-oriented)-based audio connections and a subset of AT commands for accepting an incoming phone call, etc. are supported. For further consideration, two Bluetooth profiles are especially interesting, concerning *BlueSnarfing* and *BlueBugging* attacks:

OBEX Object Push Profile (OPP)

The *Object Push Profile* (OPP) provides basic functions for exchange of binary objects, mainly used for vCards in Bluetooth. vCard is a file format standard for electronic business cards. Since vCards are not worth being especially protected, no authorisation procedure is performed before OPP transactions. Supported OBEX commands are connect, disconnect, put, get and abort.

Synchronisation Profile (SYNCH)

The *Synchronisation Profile* (SYNCH) provides functions for exchange of *Personal Information Manager* (PIM) data and was adopted from the IrDA infrared specification. In Bluetooth, especially private data, like the address book, calendar, etc. is sent using the SYNCH profile, thus certain security measures have to be setup in order to make use of SYNCH transactions, namely performing a pairing process to authenticate the opposite device, based on a link key.

Trusted Devices

The Bluetooth specification defines several possible relations between Bluetooth Devices. A paired device may get explicitely marked as a *trusted device*, which means that *e.g.* no authentication based on the link key is required for that device, in order to access certain services. A weak implementation of the trusted devices feature leads to the *HeloMoto* vulnerability, which ocurred on some Motorola mobile phones.

SPAM ATTACKS

Nowadays, E-mail (Electronic mail) communication plays a great role in the human life due to its fast and free availability, lower or free cost. It is more useful for many corporate because of some features like newsletters, business correspondence, E-mail marketing, Advertisements etc. Like Freelancer.com Support use e-mail service for business correspondence to send the e-mails and messages to its authorised members.

Google news alerts use it for the newsletter. Naukri.com, DevNetworkIndia.org and etc. use e-mail service for the new jobs advertisements massively. Inkfruit, ZoomIn, Fashnvia.com (India) and etc. use e-mail service for their product marketing and their advertisements. Many times, these mails like Product advertisements, job advertisements, news alerts are meaningful for the e-mail users but sometimes, they generate spam mails over the mail-inbox.

Today, E-mail and chat services are the most common, instantaneous and successful Internet applications, which are threatened by spam mails and spam chats. These Service can be accessed using mobile Internet or low speed Internet. Spam mails can be an advertisement or notification of porn Web site, porn video, phishing Web site, Nigerian scam, medicines advertisements, adult content etc.

Spammers collect e-mail addresses from chartrooms, public networking web sites, customer lists, newsgroups, and worms, viruses which harvest users' address books, and are sold to other spammers. They also use a practice known as "e-mail appending" or "epending" in which they use known information about their target (such as a postal address) to search for the target's e-mail address. Much of spam is sent to invalid e-mail addresses.

Spam averages 78 per cent of all e-mail sent. The spam detection problem seems more serious over mailboxes today. Without a spam filter, one e-mail user might receive over hundreds of mails daily and find that most of them are of spam category. Spam mails consume unnecessary traffic over the Internet as well as e-mail service provider. Moreover, receiving spam mails are with no use for e-mail users. In the employed system, a highly simplified architecture of artificial neural networks is used to detect the misbehaviour of incoming mails.

An artificial neural network is a mathematical model which works on the principles of biological neural networks. Generally it is referred as neural network (NN). Using neural network model; we can easily map the complex inputs with the complex outputs.

Some of the silent features of ANN are as follows:

- They represent a highly connected network of neurons - the basic processing unit.
- They operate in a highly parallel manner.
- Each neuron does some amount of information processing.
- It derives inputs from some other neuron and in return gives its output to other neuron for further processing.
- This layer-by-layer processing of the information results in great computational capability.
- As a result of this parallel processing, ANNs are able to achieve great results when applied to real-life problems.

A typical architecture of neural network is depicted in figure.

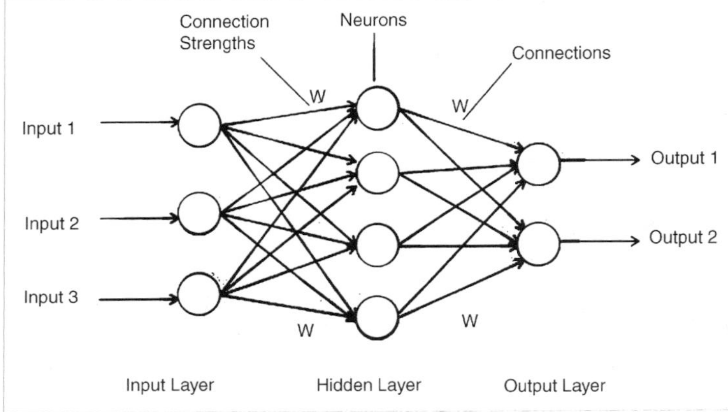

Fig. Architecture of Neural Network.

Neural network performs its operations in two phases: learning phase and testing phase.

LEARNING PHASE

In the proposed methodology, we have taught several SQL attacks to the network in a supervised manner. We entrust the system with several variants of any attack and assign it a particular *label.*

Thus we can see that system learns by feeding various patterns of the same attack. During the *training process of neural network*, matrix of inbox mails and spam mails is used as input matrix to the neural network. In the proposed methodology, the input matrix is updated after defined time interval. Any neural network adjusts the weights of attacks in order to learn in a supervised or unsupervised manner.

In our method of learning, each candidate attack taught to the network is associated with a weight matrix. Weight matrix associated with the kth spam is assigned the label Wk. Weight matrix is updated with the progress of the learning of the spam mail. This matrix is initialised to zero when learning phase starts.

An input pattern corresponding to the spam is taught to the submitted to the network.According to information compiled by Commtouch Software Ltd., E-mail spam for the first quarter of 2010 can be broken down as follows.

Table. E-mail Spam by Topic.

Pharmacy	81%
Replica	5.40%
Enhancers	2.30%
Degrees	1.30%
Casino	1%
Phishing	2.30%
Weight Loss	0.40%
Other	6.30%

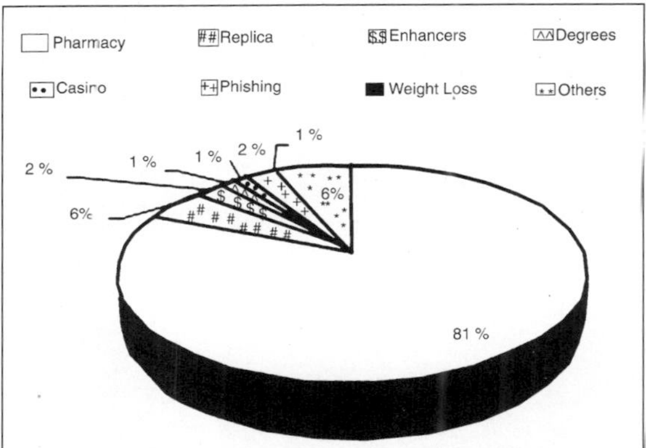

Fig. Spam e-mails Distribution by Topic.

Due to following characteristics, currently the identification process of spam mails is a difficult problem.

- Spam heterogeneity
- Spam definition

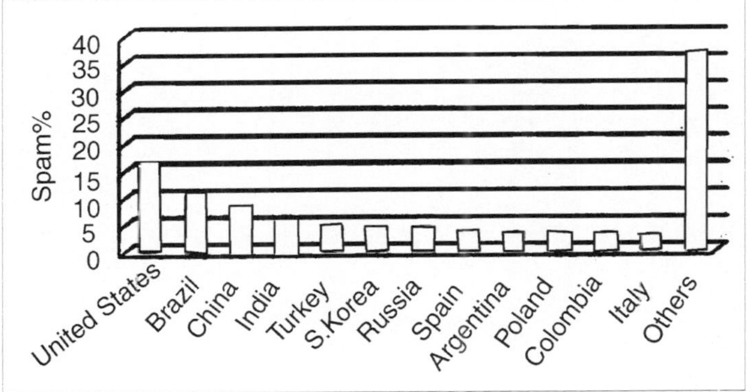

Fig. Represents the Spam Distribution over Various Countries.

By continent, Asia continues to dominate in spam, with more than a third of the world's unsolicited junk e-mail relayed by the region. Asia covers 34.8

per cent spam mails over all the spam mails. The breakdown of spam relaying by continent is as follows.

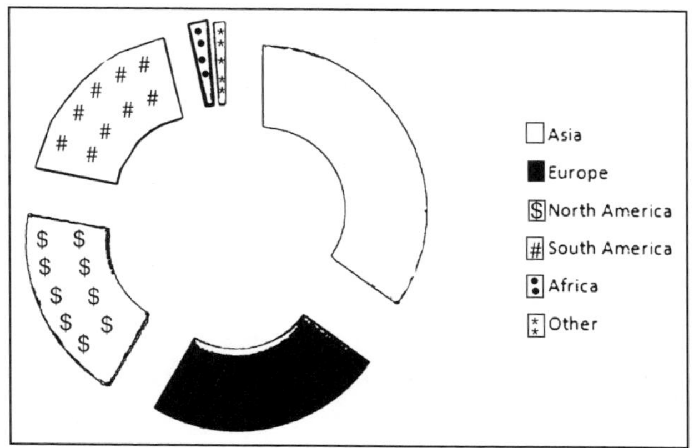

Fig. Spam Distribution over Various Regions.

SPAMMER APPROACHES AND THEIR ATTACK

There are many techniques adopted by the spammer or attackers to collect and store the e-mail addresses or personal information etc. Some of those approaches are from posts to UseNet with e-mail address, from mailing lists, from web pages, from various web and paper forms, via an Ident daemon, from a web browser, from IRC and chat rooms, from finger daemons, from AOL profiles, from domain contact points, by guessing and cleaning, from white and yellow pages, from a previous owner of the e-mail address, by having access to the same computer, using social engineering, from the address book and e-mails on other people's computers, buying lists from others, by hacking into sites and etc.

Delete all spam messages now (messages that have been in Spam more than 30 days will be automatically deleted)

Charity Donation	**MID YEAR PROMO ALERT** - Your E-L.D won the sum of 1000000 00usd on our Mid Year O	Jul 23
utaosa8331	**Original boosters for men** - http://www.refillyle77t.ru	Jul 23
MICROSOFT CUSTOMER SER\	**REFNO.:MS/75-A08055161/2010** - MICROSOFT CUSTOMER SERVICE REFNO. MS/75-A(	Jul 23
MICROSOFT CUSTOMER SER\	**REFNO:MS/75-A08055161/2010 !!** - MICROSOFT CUSTOMER SERVICE REFNO. MS/75-/	Jul 23
PHP Classes	**[PHP Classes] New class daily digest of 2010-07-22** - PHP Classes elePHPant Icontem I	Jul 23
PharmacyForMen	**gauravtakswm, you win a 80% discount. American** - If you are unable to see the messa	Jul 23
atodi7203	**Wholesale drugs for sex** - http://www.refillyle77t.ru	Jul 22
• » αнυзα тнє ѕιℓєηт кιℓ.	**orkut - • » αнυзα тнє wants to be your friend on orkut!** - Hi Gaurav Tak, • » αнυзα тнє ѕιℓєηт	Jul 22
Admail	**Shift the way you move.** - YouMint AdMail To: gauravtakswm@gmail.com (Code- mwsk) :	Jul 22
CheaperViagra with brand.	**Special discount for gauravtakswm. and careful evidence Association** - If you are una	Jul 22
PHP Classes	**[PHP Classes] New class daily digest of 2010-07-21** - PHP Classes elePHPant Icontem I	Jul 22
pixawyo9064	**Best meds for best sex** - http://www.drugstimothy69c.ru	Jul 22
Best-Store of MalePills	**User gauravtakswm was chosen for 70% discounts. his m toll of** - Issue 151 / July 22, 2	Jul 21
Best-Store of MalePills	**User gauravtakswm was chosen for 70% discounts. States major is the** - Issue 110 / Ju	Jul 21
me	**Only trustworthy pills for sex** - http://www.pillpalmer25c.ru	Jul 21
Admail	**Find a match in your community & profession.** - YouMint AdMail To: gauravtakswm@gn	Jul 21
me	**Dear gauravtakswm@gmail.com VIAGRA © Official Site -20%** - Click here. Dear gaurav	Jul 21
Best-Store of MalePills	**User gauravtakswm was chosen for 70% discounts. concerned National Grove** - Issue	Jul 21
PHP Classes	**[PHP Classes] Weekly newsletter of Wednesday - 2010-07-21** - PHP Classes elePHPan	Jul 21
ComTechService	**Why we stopped our communication? "I expected more, Olga!** - 108188A69AAD711	Jul 21
GaneshaSpeaks	**Capricornians, your perfect gemstone** - View this mailer online Hello Capricornians, You	Jul 21

Fig. A Spam Box Folder Over the Mailbox.

With a marketing service, a person can arrange his contacts by certain demographics so that he can create custom mailing lists. This means that he can have some newsletters that go to all customers while also having some that only go to women or men or people with a history of shopping in a particular category.

These tailored mailing lists ensure that your messages are only received by customers who may be interested in the subject matter, keeping those who likely would not be from feeling as though they are being spammed and unsubscribing. Currently, a lot of social networking sites exits over WWW. Some sites are really useful but some creates spam mails over the mailbox. With social networking sites,when a person joins some social networking Web site (like shtyle.fm, yaari.com, indiarocks.com, mycantos.com, facebook.com, tagged.com etc.), then these social site use some script to approach contacts (contact mail list) of that person and send invitation to his contacts to join the same social site. Many times they fill spam mails in peoples' inbox using this approach. There are also many several attacks over the mailbox by the spammers. Some spammers generate spam mails over the mailbox using the manual script but some use machine generated scripts to generate the spam mails.

RELATED WORK

In literature, there are many techniques described for the detection of spam and mail filtering. Some of the techniques are described as follows: A Rule approach has been proposed for the detection of spam mails. The discussed approach uses the training and testing phases of data. Moreover, the stale and obsolete spam rules suspend during the training.

This action is used for improving the spam filtering efficiency. However, the time complexity is higher due to the rules generation and their execution. E. Damiani *et al.* discussed some basic properties of the spam mails. They focused on the reasons of the popularity of spam mails. The uses of the digests in the proposed approach to identify spam mails in a privacy-preserving way is a fundamental technique for collaborative ltering. A social network is constructed based on e-mail exchanges between various users. Spammers are identified by observing abnormalities in the structural properties of the network.

Many times spammer uses the public social sites for increasing their mail list database. However, it is a reactive mechanism since spammers are identified after they have already sent spam. In a novel approach has been discussed, which creates a Bayesian network out of e-mail exchanges to detect spam. Though Bayesian classifiers can be used for detecting spam e-mails, they inherently need to scan the contents of the e-mail to compute the probability distributions for every node in the network.

Since many times it is not possible, to detect spam mails for the particular inbox and its requirement for filtering the spam mails. Nitin Jindal *et al.* discussed an approach of review spam. Review spam is quite different from Web page spam and e-mail spam, and thus requires different detection techniques.There is an effective technique to detect the spam mail that is 'Fast Effective Botnet Spam Detection'. It uses the header information of mails to detect the spam mails. It is useful for both 'Text based spam' as well as 'image based spam'. It analyses the sender IP address, sender e-mail address, MX records and MX hosts. One approach is also described to detect the spam mails, it use the Bayesian calculation for single keyword sets and multiple keywords sets, along with its keyword contexts to improve the spam detection.

PROPOSED METHODOLOGY

Before proposing a new methodology for spam detection, we are aware of this fact that most of time spam mails and scams are spread out using the machine generated script. In this paper, we are proposing a new query based cross layer approach for the above that is based on the above facts and some other spam features.

Our system uses some knowledge base and query generation using the history of previous mails and spam mails which is specific for the each user or its mailbox. Using the knowledge base, detection of spam mails is performed. It also maintains some keywords list, which can easily be pointed out as some words or content in the incoming mail, then perform the detection operation. Many times when a person clicks a URL which is present in his mailbox, (that URL has been provided by the spammers) then mail address of the person is captured by the spammer and is easily inserted in spammer's database. Proposed spam detection approach, follow the few steps to indentify the spam mails.

ANALYSE THE MAIL CONTENT

Firstly, proposed approach analyse the mail content and sender mail address of the mail, then cross analyse and compare the content and sender address of the previous spam mails if content and sender address both are already present in any of the previous spam mails then it directly declares the mail as *"a spam"* (a spam is already present with the same sender and same mail content). If the some fraction of incoming mail content matches with the any previous spam mail then mail is filtered using the spam threshold value (St).

The spam threshold value can be defined as the mathematical value which decides the performance and accuracy of spam detection system. It can be different for various systems.

It is used to indentify the spam mails with the partially matching case.

- If St =0.7 and matching fraction of the content of mail matches with the previous declared spam mails is greater than equal to 0.7, then the mail is declared as *"a spam"*.
- *Matching fraction of the content= max.(NM1/N1, NM2/N2, …., NMp/Np)*
- NMp: Total number of exactly matched words of incoming mail with the pth spam mail.
- Np: Total number of words in p-th spam mail.
- P: The total no. of recent mails which are available in the spam mail list corresponding to that user.

Using the analysis step, following mail from PHP-classes is detected as spam mail because it was already present in the spam folder and user never communicated with the sender mail id.

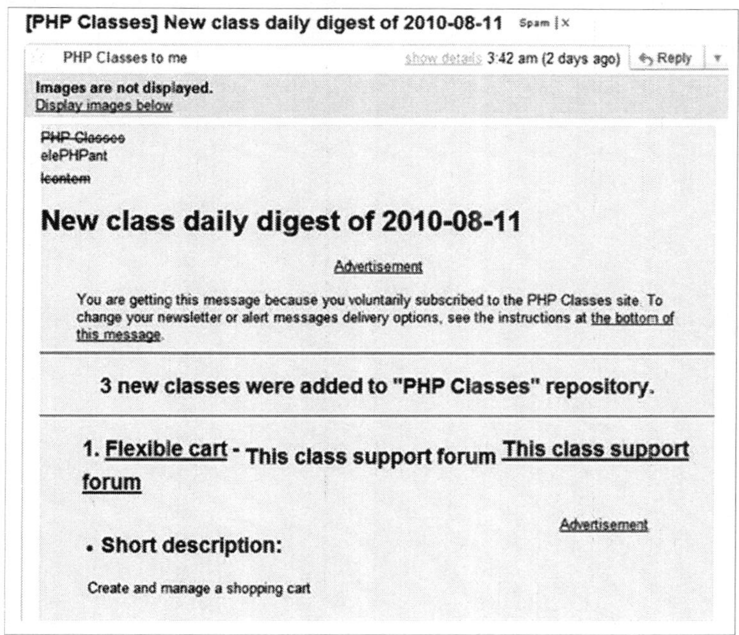

Fig. A Spam mail from the PHP Classes.

TRUSTED KNOWLEDGE BASE

Knowledge Base is always a good, efficient and faster approach to give the results based on historical data. It is used some queries to execute the results. It also follow some update operation to make the result efficient based on the system requirements. In the Trusted Knowledge Base, database of trusted sender is stored over the inbox based on the frequency of the communication of mails. The Knowledge Base is also updated upon the requirement of inbox or threshold count of incoming mails. This Knowledge Base is responsible to the detection of spam mails when sender of incoming is already kept in the trusted zone. If the sender is not the trusted sender then next steps would be executed to indentify the spam mails.

KEYWORDS KNOWLEDGE BASE

To execute this step, A knowledge base is maintained at mail server for each user which stores the spam keywords (already defined by the specific user). During this step, proposed approach analyses the keywords of mails with the keywords knowledge base of spam which is prepared by the particular user for detection of spam. Using the result it decides that incoming mail belongs to the spam category or not. If incoming mail has not been declared as "*spam*" then execute the other steps to indentify the spam mails.

SENDER MAIL ADDRESS

Our proposed methodology extract the sender mail address using the mail header (check the *from* field or *reply-to* field to get the sender e-mail address) and analyse it to indentify the spam. Using the sender e-mail address, system finds that have any communication been done previously between receiver and sender or not? If receiver has already communicated with that mail address, then mail is declared as "*not a spam*". But if receiver has never communicated, then system explores the contact list of the receiver.

If the sender mail address already present in the contact list then the mail is declared as "*not a spam*".This step is very useful with the public networking site because many times networking sites send invitation using someone contacts.

SENDER LOCATION

This step is useful when mail user receive a mail from the another country which already belongs to the spam mail country. Our approach finds the sender mail server location and then compares the location with the spam mails location. Using this step, we are able to filter out some lottery spam and some Nigerian scams too. Using this step following mail is easily detected as spam mail because nation of mail inbox is INDIA and incoming mail server exists in US and receiver has never communicated with the US mail sender so it can be detected as spam mail. Many mail server use the sender location approach to indentify the spam so they ask to the users country and location at the time of mail registration.

MISBEHAVIOUR OF INCOMING MAIL

This step is executed using the artificial neural network. Artificial Neural Network (ANN) is a scientific discipline that is concerned with the design and development of algorithms that allow computers to adapt their behaviour based on data. ANN automatically learns to recognise complex patterns and makes intelligent and efficient decisions based on data.

In the spam filtering ANN learns the complex pattern of mails and makes intelligent, efficient decisions based on the incoming mail. Proposed methodology executes training phase testing phase using sample set of the mailbox to complete this step. During this step, we are able to predict any misbehaviour event of incoming mails; Machines generated mails, flood of mails over inbox. Misbehaviour can be predicted using the time factor, some sender mail address, some attacks. To detect the Misbehaviour, training phase is executed after each threshold value of incoming mail over inbox.

CROSS VALIDATION

During this step, system will verify the sender that sender is a genuine human user or machine generated user using some cross request.

If the incoming mail is machine generated e-mail, it implies that sender is not human user. So the machine generated mails are not able to validate their identity. Most of the spam mails are detected during this step.

CYBER-ATTACKS AND THE INSURANCE INDUSTRY

As an industry dedicated to accepting risks that people and businesses want or need to shed, the insurance industry is unsurprisingly interested in the increasing risk of cyber-attack. As these risks became larger and more evident with the growth of the Internet, the insurance industry's reaction was essentially twofold. The initial reaction was largely to make it clear that existing business insurance did not include coverage of cyber-risks. The premiums charged for existing types of business insurance essentially did not account for the risk from some form of cyber-attack and thus to cover these risks at the existing lower premium rate would have been economically damaging to the insurance company. In general, the reaction of excluding a new risk once it becomes known is quite common in the insurance industry. One can see it, for example, in the reaction to the 9/11 attacks and in the industry's reaction to the increase of homeowners' claims for mold damage, particularly in Texas. In both cases, these risks were presumed to be included in policies when they were low frequency and low cost risks. Once it became clear that they were not such low frequency and low cost risks, insurance contracts began to specifically exclude them.

The second reaction to this new cyber-risk was to introduce specific policies to cover those risks that had been excluded from traditional business insurance coverage. This largely began occurring in 1999 although some coverage was offered as far back as 1997. The market leader in cyber-risk policies, AIG, is estimated to have approximately 70 per cent of the market for cyber-risk insurance with approximately 2,500 policies issued. Other companies writing policies include Chubb, St. Paul, Zurich American, Hartford, and Ace Ltd. The total premium for such policies has been estimated to be between $60 million and $120 million in 2002. These numbers are, however, quite different compared to those found in other types of commercial insurance. For example, general business liability insurance premiums totaled more than $30 billion in 2002, and AIG is able to lead the market for commercial lines with only 9 per cent of the total commercial market in 2002. Estimates for growth in cyber-insurance coverage are substantial, with the Insurance Information Institute seeing $2 billion in premiums by 2007 or 2008, while Conning and Co. projects a 100 per cent annual growth rate and a total premium volume as high as $6 billion by 2006.The policies offered by the companies in this area vary greatly as to the terms and coverages. There is no standard cyber-insurance policy. Policies can include both first party and third party risks with most companies apparently showing a preference for covering third party risks before covering first party risks. This seems to be due to a faith that the computer systems under a company's direct control are sufficiently secured to prevent direct loss of company data or the like. Risks that can be covered include: network security (damage due to direct attack on a network/transmission of a virus/unauthorized access), web content (copyright infringement/libel or slander claims from material posted on a Web site), business interruption (lost income due to loss of computer function after an attack), cyber-extortion (settlement of an extortion attempt against a network), and public relations (cost of repairing a company's image after a cyber-attack).

The principal challenge facing the insurance industry in this realm is a lack of data. Insurance pricing rests critically on an understanding of the risks that are being transferred, particularly the frequency of the risk and the possible damages that could result. With enough experience and data, the insurance industry can be extremely accurate in its predictions and very efficient at dealing with risk, even with risks that might be very rare or very damaging. The risks to be covered by cyber-insurance, however, were not only unexpected, but also are to a large degree qualitatively different from what has been seen in the past. This leads to a situation where insurers are writing policies without the type of information that they prefer, particularly when compared to lines like fire or auto where insurers have long historical experience. AIG might estimate, as it has, that computer viruses caused $13 billion in damage in 2001. However, this would only be the beginning of the questions that might need to be answered. What is the likely frequency of such attacks? Is this number a high number or low number compared to what the costs might be in the future? What steps has a particular company taken to mitigate the damage from a future attack and will these steps be successful in doing so? Successfully pricing insurance in the long run demands answers to such questions. The experience that a few years have given the companies is important and the estimates now are more accurate than they were five years ago, but more experience is certainly needed before insurers will as comfortably write cyber-risk polices as they write other lines today.

CYBER-TERROR THREAT

In order to assess the macroeconomic effects of a cyber-attack on computers it may first be useful to examine how computers contribute to economic activity. It is that contribution that is presumed to be at some risk.

Robert Solow, a major contributor to the theory of economic growth, is often quoted for his remark that the effect of computers can be seen everywhere but in the productivity statistics. Through the 1980s and early 1990s, there seemed to be no big payoff from the growing stock of computers. That presented a puzzle to those who expected significant returns. But it is now believed that computers have had much to do with an acceleration in productivity growth that began in the mid-1990s.

Consumers have come to expect a rapid rate of innovation in the manufacture of computers. It is also widely expected that the speed and memory capacity of those computers will continue to improve rapidly. Such a rapid rate of technological advance in the development and manufacture of computers was predicted in 1965 by Gordon E. Moore, one of the co-founders of Intel Corporation. Specifically "Moore's Law" predicted that the number of transistors that could be put on a computer chip would double every 18 months. Whether or not that prediction was a self-fulfilling prophecy may be open to question, but the fact is that the pace of technological advance in the manufacture of computers has vindicated Moore's Law over time.

Because of the rapid innovation in the production of computer chips, the prices of computers, as well as other goods related to information processing and communications, sometimes referred to collectively as information technology (IT), have been falling steadily for some time. Between 1959 and 1995, computer prices fell at an average annual rate of nearly 16.9 per cent, and between 1995 and 2002 prices fell at an annual rate of 20.1 per cent.

These price declines reflect substantial improvements in the quality of computers. The Bureau of Labour Statistics (BLS) has developed a procedure for estimating price indexes for goods whose characteristics are changing rapidly. These are referred to as "hedonic" price indexes. Hedonic price indexes attempt to estimate a statistical relationship between prices and a set of characteristics, such as memory and processor speed.

These price indexes are important to the measurement of productivity, because estimating price change is necessary to estimating change in real output and thus productivity. If the rate of price decline in computers is overestimated, then measures of productivity will be overstated. Most studies estimate that, in the late 1990s, prices for personal computers alone fell at an annual rate of somewhere between 30 per cent and 40 per cent.

Rapid declines in computer prices have, not surprisingly, stimulated a surge in investment. Although there are data back to 1959, production of computers was negligible until the 1980s. Thus, even though real output of IT equipment was increasing rapidly, it did not account for a very large share of total output until recently.

Computers have affected growth in productivity in at least two ways. *First*, there has been rapid productivity growth in the production of computers which, as computers accounted for an increasing share of total production, tended to raise the overall measure of productivity growth. *Second*, the sharp drop in computer prices has stimulated increased investment in computers, which has contributed to an increase in the overall amount of capital available to the workforce. This is often referred to as "capital deepening." Increases in the capital stock generally tend to raise worker productivity.

In part because of increased spending on IT equipment, the overall rate of investment spending rose significantly in the 1990s. Prior to the recent acceleration in productivity growth, most analyses found that computers yielded little benefit. One reason is that, until recently, computers accounted for a relatively small share of the total capital stock.

But, that view has now changed. Economists are encouraged that the acceleration in productivity growth of the late 1990s may mean that the economy is on a higher growth path and many believe that computers have had a lot to do with it.

Two recent studies found considerable evidence that the computer, or more generally IT equipment, is behind most of the recent acceleration in productivity growth. There is also evidence of a modest "spillover" into other sectors of the economy. In other words, investment in computers can raise the productivity of the workers who use them, but it may also lead firms to change the way they operate leading to further productivity gains.

The first study, by Oliner and Sichel at the Federal Reserve Board, found that of a 0.9 percentage point increase in the growth rate of total factor productivity from the first half of the 1990s to the second half, all could be accounted for by advances in the production of computers themselves and the also by the use of those computers.

NEW GENERATION ATTACKS

SMURF ATTACKS

These techniques are named after the Programmes that launch the attacks. In a Smurf attack, the hacker sends out an ICMP echo request packet, or "ping" command to a computer network with the return IP address of the targeted victim. The network's server broadcasts the "ping" through the system's network and the computers send a reply back. If the network is large enough, those packets will swamp the victim's computer and possibly bring the computer down.

Fraggle

The Fraggle attacks are similar to the Smurf attacks, except they use UDP echo packets to overwhelm a network computer.

Papasmurf

Papasmurf combines Smurf and Fraggle by launching ping requests with ICMP echo packets and UDP echo packets. This program's two-headed assault makes it more difficult for administrators to defend themselves.

DISTRIBUTED DENIAL OF SERVICE ATTACKS

Distributed Denial of Service attacks ("DDoS") are a natural development in the search for more effective and debilitating denial of service attacks. Instead of using just one computer to launch an attack, the hacker enlists numerous computers to attack the target computer from numerous launch points. Prior to an attack, the hacker places a daemon, or a small computer Programme, on an innocent third-party computer. These third-party computers are often referred to as "zombies" or "soldiers." The "slave" daemons are remotely controlled by the "master" Programme to launch attacks against certain servers. By distributing the source of attacks across a wider array of zombie computers, the attacker has made it more difficult for the target server to block off the attack routes.

Trinoo (June 1999)

On August 17, 1999, a Trinoo network of at least 227 systems was used to flood a single server at the University of Minnesota, including more than 100 compromised computers at the University of Washington. The attack rendered the system inoperable for two days.

There has been speculation that Trinoo was one of the Programmes that brought down Yahoo and other major Internet sites in February 2000. Trinoo is used to create distributed denial of service UDP flood attacks. There is concern that Trinoo could enlist common desktop computers in a DDoS attack by loading a daemon on the local computer through an e-mail attachment. According to one estimate, Trinoo networks are "being set up on hundreds, perhaps thousands, of systems that are being compromised by remote buffer overrun exploitation."

After the attacker has placed the daemons on the intermediary computers, master Programmes are set up on other computers to act as commanders to call "the troops" into action. The attacker only needs to access the master

Programmes, via telnet, to launch the massive, coordinated attacks. Both the slave and master Programmes are password controlled to prevent system administrators from taking control of the Trinoo network. Once the attacker has accessed the master, he only needs to enter the IP address of the targeted server in a "dos IP" command to wake up the daemon "zombies" that begin launching their massive queries at the target. The attacker is also able to launch attacks against multiple targets using the "mdos" command. Finally, the attacker can set a time limit for the DoS attack.

Tribe Flood Network (August 1999)

Tribe Flood Network, ("TFN"), is a DDoS Programme written by a German hacker that is capable of launching ICMP, SYN Flood, UDP Flood and Smurf attacks. In late August, 1999, DDoS attackers began to shift from Trinoo to TFN. Using TFN, a single attacker can launch an attack from dozens of computers on which the attacker has surreptitiously placed the TFN daemon. The attacker remotely controls the TFN client network using a variety of connection methods, including telnet TCP connections. Unlike various versions of Trinoo, TFN clients do not require a password to be activated, although the client sends commands to the daemon in an ICMP packet. However, there is no telnet TCP or UDP-based communication between the client and the daemon, making detection of the client's call to action more difficult to detect on the client, or master, system.

Tribe Floodnet 2k (January 2000)

Tribe Floodnet 2k ("TFN2K") is an updated version of the TFN DDoS attack tool. According to Mixter, the German hacker who wrote the Programme, TFN2K still contains the popular features of the original TFN, including the client/server functionality, stealth, and encryption techniques. However, Mixter added several new features that make the system more robust and deadly, including remote one-way command instructions to the distributed servers who go on to launch the attacks. Also, TFN2K boasts stronger encryption between the client and the server.

Stacheldraht (October 1999)

The most recent advance in DDoS attacks has come in the form of Stacheldraht, a German word for "Barbed Wire." Stacheldraht has the ability to automatically update the daemon Programmes, reducing the attacker's risk of intrusion. Stacheldraht was based on the source code from Tribe Flood Network, with at least two significant new features. The communication between the attacker and the Stacheldraht masters are encrypted and the daemons can be automatically updated by the masters. One of the weaknesses of TFN was the attacker's connection to the master Programme located on the remote computers. Stacheldraht combines Trinoo's master/daemon control features with TFN's ICMP flood, SYN flood, UDP flood, and Smurf attacks. The attackers control the master computers through encrypted clients, and each master can control up to 1000 daemons that are installed on innocent third-party computers. The attack begins in the preparation stage, called the "mass-intrusion phase," where large numbers of computers are compromised. The attacker places the Stacheldraht daemons on the compromised systems and the daemons lie in wait for the command to attack. The third-party computers are also victims in these attacks because the systems have been compromised and they use up bandwidth and processing power.

TRACKING DOWN THE ATTACKERS

The Federal Bureau of Investigation ("FBI") has had a very difficult time locating the origin of the attackers because of the networked nature of the Internet, the spoofing of the DoS packets, and the procedural difficulty of organizing an investigation that involves countless jurisdictions. One method used to track the attacker is to start from the targeted server and locate the immediate server that sent the packet. However, because the packet was carrying "false identification," each subsequent router along the network could lead the investigator astray.

Because the packet's "false papers" hide the true origin of the packet, it is difficult to reconstruct the origin of the spoofed packets after the fact. In order to determine where the packet came from, the investigators must set up a filer, or "trace and trap," before they arrive at that particular router. This is complicated by fact that the packet could cross as many as thirty different routers owned by ten different companies in several different legal jurisdictions. In the February, 2000 attacks on the major Internet sites, the authorities have identified several university computers that were compromised and used to attack the targeted servers.

The actual technique of spoofing can be complicated. For example, a traditional method of spoofing was to initiate a DoS attack on Computer B, the computer that one eventually wants to spoof. When Computer B is overwhelmed, it is not able to respond to requests from Computer C that it is requesting ACKs, or confirmation — trying to confirm they are who they said they are. The TCP tags each datagram with a sequential number. If Computer C receives a packet that is out of sequence, it will discard the packet or hold, depending on how close the packet is to the number it is looking for. The hacker, using Computer A, estimates the number that Computer C is looking for and pretends to be sending packets from Computer B by using Computer B's information or identification. Computer B is unable to stop this use of his identification because he is spending all of his time answering the false packets from another computer that the hacker has set up to send the packets.

THE CFAA AND DENIAL OF SERVICE

In any criminal law analysis, the specifics of the crime will determine which statutory section can be successfully applied. For example, the exact definition of an "intrusion" can determine whether inserting a debit card into a exterior cash machine constitutes burglary. The individual characteristics of a Denial of Service attack may also change which computer crime statutes can be applied to the attack. For example, in the above TFN2K example where the attacker used Computer A to plant "servers" on Computers B, C, and D to attack Computer F, will a traditional hacking statute be applicable for the attack on Computer F? Under 18 U.S.C. § 1030(a)(5)(B) and (C), the statute prohibits "access" of a protected computer. However, are these anti-hacking statutes applicable to an attacker whose intent was to "deny access" to, rather than to merely access, the computer?

The CFAA is the primary federal anti-hacking statute, and contains seven main sections. The first section, § 1030(a)(1), protects against the knowing access of government computers to obtain classified information. This section is not applicable.

The second section, § 1030(a)(2), proscribes the intentional access of a computer without, or in excess of authorization, to thereby obtain information from a financial institution, the federal government, or any protected computer involved in interstate or foreign communications—essentially any computer connected to the Internet. This section is concerned with the protection of information. The point of all of the DoS attacks is not to obtain information, but rather to bring the system down.

The third section, § 1030(a)(3), is concerned with the intentional and unauthorized access of government computers or computers used by the government. In a standard DoS attack where only one computer is used to attack another, this section is unlikely to be invoked unless the attacker targeted a computer that "is used by or for the Government of the United States and such conduct affects that use by or for the Government of the United States."

However, in a DDoS attack, there is a better chance that this section may be relevant if the attacker placed an attack daemon on a § 1030(a)(3) protected computer. Many university computers, for example, are used by the federal government. Even slight activity by the daemon on the university computer could "affect" the government's use of the computer.

The access and fraudulent use of a protected computer and is triggered if the value of the use obtained exceeds $5,000. Congress intended this subsection to apply, for example, to use by hackers who take over a supercomputer to run a password-breaking Programme. The "zombie" computers who were infected by the daemon and enlisted into the attack suffered a loss of processor power and bandwidth. This subsection could be applied against the attacker for each computer the hacker enlisted in the assault. With the subsection providing for a jail term for up to five years per instance, a hacker who plants hundreds of daemons could be liable for an extensive prison sentence.

One of the critiques of this subsection is the $5,000 damage threshold. Prosecutors have found that the $5,000 damage requirement is often both difficult to establish and an impediment to investigation. It is sometimes speculative to assess $5,000 damages if the attacker only used the computer to launch attacks. In *United States v. Middleton*, the defendant challenged the government's theory of calculating the $5,000 in damages to Slip.net, an Internet Service Provider ("ISP"). The court held that the government's theory of loss "will be that the damage caused by defendant to the Slip.net computers caused Slip.net employees to expend time to investigate, identify, and correct the damage caused by Middleton, and take other security related steps." The court agreed with the government "that the time the employees expended can be fairly valued at a figure of at least their hourly wage or salary, plus the value of benefits and overhead" provided adequate explanation of the government's theory.

In addition to the uncertainty concerning the factors used to calculate the $5,000, federal authorities currently have to wait for a damage assessment to determine if there is federal jurisdiction, delaying time-sensitive investigations. For example, if a DoS attack is launched on a California web site, but the attack originated in New York, was routed through a server in New Jersey, and bounced off a computer in Wisconsin on its way to California, investigators may be required to petition the court in each jurisdiction for an order to place a trace on the activity. Under a new legislative proposal by Senators Charles Schumer and Jon Kyl, the federal government would unambiguously permit federal jurisdiction as soon as the attack occurs, rather than waiting for the damage assessment. Also, damage estimates below $5,000 will be treated as a misdemeanor, while damage above $5,000 will still be treated as a felony. Finally, proposed legislation specifies that the costs of responding to the attack, damage assessment costs, repair to the system and lost revenue from the interruption of service will be counted Towards the $5,000 damage amount. Under the present statute, the damage calculation method is unclear and there has been little judicial precedent to provide guidance for allowable damage factors.

The main anti-hacking subsection. Subsection 1030(a)(5)(A) applies to whomever "knowingly causes the transmission of a Programme, information, code, or command, and as a result of such conduct, intentionally causes damage without authorization, to a protected computer." The DoS and DDoS attacker would be liable under this subsection both to the "zombie" systems and the targeted systems. The attacker causes the transmission of a Programme on the "zombie" system and intentionally causes damage. The attacker also causes the transmission of information, the packets, and code, the datagrams that intentionally cause damage. This subsection provides serious sentencing guidelines. A first-time conviction can subject the attacker to up to five years in prison for each occurrence. According to United States Sentencing Commission, "[i]f the defendant is convicted under 18 U.S.C. Section 1030 (a)(4) or (5), the minimum guideline sentence, notwithstanding any other adjustment, shall be six months' imprisonment."

Section 1030(a)(5)(B) prohibits unauthorized access that recklessly causes damage to a protected computer. Violation of this subsection is also a felony. However, the standard of reckless disregard is below the intentional damage provided under § 1030(a)(5)(A). If the prosecutor can show that the damage was intentional, as all DoS and DDoS attacks are, then the reckless disregard is unnecessary.Section 1030(a)(5)(C) covers negligent damage to a protected computer. There is almost no conceivable scenario where this subsection could be used. Congress intended to punish the activity of hackers who do not intend to harm the systems but accidentally cause harm to the computer in the process.

To only punish intentional harm would condone hacking into systems as long as no harm was done to the system. However, in DoS and DDoS attacks, there could be no other reason a person would plant a daemon on another computer, or launch a DoS attack against another computer. Perhaps it is feasible that a curious computer user would enter a large ping command for another computer without a full understanding of the consequences. However, such conduct would be more reckless than negligent.

The unauthorized trafficking of computer passwords and is not relevant to DoS attacks. Likewise, § 1030(a)(7) covers extortion threats against computer or network owners. This subsection would only be invoked if the attacker threatened to launch a DoS attack against the victim unless the victim pays the attacker "any money or other thing of value."

DoS Summary

Denial of Service attacks represent a significant threat to the stability of our network infrastructure because of the inherent vulnerability in the TCP/IP 3-handshake reliable protocol. Successful prosecution of the perpetrators should raise the awareness that DoS and DDoS are very serious crimes with serious consequences.

Also, system administrators are likely to collaborate in devising plans for rapid network response to thwart the source of the attacks. However, where the system administrator's carrot may be minimized damage to their systems, the stick may be potential tort liability for allowing their system to be used in an attack against another server.

The tort standard of negligence could be: would a "reasonably prudent system administrator" have allowed a hacker to place a DDoS daemon on his system, and "but for" his negligence, the targeted server would not have been overloaded without his contribution? If the "zombie" computers were held liable for negligent administration of their servers, this also may help secure the Internet against DDoS attacks. Finally, the CFAA provides for a civil action for those who suffer any damage or loss against someone who violates 18 U.S.C. § 1030(a). The laws are in place to address the issue. Unfortunately, the greatest impediment to prosecuting will continue to be technical difficulty of tracing the route of the attack back to the perpetrator.

SECURITY AND DATA INTEGRITY THREATS

The range of means by which the security and integrity of computing resources can be threatened is very broad, and encompasses:

- Operator error (for example a user inadvertently deleting the wrong file).
- Hardware or media failure (either as a result of wear-and-tear, old age or accidental damage).
- Theft or sabotage (of hardware and/or data or its media).
- Hackers (who obtain unauthorised online access via the Internet).
- Malware (any form of virus, and including "Trojan" e-mail attachments that users are encouraged to open).
- Power surges and/or outages (which are one of the most common means of hard disk corruption and hardware damage).
- Flood, fire, storm or other natural disasters.
- Fraud or embezzlement.
- Industrial espionage.
- Terrorism.

Physical Security Measures

Given the breadth of the human reliance on computer technology, physical security arrangements to try and ensure that hardware and storage media are not compromised by theft or unauthorised access are more important today than ever before. And yet surprisingly they still often not taken seriously enough. Indeed, the number of high-profile instances of CDs, DVDs, hard disks and laptops going missing from government offices in the United Kingdom over the past year is quite staggering. Not least due to advances in mobile and cloud computing, computing resources are more vulnerable to theft than ever before. Twenty or more years ago, most computer equipment and data lived in a secure IT "glass house" well out of the reach of the casual thief, and with the hardware involved of little or no street value anyway. However, this is obviously no longer the case.

Personal and business data is now stored across a wide range of organisational, cloud vendor and personal locations, more work is conducted at home than since the rise of the modern city, and IT departments therefore have a right to be nervous. At the very least, physical computing security measures—such as external building safeguards and the control of access to areas of a building where computers are located—should be subject to regular formal updating and review. Most large organizations—particularly in the public sector—have a horror story or several to tell of computer equipment that has "walked". Many such stories suggest that people who walk out of buildings with computer equipment under their arm are rarely challenged (and sometimes even assisted!). Locking-down computer equipment and/or ensuring adequate door and window security at all computer locations should today just be pure common sense.

Physical security also needs to be particularly carefully considered in semi-public locations (such as many open plan offices). For example, it needs to be considered how easy it would be for somebody to gain access to a PC, insert a USB memory stick, and walk away with valuable or sensitive data. Large corporate data centres in which the computer equipment is located in an air conditioned room typically have fire control systems that will hermetically seal the location and put out a fire using an inert gas. In smaller companies and domestically this clearly is not an option. However, whilst computers themselves may be at risk from fire (and indeed the cause of a fire!), back-up media can be protected in a fire safe, and/or via off-site storage. The physical security ofstorage media against the threats of fire, flood and other forms of damage.

Alongside theft, fire and flood, the other most significant threat that can damage computer equipment and/or the data held on it comes from power surges (voltage spikes) or power outages (brown-outs or black-outs). Many hard disk failures in particular are thought to be linked to power surge or outage issues of which users are often unaware. To protect against this very real but often ignored threat to computer equipment and data, a power surge protector and/or uninteruptable power supply (UPS) unit can be employed. Surge protectors are relatively cheap and protect against voltage spikes. They are today often built into multi-socket outlets with an insurance guarantee included for the connected equipment.

For even greater protection, a UPS unit includes a rechargeable battery that will continue to power a computer and key peripherals during a mains power brown-out or black-out. Software is usually also used to permit a controlled shut-down of equipment when a power black-out occurs. UPS units are more expensive than surge protectors, somewhat bulky, and often very heavy. However, for a server or key personal computer (such as one used to run a business or key part thereof) they are also a very good investment.

Minimising the Impact of Error, Failure or Loss

Whilst physical threats need to be protected against, most data is lost or corrupted following user error or hardware failure. The best defence against this is an appropriate back-up strategy, triggered on both a time and event basis and with appropriate physical resilience. In other words, users need to ensure that they take regular backs-ups at regular intervals and before and after making key data changes. They also need to store multiple back-ups on different media in different locations. There is no such thing as a permanent store of any form of computer data. Nor is any storage location entirely safe (although the cloud data centres run by Google, Amazon, IBM, Microsoft and other computing industry giants are pretty well protected these days!). Whilst any back-up strategy does require the selection of appropriate storage media, user education is often an equally key a consideration. Taking regular back-ups is at best only half of the story. Far too many individuals and businesses keep their back-up media—be they removable hard drives, optical disks and even USB memory sticks, in an entirely insecure manner in the same physical location as their computer. Even in corporate IT departments this has been known. Such practice has to significantly reduce the value of back-ups.

When making their disaster recovery plans and addressing the key computer security questions, the location of back-up media needs careful consideration. Even on a domestic level, most households could keep a few writable CD or DVD disks (or even SD cards) of key back-ups (including photographs and their music collection) in a secure location (in the roof or under a floorboard or with family and friends or wherever), and which would provide significantly increased data storage resilience. However, unfortunately most people still only ever think of this kind of simple strategy after it is too late.

Passwords and Appropriate User Authentication

Physically protecting computer equipment and data against damage or loss is a large element of computer security. However, another large element is limiting access to all or part of a system or data store to authorised users only.

In the broadest of terms, user authorisation within any security system can be verified via one three means:

- Something known by the individual (a piece of information such as a password)
- Something possessed by the individual (a physical token such a credit, security or ID card), or
- A biometric characteristic of the individual (for example their signature, finger print, retinal scan or DNA).

For good security, two of the above measures should be employed for what is known as "two-factor security". For example, to obtain money from a bank cash machine both a card and a PIN (personal identification number password) are required. Where computer security is concerned, one measure of user verification will almost always be a password given the relative technical ease with which this can be implemented. Computer keyboards, mobile computers and dedicated input devices that include finger print readers are also becoming more common, and can be combined with passwording to achieve two-factor security. ID cards and even retinal scans are also used in conjunction with passwords on high-end security systems. However, any system that requires a token or biometric to be read has proved difficult to rollout en-mass. This said, recently some banks have started to provide each customer with a reader device into which their bank card is inserted. This allows for two-factor security, as the unit displays a number for each transaction that is uniquely in sequence with their bank.

Today at least, and probably in practice for many years to come, one-factor security based on passwords is all that is available for identifying authorised users in the majority of computing situations. This in turn means that users must be educated to use strong passwording—or in other words, to choose and use passwords in a manner that makes the password difficult to either fathom or otherwise obtain by an unauthorised party.

To be classed as "strong", passwords,

- Should be at least six and preferably eight or more characters in length.
- Should be mixed case alphanumeric (a mix of apparently random upper and lower case letters and numbers is best).
- Should be changed regularly (at least every three months is a common rule).
- Should be known only to the user.
- Should not be obviously related to the user.
- Should be different for each application used.
- Should not be based on data (such as a favourite place) listed publically on Facebook or another social networking site, and
- Should not be written down (let alone stuck on a post-it note on the side of a computer!)

Users should also try and ensure password security by following the measures as outlined below under "Internet Security".

Maintaining Confidentiality

In part the confidentiality of data is protected via physical security measures and appropriate user authentication precautions as already outlined above. However, effective security should plan for what happens if these measures fail, and how data confidentiality can be protected even if computer equipment or media fall into the wrong hands. This is particularly important when it comes to the protection of sensitive information such as financial data. The confidentiality of the data on stolen hardware or of data accessed by unauthorised users can be protected via encryption. For example, software such as the open-source TrueCrypt (available from www.truecrypt.org) can be used to encrypt the data on any storage device (for example a USB key carried in your pocket). Office documents can also or alternatively be protected by securing them with a password. This can be a particularly sensible thing to do when e-mailing sensitive documents, or posting them by snail mail on removable media. In an office package such as the freely downloadable OpenOffice, password protecting a file is as simple as ticking the "save with password" option when selecting "Save As".

Data confidentiality also needs to be protected on output and disposal. In the case of the former, in an open plan office environment precautions should be taken when sending documents containing confidential information to a communal network printer. In the case of the latter, printed output containing sensitive data needs to be disposed of securely (eg via shredding and/or incineration), as do waste media (such as discarded optical disks). At the end of a computer's life or when components are being upgraded, care also needs to be taken to ensure that discarded hard disk drives (including those located in external hard drive units) are appropriately erased before disposal.

Internet Security

The connection of most computers in the world to the Internet, coupled with the growth of cloud computing, has inevitably broadened significantly the scope of computer security and control vulnerabilities. Before the widespread adoption of personal computers, rogue programmers with malicious or criminal intent would try to "hack" into big computing facilities via the phone network. Then, once personal computing really took told, the focus for many such malicious programmers shifted to writing computer viruses that could be unknowingly distributed on floppy disks, and which could hence disrupt the operation of those millions of computers not connected to the telephone network.

Today, this situation has evolved again, with many personal computers having an "always on" broadband connection which makes them potentially prone to unauthorised access via a computer network. And on top of this, the virus writers are still at work, the fruits of their corruptive programming labours now distributed both online and via physical storage media.

Whilst there are very real security risks associated with both the consumer and business use of the Internet, it is also the case than many such security concerns are perceptual. To an extent, all that has really changed over the past few years has been the willingness of people and organizations to conduct their affairs over the world-wide web. The sensible use of a credit card over the web is not that much more secure that it was five years ago. The fact that it has become the norm is therefore due to the fact that the risk/benefit ratio of doing e-business has shifted significantly in favour of the "benefit" side in the eyes of the value-seeking majority. Care, of course, does need to be taken. For a start these days it is foolish in the absolute extreme to run any computer with an Internet connection without antivirus software. Such software—such as the range of Norton security software available from www. symantec.com—is most usually commercially purchased with a yearly subscription for regular updates to its virus definition database. However, it is possible to obtain antivirus software for free. Indeed, my own current recommendation for PC owners is to install Microsoft Security Essentials. For most people this is a very good option, does not hog resources, comes from a reputable organization—and is free!

In addition (though often bundled with) antivirus software, all computers with a potentially always-on Internet connection should be protected via a firewall. Whilst antivirus software is intended to detect and prevent infestation with malicious software (including viruses and other "malware"), the job of a firewall is to regulate the network communications a computer receives, permitting or denying such communications based on how trusted the communications source is considered to be.

Firewalls can be implemented via either hardware or software. A personal computer firewall will almost certainly be software based, although increasingly some form of hardware firewall is being incorporated into wireless ADSL routers (wireless access points). Like antivirus software, a firewall needs to be regularly updated with the latest threat information to be most effective. Windows XP, Vista and Windows 7 all include a software firewall, although many people choose to adopt third party firewall software as an alternative to this.

In addition to antivirus software and a firewall, user vigilance and even plain common sense provide one of the most effective defences against potential Internet-related security vulnerabilities. For example, users should be educated never to open unsolicited (spam) e-mails, and doubly-so never to open any e-mail attachments included with such e-mails (and as may be automatically opened by some configurations of e-mail software). Viruses and other malware (such as "sniffer" software intended to record and communicate usernames and passwords) can be attached as "Trojan" (horses) to e-mails. However, it is only when the user opens such messages and executes their attachments that corruption or security risks can occur.

Users also need to ensure that they use strong passwording when setting up accounts for web transactions. They should also never permit their browser software to remember their login details for a Web site unless they are absolutely certain of who else may have access to the computer they are using. Indeed, it is still potentially unwise to let even a single-user PC remember passwords for activities such as online shopping or online banking. This is because the theft of the PC would permit direct access to the user's bank and other online accounts. Talking of online transactions, users should also be careful only to conduct business online with trusted web sites and over secure (encrypted) connections. Trusted web sites are those that are well known, have an established trading history, and which advertise contact points for both online and off-line customer support. Secure connections can be identified by looking for the letters "HTTPS" (a secure version of the hypertext transfer protocol that facilitates web communications) at the start of the web address seen at the top of a web browser window. HTTPS connections exchange digital certificates to encrypt communications via what is known as a "secure socket layer" (SSL). As a basic rule, never enter your credit card details into a web page without first checking that the address of the page starts "HTTPS".

For users of cloud computing services such as SaaS applications, all of the above points relating to good Internet security clearly apply. Computing in the cloud is still deemed by many to be risky. However, it can also bring security advantages as user data is protected off-site in large vendor data centres. For example users of Google Docs are always safe in the knowledge that their files are always securely stored on two different servers in two different data centres. For private individauls and small companies, such a high level of off-site data protection and replication is hard to achieve by other means.

In addition to using antivirus software, a firewall, strong passwords, and uploading regular operating system and browser updates, it is doubly important for users of the cloud to ensure the security of the computer they use to access their chosen online services. In particular care needs to be taken to make certain that they never leave active accounts on a device that may be stolen or otherwise accessed by inappropriate users. For example, files held in Google Docs or indeed another other SaaS application are not at all secure if a user leaves their netbook or smartphone in a public place and all anybody has to do to gain access is to boot up the machine and visit the appropriate web address. SaaS users who share desktop PCs—or who for example use public desktop computers in cyber cafes—ought also to be very careful indeed to ensure that they log-out from cloud services whenever they finish using them.

Disaster Recovery Planning

Both individuals and in particular businesses should have plans in place to cover the eventuality of hardware failure or loss and/or data loss or corruption. Such disaster recovery or "business continuity" plans need to address how data would be recovered, what hardware would be used to run critical applications, and by whom. Such plans particularly need to take into account any current use of out-of-date software applications that may not be able to be replaced and/or run on replacement hardware and operating systems. To recover back-ups of data that cannot be run on any available hardware and software will not in any way ensure business continuity! Depending on the types of threat they are intended to cover, disaster recover plans may rely on one of a mix of strategies (and a mix is arguably often best). One option is on-site standby, where duplicate systems exist that can be used to run critical operations (provided that data is still available or can be recovered). Such duplicate systems need not necessarily be standing idle waiting for disaster (as they would be in a nuclear power station), but may be everyday systems used in one part of the business that are prepared to run key applications from other parts of a business if the need arises. As an alternative to on-site standby, some sort of off-site standby is very common. If a company has multiple buildings or premises, then it makes sense both to hold off-site back-ups across these locations, and to ensure that key system functionality can be duplicated across sites.

Some businesses also have "reciprocal agreements" with other companies to make use of their computers to run key operations in the event of a disaster (such as a fire that destroys their premises). Often small and medium-sized companies make such reciprocal agreements with nearby schools who have suitable computer suites which they are prepared to offer as an off-site standby provision for a reasonable cost. For larger organizations, or those highly dependent on computing continuity, "hot-site agreements" can be made with firms that offer commercial disaster recovery as a service, and who can deliver (for a price) portable working computer rooms at very short notice.

As a final element of disaster recovery planning, replacement purchase plans should be in place. In the event of fire or theft, the last thing most individual users or companies would want to be thinking about is where to purchase new computer equipment from, and what specification to choose. Not least this is an issue because direct-specification let alone exact-model replacements for any items of computer hardware or software more than a year old are incredibly unlikely to be available.

Data Protection Legislation

We live in a world where data is held on everybody and used and inter-linked for a very wide range of purposes. In an attempt to provide some redress against inappropriate data use, in the United Kingdom the Data Protection Act (DPA) 1998 protects data held on living individuals. Any individual can submit a subject action request to any party that holds data on them. This allows them to obtain a copy of all data held on them within 40 days of the subject action request being received. Following a subject action request, individuals can challenge the validity of the data held on them, and if appropriate can claim compensation relating to any inaccuracy or misuse.

The Data Protection Commissioner is charged with ensuring that all data in the UK "shall be obtained and subsequently processed in a fair and lawful manner". All organizations have to have a "data controller" who, with a few limited exceptions, must register all data stored with the Data Protection Commissioner. They must also be open about the data's purpose, and ensure its accuracy and security. Whilst the Data Protection Act protects individuals on whom data it held, it does not protect data itself or computer systems. Such protection is provided in the United Kingdom by the Computer Misuse Act (CMA) 1990. This created three levels of offence, and which make it illegal to gain unauthorised access to computer material; to gain unauthorised access with intent to commit or facilitate further offences; and to make an authorised modification of computer material. The last of these offences in theory at least makes it illegal to write and distribute computer viruses.

9

Cyber Security and Cyber Crime

Cyber security plays an important role in the ongoing development of information technology, as well as Internet services. Enhancing cyber security and protecting critical information infrastructures are essential to each nation's security and economic well-being.

Making the Internet safer (and protecting Internet users) has become integral to the development of new services as well as governmental policy. Deterring cyber crime is an integral component of a national cyber security and critical information infrastructure protection strategy. In particular, this includes the adoption of appropriate legislation against the misuse of ICTs for criminal or other purposes and activities intended to affect the integrity of national critical infrastructures. At the national level, this is a shared responsibility requiring coordinated action related to the prevention, preparation, response, and recovery from incidents on the part of government authorities, the private sector and citizens. At the regional and international level, this entails cooperation and coordination with relevant partners. The formulation and implementation of a national framework and strategy for cyber security thus requires a comprehensive approach. Cyber security strategies – for example, the development of technical protection systems or the education of users to prevent them from becoming victims of cyber crime – can help to reduce the risk of cyber crime. The development and support of cyber security strategies are a vital element in the fight against cyber crime. The legal, technical and institutional challenges posed by the issue of cyber security are global and far-reaching, and can only be addressed through a coherent strategy taking into account the role of different stakeholders and existing initiatives, within a framework of international cooperation.

In this regard, the World Summit on the Information Society (WSIS) recognised the real and significant risks posed by inadequate cyber security and the proliferation of cyber crime. Paragraphs 108-110 of the *WSIS Tunis Agenda for the Information Society* set out a plan for multi-stakeholder implementation at the international level of the *WSIS Geneva Plan of Action* describing the multi-stakeholder implementation process according to eleven action lines and allocating responsibilities for facilitating implementation of the different action lines. At the WSIS, world leaders and governments designated ITU to facilitate the implementation of WSIS Action Line C5, dedicated to building confidence and security in the use of ICTs.In this regard, the ITU Secretary-General launched the Global Cyber security Agenda (GCA) on 17 May 2007, alongside partners from governments, industry, regional and international organizations, academic and research institutions. The GCA is a global framework for dialogue and international cooperation to coordinate the international response to the growing challenges to cyber security and to enhance confidence and security in the Information Society. It builds on existing work, initiatives and partnerships with the objective of proposing global strategies to address today's challenges related to building confidence and security in the use of ICTs. Within ITU, the Global Cyber security Agenda complements existing ITU work programmes by facilitating the implementation of the three ITU Sectors' cyber security activities, within a framework of international cooperation.

The GCA main strategic goals, built on five work areas:

- Legal Measures;
- Technical and Procedural Measures;
- Organizational Structures;
- Capacity Building; and
- International Cooperation.

The fight against cyber crime needs a comprehensive approach. Given that technical measures alone cannot prevent any crime, it is critical that law enforcement agencies are allowed to investigate and prosecute cyber crime effectively. Among the GCA work areas, "Legal measures" focuses on how to address the legislative challenges posed by criminal activities committed over ICT networks in an internationally compatible manner.

"Technical and Procedural Measures" focuses on key measures to promote adoption of enhanced approaches to improve security and risk management in cyberspace, including accreditation schemes, protocols and standards. "Organizational Structures" focuses on the prevention, detection, response to and crisis management of cyberattacks, including the protection of critical information infrastructure systems.

"Capacity Building" focuses on elaborating strategies for capacity-building mechanisms to raise awareness, transfer knowhow and boost cyber security on the national policy agenda. Finally, "International cooperation" focuses on international cooperation, dialogue and coordination in dealing with cyber-threats. The development of adequate legislation and within this approach the development of a cyber crime-related legal framework is an essential part of a cyber security strategy. This requires first of all the necessary substantive criminal law provisions to criminalise acts such as computer fraud, illegal access, data interference, copyright violations and child pornography. The fact that provisions exist in the criminal code that are applicable to similar acts committed outside the network does not mean that they can be applied to acts committed over the Internet as well.

Therefore, a thorough analysis of current national laws is vital to identify any possible gaps. Apart from substantive criminal law provisions, the law enforcement agencies need the necessary tools and instruments to investigate cyber crime. Such investigations themselves present a number of challenges. Perpetrators can act from nearly any location in the world and take measures to mask their identity. The tools and instruments needed to investigate cyber crime can be quite different from those used to investigate ordinary crimes.

THE PILLARS OF CYBER SECURITY

The Global Cyber security Agenda has seven main strategic goals, built on five work areas:

- Legal Measures;
- Technical and Procedural Measures;
- Organizational Structures;
- Capacity Building; and
- International Cooperation.

Issues related to cyber crime play an important role in all five pillars of the Global Cyber security Agenda. Among these work areas, the Legal Measures work areas focuses on how to address the legislative challenges posed by criminal activities committed over ICT networks in an internationally compatible manner.

LEGAL MEASURES

Within the five pillars the legal measure are probably the most relevant with regard to an Anti-Cyber crime Strategy. This requires first of all the necessary substantive criminal law provisions to criminalise acts such as computer fraud, illegal access, data interference, copyright violations and child pornography. The fact that provisions exist in the criminal code that are applicable to similar acts committed outside the network does not mean that they can be applied to acts committed over the Internet as well.

Therefore, a thorough analysis of current national laws is vital to identify any possible gaps. Apart from substantive criminal law provisions, the law enforcement agencies need the necessary tools and instruments to investigate cyber crime. Such investigations themselves present a number of challenges. Perpetrators can act from nearly any location in the world and take measures to mask their identity. The tools and instruments needed to investigate cyber crime can be quite different from those used to investigate ordinary crimes. Due to the international dimension of cyber crime it is in addition necessary to develop the legal national framework to be able to cooperate with law enforcement agencies abroad.

TECHNICAL AND PROCEDURAL MEASURES

Cyber crime-related investigations very often have a strong technical component. In addition the requirement of maintaining the integrity of the evidence during an investigation requires precise procedures. The development of the necessary capacities as well as procedures is therefore a necessary requirement related to fight against cyber crime. Another issue is the development of technical protection systems. Well-protected computer systems are more difficult to attack. Improving technical protection by implementing proper security standards is an important first step. For example, changes in the online banking system (*e.g.,* the switch from TAN to ITAN) have eliminated much of the danger posed by current "phishing" attacks, demonstrating the vital importance of technical solutions. Technical protection measures should include all elements of the technical infrastructure – the core network infrastructure, as well as the many individually connected computers worldwide.

Two potential target groups can be identified for protecting Internet users and businesses:

- End users and businesses (direct approach); and
- Service providers and software companies.

Logistically, it can be easier to focus on protection of core infrastructure (*e.g.,* backbone network, routers, essential services), rather than integrating millions of users into an Anti-Cyber crime Strategy. User protection can be achieved indirectly, by securing the services consumers use – *e.g.,* online banking. This indirect approach to protecting Internet users can reduce the number of people and institutions that need to be included in steps to promote technical protection. Although limiting the number of people that need to be included in technical protection might seem desirable, computer and Internet users are often the weakest link and the main target of criminals. It is often easier to attack private computers to obtain sensitive information, rather than the well-protected computer systems of a financial institution.

Despite these logistical problems, the protection of end-user infrastructure is vital for the technical protection of the whole network. Internet Service Providers and product vendors (*e.g.* software companies) play a vital role in the support of anticyber crime strategies. Due to their direct contact with clients, they can operate as a guarantor of security activities (*e.g.,* the distribution of protection tools and information on the current status of most recent scams).

ORGANIZATIONAL STRUCTURES

An effective fight against cyber crime requires highly developed organizational structures. Without having the right structures in place that avoids overlapping and is based on clear competences it will hardly be possible to carry out complex investigations that require the assistance of different legal as well as technical experts.

CAPACITY BUILDING AND USER EDUCATION

Cyber crime is a global phenomenon. In order to be able to effectively investigate offences harmonisation of laws and the development of means of international cooperation needs to be established. In order to ensure global standards in developed countries as well as in developing countries capacity building is necessary. In addition to capacity building user education is required. Certain cyber crimes – especially those related to fraud, such as "phishing" and "spoofing" – do not generally depend on a lack of technical protection, but rather lack of awareness by victims.

There are various software products that can automatically identify fraudulent web sites, but until now, these products cannot identify all suspicious web sites. A user protection strategy based only on software products has limited ability to protect the users. Although the technical protection measures continue to develop and the products available are updated on a regular basis, such products cannot yet substitute for other approaches.

One of the most important elements in the prevention of cyber crime is user education. For example, if users are aware that their financial institutions will never contact them by e-mail requesting passwords or bank account details, they cannot fall victim to phishing or identity fraud attacks. The education of Internet users reduces the number of potential targets.

Users can be educated through:

- Public campaigns;
- Lessons in schools, libraries, IT centres and universities;
- Public Private Partnerships (PPPs).

One important requirement of an efficient education and information strategy is the open communication of the latest cyber crime threats. Some states and/or private businesses refuse to emphasize that citizens and clients respectively are affected by cyber crime threats, in order to avoid them losing trust in online communication services. The United States Federal Bureau of Investigation has explicitly asked companies to overcome their aversion to negative publicity and report cyber crime. In order to determine threat levels, as well as to inform users, it is vital to improve the collection and publication of relevant information.

INTERNATIONAL COOPERATION

In a large number of cases data transfer processes in the Internet affect more than one country. This is a result of the design of the network as well as the fact the protocols that ensures that successful transmissions can be made, even if direct lines are temporarily blocked. In addition a large number of Internet services (like for example hosting services) are offered by companies that are based abroad. In those cases where the offender is not based in the same country at the victim, the investigation requires cooperation between law enforcement agencies in all countries that affected. International and transnational investigations without the consent of the competent authorities in the countries involved are difficult with regards to the principle of National Sovereignty.

This principle does in general not allow one country to carry out investigations within the territory of another country without the permission of the local authorities. Therefore, investigations need to be carried out with the support of the authorities in all countries involved. With regard to the fact that in most cases there is only a very short time gap available in which successful investigations can take place, the application of the classic mutual legal assistance regimes involves clear difficulties when it comes to cyber crime investigations.

This is due to the fact that mutual legal assistance in general requires time consuming formal procedures. As a result improvement in terms of enhanced international cooperation plays an important and critical role in the development and implementation of cyber security strategies and anti-cyber crime strategies.

CYBER SECURITY AS SCIENCE

A science of cyber security has to deal with a combination of peculiar features that are shared by no other area of study. First, the background on which events occur is almost completely created by humans and is digital. That is, people built all the pieces. One might have thought that computers, their software, and networks were therefore completely understandable. The truth is that the cyber-universe is complex well beyond anyone's understanding and exhibits behaviour that no one predicted, and sometimes can't even be explained well. On the positive side, the cyber-universe can be thought of as reduced to the 0s and 1s of binary data. Actions in this universe consist of sequences of changes to binary data, interleaved in time, and having some sort of locations in space. One can speculate as to why mathematics is so effective in explaining physics, but the cyber-world is inherently mathematical. Mathematics is a natural way for reasoning about it and this point of view is a theme that appears repeatedly in this report. Second, cyber security has good guys and bad guys. It is a field that has developed because people have discovered how to do things that other people disapprove of, and that break what is thought to be an agreed-upon social contract in the material world. That is, in cyber security there are adversaries, and the adversaries are purposeful and intelligent.

Thus, the reasoning in cyber security has to be both about the constructed universe and the actions and reactions of the adversaries. Definitions and concepts will shift over time in cyber security, as in all sciences. A successfully chosen name is a bridge between scientific knowledge and common sense, between new experience and old habits. The conceptual foundation of any science consists of a complicated network of names of things, names of ideas, and names of names. It evolves itself, and its projections on reality changes.

This quote echoes the observations of a presentation to JASON by Peter Gallison of Harvard in which he compared the type of science encountered in cyber security to a "Manichaean science" or science in the presence of adversaries. Particularly important for this type of science (and indeed any branch of science) was the development of a common language so that precise arguments could be formulated that addressed directly the problems of interest. We emphasize this point because the definition of cyber security itself is imprecise. The subject includes correctness properties like confidentiality and integrity, and liveness properties such as are associated with denial-of-service attacks, together with a growing set of unpleasant surprises.

SECURITY DEGRADES OVER TIME

We observed earlier that success in cyber security requires constant attention. Not only do the threats and attacks change, but the old techniques tend to become less effective. Technology advances, and the properties of the security system become better understood.

Unix Passwords

The original UNIX passwords were up to 8 ASCII non-control characters. The passwords aren't stored directly. Rather hashes (some one-way function) are stored. In modern systems these hashes aren't easily read, but if a machine is compromised, then the hashes can be taken away, and one can attempt to break passwords by making up likely candidates, applying the one-way function, and seeing if the result matches any of the hashes.

There are about 2 original UNIX passwords, which seemed like quite a lot at the time. Nowadays, one could imagine trying about 32 million guesses (2) per second on a single CPU core, so testing the entire space would only take about 3 days on 1,000 cores. That's not a particularly large computer, but the calculation is also embarrassingly parallel, so the 1,000 cores could be 1,000 machines in a (small) botnet. Or one could use 9,000 machines, still not a large botnet, and do the whole calculation in one night. For completeness we note that there has been a lot of work on making it harder to guess passwords; for instance, by using much slower one-way functions and much larger spaces. Another approach is to force people to use more complex passwords, but that has other sociological ramifications which are unfortunately very difficult to deal with in terms of any science. An extreme version turned up in the recent Russian spy case, where "Ricci said the steganographic programme was activated by pressing controlalt-E and then typing in a 27-character password, which the FBI found written down on a piece of paper during one of its searches."

Lock Bumping

A second example of security decreasing over time comes from the common locks people use on doors. A simple technique called "lock bumping" makes all these locks quite easy to open with just a little practice. The locks were, of course, vulnerable, but it didn't much matter until the technique was popularized starting about 2005. There are plenty of explanatory videos online. The implication for cyber-security is that the nature of the attack can change over time. It will not in general be possible to anticipate all attacks. For this reason it becomes necessary to constantly survey the extant modes of attack to understand the nature of current technology as well as continually attack one's own systems in the hopes of finding heretofore undiscovered attacks.

The Role of Secrecy

All security regimes include some secrets. The TSA doesn't explain everything it is looking for; the credit card processors don't fully explain their criteria, and so on. In the computer science community, security by obscurity is generally considered bad, probably based on examples of awed cryptography. There seems to be little theoretical work on this subject. We mention a few examples of keeping (and not keeping) secrets.

Commercial anti-virus programmes, of the sort that run on your home computer, reveal some of the weaknesses of totally public defences. In principal, a malware author could just buy these, and adjust the malware until none of them detect it. The market has made this easier; there are online services that for a fee will run uploaded malware through a large number of commercial programmes, and report the result.

Game theory and economics teach us that keeping our private valuations secret sometimes adds value. Much effort has gone into auction mechanisms that get bidders to reveal their private valuations. On the other hand, under various circumstances, this "asymmetric information" can lead to lemon markets, where either no market exists, or only people who are forced to will trade in the market. Secrecy might also be required by the rules. For instance, the DoD might use logs of network traffic to tune its network defences. These logs might easily contain material that should not be made public. For these reasons, there may be some benefit in exploring the role an enhanced role for secrecy and obfuscation, particularly for DoD systems.Finally, one might ask if keeping the source code secret adds much to security. First, there may be other reasons for keeping source code secret, such as the trade secrets incorporated in it. Certainly attackers with source code are likely to proceed differently, as they have a better chance of finding attacks based on logical errors, and this would be especially valuable for targeted attacks. On the other hand, there seems to be no particular shortage of effective attacks when source code is unavailable. But the code owner may have no realistic alternatives to making the source available. As an example consider the following announcement: "The agreement that we signed with the FSB is an extension of Microsoft's Government Security Programme (GSP)," Microsoft said in a statement on Friday. "The purpose of the GSP is to increase trust with national governments. In the case of the Russian agreement, GSP participation will facilitate the development of the next generation of secured solutions for Russian government agencies based on the latest Microsoft technologies and Russian cryptography."

BLUETOOTH SECURITY

ATTACKS AGAINST BLUETOOTH

In the last few years, with growing popularity of the Bluetooth wireless technology, also the interest in abusing (wireless) network connections has risen. Often an adversary's goal is to eavesdrop personal data, to use third parties' devices for his own purpose, or just the drive of hacking into a computer system, PDA or cell phone. Whatever an adversary's goal may be, at first it might be helpful, to gather some information on his potential victim. Is it a cell phone? Is it perhaps vulnerable to a known software vulnerability? Which services does the aimed device provide, which might get exploited within any further stages of the attack? Such questions might get answered via some portion of social engineering, but the adversary has also access to a growing number of useful tools.

ATTACKER'S TOOLS

Making use of services provided by the Bluetooth architecture itself might seem the easiest way to collect information about the victim. The *Service Discovery Protocol* (SDP) may grant some useful information to the adversary. Which "ports" are open with programmes listening to them, waiting for example for OBEX requests, serving voice data and so on. Therefore, the tools *BTScanner* and *hcitool* should be mentioned as frontends for the *bluez-utils* Bluetooth stack on Linux platforms, providing basic information about devices within operating range, such as device addresses, device classes and names. The most direct way to detect provided services via SDP is *sdptool*, another frontend for bluez-utils. On Microsoft Windows platforms, the *BlueScanner* should be mentioned, collecting information like device type and provided services of detected devices. BlueScanner uses, in contrast to the console programmes, a graphical user interface. All those tools share a significant problem: The attacker normally depends on a laptop, which might become noticed by a potential victim. One quite successful attempt to turn an adversary's mobile phone into a suitable auditing tool has been done with Blooover, an application, which is presented as follows.

BLOOOVER

Blooover, a Java application for mobile phones, is developed by the trifinite group [tri07]. It is available for some mobile phones and requires J2ME. Blooover is able to do security audits on mobile phones, checking known vulnerabilities. Additionally, it is capable of executing a *BlueSnarf* and a limited *BlueBug* attack.Roughly, BlueSnarfing enables an adversary, to retrieve private data from the targeted mobile phone, such as pictures, the calendar or address book, while BlueBugging aims at taking remote control over a mobile phone. The latter one would potentially cause financial damage for the victim, thus it is not possible to write SMS or initiating phone calls with Blooover.

BACKTRACK

BackTrack, a Slax-based Linux distribution [bac07], available as a live-cd goes one step further, providing several more complex automated attacks on Bluetooth devices.

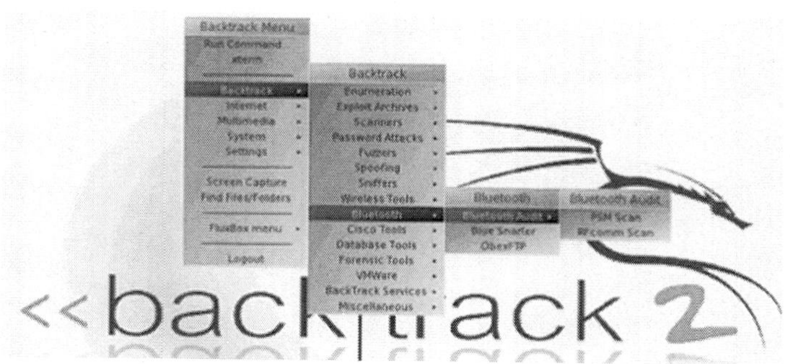

Fig. BackTrack Livecd with Dluxbox Interface

The BackTrack disc is packed with a large amount of security-related software, ranging from network analysis tools like *ettercap* and *wireshark* to a series of (partly) automated attacks, including attacks on Bluetooth devices, such as BlueSnarf or BlueBug. The most relevant of those attacks and/or vulnerabilities of Bluetooth or insecure implementations will be presented, closing with a conclusion on Bluetooth security.

BTCRACK

BTCrack [nru07] has been published at 23C3, a German hacker congress. It serves a graphical interface for a passive attack, which aims at eavesdropping messages in a pairing process between two devices, in order to retreive the Bluetooth PIN and generated link key.

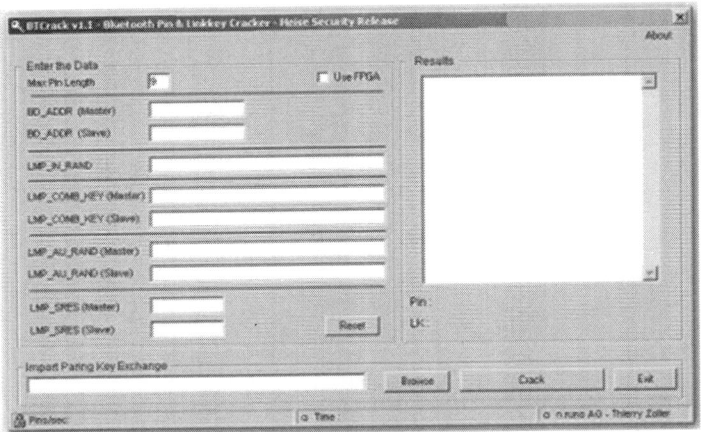

Fig. BTCrack Interface

An adversary is able to enter previously discovered Bluetooth device addresses, in order to enforce re-pairing between the two target devices. Subsequently, the whole pairing communication is eavesdropped, allowing the programme to do an exhaustive search on the Bluetooth PIN used within the pairing process.

BLUESNARF

The *BlueSnarf* attack exploits a weak Bluetooth implementation on some mobile phones, especially the implementation of *OBEX* (object exchange protocol) which is generally used by the OBEX PUSH profile, as by the Synchronisation Profile. Normally, no authentication or authorisation is required in OPP, as only vCards are transferred through OPP, if implemented correctly. The vulnerability in insecure implementations on certain mobile phones now provides an OPP and also a SYNCH profile, which both have access to the same OBEX stack, which maps requests through the secured SYNCH profile and those through the OPP profile to the same filesystem.

A possible attack may be done as follows. At first, the adversary connects to an OBEX push profile, which he might have detected within a previously done SDP scan. Now, in insecure OBEX implementations, he is able to execute a successful OBEX GET request for known filenames, like telecom/pb.vcf or whatever the adversary might expect to find on the target device. This results in a hidden download of private data. As for the use of the OPP, no pairing process with the adversary's device is necessary, the user is not aware of being spied out via Bluetooth. Combined with the advantages of a *long distance attack*, the adversary does not even have to be within range of sight to his target. This physical extension of the effective operating range of a Bluetooth device makes all of the attacks presented in this seminar work, much more effective. Instructions to modify a Bluetooth Dongle in such a way to reach operating ranges around several hundred meters are available on the internet. The trifinite group [tri07] has succesfully done a *long distance snarf* over a distance of 1.78 km. A list of mobile phones vulnerable to BlueSnarf attacks is available.

BLUESNARF++

BlueSnarf++ is an enhancement of the previously presented *BlueSnarf* attack, where the adversary had to deal with the OBEX push daemon in order to gain private data from the target device. In the BlueSnarf++ attack, the adversary instead connects to an OBEX FTP server, which is normally used for easier file transfers and, to the adversary's pleasure, is available on some of the vulnerable mobile phones. To fix the security vulnerabilities concerning BlueSnarf, respectively BlueSnarf++, the user is normally dependent on the applicable firmware update from the manufacturer (mainly affected were mobile phones by Nokia and Sony Ericsson who, today, cooperate with the trifinite group in security concerns).

BLUEBUG

For a better understanding of how the *BlueBug* attack works, a short introduction into the *RFCOMM* protocol will be given. RFCOMM is a protocol on top of L2CAP within the Bluetooth protocol stack, which emulates serial RS-232 interfaces via Bluetooth connections. Up to 60 connections via RFCOMM may get established simultaneously for one device, called *RFCOMM channels.* While L2CAP and, on a lower level, the base band, are responsible for establishing a synchronous or asynchronous data connection, RFCOMM emulates a "virtual" serial connection between two communication endpoints. Now, what the adversary needs to know of a vulnerable device [the07], is the Bluetooth Device Address, *BD ADDR*. The adversary connects to RFCOMM–channel 17, where vulnerable mobile phones provide an open backdoor, in the form of an AT-parser which requires no authentication procedure. AT commands are a powerful tool for remote control of communication devices, like analog or ISDN modems, or, like in this case, mobile phones with a Bluetooth interface. The adversary is able to execute most tasks a normal user of the mobile phone were able to do, like initiating phone calls (especially numbers like 0190..., which could be of economic interest for the adversary), reading or writing SMS or gathering the victim's private data.:

```
# scan for bluetooth devices:
oscar@darkside $ hcitool scan
Scanning...
00:0E:6D:10:1D:B6 Nokia 6310i
00:05:7A:01:A3:80 Airbus A380
00:06:6E:21:69:C2 Bluespoon AX
00:0F:DE:6C:61:04 T610
```

```
# bind channel 17 of target device to/dev/rfcomm42:
oscar@darkside $ rfcomm bind 42 00:0E:6D:10:1D:B6 17
# connect to AT terminal via, for example, cu:
oscar@darkside $ cu -l/dev/rfcomm42
Connected.
AT+CPBS="ME"
OK
AT+CPBR=1
+CPBR: 1,"",,"Paris Hilton"
OK
Disconnected.
```

This example was only presented to show, what simple set of commands on the console answer an adversary's purpose of retrieving private data or executing any AT commands on a vulnerable mobile phone. The bounds of BlueBug are only limited by the adversary's creativity and the capability of the supported set of AT commands on the target device. An overview of AT commands for GSM devices can be found in [Tra07]. The solution to RFCOMM-based attacks is, as in most cases, a firmware update fixing the insecure RFCOMM-channel.

BLUEJACKING

BlueJacking is not an attack against Bluetooth or any implementation in terms of breaking into another device, stealing private data or otherwise dealing damage to the "victim". Instead, it uses the ability of Bluetooth mobile phones to send socalled vCards, a file format, which is intended to exchange personal information in the form of an electronic business card. Now it has come quite into fashion to abuse this mechanic to send—free of charge—messages via Bluetooth, such as "You were BlueJacked!". Users who are not familiar with BlueJacking might draw the conclusion, their mobile phone were infested with a mobile phone virus, or they were followed by a stalker. Users who feel disturbed by the way, primarily teenagers, abuse the vCard service for BlueJacking, should turn off Bluetooth connectivity on their mobile phones, only reactivating it, whenever needed.

HELOMOTO

HeloMoto is a combination of BlueSnarf and BlueBug attacks, exploiting a flawed implementation of "trusted devices" in some Motorola mobile phones, which led to the attack's name. At first, the adversary connects to an OBEX push profile, as it is done in BlueSnarf. If there is no vulnerable implementation of OBEX that would allow a BlueSnarf attack, HeloMoto makes use of the "trusted devices" feature, defined in Bluetooth. The adversary now attempts to send a vCard to the target device, as it is done in BlueJacking and immediately cancels the request. In consequence of the Helo- Moto vulnerability, his device remains within the "trusted devices" history, while the owner of the target device is not aware of being attacked. Finally he uses the status of a "trusted device" to execute AT commands, as it is done in BlueBugging. Again, owners of a vulnerable device depend on a firmware update by Motorola, or otherwise should simply deactivate Bluetooth.

BLUESMACK

BlueSmack is a Denial of Service (DoS) attack, hence it is directed at the availability of a Bluetooth device. The attack is done similarly to the "Ping of Death" against IP-based devices. The adversary sends an L2CAP echo request (ping) of large size, approximately 600 bytes to a Bluetooth device with limited hardware resources. Those devices (especially known for such a behaviour is the iPaq) reserve an input buffer of fixed length (around 600 bytes). When receiving such a malicious ping request, the input buffer overflows, which normally leads to a seqmentation fault and, by this, to the immediate knock-out of the target device. On a linux computer, this can be done simply using the bluez-utils' l2ping command with -s <num> option, defining the packet length.

CRACKING THE BLUETOOTH PIN

Without exception, the previous attacks were focused on certain insecure Bluetooth implementations which could usually been fixed by firmware update. The following attack instead exploits the Bluetooth security architecture itself and was presented by Yaniv Shaked and Avishai Wool in [SW05]. Roughly spoken, the attack aims at eavesdropping the whole communication through the pairing process between two Bluetooth devices, in order to extract the initialisation key, Kinit, using it for an exhaustive search on the Bluetooth PIN. Generally, Bluetooth aspires confidentiality and authenticity. We will take a closer look at the cryptographic functions used to accomplish those security targets within the Link Managing Protocol, while discussing the attack. In order to establish a secure Bluetooth connection between two devices, an enquiry routine has to detect the opposite's Bluetooth device address, BD ADDR. Subsequently, in both devices have to be entered the same Bluetooth PIN, depending on the device type.

Some devices with limited memory or user interface capability have a fixed PIN, which is in most cases 0000, which will be discussed later on. Important for the establishment of a connection is, that at least one device must have a variable PIN, that has eventually to be set to the second device's fixed PIN. Now everything is set up correctly for the following steps within the pairing process:

- Creation of an initialization key, Kinit, which is used to confidentially exchange random values

- Creation of a link key Kab, which is a function of the input of A and B; discarding of Kinit
- Mutual Authentication via simple challenge-response scheme, based on Kab

All algorithms used during the pairing process, namely E22, E21 and E1 are based on the *SAFER+* block cipher. SAFER+ operates with a block size of 128 bits and three different key lengths: 128, 192 or 256 bits. Bluetooth uses the SAFER+ with 128 bit key length. As the inner design of SAFER+, respectively the derived Bluetooth algorithms are not essentially important for the following attack, they are used as "black boxes" in this seminar work.

CREATION OF KINIT

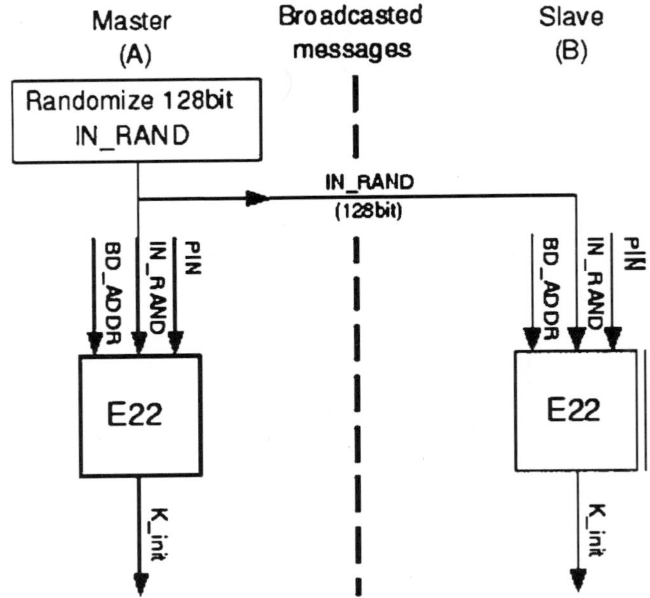

Fig. Generation of Kinit Using E22

We assume, that the same PIN has been entered into both Bluetooth devices correctly.

Now the Master device A chooses a pseudorandom number of 128 bits length (IN RAND) and sends it to the Slave B. Subsequently the Kinit key is created on both devices, using the E22 algorithm:

The Kinit key generated by E22 is only used in the following to confidentially exchange random values. Those values are used to agree on a link key, which is a function of inputs from both devices, A and B. After the creation of Kab, the link key, Kinit is discarded, leaving Kab as the shared secret for subsequent communication.

CREATION OF KAB

After exchanging the initialization key, Kinit, the devices agree on the link key Kab. Both devices choose a 128 bit random number, LK RANDA, respectively LK RANDB, xor it bitwise with Kinit and send it to their communication partner.

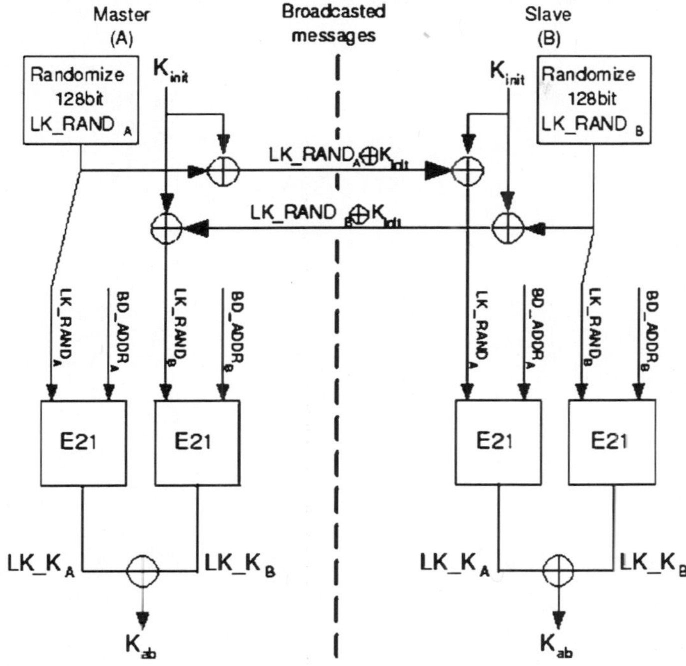

Fig. Generation of Kabusing E21

Using the self-inverse xor function again, the random values are decrypted and used to generate the link key using the E21 algorithm. Now both devices share a link key and Kinitis discarded. Finally a mutual (device) authentication, based on Kab is done.

MUTUALAUTHENTICATION

In order to authenticate the opposite device, a mutual authentication based on a challenge-response scheme is performed. Therefore, one of the devices is the verifier A, leaving the other device as the Claimant B. Now, B claims to know the corresponding link key which A likes to verify.

The verifier A choses a 128 bit random number AU RANDA as a challenge and sends it to B, who responds with the 32 bit word SRES/A, using AU RANDA, BD ADDRB and Kab as input values for the E1 algorithm. Then, A computes a value SRESA, using the same input for E1, as B is expected to take. If SRES/A and SRESA are different, A immediately halts the session, leaving B the possibility to authenticate again, after a certain amount of time. After each unsuccessful attempt, this amount of time is increased exponentially, which is done to prevent brute force attacks. Otherwise, roles for verifier and claimant are switched and the entire process is repeated.

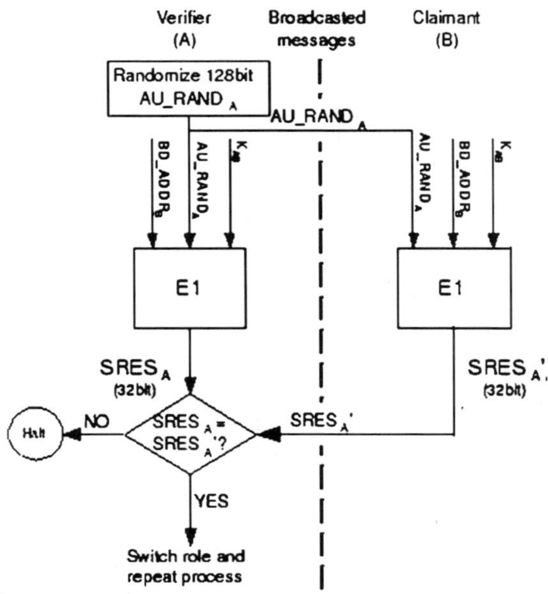

Fig. Mutual Authentication Using E1

ATTACKING THE PAIRING PROCESS

In [SW05], the following passive attack against the pairing process between two Bluetooth devices is documented. Let us assume the adversary was able to eavesdrop the whole communication within the pairing process between two devices A and B:

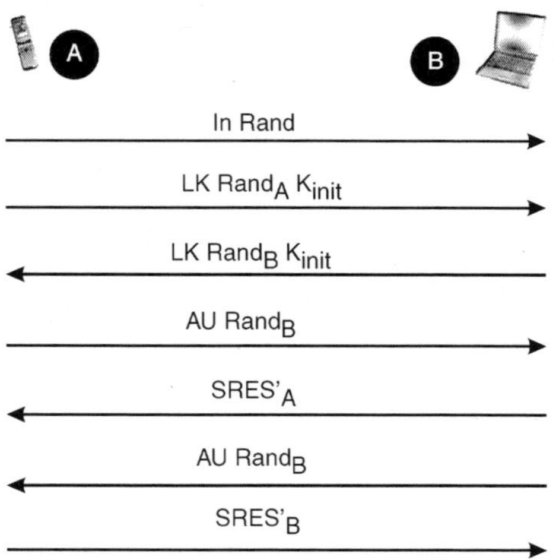

Fig. Eavesdropping of the Pairing Process

Now the adversary is able to do an exhaustive search within the space of possible Bluetooth PINs. Knowing IN RAND and BD ADDR, the adversary feeds E22 with those values, together with the PIN "candidates", chosen by his brute force algorithm, receiving a hypothesis for Kinit. Subsequently, the adversary decrypts the first two messages within the mutual authentication process, resulting in a hypothesis for LK RANDA and LK RANDB. Due to LK RANDA and LK RANDB being the only secret information used in E21 to calculate the link key, the adversary computes a hypothesis for Kab. Now the adversary is able to use the last few messages to prove, whether his hypothesis for Kab is correct or not. He feeds E1 with the challenges AU RANDA, respectively AU RANDB and compares his result with the corresponding SRESA or SRESB message. This process is repeatedly done until the correct Bluetooth PIN used by A and B is found. The entire attack looks like this:

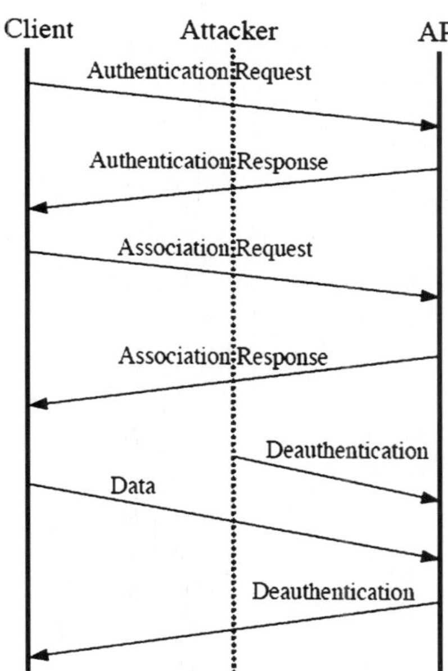

Fig. Cracking the Bluetooth PIN - Algorithm

Attack is more powerful than it might appear at a first glance. While generally the pairing procedure for two devices is not frequently repeated, Bluetooth grants the possibility to "forget" a link key, due to limited memory. By this, the adversary is able to enforce a repairing process, which still requires to inject a specific message at a certain point in the protocol run, what needs a custom device in general. Additionally, the attack is rather efficient. Due to some algebraic optimisation of needed computations, cracking a 4-digit Bluetooth PIN with a Pentium IV 3GHz takes approximately 63 milliseconds. Since this attack is aiming directly at the Bluetooth security architecture itself, instead of against a vulnerable implementation, it is not possible to fix this problem through a simple firmware update. Instead, the user should be aware of the possible risks when being prompted to reenter the PIN for an existing connection and, whenever possible, use a PIN of considerably more than 4 digits. Finally it should be mentioned, that devices using a fixed PIN(which is generally 0000) are - due to obious reasons - an open door for any adversary.

This holds for devices like headsets, printers, etc. In this case, the user should be aware of the fact that no effective method for providing confidentiality is applied to such connections, because further authentication and encryption is based on the insecure link key Kab, or even a fixed unit key.The most important practical attacks against Bluetooth have been presented in this seminar work. Those attacks either exploit the Bluetooth architecture itself, a short PIN, or a weak implementation. While insecure software on embedded devices generally leads to compromised private data, gaining remote control over a cell phone, or, at least, a simple knockout due to a DoS attack like BlueSmack, the power of an attack grows with the complexity of the target.

When a buffer overflow or similar vulnerabilities occur in Bluetooth protocol stacks or application software for a personal computer or MAC, the adversary might even be able to execute arbitrary code. Concerning the Bluetooth specification [SIG04], some security-by-obscurity elements have been promoted, as things like frequency hopping or the limitation to short operating ranges have been advertised as security features. When considering previous attacks like the long distance snarf or successful attempts of mounting an embedded bluetooth device on a modified rifle, for large distance attacks, those features seem to create a false awareness of security. Additionally, the key management in Bluetooth seems to draw its security partly from the big issues of perfoming practical attacks.

The link key, which is used to authenticate an opposite device and to compute encryption keys, is promoted as a shared secret of 128 bits length, which is not true. Since it is based on a Bluetooth PIN, the effective key space of Kab can generally be reduced to 10^4 (approximately 13 to 14 bits), which essentially is, what Shaked and Wool did in their attempt to attack the pairing process. Finally, the weakest link within the system "Bluetooth" often seems to be the user, who is not always aware of potential security risks and chooses short PINs or permanently leaves Bluetooth connectivity switched on. Combined with the fact that auditing tools and tools for automated attacks on Bluetooth devices get improved steadily, Bluetooth seems to be an interesting issue in the future, especially, if Bluetooth will go on receiving an increasing popularity.

INHERENT RISKS WITH BLUETOOTH DEVICES

It is a very nice technology but the security issue has to be taken into serious consideration. Risks are inherent to any wireless technology. And the most significant risk in the wireless technology is that the underlying communication medium is open to everybody, including authentic users as well as the intruders. Bluetooth used short-range radio which is very vulnerable.

For instance, if the intruders had the frequency to connect to your PC, they can use their own Bluetooth technology monitor and mouse to get access. So they can have all information in your PC. And if the attackers' headsets connected to your mobile phone by hacking the frequency, you will never know somebody bugged you phone and everything will be unsafe. Therefore we need to put extra efforts in security section to make sure the technology is safe for the users. The Bluetooth technology needs to sort out the following specific threats

- All the vulnerabilities that exist in a conventional wired network apply to wireless technologies.
- Malicious entities may gain unauthorized access to an agency's computer network through wireless connections, bypassing any firewall protections.
- Sensitive information that is not encrypted (or that is encrypted with poor cryptographic techniques) and that is transmitted between two wireless devices may be intercepted and disclosed.
- DoS attacks may be directed at wireless connections or devices.
- Malicious entities may steal the identity of legitimate users and masquerade as them on internal or external corporate networks.
- Sensitive data may be corrupted during improper synchronization.
- Malicious entities may be able to violate the privacy of legitimate users and be able to track their movements.
- Malicious entities may deploy unauthorized equipment (*e.g.*, client devices and access points) to surreptitiously gain access to sensitive information.
- Handheld devices are easily stolen and can reveal sensitive information.
- Data may be extracted without detection from improperly configured devices.
- Viruses or other malicious code may corrupt data on a wireless device and subsequently be introduced to a wired network connection.
- Malicious entities may, through wireless connections, connect to other agencies or organizations for the purposes of launching attacks and concealing their activities.
- Interlopers, from inside or out, may be able to gain connectivity to network management controls and thereby disable or disrupt operations.
- Malicious entities may use third-party, untrusted wireless network services to gain access to an agency's or other organization's network resources.
- Internal attacks may be possible via ad hoc transmissions.

SECURITY ARCHITECTURE

Because of these many new risks that a new technology like Bluetooth creates, a good security design is essential for it to be successful. However, since Bluetooth is a relatively recent invention, and we are well aware of the security risks and needs for technologies in today's world (especially having the similar 802.11 wireless technology available to examine), the architecture of Bluetooth security was very well thought out to begin with. Thus, Bluetooth is considered a relatively secure form of communication, especially when considering it uses a wireless medium.

The design of secure interaction between devices in Bluetooth consists of the following phases:

An initial phase, called pairing, in order to establish a "link" key, which will then be used for encryption and decryption for secure connections. This is the most dangerous stage of connecting 2 Bluetooth devices together; as if an attacker can spy on this part of the interaction then he may be able to establish what the link key. During this pairing, an initialisation key is generated based on each device's address, and a PIN which is shared between the devices. Once pairing has occurred, each device considers the other to be "trusted", and thus it grants it access to certain things on itself. Due to the fact that someone spying on this would be able to determine what the initialization key, and thus the link key, the Bluetooth Special Interests Group (SIG) recommend that this stage is carried out in private, and that PIN should be long and manually input if possible. The PIN should also random and not common PINs like "0000".

Using this initialisation key, the devices then agree on a link key which they will use to establish a secure connection between each other when needed. There are 2 types of link key. The first is a unit key, where a device's individual unit key (which every Bluetooth device has) is chosen as the link key. This method clearly allows other a device to spy on data being transferred between a device it is trusted by and some other device, or even to send false data to another device by impersonating using the unit key. The other method is combination keys, in which an individual link key is generated for each individual link between 2 devices, based on each of their Bluetooth addresses. Whenever a device wishes to access another Bluetooth device, it gets the other to send it a challenge.

It then encrypts this challenge using the link key along with other information and returns a partial result to the device he wishes to access. This other device then verifies the partial result and communication can take place using encrypted wireless interaction. This can then be mirrored in reverse to complete a mutual pairing. When data is then being communicated, the link key is used to help generate a ciphering for an E0 encryption algorithm, which again makes it more secure as the link key is not used directly for encryption or decryption during the communication.

KNOWN SECURITY ISSUES

Given that this Bluetooth security has been well thought out and the scope for a hacker to be able to attain the link key is minimal (especially if Bluetooth SIG's recommendations are taken aboard), any security compromises must take a different form than trying to obtain or guess the decryption key. Currently there are just a few known methods for bypassing Bluetooth's security measures.

One method of hacking Bluetooth has been named "bluesnarfing", and, as with most Bluetooth hacks, the reason for its existence is a fault of the way Bluetooth is implemented on certain mobile phones, and in this case the way in which the object exchange (OBEX) protocol is implemented. What it does is it can silently access these mobile phones contacts, calendar and pictures without the owner ever knowing - a clear violation of the owner's security expectations. Nokia is one of a few mobile phone companies who have acknowledged that some of their devices have this fault, and have addressed it with updated firmware for the faulty products.

Another method is that of "backdoor" hacking. This is where a device which is no longer trusted can still gain access to the mobile phone and gain access to data as with bluesnarfing, or also use services like WAP etc.

A third flaw in some mobile phones allows for a hacker to use a method called "bluebugging" in order to hack into the owner's phone. It is possibly the most dangerous of the attacks, and allows hackers to send/read SMS, call numbers, monitor phonecalls and also do everything that backdoor and bluesnarfing allows. This is a separate vulnerability from bluesnarfing and does not affect all of the same phones as bluesnarfing. The seemingly harmless "Bluejacking" is a different style of attack. It works on the fact that during the initialization process, when a device wishes to be paired with you, a message containing the device's name and whether you want to pair with this device is displayed. To many people this is just an innocent joke to get a reaction out of someone by renaming their phone and then sending them a clever anonymous message and watching their reaction. However, if a malicious individual names their phone something like "Click accept to win!!" then they can gain access to someone's Bluetooth device if an owner falls for the trick.

As with computers, there is also the risk of worms and viruses. One such worm is the Cabir worm, which tries to pair the Bluetooth device it's on to any in the vicinity, and if successful it will install itself on the paired device. Once it is there, it will attempt to repeat this process, and also when the device is switched on, the worm will drain the battery by scanning for enabled Bluetooth devices. There is also the possibility for Denial of Service (DoS) attacks on Bluetooth devices. This works exactly the same way that traditional DoS attacks work, with a hacker sending invalid Bluetooth requests and his occupying a devices Bluetooth channel so it cannot communicate with any other Bluetooth devices. The first three of these issues are purely faults of the manufacturers of particular mobile phones, and firmware has been released since their discovery to correct any faulty models. These problems illustrate the dangers of using Bluetooth devices if they are not implemented properly. Indeed, they can all be solved, for most phones, by switching the phone into "invisible" mode so that it will not be recognised by other Bluetooth devices. Switching off the Bluetooth capability when you're not using it is another more extreme option. The Bluejacking and Cabir worm issues can only hack someones phone if they agree to be paired with the device, and in the case of the cabir worm if they then also agree to install the software that it tries to install. There are also security updates and antivirus software readily available for users. These user security measures show that, as with any technology, there is responsibility on the user to take care of their device, and if they do so they should not be at a large risk. Generally, Bluetooth is accepted as a well-designed and secure medium of transfer, so long as their users take care of their devices.

THE FUTURE

The SIG outlined in its roadmap through to 2006 to continue to tackle issues of privacy and security. Nokia and Ericsson have both developed software upgrades for phones vulnerable to Bluetooth attacks. Both companies have also made sure that new phones coming to market will be able to defend against attacks. Although consumers are still advised to use long PIN codes to decrease the risk of a security violation. Most experts regard Bluetooth as still being the most secure form of wireless networking today. Bluetooth is considered more secure than any other wireless technology, such as 802.11 networks and Wi-Fi which is vulnerable to security threats due to its weak WEP and WPA protocols. Everything considered Bluetooth is expected to become more pervasive as demand for wireless grows.

CRITICAL INFRASTRUCTURE PROTECTION

The Internet infrastructure relies on primarily on the Border Gateway Protocol (BGP) and the Domain Name System (DNS). The secure remote administration of routers relies mostly on the Secure Shell (SSH) protocol.

Attacks against any of these technologies may impact on the availability of Internet-based services. As we do not know how to guarantee software correctness, it is a reasonable to assume that exploitable programming errors exist in applications.

To reduce the ability of an adversary to cause damage, we need to limit the impact of such programming errors. We offer *Privilege Separation* as one solution.

Services that authenticate remote users to system resources are difficult to contain via external application confinement mechanisms. Privilege

Separation is a protection mechanism at the application level that separates the privileged code path from the unprivileged code path. An adversary interacts with the unprivileged part only; an exploitable programming error in the unprivileged code path does not lead to immediate privilege escalation.

Privilege separation may also be employed to increase the resilience of domain name service implementations like bind. Privilege Separation is very portable as most modern Unix operating system provide address space protection between processes and inter-process communication, privilege separation.

INTRUSION PREVENTION

While Privilege Separation increases an application's resilience against programming errors, it does not prevent all possible intrusions. Many system services and applications perform specific tasks. By confining applications to only those operations that required for its correct execution, we prevent adversaries who gain control over these system services from causing damage to the system.

In Unix operating systems, persistent changes are possibly only via *System Calls*. By carefully monitoring and restricting an application's system calls, we can limit or even prevent an adversary from causing damage. We offer *Systrace* as solution. Systrace provides fine-grained application confinement based on configurable security policies. Additionally, it can detect and prevent intrusions. It also records audit trails that can used in forensic analysis.

Threat Assessment

The impact of new security problems can be reduced by early threat detection. Threat detection and assessment allows us to quickly identify so far unknown attacks, prioritize their threat and protect vulnerable systems. Honeypot technology serves this purpose by providing computer systems that we expect to be compromised. The honeypot systems are network sensors that allows us to detect new attacks.

As computer security problems are inherently repeatable, we obtain threat detection by populating our network with honeypots. New attacks can easily be identified by monitoring the state of deployed honeypots including new worms or widespread scans for vulnerabilities.

MODEL OF CYBER-PROTECTION

The cyber-threat to British business and government is growing. Statistics from Symantec, the internet protection software company, show that during 2010 over 286 million unique malicious Internet threats were observed globally, with a 93 per cent increase in the volume of web-based attacks from the previous year. This translates to a growing economic threat, with the UK's Office of

Cyber Security and Information Assurance estimating the cost of cyber-crime to British business at over £20 billion a year. This rising burden on the British economy cannot be ignored or dismissed as an acceptable cost of conducting business online.

There is also widespread acknowledgement that better public-private cooperation is an important element in improving security in cyberspace. At a meeting in February hosted by the Prime Minister, representatives from a cross section of British industry and government ministers agreed on the need for increased information sharing as part of a new approach to protecting the UK's economic and national security interests against cyber threats.

Research conducted by RUSI's Cyber-Security Programme has confirmed the need for sharing information on threats and responses, not just between government and industry, but between companies and other organisations, especially across sector boundaries. This research has also shown that it is vital to extend protection beyond what is traditionally perceived to be national infrastructure (*e.g.*, defence, telecommunications, food and water supply) to include often neglected sectors. These overlooked areas of vulnerability encompass those sectors which act as service providers (*e.g.*, lawyers and accountants) and collaborators (in particular academia), and potentially represent weak links in the cyber-security chain. Moreover, these sectors also represent vital components of the economy, and should be protected accordingly. Any critical breach of security from these companies, such as the theft of sensitive client data from a law firm or a doctor's practice, could have a damaging impact upon public confidence in the industry as a whole. Furthermore, sectors such as academia are entirely based upon the knowledge they generate through research, and hence it is vital to safeguard this from theft. There is therefore a clear need to extend protection across and within sectors to provide collective security. RUSI's research has, however, also revealed equally widespread agreement among stakeholders and others that effective information sharing is hard to achieve, and that the costs often outweigh the benefits, as highlighted in Thomas and Walport's Data Sharing Review for the Ministry of Justice. This problem afflicts many areas where collective action is crucial for security (not just cyberspace), but is rarely acknowledged publicly. The idea is attractive, but there are many examples in various fields of systems that fail to deliver. However, RUSI's research into models for information sharing shows that, whilst it is undoubtedly challenging to do it well, outstandingly effective and efficient systems do exist, and a study of these can help identify the criteria that are key to success.

UNDERSTANDING THE REQUIREMENT

The overarching problem for security in cyberspace is that whilst a networked world brings many benefits, those benefits are accompanied by risks.

How do we manage those risks intelligently and efficiently? The immediate problem is that our knowledge of those risks is dispersed, and our understanding fragmentary.

Without adequate knowledge, countermeasures will be ineffectual, if not counter-productive, and policy will be based merely on plausible ideas and guesswork. Success will be the result of luck, not judgement. But from greater shared knowledge will follow better countermeasures (both in their design and implementation) and better policy. Thus the absolutely necessary precursor to any sensible intervention in cyber-security is: Get knowledge.

Genuine knowledge is rooted in accurate, timely information, but how are we to understand 'information sharing'? It covers a wide range of actions, from the exchange of high-level generalised conclusions (*e.g.* at conferences or liaison meetings) to the automated transfer of large volumes of data. We would suggest that the latter is not appropriate in this instance, two major objections being the horrendous privacy implications and the technical infrastructure needed. High-level exchanges have their place but experience (*e.g.* from financial crime) suggests that by themselves they are inadequate. The answer lies somewhere between these two extremes: in essence, the reporting of incidents by individuals at the operational level. This does not rule out deeper analysis and higher level exchanges, but is a necessary precursor: a firm foundation of hard information on which they can be based. There is, indeed, much good co-operation and information sharing already in the field of cyber security, often of an informal sort. But this activity tends to be confined to a particular sector (*e.g.*, banking or academia) and even then it is rarely comprehensive. The sharing of knowledge is fairly high level or anecdotal: what is lacking is a foundation of hard information upon which a solid body of knowledge can be built. It will be important, however, to ensure that any new initiative(s) do not harm or disrupt the good work that is already being done: they should enhance and improve, not replace. Especially important will be avoiding a form of moral hazard where reporting, analysing and solving problems become 'someone else's business'. This will easily happen if the wrong model is adopted. Systemic flaws produce perverse outcomes, no matter how commendable the aims or how strong the commitment to them.

Principles

There are several guiding principles upon which we believe any solution to the problem of wider cyber security should be based.

The first is that the process should be fundamentally based upon active collaboration between the public and private sectors, whereby the government and its relevant agencies are equal stakeholders rather than controlling entities. This is designed to ensure a more level playing field to engender trust between public and private agencies, and to help facilitate greater information sharing, to the mutual benefit of all. The second principle concerns the shifting of responsibility for cyber security from central government agencies to companies themselves. This is designed to empower companies so that they may look after their own interests and not have to rely on the resources and direction of some central entity. This will help overcome the crucial time delay which occurs whenever companies at the periphery have to defer to the centre, thus reducing the vital time between detection and response to cyber incidents, where action will need to be taken within minutes rather than hours. Therefore companies should be provided with the tools and education to protect themselves from the most prevalent threats, and also trained to recognise serious incursions so that the rest of the community can be alerted and the relevant government agencies quickly involved.

In relation to this, the third principle argues for the creation of an environment which encourages collective security that can be collectively enforced, rather than security controlled and enforced from a central entity. An ideal model of cyber security would facilitate, rather than direct, information-sharing between companies across non-traditional sector boundaries, and would encourage a culture of 'cyber-hygiene' amongst its members. Member organisations would thus be nudged into practicing better cyber security as part of a collective community of security, with any central agency only intervening when necessary.

The fourth and perhaps the most important principle concerns the operator 'at the coalface'. This is the person who will spot and report incidents. If the system is designed so that their interest and intelligence is engaged, it will succeed. If not, a 'box-ticking' mentality will prevail and the information entering the system will be of poor quality, which will be devastating. Positive and negative factors come into play. The most important positive factor is that the system helps the operator to do their job better: they have access to the reports it contains and can use them to locally implement better countermeasures. This is a powerful incentive to contribute to the body of information themselves. On the negative side there must be no undue obstacles or disincentives to report. Reporting must be easy, quick, not (primarily) a compliance issue, and not governed by arbitrary targets.

Comparable Models

When considering the feasibility of putting these principles into practice, it is instructive to look towards existing collective security and information sharing arrangements. Public sector models such as the Serious Organised Crime Agency's Suspicious Activities Reports (SAR) system whilst playing a vital role in combating financial crime in the UK, are incompatible with our stated principles because they employ a top-down centralised approach, with private companies relegated to merely passing on information to assist law enforcement. Furthermore the SARs regime is part of a large and costly public-sector body, which is at odds with our vision of a small and nimble public-private sector collaborative entity.

A workable model can be found in Information Sharing and Analysis Centres (ISACs), which are organisations usually set up by the owners and operators of an infrastructure within a sector to provide information analysis and data dissemination. An example of this model that can be seen in practice in the UK is CIFAS-the UK's Credit Industry Fraud Advisory Service, which is a privately run organisation consisting of over 260 UK organisations, predominantly drawn from the private sector, and is the world's first non-profit fraud prevention data-sharing scheme. This model closely adheres to our stated principles as a relatively small organisation, entirely funded through membership fees, which facilitates information sharing between public and private agencies and across different sectors such a retail and finance. It also helps to empower and educate its members about fraud prevention by providing them with reports concerning the latest fraud trends and threats, and offers a multitude of staff training and even (jointly with a university) a foundation degree in Fraud Management. CIFAS provides an attractive model of collective security whereby the system empowers and educates its members whilst also facilitating information sharing, with the centre intervening and disciplining members only in cases of serious misconduct.

THE CYBER SECURITY STRATEGY

The Federal Government aims at making a substantial contribution to a secure cyberspace, thus maintaining and promoting economic and social prosperity in Germany. Cyber security in Germany must be ensured at a level commensurate with the importance and protection required by interlinked information infrastructures, without hampering the opportunities and the utilization of the cyberspace. In this context the level of cyber security reached is the sum of all national and international measures taken to protect the availability of information and communications technology and the integrity, authenticity and confidentiality of data in cyberspace.

Cyber security must be based on a comprehensive approach. This requires even more intensive information sharing and coordination. The Cyber Security Strategy mainly focuses on civilian approaches and measures. They are complemented by measures taken by the Bundeswehr to protect its capabilities and measures based on mandates to make cyber security a part of Germany's preventive security strategy. Given the global nature of information and communications technology, international coordination and appropriate networks focusing on foreign and security policy aspects are indispensable. This includes cooperation not only in the United Nations, but also in the EU, the Council of Europe, NATO, the G8, the OSCE and other multinational organizations. The aim is to ensure the coherence and capabilities of the international community to protect cyberspace.

PROTECTION OF CRITICAL INFORMATION INFRASTRUCTURES

The protection of critical information infrastructures is the main priority of cyber security. They are a central component of nearly all critical infrastructures and become increasingly important. The public and the private sector must create an enhanced strategic and organizational basis for closer coordination based on intensified information sharing. To this end, cooperation established by the CIP implementation plan is systematically extended, and legal commitments to enhance the binding nature of the CIP implementation plan are examined.

With the participation of the National Cyber Security Council (cf. objective 5), the integration of additional sectors is examined and the introduction of new relevant technologies is considered to a greater extent. Whether and where protective measures have to be made mandatory and whether and where additional powers are required in case of specific threats have to be clarified, too. Furthermore we will examine the necessity of harmonizing rules to maintain critical infrastructures during IT crises.

STRENGTHENING IT SECURITY IN THE PUBLIC ADMINISTRATION

The public administration will further enhance the protection of its IT systems. State authorities have to serve as role models for data security. We will create a common, uniform and secure network infrastructure in the federal administration ("federal networks") as a basis for electronic audio and data communication. We will continue to press ahead with the implementation plan for the federal administration. Should the IT security situation get worse, this plan may be aligned accordingly. Effective IT security requires powerful structures in all federal authorities. For this reason resources must be deployed appropriately at central and local level. To facilitate implementation through uniform action by authorities, joint investments into the Federal Government's IT security will be made regularly in line with budgetary possibilities. Operational cooperation with the federal Länder, particularly with regard to CERTs (computer emergency response teams), will be further intensified by the IT planning council.

NATIONAL CYBER RESPONSE CENTRE

To optimize operational cooperation between all state authorities and improve the coordination of protection and response measures for IT incidents we will set up a National Cyber Response Centre. It will report to the Federal Office for Information Security (BSI) and cooperate directly with the Federal

Office for the Protection of the Constitution (BfV) and the Federal Office of Civil Protection and Disaster Assistance (BBK). Cooperation in the National Cyber Response Centre will strictly observe the statutory tasks and powers of all authorities involved on the basis of cooperation agreements. The Federal Criminal Police Office (BKA), the Federal Police (BPOL), the Customs Criminological Office (ZKA), the Federal Intelligence Service (BND), the Bundeswehr and authorities supervising critical infrastructure operators all participate in this centre within the framework of their statutory tasks and powers.

Quick and close information sharing on weaknesses of IT products, vulnerabilities, forms of attacks and profiles of perpetrators enables the National Cyber Response Centre to analyse IT incidents and give consolidated recommendations for action. The interests of the private sector to protect itself against crime and espionage in cyberspace should also be adequately taken into account.

At the same time respective responsibilities must be observed. Every stakeholder takes the necessary measures in its remit on the basis of the jointly developed national cyber security assessment and coordinates them with the competent authorities as well as partners from industry and academia. Since security preparedness is best achieved by early warning and prevention, the Cyber Response Centre will submit recommendations to the National Cyber Security Council both on a regular basis and for specific incidents. If the cyber security situation reaches the level of an imminent or already occurred crisis, the National Cyber Response Centre will directly inform the crisis management staff headed by the responsible State Secretary at the Federal Ministry of the Interior.

A NETWORK MODEL FOR CYBER SECURITY

A well-balanced cyber security policy framework is highly complex. Such a policy framework has no bounds or limits—geographical or jurisdictional. It necessarily encompasses a full spectrum of business, societal, and governmental interests. Although cyber security policy will inevitably address grave concerns about national and global security, as well as well-organized criminal activity, it is fundamentally about creating the very underpinnings of stable economic growth and open, transparent, just, and vibrant societies.

A "network model"—essentially, a communications network—illustrates how actors in the public and private sectors can work together to manage future cyber risks. Rather than focus on institutions and functions, the focus is on processes, procedures, and information flows within these sectors. In other words, the framework promotes thinking in terms of functions, rather than titles or national or international institutions. The focus on information flows is intended to help policymakers and other stakeholders visualize the systemic, inter-related nature of cyber security and how the actions of individual entities are likely to impact the decisions and responses of other participants in the network. It should be noted that such a model may require significant changes in traditional roles of intelligence and (inter)national security agencies, requiring them to operate on a more collaborative, interinstitutional basis.

The network model is based on three types of nodes or groups of stakeholders (policymakers, policy implementers, and operational personnel), which exchange three types of information on cyber-security: assessments, responses, and policy. Information exchange occurs both among the nodes, as well as between individual nodes and their peers in outside organizations at all levels. The model operates in the same way at four different levels, as risk management generally has the same components, regardless of whether it is conducted at the level of a firm, industrial sector, nation, or international organization. First, it requires communications across "organizational" boundaries. Second, it requires information exchange between stakeholders at different levels in the same organization and with other organizations regarding threats that have been encountered and handled. Third, procedures for handling such incidents are required and, fourth, legal or law enforcement sanctions may need to be applied.

At the national level, the major network "nodes" are central coordinating bodies, telecommunications regulators and e-economy ministries, intelligence agencies, law enforcement bodies, and national and governmental Computer Emergency Response Teams (CERTs) and Information Sharing and Analysis Centres (ISACs).

The model works at the international level, where the top-level node is comprised of multinational firms, political and military alliances, which coordinate with such international bodies as the ITU, G8, and the United Nations and its specialized agencies. The implementation node in the international model is comprised of individual national ministries (telecommunications, intelligence, e-economy, and defence ministries, together with law enforcement bodies) and the operational level of national firms (including software and hardware vendors), CERTs, and national defence organizations.

The drivers of various information exchanges—the factors that shape and influence critical flows of information—include regulatory requirements, liability obligations, and market signals (*e.g.*, risk-related information through which the performance of a network may be influenced). Each national networked relationship may operate with its own unique set of additional drivers. Policymakers may further shape certain drivers to influence node behaviour and performance. It may be possible, for example, to strengthen the influence of market-related drivers by using government procurement policies. Insurance and rating companies may use liability strategies to influence the cost of capital and the incentives for security-related investments.

PROMOTING AUTOMATION OF SECURITY

Several commenters to the NOI discussed how they use automated methods to detect potentially dangerous web behaviour in order to prevent users from exposing themselves to risk suggesting that others could be doing the same. These entities said that they also were providing incentives to the owners of bad web sites to reform.

By some accounts, approximately 80 per cent of successful online attacks are attributable to known vulnerabilities that can be addressed with implementation of widely agreed upon industry standards, proper configurations and patches. As more computing services are based in the cloud and move further away from centralized enterprises, automating security will likely become even more important than it is today. Enterprise and service delivery will need to address vulnerabilities easily and quickly in order to assure customers of security. In particular, the automated sharing of threats and related signature information among government agencies, among the private sector, and between public and private entities is becoming more commonplace.

With leadership from NIST, the National Security Agency (NSA), DHS and the U.S. CIO Council, the U.S. government leads efforts to automate configuration and vulnerability management. The private sector has also begun to adopt automation protocols such as Security Content Automation Protocol (SCAP) and Continuous Monitoring. These efforts offer enterprises of all sizes the ability to better update security compliance at potentially lower costs and pave the way for future automated protocols.

The security automation initiative is a public/private collaboration that spans multiple government agencies, more than 30 security tool vendors, and a host of end user organizations. The goal of the project is to enable the efficient and accurate collection, correlation, and sharing of security relevant information including software vulnerabilities, system configurations and network events across disparate systems in the enterprise.

Security automation work currently supports reference data such as the National Vulnerability Database (NVD), which provides software vulnerability information to users worldwide, and system configurations such as the U.S. Government Configuration Baseline (USGCB) through the Technology Infrastructure Sub-committee of the CIO Council. Standardization of security information has created opportunities for innovation in the private sector and research into new information domains like network events and asset management is expected to foster additional innovation in those markets. Through procurement strategies, the U.S. government can continue to provide tools for leveraging security automation technologies, leveraging existing vendor investment while encouraging additional investment in support of new specifications and standards.

THE FUTURE OF CYBER SECURITY

The product of human ingenuity and innovation, cyberspace now delivers a range of critical services to more citizens around the world than ever before. Yet, the online world as we know it stands at the threshold of unprecedented change.Being invited to speak at the EastWest Institute's Worldwide Security Conference in Brussels this week provided an opportunity to examine the needs faced by the global security community as we prepare to meet the needs of the Internet's next billion users. The International Telecommunication Union (ITU) reported that the number of Internet users reached the two billion threshold in March of this year and according to a Boston Consulting Group report, another billion are expected to come online in the next four years, bringing the total number of Internet users worldwide to about three billion by 2015.

Planning to ensure that our online world—cyberspace—is trustworthy, resilient and secure as we move into this uncertain future, policy leaders need to consider the fundamental changes that are occurring in cyberspace, and the policy issues that these changes will likely present and that will need to be addressed. Looking towards the future of three billion users, four factors will fundamentally change the future of cyberspace security: people, devices, data, and cloud services.

THE GLOBAL ONLINE POPULATION EXPANDS

The emergence of the next billion Internet users will impact security in two ways. Most important will be the impact of the demographic characteristics of these users. Consider that the next billion users will (1) be younger, (2) spend more time online, (3) be more mobile, (4) see the world through social media and apps, and (5) make greater use of natural interfaces. These five factors could hasten the onset of totally digital lifestyles making connectivity seemingly as essential as oxygen. The next billion could also help foster new innovation in the development and application of technology.

Separately, however, this emerging user population also represents a greatly expanded "target rich" environment for cybercriminals that want to exploit their data, social networks, and devices via botnets or other means.

Internet of Things to Immersive Computing

These new users will require new devices. According to The Boston Consulting Group, the number of Internet-connected devices is predicted to exceed 15 billion—twice the world's population–by 2015, and to soar to 50 billion devices by 2020. "Devices" of course refers to more than smart phones, netbooks and tablets. It also systems such as smart grids, intelligent transportation, Health care monitoring, smart manufacturing, and environmental sensors.

The advent of powerful wireless devices that both run infrastructure and deliver infrastructure services, including providing access to cloud services, means that cybercriminals and other threat actors need not merely target traditional, and increasingly protected, commercial software and consumer applications to execute attacks with significant consequences. Attackers may well target the embedded software, firmware and hardware in these devices to attack the infrastructure or seize control of the devices and turn them into sensors that can report status, collect personally identifiable information, or conduct other espionage.

Data: Rapid Increases in Understanding

The striking growth in the number of users and devices will also produce an exponential growth in the amount of data that is being generated, stored, analysed and transformed into innovation and knowledge. Analysing large data sets—so-called big data—will become a key basis of competition, underpinning new waves of productivity growth, innovation, and consumer surplus, according to research by MGI and McKinsey's Business Technology Office.

However, such data sets also represent attractive targets for organized cyber criminals and other threat actors. From a security standpoint, safeguarding these huge data sets, protecting privacy and integrity, will require concerted global effort requiring collaboration among governments, the private sector, and users.

Cloud Computing: The Information Society Enabler

With an exponentially growing community of increasingly mobile users, cloud computing will commensurately grow in importance. It will fundamentally change how businesses operate, how every manner of services are delivered, and even how lives are lived. On the positive side, the security best practices implemented by an effective cloud provider may rival or surpass the measures that cloud customers might themselves be able to provide, resulting in enhanced security. Yet there are global issues that will need to be addressed in terms of transparency and jurisdiction to enable cloud services that are both secure and scalable to service the needs of this expanded user community across multiple countries.

Reducing the Cyber-attack Surface

Reducing the cyber-attack surface can be achieved by industry and government working inpartnership to make the ICT infrastructure less susceptible to attack and compromise. One important way to achieve this is through concerted action to address risks in the supply chain for information and communications technology products and services. Vendors and service providers need to build and maintain world-class approaches to secure software and hardware development methodologies. Microsoft began this journey over 10 years ago and has openly shared its Security Development Lifecycle.

The non-profit alliance SAFECode provides a platform for companies to share, both within the software development community and more broadly, information on secure software development techniques that have proven to be effective as well as those that have not. Industry needs to do more.

For their part, governments need to understand the nature of ICT supply chain risk more clearly and work collaboratively with one another and with vendors to develop a common risk management framework rooted in core principles that both address supply chain integrity concerns and preserve the fruits of global free trade. Such a system should be risk-based,transparent, flexible, and should recognize the realities of reciprocal treatment in the global economic environment.

Improving Internet Health

Improving Internet health requires a global, collaborative approach to protecting people from the potential dangers of the Internet. Despite the best efforts at education and protection, many consumer computers host malware and may be part of a "botnet," unbeknownst to their legitimate owners. There is currently no concerted mechanism to shield users from or help them mitigate these risks. Such infected computers do not simply expose their owners' valuable information and data; they place others at risk too. This threat to greater society makes it is essential that the technology ecosystem take collective action to combat it. Work has been underway in industry circles to build cooperation among various stakeholder groups including ISPs, software vendors, and others; to leverage investments made in key regions of the world; and to create a future roadmap for an Internet health system. The active discussions of cyber security policy and legislation now underway in many nations afford a ripe opportunity to promote this Internet health model. As part of this discussion, it is important to focus on building a socially acceptable model. While the security benefits may be clear, it is important to achieve those benefits in a way that does not erode privacy or otherwise raise concern.

CYBER SECURITY THREATS IN COUNTER- ATTACKS

Many people have proposed methods of "counter-attack" or "active response" to deal with today's cyber security threats. There is a common belief that traditional approaches to the problem are inadequate. Patching software vulnerabilities is labour intensive, so many people don't do it until there's an attack. The legal system is slow to respond, courts lack the necessary technical expertise, and prosecutions do not occur often enough to deter attacks.

HISTORY OF CYBER SECURITY

The history of successful counter-attacks in the world of cyber security is a short one. There are an increasing number of papers and publications which make proposals, but concerns over legal issues as well as technical challenges have kept the list of successes small. In Sept. 1998, the Pentagon is reported to have counter-attacked some activists who were doing a Denial of Service attack of the Department of Defence's web sites, responding to their requests with an applet which ran on the attackers' machines and forced them to reboot.

In 1999, a California ISP Conxion wrote a script which caused DoS packets sent to the World Trade Organization's web site to be sent back to the attackers.

Of course, such an attack would not have worked if the attackers had used what's known as "IP address spoofing", which would have made the packets appear that they came from a different computer from where they did.

In 2001, several defences were created in response to the Code Red II worm. One, called CRclean, if it received a probe from the worm, would make use of a back door which the worm placed on the infected machine to load a neutralizing agent and halt the spread of the worm. But it would also install itself on that machine. Another, called CodeGreen, would actually scan the internet for computers with the IIS vulnerability that allowed CodeRed, then download the patch and place it on the machine, and clean up the back doors.

It is clear that there are serious legal and ethical issues with both of these worms, even the former, which is still a worm even though it only reacts to attacks. In 2003, the Welchia worm was released onto the Internet. Welchia would remove the Blaster worm and patch the vulnerability that Blaster used to spread. However, Welchia also caused severe network congestion.

In late 2004, Lycos Europe got fed up with spammers and launched a popular campaign called "Make Love Not Spam" which attracted over 100,000 users. Users could install a screen saver on their desktop which would send requests to web sites which were known to advertise via spam. This effort was sucessful in causing some of the sites to change locations. (http://www.makelovenotspam.com) Lycos reportedly got around the illegality of DDoS attacks by claiming to only take 95 per cent of the target sites' bandwidth, though, David Dittrich finds this reasoning dubious at best. Lycos ended this campaign in December 2004. Some companies such as Symbiot Security are currently developing counter attack tools and devices, but there is a lot of skepticism about deployment of devices because of liability concerns.

Cyber Security Incident Response

Counter-attacks are part of the overall process of cyber security incident response. This consists of five stages:

1. Intrusion detection.
2. Identifying the attacker.
3. Defending against the attack.
4. Designing and deploying a counter-attack.
5. Post-conflict investigation and support.

Intrusion Detection: Intrusion detection first identifies if there is an intrusion or intrusion attempt in the network or machine connected to network. Monitoring can be done on the network or on end-hosts. Firewalls and virus scanners also contribute. There are various techniques, such as anomaly detection, and policy-based approaches.

Identifying the Attacker

This very important step towards counter-attack, basically knowing who your enemy is and where is he located. Identifying the attacker can be difficult, since an attacker may use one compromised host to attack another. Also, with today's network architecture it can be quite difficult to locate the real attacker. Packets can be sent with spoofed source addresses, and tracing them through multiple hops and different autonomous systems can be a complicated process. Finding out the specific server and location can be critical in determining what the counter-attack would be.

Defending against the Attack: Before an attack, software patches are used to fix vulnerabillities. More interesting are defences once an attack against a real vulnerability has happened. Diversions can be set forth to surprise an attacker. Or once the attack has been detected, countermeasures can be put in place to stop further damage. Also, diversion tactics like Honey Pots can be used to keep the rest of the network safe. The information from these diversions (or information gained during the delays caused by these tactics) can be harnessed to engineer a specific counter-attack.

Designing and Deploying a Counter-Attack: Counter-attacks take a surprising variety of forms. Designing a counter- attack should take into account the following factors: the method of attack; the support of the network infrastructure (*i.e.* are ISPs performing egress filtering); collateral damage; and costs.

Post-Counter-Attack Investigation and Support: In order to aid the post-counter-attack investigation a counter- attack should have inbuilt mechanism to log its trail and its operation history. Ideally, it will also provide a means of discovering the hacker's techniques and identity. The more risk hackers have of being discovered, the less likely they are to go hacking.

Anti-worms

A worm spreads itself by sending out packets which look for certain responses from computers. It will analyse those responses to deduce if it thinks the replying machine has the vulnerability that it exploits. These packets represent a worm's 'signature'. The machine the worm is targeting can detect the signature of the worm and thus know its mode of propagation. An anti-worm is generated, which exploits the same vulnerabilities as the original worm or uses the back doors opened by the original worm. The antiworm would either fix the attacking host, neutralize the worm, or bring it down gracefully, potentially informing the owner. It may also install itself for further propagation.

In addition to the stated goal, an anti-worm adheres to following guidelines to minimize collateral damage:

- It is bug-free and does leave other vulnerabilities that could be exploited further.
- It can be uninstalled gracefully when owner asks for it.
- It makes minimal changes to host that it operates on.
- It should not be able to be used for propagating malicious content.

The countermeasure, or 'Neutralizing Agent' used, can take several forms. For example, it could patch the vulnerability and remove the botnet or worm. Less invasive changes include blocking the port over which the worm sends messages, or using a mutex and rebooting the machine to lock the botnet from being able to execute.

Also, one would have to remove any backdoors left by the worm.

In addition, deployment strategy of the anti-worm will determine its effectiveness and collateral damage it may cause.

- *Active Deployment*: The anti-worm is itself a worm; it propagates across the network by scanning and seeking exploited vulnerabilities. This is the fastest way to remove the original worm from the network, but this also causes the most collateral damage by affecting the network traffic a lot.
- *Passive Deployment*: The anti-worm waits on a host till another host attacks it, and then the anti-worm cures only the attacking host. Collateral damage is bare minimum, but the anti-worm is left behind on the new host.
- *Controlled Deployment*: The anti-worm propagation is control via some statistic of number of infected/vulnerable host to number host it cured. This can be very effective and efficient.
- *IDS base Deployment*: The anti-worm uses the intrusion detection sensors which monitor traffic and may deploy an anti-worm against an attacker. As with passive deployment, collateral damage is limited to computers actively launching attacks, but this is less invasive because it does not leave a worm, it just neutralizes the machine.

Spam

Spam is unsolicited e-mail. A virus is a programme which, when executed, installs malware such as root-kits, key-stroke loggers, etc. These programmes are then used to send sensitive information to the attacker without the user's consent. Both spam and viruses spread through e-mail and require human interaction to activate them. E-mail servers as well as the hosts can detect spam with the help of spam detectors like Symantec's TurnTide. Once the spam is identified one counter attack is achieved by automatic flooding of the Sender Server with bounced e-mails and mail notification to server's administrator. (Even if sender addresses are spoofed, one may be able to identify the last mail server that forwarded a message.)

Botnet

An attacker establishes a botnet by first spreading a virus or worm that takes over the vulnerable hosts. Each worm or virus then calls Home to tell that it has successfully captured the Host. It also establishes a command channel such that the Attacker through the home can control the host. Botnets can be used for DDOS attacks, phishing etc.

Counter-Attack

- Counter-attack involves identifying the attacker by monitoring the compromised Host and intercepting its communication to the Home machine. The Home machine is probably the attacker's base or intermediate node for communication between the host and the attacker base machines. Once that machine is identified, you hack back into that machine bring it down. For hacking back, you can use same techniques as used by the hackers to take control of the attacking machine.
- Taking down the Home machine only removes the attacker for a short duration, the network of compromised hosts still exists. A more effective counter-attack would be to takeover or monitor the command channel for communication between the Home and other compromised hosts. If possible, identify other compromised hosts and fix them or take them down as preventive measure.

THREATS AND COUNTERMEASURES

This chapter analyses Web application security from the perspectives of threats, countermeasures, vulnerabilities, and attacks. The following set of core terms are defined to avoid confusion and to ensure they are used in the correct context.

- *Asset*. A resource of value such as the data in a database or on the file system, or a system resource
- *Threat*. A potential occurrence — malicious or otherwise — that may harm an asset
- *Vulnerability*. A weakness that makes a threat possible
- *Attack (or exploit)*. An action taken to harm an asset
- *Countermeasure*. A safeguard that addresses a threat and mitigates risk

This chapter also identifies a set of common network, host, and application level threats, and the recommended countermeasures to address each one. The chapter does not contain an exhaustive list of threats, but it does highlight many top threats. With this information and knowledge of how an attacker works, you will be able to identify additional threats. You need to know the threats that are most likely to impact your system to be able to build effective threat models.

UNDERSTANDING THREAT CATEGORIES

While there are many variations of specific attacks and attack techniques, it is useful to think about threats in terms of what the attacker is trying to achieve. This changes your focus from the identification of every specific attack — which is really just a means to an end — to focusing on the end results of possible attacks.

STRIDE

Threats faced by the application can be categorized based on the goals and purposes of the attacks. A working knowledge of these categories of threats can help you organize a security strategy so that you have planned responses to threats. STRIDE is the acronym used at Microsoft to categorize different threat types. STRIDE stands for:

- *Spoofing*. Spoofing is attempting to gain access to a system by using a false identity. This can be accomplished using stolen user credentials or a false IP address. After the attacker successfully gains access as a legitimate user or host, elevation of privileges or abuse using authorization can begin.
- *Tampering*. Tampering is the unauthorized modification of data, for example as it flows over a network between two computers.
- *Repudiation*. Repudiation is the ability of users (legitimate or otherwise) to deny that they performed specific actions or transactions. Without adequate auditing, repudiation attacks are difficult to prove.
- *Information disclosure*. Information disclosure is the unwanted exposure of private data. For example, a user views the contents of a table or file he or she is not authorized to open, or monitors data passed in plaintext over a network. Some examples of information disclosure vulnerabilities include the use of hidden form fields, comments embedded in Web pages that contain database connection strings and connection details, and weak exception handling that can lead to internal system level details being revealed to the client. Any of this information can be very useful to the attacker.
- *Denial of service*. Denial of service is the process of making a system or application unavailable. For example, a denial of service attack might be accomplished by bombarding a server with requests to consume all available system resources or by passing it malformed input data that can crash an application process.

- *Elevation of privilege*. Elevation of privilege occurs when a user with limited privileges assumes the identity of a privileged user to gain privileged access to an application. For example, an attacker with limited privileges might elevate his or her privilege level to compromise and take control of a highly privileged and trusted process or account.

NETWORK THREATS AND COUNTERMEASURES

The primary components that make up your network infrastructure are routers, firewalls, and switches. They act as the gatekeepers guarding your servers and applications from attacks and intrusions. An attacker may exploit poorly configured network devices. Common vulnerabilities include weak default installation settings, wide open access controls, and devices lacking the latest security patches. Top network level threats include:

Information Gathering

Network devices can be discovered and profiled in much the same way as other types of systems. Attackers usually start with port scanning. After they identify open ports, they use banner grabbing and enumeration to detect device types and to determine operating system and application versions. Armed with this information, an attacker can attack known vulnerabilities that may not be updated with security patches.

Countermeasures to prevent information gathering include:

- Configure routers to restrict their responses to footprinting requests.
- Configure operating systems that host network software (for example, software firewalls) to prevent footprinting by disabling unused protocols and unnecessary ports.

Sniffing

Sniffing or eavesdropping is the act of monitoring traffic on the network for data such as plaintext passwords or configuration information. With a simple packet sniffer, an attacker can easily read all plaintext traffic. Also, attackers can crack packets encrypted by lightweight hashing algorithms and can decipher the payload that you considered to be safe. The sniffing of packets requires a packet sniffer in the path of the server/client communication.

Countermeasures to help prevent sniffing include:

- Use strong physical security and proper segmenting of the network. This is the first step in preventing traffic from being collected locally.
- Encrypt communication fully, including authentication credentials. This prevents sniffed packets from being usable to an attacker. SSL and IPSec (Internet Protocol Security) are examples of encryption solutions.

Spoofing

Spoofing is a means to hide one's true identity on the network. To create a spoofed identity, an attacker uses a fake source address that does not represent the actual address of the packet. Spoofing may be used to hide the original source of an attack or to work around network access control lists (ACLs) that are in place to limit host access based on source address rules.

Although carefully crafted spoofed packets may never be tracked to the original sender, a combination of filtering rules prevents spoofed packets from originating from your network, allowing you to block obviously spoofed packets.

Countermeasures to prevent spoofing include:

- Filter incoming packets that appear to come from an internal IP address at your perimeter.
- Filter outgoing packets that appear to originate from an invalid local IP address.

Session Hijacking

Also known as man in the middle attacks, session hijacking deceives a server or a client into accepting the upstream host as the actual legitimate host. Instead the upstream host is an attacker's host that is manipulating the network so the attacker's host appears to be the desired destination.

Countermeasures to help prevent session hijacking include:

- Use encrypted session negotiation.
- Use encrypted communication channels.
- Stay informed of platform patches to fix TCP/IP vulnerabilities, such as predictable packet sequences.

Denial of Service

Denial of service denies legitimate users access to a server or services. The SYN flood attack is a common example of a network level denial of service attack. It is easy to launch and difficult to track. The aim of the attack is to send more requests to a server than it can handle. The attack exploits a potential vulnerability in the TCP/IP connection establishment mechanism and floods the server's pending connection queue.

Countermeasures to prevent denial of service include:

- Apply the latest service packs.
- Harden the TCP/IP stack by applying the appropriate registry settings to increase the size of the TCP connection queue, decrease the connection establishment period, and employ dynamic backlog mechanisms to ensure that the connection queue is never exhausted.
- Use a network Intrusion Detection System (IDS) because these can automatically detect and respond to SYN attacks.

ANATOMY OF AN ATTACK

By understanding the basic approach used by attackers to target your Web application, you will be better equipped to take defensive measures because you will know what you are up against. The basic steps in attacker methodology are summarized below and illustrated in Figure below:

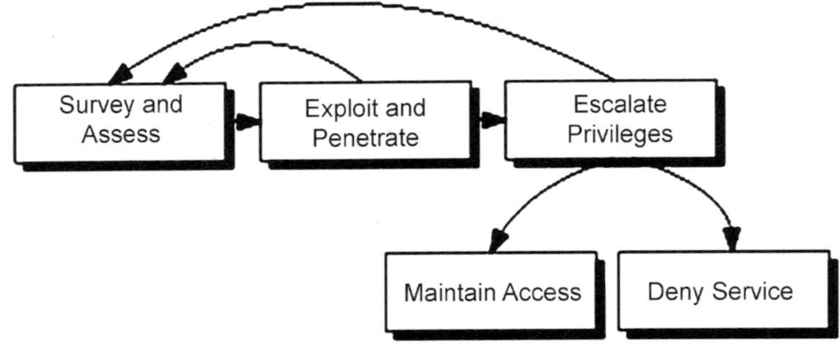

Fig. Basic Steps for Attacking Methodology

Survey and Assess

Surveying and assessing the potential target are done in tandem. The first step an attacker usually takes is to survey the potential target to identify and assess its characteristics. These characteristics may include its supported services and protocols together with potential vulnerabilities and entry points. The attacker uses the information gathered in the survey and assess phase to plan an initial attack.

For example, an attacker can detect a cross-site scripting (XSS) vulnerability by testing to see if any controls in a Web page echo back output.

Exploit and Penetrate

Having surveyed a potential target, the next step is to exploit and penetrate. If the network and host are fully secured, your application (the front gate) becomes the next channel for attack.

For an attacker, the easiest way into an application is through the same entrance that legitimate users use — for example, through the application's logon page or a page that does not require authentication.

Escalate Privileges

After attackers manage to compromise an application or network, perhaps by injecting code into an application or creating an authenticated session with the Microsoft® Windows® 2000 operating system, they immediately attempt to escalate privileges.

Specifically, they look for administration privileges provided by accounts that are members of the Administrators group. They also seek out the high level of privileges offered by the local system account.

Using least privileged service accounts throughout your application is a primary defence against privilege escalation attacks. Also, many network level privilege escalation attacks require an interactive logon session.

Maintain Access

Having gained access to a system, an attacker takes steps to make future access easier and to cover his or her tracks. Common approaches for making future access easier include planting back-door programmes or using an existing account that lacks strong protection. Covering tracks typically involves clearing logs and hiding tools. As such, audit logs are a primary target for the attacker.

Log files should be secured, and they should be analysed on a regular basis. Log file analysis can often uncover the early signs of an attempted break-in before damage is done.

Deny Service

Attackers who cannot gain access often mount a denial of service attack to prevent others from using the application. For other attackers, the denial of service option is their goal from the outset. An example is the SYN flood attack, where the attacker uses a programme to send a flood of TCP SYN requests to fill the pending connection queue on the server. This prevents other users from establishing network connections.

HOST THREATS AND COUNTERMEASURES

Host threats are directed at the system software upon which your applications are built. This includes Windows 2000, Microsoft Windows Server 2003, Internet Information Services (IIS), the.NET Framework, and SQL Server depending upon the specific server role. Top host level threats include:

Viruses, Trojan Horses, and Worms

A virus is a programme that is designed to perform malicious acts and cause disruption to your operating system or applications. A Trojan horse resembles a virus except that the malicious code is contained inside what appears to be a harmless data file or executable programme. A worm is similar to a Trojan horse except that it self-replicates from one server to another. Worms are difficult to detect because they do not regularly create files that can be seen. They are often noticed only when they begin to consume system resources because the system slows down or the execution of other programmes halt. The Code Red Worm is one of the most notorious to afflict IIS; it relied upon a buffer overflow vulnerability in a particular ISAPI filter.

Although these three threats are actually attacks, together they pose a significant threat to Web applications, the hosts these applications live on, and the network used to deliver these applications. The success of these attacks on any system is possible through many vulnerabilities such as weak defaults, software bugs, user error, and inherent vulnerabilities in Internet protocols.

Countermeasures that you can use against viruses, Trojan horses, and worms include:

- Stay current with the latest operating system service packs and software patches.
- Block all unnecessary ports at the firewall and host.
- Disable unused functionality including protocols and services.
- Harden weak, default configuration settings.

Footprinting

Examples of footprinting are port scans, ping sweeps, and NetBIOS enumeration that can be used by attackers to glean valuable system-level information to help prepare for more significant attacks. The type of information potentially revealed by footprinting includes account details, operating system and other software versions, server names, and database schema details.

Countermeasures to help prevent footprinting include:

- Disable unnecessary protocols.
- Lock down ports with the appropriate firewall configuration.
- Use TCP/IP and IPSec filters for defence in depth.
- Configure IIS to prevent information disclosure through banner grabbing.
- Use an IDS that can be configured to pick up footprinting patterns and reject suspicious traffic.

Password Cracking

If the attacker cannot establish an anonymous connection with the server, he or she will try to establish an authenticated connection. For this, the attacker must know a valid username and password combination. If you use default account names, you are giving the attacker a head start. Then the attacker only has to crack the account's password. The use of blank or weak passwords makes the attacker's job even easier.

Countermeasures to help prevent password cracking include:

- Use strong passwords for all account types.
- Apply lockout policies to end-user accounts to limit the number of retry attempts that can be used to guess the password.
- Do not use default account names, and rename standard accounts such as the administrator's account and the anonymous Internet user account used by many Web applications.
- Audit failed logins for patterns of password hacking attempts.

Denial of Service

Denial of service can be attained by many methods aimed at several targets within your infrastructure. At the host, an attacker can disrupt service by brute force against your application, or an attacker may know of a vulnerability that exists in the service your application is hosted in or in the operating system that runs your server.

Countermeasures to help prevent denial of service include:

- Configure your applications, services, and operating system with denial of service in mind.
- Stay current with patches and security updates.
- Harden the TCP/IP stack against denial of service.
- Make sure your account lockout policies cannot be exploited to lock out well known service accounts.
- Make sure your application is capable of handling high volumes of traffic and that thresholds are in place to handle abnormally high loads.
- Review your application's failover functionality.
- Use an IDS that can detect potential denial of service attacks.

Arbitrary Code Execution

If an attacker can execute malicious code on your server, the attacker can either compromise server resources or mount further attacks against downstream systems. The risks posed by arbitrary code execution increase if the server process under which the attacker's code runs is over-privileged. Common vulnerabilities include weak IIS configuration and unpatched servers that allow path traversal and buffer overflow attacks, both of which can lead to arbitrary code execution.

Countermeasures to help prevent arbitrary code execution include:

- Configure IIS to reject URLs with "../" to prevent path traversal.
- Lock down system commands and utilities with restricted ACLs.
- Stay current with patches and updates to ensure that newly discovered buffer overflows are speedily patched.

Unauthorized Access

Inadequate access controls could allow an unauthorized user to access restricted information or perform restricted operations. Common vulnerabilities include weak IIS Web access controls, including Web permissions and weak NTFS permissions.

Countermeasures to help prevent unauthorized access include:

- Configure secure Web permissions.
- Lock down files and folders with restricted NTFS permissions.
- Use.NET Framework access control mechanisms within your ASP.NET applications, including URL authorization and principal permission demands.

AUTHENTICATION MECHANISMS

Depending on your requirements, there are several available authentication mechanisms to choose from. If they are not correctly chosen and implemented, the authentication mechanism can expose vulnerabilities that attackers can exploit to gain access to your system. The top threats that exploit authentication vulnerabilities include:

Network Eavesdropping

If authentication credentials are passed in plaintext from client to server, an attacker armed with rudimentary network monitoring software on a host on the same network can capture traffic and obtain user names and passwords.

Countermeasures to prevent network eavesdropping include:

- Use authentication mechanisms that do not transmit the password over the network such as Kerberos protocol or Windows authentication.
- Make sure passwords are encrypted (if you must transmit passwords over the network) or use an encrypted communication channel, for example with SSL.

Brute Force Attacks

Brute force attacks rely on computational power to crack hashed passwords or other secrets secured with hashing and encryption. To mitigate the risk, use strong passwords. Additionally, use hashed passwords with salt; this slows down the attacker considerably and allows sufficient time for countermeasures to be activated.

Dictionary Attacks

This attack is used to obtain passwords. Most password systems do not store plaintext passwords or encrypted passwords. They avoid encrypted passwords because a compromised key leads to the compromise of all passwords in the data store. Lost keys mean that all passwords are invalidated. Most user store implementations hold password hashes (or digests). Users are authenticated by re-computing the hash based on the user-supplied password value and comparing it against the hash value stored in the database.

If an attacker manages to obtain the list of hashed passwords, a brute force attack can be used to crack the password hashes. With the dictionary attack, an attacker uses a programme to iterate through all of the words in a dictionary (or multiple dictionaries in different languages) and computes the hash for each word. The resultant hash is compared with the value in the data store. Weak passwords such as "Yankees" (a favourite team) or "Mustang" (a favourite car) will be cracked quickly. Stronger passwords such as "? You' LlNevaFiNdMeyePasSWerd!", are less likely to be cracked.

Note Once the attacker has obtained the list of password hashes, the dictionary attack can be performed offline and does not require interaction with the application.

Countermeasures to prevent dictionary attacks include:

- Use strong passwords that are complex, are not regular words, and contain a mixture of upper case, lower case, numeric, and special characters.
- Store non-reversible password hashes in the user store. Also combine a salt value (a cryptographically strong random number) with the password hash.

Cookie Replay Attacks

With this type of attack, the attacker captures the user's authentication cookie using monitoring software and replays it to the application to gain access under a false identity.

Countermeasures to prevent cookie replay include:

- Use an encrypted communication channel provided by SSL whenever an authentication cookie is transmitted.
- Use a cookie timeout to a value that forces authentication after a relatively short time interval. Although this doesn't prevent replay attacks, it reduces the time interval in which the attacker can replay a request without being forced to re-authenticate because the session has timed out.

Credential Theft

If your application implements its own user store containing user account names and passwords, compare its security to the credential stores provided by the platform, for example, a Microsoft Active Directory® directory service or Security Accounts Manager (SAM) user store. Browser history and cache also store user login information for future use. If the terminal is accessed by someone other than the user who logged on, and the same page is hit, the saved login will be available.

Countermeasures to help prevent credential theft include:

- Use and enforce strong passwords.
- Store password verifiers in the form of one way hashes with added salt.
- Enforce account lockout for end-user accounts after a set number of retry attempts.
- To counter the possibility of the browser cache allowing login access, create functionality that either allows the user to choose to not save credentials, or force this functionality as a default policy.

10

Cyber Terrorism and its Network

CYBERTERRORISM

WHAT IS CYBERTERRORISM?

Cyberterrorism is the convergence of cyberspace and terrorism. It refers to unlawful attacks and threats of attack against computers, networks, and the information stored therein when done to intimidate or coerce a government or its people in furtherance of political or social objectives. Further, to qualify as cyberterrorism, an attack should result in violence against persons or property, or at least cause enough harm to generate fear. Attacks that lead to death or bodily injury, explosions, or severe economic loss would be examples. Serious attacks against critical infrastructures could be acts of cyberterrorism, depending on their impact. Attacks that disrupt non-essential services or that are mainly a costly nuisance would not.

Numerous scenarios have been suggested. In one, a cyberterrorist attacks the computer systems that control a large regional power grid. Power is lost for a sustained period of time and people die. In another, the cyberterrorist breaks into an air traffic control system and tampers with the system. Two large civilian aircraft collide. In a third, the cyberterrorist disrupts banks, international financial transactions, and stock exchanges. Economic systems grind to a halt, the public loses confidence, and destabilization is achieved. While none of these or similar scenarios has played out, many believe it is not a question of "if" but "when."

Terrorists in Cyberspace

Terrorists have moved into cyberspace to facilitate traditional forms of terrorism such as bombings. They use the Internet to communicate, coordinate events, and advance their agenda. While such activity does not constitute cyberterrorism in the strict sense, it does show that terrorists have some competency using the new information technologies. By 1996, the headquarters of terrorist financier Osama bin Laden in Afghanistan was equipped with computers and communications equipment. Egyptian "Afghan" computer experts were said to have helped devise a communication network that used the Web, e-mail, and electronic bulletin boards. Hamas activists have been said to use chat rooms and e-mail to plan operations and coordinate activities, making it difficult for Israeli security officials to trace their messages and decode their contents. The Revolutionary Armed Forces of Columbia (FARC) uses e-mail to field enquiries from the press.

The Web is especially popular as a medium for reaching a global audience. For example, after the Peruvian terrorist group Tupac Amaru stormed the Japanese Ambassador's residence in Lima on December 17, 1996 and took 400 diplomatic, political, and military officials as hostage, sympathizers in the United States and Canada put up solidarity Web sites. One site included detailed drawings of the residence and planned assault.

In February 1998, Hizbullah was operating three Web sites: one for the central press office, another to describe its attacks on Israeli targets, and the third for news and information. That month, Clark Staten, executive director of the Emergency Response and Research Institute (ERRI) in Chicago, testified before a U.S. Senate subcommittee that "even small terrorist groups are now using the Internet to broadcast their message and misdirect/misinform the general population in multiple nations simultaneously." He gave the subcommittee copies of both domestic and international messages containing anti-American and anti-Israeli propaganda and threats, including a widely distributed extremist call for "jihad" (holy war) against America and Great Britain.

In June 1998, *U.S. News and World Report* noted that 12 of the 30 groups on the U.S. State Department's list of terrorist organizations are on the Web. Now, it appears that virtually every terrorist group is on the Web. Forcing them off the Web is impossible, because they can set up their sites in countries with free-speech laws. The government of Sri Lanka, for example, banned the separatist Liberation Tigers of Tamil Eelam, but they have not even attempted to take down their London-based Web site.

Many terrorists are using encryption to conceal their communications and stored files, compounding the difficulties of providing effective counter-terrorism. Hamas, for example, reportedly has used encrypted Internet communications to transmit maps, pictures, and other details pertaining to terrorist attacks.

Ramsey Yousef, a member of the international terrorist group responsible for bombing the World Trade Center in 1994 and a Manila Air airliner in late 1995, encrypted files on his laptop computer. The files, which U.S. government officials decrypted, contained information pertaining to further plans to blow up eleven U.S.-owned commercial airliners in the Far East. The Aum Shinrikyo cult, which gassed the Tokyo subway in March 1995, killing 12 people and injuring 6,000 more, also used encryption to protect their computerized records, which included plans and intentions to deploy weapons of mass destruction in Japan and the United States.

CYBERSPACE ATTACKS

Governments are particularly concerned with terrorist and state-sponsored attacks against the critical infrastructures that constitute their national life support systems. The Clinton Administration defined eight: telecommunications, banking and finance, electrical power, oil and gas distribution and storage, water supply, transportation, emergency services, and government services.

There have been numerous attacks against these infrastructures. Hackers have invaded the public phone networks, compromising nearly every category of activity, including switching and operations, administration, maintenance, and provisioning (OAM&P).

They have crashed or disrupted signal transfer points, traffic switches, OAM&P systems, and other network elements. They have planted "time bomb" programmes designed to shut down major switching hubs, disrupted emergency 911 services throughout the eastern seaboard, and boasted that they have the capability to bring down all switches in Manhattan. They have installed wiretaps, rerouted phone calls, changed the greetings on voice mail systems, taken over voice mailboxes, and made free long-distance calls at their victims' expense — sticking some victims with phone bills in the hundreds of thousands of dollars. When they can't crack the technology, they use "social engineering" to con employees into giving them access.

In March 1997, one teenage hacker penetrated and disabled a telephone company computer that serviced the Worcester Airport in Massachusetts. As a result, telephone service to the Federal Aviation Administration control tower, the airport fire department, airport security, the weather service, and various private airfreight companies was cut off for six hours.

Later in the day, the juvenile disabled another telephone company computer, this time causing an outage in the Rutland area. The lost service caused financial damages and threatened public health and public safety. On a separate occasion, the hacker allegedly broke into a pharmacist's computer and accessed files containing prescriptions.

Banks and financial systems are a popular target of cyber criminals. The usual motive is money, and perpetrators have stolen or attempted to steal tens of millions of dollars.

In one case of sabotage, a computer operator at Reuters in Hong Kong tampered with the dealing room systems of five of the company's bank clients.

In November 1996, he programmed the systems to delete key operating system files after a delay long enough to allow him to leave the building. When the "time bombs" exploded, the systems crashed.

They were partially restored by the next morning, but it took another day before they were fully operational. However, the banks said the tampering did not significantly affect trading and that neither they nor their clients experienced losses.

In another act of sabotage against a critical infrastructure, a fired employee of Chevron's emergency alert network disabled the firm's alert system by hacking into computers in New York and San Jose, California, and reconfiguring them so they'd crash. The vandalism was not discovered until an emergency arose at the Chevron refinery in Richmond, California, and the system could not be used to notify the adjacent community of a noxious release. During the 10-hour period in 1992 when the system was down, thousands of people in 22 states and 6 unspecified areas of Canada were put at risk.

An overflow of raw sewage on the Sunshine Coast of Australia in June was linked to a 49-year-old Brisbane man, who allegedly penetrated the Maroochy Shire Council's computer system and used radio transmissions to create the overflows. The man faced 370 charges that included stealing, computer hacking, and use radio communications equipment without authority.

Government computers, particularly Department of Defence computers, are a regular target of attack. Detected attacks against unclassified DoD computers rose from 780 in 1997 to 5,844 in 1998 and 22,144 in 1999.

Politically and Socially Motivated Cyberattacks

There are a few indications that some terrorist groups are pursuing cyberterrorism, either alone or in conjunction with acts of physical violence. In February 1998, Clark Staten told the Senate Judiciary Committee Subcommittee on Technology, Terrorism, and Government Information that it was believed that "members of some Islamic extremist organizations have been attempting to develop a 'hacker network' to support their computer activities and even engage in offensive information warfare attacks in the future." In November 1998, the *Detroit News* reported that Khalid Ibrahim, who claimed to be a member of the militant Indian separatist group Harkat-ul-Ansar, had tried to buy military software from hackers who had stolen it from Department of Defence computers they had penetrated. The attempted purchase was discovered when an 18-year-old hacker calling himself Chameleon attempted to cash a $1,000 check from Ibrahim. Chameleon said he did not have the software and did not give it to Ibrahim, but Ibrahim may have obtained it or other sensitive information from one of the many other hackers he approached. Harkat-ul-Ansar declared war on the United States following the August cruise-missile attack on a suspected terrorist training camp in Afghanistan run by bin Laden, which allegedly killed nine of their members.

The Provisional Irish Republican Army employed the services of contract hackers to penetrate computers in order to acquire home addresses of law enforcement and intelligence officers, but the data was used to draw up plans to kill the officers in a single "night of the long knives" if the British government did not meet terms for a new cease-fire. As this case illustrates, terrorists may use hacking as a way of acquiring intelligence in support of physical violence, even if they do not use it to wreak havoc in cyberspace.

Potential Threat

To understand the potential threat of cyberterrorism, two factors must be considered: first, whether there are targets that are vulnerable to attack that could lead to violence or severe harm, and second, whether there are actors with the capability and motivation to carry them out.

Looking first at vulnerabilities, several studies have shown that critical infrastructures are potentially vulnerable to cyberterrorist attack. Eligible Receiver, an exercise conducted by the Department of Defence in 1997 with support from National Security Agency penetration testing teams, found the power grid and emergency 911 systems had weaknesses that could be exploited by an adversary using only publicly available tools on the Internet. Although neither of these systems were actually attacked, study members concluded that service on these systems could be disrupted. Also in 1997, the President's Commission on Critical Infrastructure Protection issued its report warning that through mutual dependencies and interconnectedness, critical infrastructures could be vulnerable in new ways, and that vulnerabilities were steadily increasing, while the costs of attack were decreasing.

Although many of the weaknesses in computerized systems can be corrected, it is effectively impossible to eliminate all of them. Even if the technology itself offers good security, it is frequently configured or used in ways that make it open to attack. In addition, there is always the possibility of insiders, acting alone or in concert with other terrorists, misusing their access capabilities. According to Russia's Interior Ministry Col. Konstantin Machabeli, the state-run gas monopoly, Gazprom, was hit by hackers in 1999 who collaborated with a Gazprom insider. The hackers were said to have used a Trojan horse to gain control of the central switchboard which controls gas flows in pipelines, although Gazprom, the world's largest natural gas producer and the largest gas supplier to Western Europe, refuted the report.

Consultants and contractors are frequently in a position where they could cause grave harm. This past March, Japan's Metropolitan Police Department reported that a software system they had procured to track 150 police vehicles, including unmarked cars, had been developed by the Aum Shinryko cult. At the time of the discovery, the cult had received classified tracking data on 115 vehicles. Further, the cult had developed software for at least 80 Japanese firms and 10 government agencies. They had worked as subcontractors to other firms, making it almost impossible for the organizations to know who was developing the software. As subcontractors, the cult could have installed Trojan horses to launch or facilitate cyberterrorist attacks at a later date. Fearing a Trojan horse of their own, last February, the U.S. State Department sent an urgent cable to about 170 embassies asking them to remove software, which they belatedly realized had been written by citizens of the former Soviet Union.

Future Prospects

In August 1999, the Center for the Study of Terrorism and Irregular Warfare at the Naval Postgraduate School in Monterey, California, issued a report titled "Cyberterror: Prospects and Implications." Their objective was to articulate the demand side of terrorism. Specifically, they assessed the prospects of terrorist organizations pursuing cyberterrorism. They concluded that the barrier to entry for anything beyond annoying hacks is quite high, and that terrorists generally lack the wherewithal and human capital needed to mount a meaningful operation. Cyberterrorism, they argued, was a thing of the future, although it might be pursued as an ancillary tool.

The Monterey team defined three levels of cyberterror capability. First is simple-unstructured: the capability to conduct basic hacks against individual systems using tools created by someone else. The organization possesses little target analysis, command and control, or learning capability.

Second is advanced-structured: the capability to conduct more sophisticated attacks against multiple systems or networks and possibly, to modify or create basic hacking tools. The organization possesses an elementary target analysis, command and control, and learning capability.

Third is complex-coordinated: the capability for a coordinated attacks capable of causing mass-disruption against integrated, heterogeneous defences (including cryptography). The organization has the ability to create sophisticated hacking tools. They possess a highly capable target analysis, command and control, and organization learning capability.

The Monterey team estimated that it would take a group starting from scratch 2-4 years to reach the advanced-structured level and 6-10 years to reach the complex-coordinated level, although some groups might get there in just a few years or turn to outsourcing or sponsorship to extend their capability.

The study examined five terrorist group types: religious, New Age, ethno-nationalist separatist, revolutionary, and far-right extremists. They determined that only the religious groups are likely to seek the most damaging capability level, as it is consistent with their indiscriminate application of violence. New Age or single issue terrorists, such as the Animal Liberation Front, pose the most immediate threat, however, such groups are likely to accept disruption as a substitute for destruction. Both the revolutionary and ethno-nationalist separatists are likely to seek an advanced-structured capability. The far-right extremists are likely to settle for a simple-unstructured capability, as cyberterror offers neither the intimacy nor cathartic effects that are central to the psychology of far-right terror. The study also determined that hacker groups are psychologically and organizationally ill-suited to cyberterrorism, and that it would be against their interests to cause mass disruption of the information infrastructure.

Thus, at this time, cyberterrorism does not seem to pose an imminent threat. This could change. For a terrorist, it would have some advantages over physical methods. It could be conducted remotely and anonymously, and it would not require the handling of explosives or a suicide mission. It would likely garner extensive media coverage, as journalists and the public alike are fascinated by practically any kind of computer attack. Indeed cyberterrorism could be immensely appealing precisely because of the tremendous attention given to it by the government and media.

Cyberterrorism also has its drawbacks. Systems are complex, so it may be harder to control an attack and achieve a desired level of damage than using physical weapons. Unless people are injured, there is also less drama and emotional appeal. Further, terrorists may be disinclined to try new methods unless they see their old ones as inadequate, particularly when the new methods require considerable knowledge and skill to use effectively. Terrorists generally stick with tired and true methods. Novelty and sophistication of attack may be much less important than assurance that a mission will be operationally successful. Indeed, the risk of operational failure could be a deterrent to terrorists. For now, the truck bomb poses a much greater threat than the logic bomb.

The next generation of terrorists will grow up in a digital world, with ever more powerful and easy-to-use hacking tools at their disposal. They might see greater potential for cyberterrorism than the terrorists of today, and their level of knowledge and skill relating to hacking will be greater. Hackers and insiders might be recruited by terrorists or become self-recruiting cyberterrorists, the Timothy McVeigh's of cyberspace.

Some might be moved to action by cyber policy issues, making cyberspace an attractive venue for carrying out an attack. Cyberterrorism could also become more attractive as the real and virtual worlds become more closely coupled, with a greater number of physical devices attached to the Internet. Unless these systems are carefully secured, conducting an operation that physically harms someone may be easy as penetrating a Web site is today.

Riptech Internet Security Report

Riptech, Inc. was founded in 1998 by a group of U.S. Department of Defence security professionals to protect its clients' network security needs. Riptech publishes a semiannual Internet Security Report based on a sample set of its more than 400 clients located in more than 30 countries throughout the world.

- During the six-month period from January – June 2002, Riptech discovered that 39 per cent of attacks appeared to be targeted at a specific organization rather than a general search for any exploitable system.
- Power and Energy, Financial Services, and High Tech companies continued to experience the highest rate of overall attack activity, and also suffered relatively higher rates of severe and highly aggressive attacks. 70 per cent of Power and Energy companies suffered at least one severe attack during the first six months of 2002, as opposed to 57 per cent during the last six months of 2001.

The Internet Security Report also includes an analysis of cyberterrorism attacks from countries included on Riptech's "Cyber-Terrorism Watch List", which includes the U.S. State Department's list of countries who are designated state sponsors of terrorism.

- Countries on the Watch List generated less than 1 per cent of all attacks detected over the past six months; 84 per cent of this activity originated in Kuwait, Pakistan, Egypt, Indonesia, and Iran.
- Attacks were detected from only three of the seven countries designated by the U.S. State Department as "State Sponsors of Terrorism." 90 per cent of this activity emanated
- from Iran, while the remaining 10 per cent was split evenly between Cuba and Sudan. Iraq, Syria, North Korea, and Libya did not show any attacks over the past six months; however, this is likely attributable to Internet connectivity and mapping restraints. Because Iraq, North Korea, Syria, and Libya, have little, if any, IP space assigned to them, it is difficult to detect attacks coming directly from these nations. Therefore, it is certainly possible that these countries are launching attacks, but they are being funneled through ISPs located in neighbouring countries.
- The average attacks per Internet capita for countries with between 100,000 and 1 million Internet users is approximately 50 per cent higher than the average rate for countries with more than 1 million Internet users.
- Iran and Kuwait top the list of attacking countries per Internet capita for countries with less than one million Internet users. The rate of attack activity from Kuwait far exceeds the rest of the top ten countries and is more than twice the mean of all of the top ten attacking countries in this category.

Deterrence and Prevention of Cyberterrorism

Section 814 of the USA Patriot Act amended 18 U.S.C. § 1030, the Computer Fraud and Abuse Act to strengthen its use against cyberterrorism.

Did these amendments go too far – or not far enough – in prosecuting cyberterrorism?

- Increased penalties for hackers who damage protected computers (from a maximum of 10 years for first offenders to a maximum of 20 years for a repeat offenders). 18 U.S.C. § 1030(c)(4).
- Clarified the *mens rea* required for 1030(a)(5) offences to make explicit that a hacker need only intend to damage the computer or the information on it, and not a specific dollar amount of loss or other special harm. 18 U.S.C. § 1030(a)(5)(B).
- Allowed the government to meet the $5,000 jurisdictional threshold for damaging a protected computer by aggregating "loss resulting from a related course of conduct affecting one or more other protected computers." 18 U.S.C. § 1030(a)(5)(B)(i).
- Added a new offence for damaging computers used for national security or criminal justice, even if that damage does not result in provable loss over $5,000. 18 U.S.C. 1030(a)(5)(B)(v).
- Expanded the coverage of the statute to include computers in foreign countries so long as there is an effect on U.S. interstate or foreign commerce, allowing speedier domestic procedures to join in international hacker investigations. 18 U.S.C. § 1030(e)(2)(B)

OBSTACLES AND OPTIONS FOR CYBER ARMS CONTROLS

The Internet has evolved from a benign research environment to a venue for crime and conflict. Increasingly, cyber spies, thieves, and vandals exploit computers and networks to disrupt service, sabotage information and systems, and steal sensitive information. Although cyber defences are improving, the number and cost of attacks seems to be rising at an even faster rate. Further, there is a real danger that cyber terrorists, hostile nations, and others will launch attacks that cause catastrophic damage, potentially leading to loss of life or widespread economic failure.

The question arises then whether an international cyber arms control treaty might diminish the criminal and national security threats, while promoting greater cyber peace. Such a treaty might pertain to the development, distribution, and deployment of cyber weapons, or it might apply only to their use. It might relate primarily to criminal law, or it might govern the conduct of nation states in the domain of international law.

The purpose of this chapter is to address obstacles and options for implementing a cyber arms control treaty. It is concerned mainly with computer network attacks and the cyber weapons deployed in those attacks. These weapons include software and methods for sabotaging systems and data and for launching computer viruses, worms, and denial-of-service attacks. After reviewing obstacles, the paper presents options for overcoming these obstacles.

Obstacles

To be effective, a cyber arms control treaty must overcome obstacles in several areas: enforcement, security, privacy, free speech, corporate liabilities and responsibilities, and foreign policy.

Enforceability

Before considering the enforceability of a cyber arms control treaty, it is worth noting that it has been extremely difficult to enforce existing criminal laws that pertain to computer network attacks. Many attacks are never detected in the first place. When they are, finding the perpetrator is seldom easy, especially when the person has looped through numerous computers in different countries. An attack against computers in one country, for example, might appear to originate from government computers in another, all the while being perpetrated by teenage hackers in a third country who had gained control over the computers. Further, many countries do not have adequate cyber crime laws, making it difficult or impossible to prosecute persons in those countries who commit acts that are illegal in their victim's county. Even if their laws are good, their investigative capability may be inadequate, or they may not agree to cooperate in an international investigation.

A cyber arms control treaty could alleviate many of these problems by promoting greater harmony of national crime laws and greater cooperation among international law enforcement agencies. Enforcement would still be non-trivial, however, as it only takes a few non-compliant countries to complicate an investigation. Further, enforcement would be problematic as it relates to the actions of sovereign states, as it can be hard to know if an attack originated from a state or non-state actor. The United States government has yet to determine who is responsible for the ongoing Moonlight Maze intrusions into Department of Defence computers other than that they are coming out of Russia.

Currently, most crime laws do not prohibit the production, distribution, or possession of cyber weapons, at least when the tools are not used in conjunction with a crime. Given that many treaties and laws restrict these activities as they pertain to certain physical weapons, particularly chemical, biological, and nuclear weapons, it is reasonable to consider whether a cyber arms control treaty should extend such restrictions to cyber weapons.

At least on the surface, it would seem to be much more difficult to enforce general prohibitions against cyber weapons, as they can be manufactured without any special physical materials or laboratory facilities. All that is required is a computer and standard software, both of which are readily available. A nation could abrogate a cyber arms control treaty one day and develop cyber weapons the next. Moreover, once produced, cyber weapons are easily copied and distributed on the Internet through electronic mail, web sites, instant messaging, peer-to-peer sharing systems, and other mechanisms. Unlike many physical weapons, software weapons can be transmitted and stored without posing any physical danger to the parties involved. Thousands of copies can be produced and transmitted to other locations at virtually no cost.

Monitoring for treaty compliance would also be hard given the rapid changes in technology and in methods and tools of attack. New computer viruses, worms, Trojan horses, denial-of-service programmes, exploit scripts, and other types of cyber weapons are continually being developed.

There are tools for detecting the presence of some cyber weapons, but they are not perfect, and cyber weapons often evolve in ways that foil detectors. Most anti-viral tools, for example, scan mainly for known viruses. One of the costliest viruses, ILOVEYOU, succeeded in part because it was new and escaped detection. Further, the presence and distribution of cyber weapons can be concealed with the use of encryption, steganography, anonymity, and other information hiding tools and methods.

Verification and monitoring for compliance would also require a level of intrusion that few if any people would find acceptable. It would be impossible to know if a government agency, for example, had access to prohibited cyber weapons without scanning all computers and storage devices owned by the agency, including all classified systems. No agency would agree to this. Scanning the personal computers of citizens likewise would be unacceptable, as it would violate human rights. The best that could be achieved would be to scan the public spaces of network servers for certain hacking tools. This might help keep the tools from some, but it would not keep them from determined individuals, who could swap them through private channels. Nor would it keep them from governments, who could develop them on their own.

Another issue is that even if the presence of a controlled cyber weapon is detected, it would be impossible to find and eliminate all copies, which might be stored on thousands of computers all over the world. Some of these servers could be located in places that are not party to a cyber arms control treaty or that operate safe havens, for example, the offshore Sealand platform, which is said to be the world's smallest sovereign territory. Hacking tools can be published through systems such as Publius that use encryption and distributed storage techniques to create an environment that is highly resistant to censorship.

Security

There is another argument against enacting cyber arms controls that prohibit the production and distribution of attack tools. Such controls would curtail research and publication in the area of computer security. It is not possible to build strong defences without knowing what attacks are possible and what vulnerabilities might be exploited, so investigating methods and tools of attack is an important element of cyber security. Indeed, it is frequently argued that "full disclosure," which includes publishing information about system vulnerabilities and the tools that exploit them, contributes to security by making the information available to everyone and not just "the bad guys." Researchers can build on each other's work, thereby accelerating progress in information security. Further, it is argued, publication pushes the vendors to fix security flaws. While the merits of full disclosure, particularly the publication of the actual tools of attack, are debatable, it must be recognized that it is not just malicious hackers who support the concept.

System administrators and security consultants would also object if the controls prohibited them from using hacking tools to test their own systems or the systems of their clients for vulnerabilities. It is common to use many of the same types of tools used by hackers for this purpose, for example, scanners, password crackers, sniffers, and network monitoring tools. The difference lies in whether the tools are used for attack or defence.

Hacking tools are also used for "active defence," that is, launching some sort of operation against the perpetrator to trace their location or abort their attack. Governments especially might object if they could not use hacking tools against adversaries that disable or penetrate systems and threaten national security.

Privacy

To investigate crimes in cyberspace, law enforcement agencies need the capability to search and seize digital evidence and to intercept network communications. To facilitate these operations, they have asked for hardware and software tools and, in some cases, additional legal authorities. In the United States, for example, the FBI developed Carnivore, now called DCS1000, to support court-authorized Internet wiretaps. When installed at a subject's Internet Service Provider, DCS1000 intercepts particular message traffic belonging to the subject, for example, all e-mail messages sent to or from the subject, as specified in the court order. In the United Kingdom, the Regulation of Investigatory Powers (RIP) bill has provisions that facilitate government monitoring of Internet traffic and provide access to encryption keys.

These law enforcement advances have raised privacy concerns. Opponents of Carnivore argue that the tool could be misused in order to conduct mass surveillance or otherwise acquire evidence that was not legally permitted, although no evidence of abuse was put forth. Opponents of RIP argue that the ability of the government to demand encryption keys sets a dangerous precedent. If a cyber arms control treaty prohibited certain cyber weapons, the process of policing the Internet for these weapons would raise additional privacy issues. Scanning the personal computers of citizens would violate the privacy laws of many nations.

Free Speech

Restrictions on cyber weapons, particularly source code and scripts, would raise significant legal issues in countries with laws protecting speech. In the United States, speech is protected under the First Amendment, and software is considered to be a type of speech.

Treating cyber weapons in the form of software differently from more general information about cyber weapons is also problematic [under the First Amendment]. For example, a programmer can translate a mathematical or English-language description of an algorithm into a working programme. Should the programme be restricted but not the description? Further, source code can be embedded in prose or poetry, as illustrated by a version of the DeCSS, with commentary, in haiku form.

Professor David Touretzky of Carnegie Mellon University has over two dozen different versions of the DeCSS on his web site, including the haiku version and a "dramatic reading" of the code. It would be extraordinarily difficult to draw a line between what could be published and what could not.

Corporate Responsibilities and Liabilities

A cyber arms control treaty could have a substantial impact on industry. Industry might be required to implement costly mechanisms to control the use or spread of cyber weapons or to investigate violations of arms control. They might also be held liable for actions taken on their network in violation of laws stemming from the treaty.

Companies, particularly service providers, are also concerned about being burdened with subpoenas and court orders originating in foreign countries. Many companies already spend considerable resources responding to requests relating to crimes in their own countries.

Foreign Policy

It will be impossible to establish meaningful cyber arms controls if nation states are opposed. Information warfare covers a much broader range of activity than computer network attacks, however. It also includes psychological operations and perception management, deception, electronic warfare, and intelligence collection.

Many of these operations are used by governments during peacetime as well as during conflicts. It is, therefore, not surprising that any attempt to impose international restrictions on information warfare would meet with resistance.

[G]overnments might oppose a cyber arms control treaty is that they might be concerned that such a treaty could preclude computer espionage operations by prohibiting network penetrations. These operations are designed to acquire access to secrets without damaging data and resources. Because technologies such as encryption are hampering the ability of intelligence agencies to intercept communications, computer espionage might be regarded as an attractive, perhaps essential, alternative. Espionage is not considered to be an act of war or aggression, and computer espionage should be similarly regarded.

Governments might also oppose any treaty that restricts their ability to develop offensive cyber weapons on the grounds that such restrictions would hamper their ability to prepare an adequate cyber defence in the event of an attack. As noted earlier, a thorough understanding of attack methodologies and tools is essential for building a strong defence, and attack tools play an important role in assessing one's own defensive posture.

The position of the United States has been that it is premature to discuss negotiating an international agreement on information warfare, and that the energies of the international community are better spent cooperating to secure information systems against criminals and terrorists. Although the government takes the state-sponsored threat seriously, it does not see this threat as something that lends itself to an international treaty.

Criminal Law vs the Law of War

There are two general options for an international treaty relating to cyber arms. One is a treaty that pertains exclusively to the domestic crime laws and procedures of the signatories. It would have no bearing on the law of war and the military operations of sovereign states. The other option is a treaty that pertains to the law of war in addition to or in lieu of domestic laws.

If nation states are not interested in pursuing a cyber arms control treaty that limits state-level operations, a possible alternative might be some sort of agreement acknowledging that the law of war applies to cyberspace. Such an agreement could confirm that a computer network attack causing damage within a sovereign state is comparable to the use of force against that state, even if it is not considered to be an armed attack. It might establish general guidelines for proportionality. For example, the use of nuclear weapons to counter a cyber attack that did not lead to loss of life or injury would clearly constitute a disproportionate response. An agreement might also establish that computer espionage operations, like other forms of espionage, are considered lawful under international law and provide conditions under which such operations could be conducted.

TECHNOLOGY-DRIVEN TERRORISM: THE NATURE OF THE CYBER TERRORIST THREAT

In the 1983 movie WarGames, Matthew Broderick's character breached the Pentagon computer system and almost started World War III. Since, then, much of the Western world has been both captivated and mystified by the idea of computer conflict, hacking and, more recently, cyber terrorism. The concept of cyber terrorism is rooted in two fields of study: information technology and asymmetric conflict. First, the modern technological revolution, originating in the 1980s, has led authors such as Alvin and Heidi Toffler to argue that information technologies are transforming industrial societies into information-based societies. Occurring primarily in developed, industrialised regions, there exists an increasing reliance upon complex networks and modern technologies for the proper functioning of society. This post-industrial period has been coined the "Information Age". Manuel Castells argues that the most recent period of the Information Age is one dominated by networks. As a new socio-political and economic configuration, "network society" consists of a "space of flows" where various transactions and encounters take place.

Second, asymmetric threats, specifically in the form of terrorism, have existed since, the dawn of warfare. Defined by the U.S., Joint Chiefs of staff as attempts to circumvent or undermine a superior military power's strengths while exploiting its weaknesses, using methods that differ from the superior military power's expected mode of operations, the recent escalation in asymmetric threats is commonly considered a result of the demonstration of U.S., military might in the first Gulf War. Not limited solely to cyber terrorism, those seeking to challenge U.S., power have recognised that conflict on the traditional battlefield using conventional military weaponry is no longer feasible. As such, the threat of cyber terrorism comes from both states and non-state actors and, though negative, is perhaps an inevitable consequence of the transition to an information-based society.

DEFINING THE BOUNDARIES OF CYBER TERRORISM

Attempts to define cyber terrorism suffer from the same dilemmas as definitions of terrorism. Generally, cyber terrorism is a result of the convergence of technology and terrorism, and consists of two mutually dependent elements. First, it refers to attacks and threats of attacks against computers, networks and the information stored within them, for the purpose of intimidating or influencing a government or society to further political or social objectives. Second, the attack results in violence against persons or property, or at least causes enough harm to generate fear.

The definition is a reinterpretation of mainstream characterisations of terrorism infused with technological terminology. While it should be noted that terrorism is still somewhat of a contested term, section 83.01 of the *Anti-Terrorism Act* provides an in-depth classification within the Canadian context. A cyber terrorist differs from a terrorist who uses technology. Cyber terrorism consists of an attack on a technological factor using another technological factor. This is distinct from a terrorist utilising technology to commit a traditional act of terrorism, and is also distinct from a terrorist using non-technological means to commit an act of terrorism against a network of computer system. For example, an act of cyber terrorism occurs when an individual or organisation uses a computer network to overload and destroy a national power-management system. Cyber terrorism does not occur when a suicide bomber destroys an electrical grid – nor does cyber terrorism occur if a terrorist uses the World Wide Web to acquire information on building a chemical weapon. Distinctions must also be made between cyber terrorism and hacktivism, the latter being a term coined by scholars to describe the marriage of hacking with political activism.

While politically motivated, hacktivism differs from cyber terrorism in that the former seeks to protest and disrupt, not to kill, physically injure, or terrify. As such, serious attacks against critical infrastructure, depending on their impact, could be acts of terrorism; whereas attacks that disrupt non-essential services would most likely not. This distinction between cyber terrorism and cyber dissent is of significance as it addresses, to a limited extent specifically in the field of computer technology, historical critiques on the inability of legal institutions in recognising legitimate and/or illegitimate dissent. In the context of terrorism contrasted with dissent, self-branded civil libertarian, Irwin Cotler, makes a persuasive argument on the differentiation by outlining some of the key principles that underpin Canada's *Anti-Terrorism Act*, while also addressing some of the concerns.

He argues that the inclusion of section 83.01(1)(b)(ii)(E) seeks to ensure that "any advocacy, protest, dissent or work stoppage activity, even if unlawful, even if attended by violence, even if it causes disruption to a public or private essential service or facility, would not be considered a terrorist activity". However, it remains to be seen whether this policy will withstand public and governmental pressure once a test case is presented to the courts.

WHY USE CYBER TERRORISM

As a result of globalisation, computerisation and the emergence of a network society, numerous authors have argued that cyber terrorism is becoming increasingly attractive to terrorists for several reasons. First, cyber terrorism is generally perceived to be more cost-effective than traditional terrorist methods. Typical computers and phone or broadband internet connections are generally much cheaper and easier to acquire than traditional types of weaponry, such as explosives and military-grade vehicles. Cyber terrorist attacks also do not result in the attacker's death, as is the case with suicide bombers, and as is potentially the case in traditional acts of terrorism.

Second, cyber terrorism possesses a certain amount of anonymity not found in more traditional forms of terrorism. The global extension of computer technologies in post-industrial societies has facilitated terrorist mobility and deployability. As such, it has become increasingly difficult for security agencies to determine the real identities of the terrorists. This complex obstacle is further enhanced by the lack of customs, borders or checkpoints within cyber space. While the fact remains that all Internet traffic passes through at least one of thirteen central servers that act as the foundation of the World Wide Web, the sheer amount of information transferred creates considerable challenges for data analysis and effective intelligence collection.

Third, the quantity and quality of targets increases as society moves towards further dependence on information technologies. The multiplicity of potential targets is already enormous, ranging from government military systems to civilian economic and scientific networks.

Fourth, cyber terrorism removes or reduces the requirement for geographical proximity to the target. This virtually eliminates the traditional requirements for physical and psychological training to avoid capture, and risk of mortality. The ability to conduct cyber terrorism remotely is a key factor in the transnational nature of committing terrorist acts and in recruiting new members.

Fifth, cyber terrorism can potentially have a direct affect on a larger number of people than traditional terrorist methods, thereby generating widespread effects and increasing awareness of particular causes. While a suicide bomber may destroy a building, killing the tens or hundreds of individuals inside, a cyber terrorist attack on a waste-management or energy system has the potential to kill or injure thousands, if not millions of people.

IS THERE A REAL THREAT

It should be emphasised that no single cyber terrorist attack has been recorded – that is, categorised as such. This begs the question of whether cyber terrorism is a real threat. Current discussions revolve around military systems, intelligence networks, government systems and critical infrastructure. First, suggestions have been put forth that cyber terrorists could compromise military systems, such as a nuclear missile launch facility, and either launch a missile or disable the entire system.

Currently, the cyber terrorism threat of this type is non-existent. Government statements indicate that major military systems, such as the Canadian Department of National Defence, the Pentagon, and nuclear launch facilities, are "air-gapped". That is, they are not physically connected to external networks such as the Internet. The implied conclusion is that computer network attacks would be ineffective against these types of military networks.

However, during a U.S., military exercise conducted by the National Security Agency (NSA), attackers using tools available on the Internet were able to gain access to several key U.S., systems. While the details remain classified, the report on the exercise concluded that military infrastructure could be disrupted and troop deployments could be hindered. Most security and intelligence systems are also protected in the same way as military infrastructure. The Canadian Security and Intelligence Service (CSIS), the Central Intelligence Agency (CIA) and the Federal Bureau of Investigation (FBI) all utilise stand-alone networks. Martin Libicki, a defence analyst at the National Defence University and RAND Corporation, indicates that this is partially rooted in the general paranoia that exists within intelligence agencies, and that such paranoia is a sound governing principle when considering cyber security. Like most military systems, security and intelligence systems in their current form are shielded from computer attack. More general government systems, in both the United States and in Canada, are further protected by the development of proprietary systems, unique to each branch of government. While this has often led to difficulties in cooperation between agencies, it has also provided protection in that only a select few individuals understand the systems well enough to violate them. In an ironic twist, inefficiency breeds security.

While government systems may be connected to external networks, such as the Internet, the proprietary nature of current computer applications in combination with screening processes for new employees ensures a relatively high level of security from the cyber terrorist threat. Critical infrastructure consists of less-protected secondary targets, such as power grids, oil pipelines, water-treatment and waste-management systems. Particularly in the United States, most of these systems are privatised and are not currently as of much a concern as military or government systems. As such, critical infrastructure systems are less secure than military, intelligence or government systems.

Concerns over the susceptibility of U.S., critical infrastructure are significant to Canadians due to the numerous connections between Canadian and U.S., systems. Additionally, 85 per cent of Canada's critical infrastructure is owned by stake holders other than the federal government. However, while critical infrastructure is possibly more vulnerable to cyber terrorism, it is still quite secure. These systems are under constant threat from natural disasters such as hurricanes, floods or tornados, and company employees are trained to act in emergency scenarios.

Nonetheless, as a consequence of openness to external networks and lower security thresholds, a cyber terrorist threat to critical infrastructure does exist. Cyber attacks differ from traditional emergencies and natural disasters in that they can be directed and concentrated at specific weak points in a computer network. Attackers were also able to gain access to power grid and emergency systems, resulting in service disruptions. Currently, it seems as though the greatest threat to the aforementioned systems comes not from cyber terrorism, but from two other factors: insider action and deregulation. Insiders possess specialised knowledge that is difficult, if not impossible, for outsiders to acquire. Disgruntled staff or vengeance-seeking former employees may possess both the resolve and the means to wreak havoc on internal computer and information systems. For example, in 2000, a disgruntled consultant hacked into a waste management control system and let loose millions of gallons of raw sewage on the town. While this potential problem may be alleviated through comprehensive employee screening processes, such security measures may be decreasingly feasible as a result of deregulation.

Second, deregulation potentially leads to an increased risk of cyber terrorism. An amplified focus on profitability has forced utility companies and other critical infrastructure businesses to move increasing proportions of their operations to the Internet in search of greater efficiency and lower costs. This may result in further risk and exposure to cyber terrorist threats.

Growing cross-border interdependency will play an increasingly important role in the vulnerability of vital networks. For example, strong links between Canadian and U.S., critical infrastructure were demonstrated during the 2003 Canada-U.S., blackout, in which a transformer station in Cleveland malfunctioned, causing power outages affecting 40 million people in Canada and the north-western United States. In sum, despite current concerns over the vulnerabilities of military, security and intelligence, government and critical infrastructure systems, the nature of these systems currently suggests that such concerns are generally unfounded, though a potential threat is present. While dangers to critical infrastructure systems exist, in the form of insider action and deregulation, a "digital Pearl Harbour" has yet to occur.

AN EXAGGERATED THREAT

The relatively insignificant threat of a cyber terrorist attack brings forth the question of why the threat is exaggerated. The reasons behind this are four-fold. First, as Dorothy E. Denning, a professor of computer science speaking before the U.S., House Armed Services Committee, has observed, "cyber terrorism and cyber attacks are sexy right now. It's novel, original, it captures people's imagination".

As such, the concept of cyber terrorism has symbolic power that creates compelling and frightening scenarios, influencing perceptions and contributing to the remaining three reasons below. In addition to the symbolic impact of cyber terrorism, the mass media frequently fail to distinguish between hacktivism and cyber terrorism, often exaggerating the threat of the latter. The two are not analogous. Additionally, misunderstandings between computer crime and cyber terrorism have also surfaced. Ambiguity about the very meaning of "cyber terrorism" has confused the public and given rise to many misrepresentations.

Third, there is a general fear of the unknown. Despite the advent of Third Wave society, many people, including most lawmakers and government officials, still do not fully understand and therefore tend to fear both computer technology and terrorism. As a result, psychological distress and the desire for self-preservation increase the likelihood of accepting unnecessary measures to combat an exaggerated threat. Fourth, some groups are eager to exploit this ignorance. National security officials are inclined to take measures to increase their presence and influence in government, while the computer technology industry, still recovering from the collapse of the high-tech bubble, seeks to regain its economic foothold.

Any response to a cyber terrorist threat requires enhanced technology, training and maintenance. Some politicians have "played the role of prophets of doom", purposely stoking fears of cyber terrorism, whether out of genuine conviction or from a desire to create public anxiety in order to advance a political agenda. While the potential threat of cyber terrorism is currently exaggerated, many analysts predict an increase in the actual threat. Looking at the various trends in military transformation, technological innovation and terrorist sophistication, the threat of cyber terrorism and computer-based attacks in expected to increase in the future for three principal reasons. First, the next generation of terrorists is now growing up in an increasingly digital world, alongside or integrated into post-industrial society, and will therefore be progressively more proficient in the use of information and computer technologies.

An example of recent activity, though not classified as cyber terrorism, is *Titan Rain,* the name given to a series of attacks against the U.S., since, 2003, in which the networks at Lockheed martin and NASA were infiltrated. Second, cyber terrorism may also become more attractive as the real and virtual worlds become more closely coupled. Increasing demands for efficiency and interoperability in critical infrastructure, government systems and potentially intelligence systems will ultimately result in elevated degrees of exposure to outside networks, and therefore cyber terrorist attacks. For example, the push by the U.S., military towards the network-centric warfare doctrine has resulted in new attempts at military transformation and integration.

The Global Information Grid, which seeks to encompass the end-to-end set of information capabilities, is a primary example. In terms of supervisory control and data acquisition (SCADA) systems, they are no longer only on stand-alone networks – connections between SCADA systems via the Internet are perceived as better for business. While SCADA systems are solely for the management and supervision of critical infrastructure (such as power-grid systems), their intentional or unintentional misuse can still cause damage. During a no-notice exercise performed by the U.S., Department of Defence, operators at a power management station were fooled by manipulated SCADA data into taking actions that would have damaged the system.

Third, success in the "war on terror" on the traditional battlefield may result in terrorists turning increasingly towards unconventional weapons such as cyber terrorism. The cost-effectiveness (in both human and economic terms), anonymity, abundance of critical targets and geographical freedom provide several incentives for terrorists to experiment with this new method. As such, while the current conjecture regarding the cyber terrorist threat is exaggerated, the expected increase in cyber terrorist activity demands that legal and technological remedies be explored.

COUNTER-TERRORISM I: SECURING A NETWORK SOCIETY—MODES OF PREVENTION

Indicating that no acts of cyber terrorism have occurred, does not necessarily imply that the potential cyber terrorist threat should not be addressed. Irwin Cotler argues that the nature of security legislation, particularly in regards to terrorism, is preventative rather than reactive– that it is necessary to stop acts of terrorism, including cyber terrorism, before they occur. While the extent and scope of preventative approaches should be questioned, the following portion of this chapter examines current and potential legal and political mechanisms at various scales for combating the threat of cyber terrorism.

EXISTING DOMESTIC LAW

Canadian domestic legal mechanisms are insufficient for addressing terrorism, and especially cyber terrorism. The transnational nature of the threat, severely limits the utility of federal or sub-federal law. Of particular interest here is the lack of geographic restrictions on acts of cyber terrorism. Not only can cyber terrorism occur from outside the territorial boundaries of the state, but acts can originate from numerous foreign states simultaneously. Therefore, domestic mechanisms such as the U.S., terrorism watch lists are either inadequate or inefficient.

The dilemma rests on the rise of the network society and increasing dependence on information and computer technologies for the production of everyday life. Additionally, considerations of national sovereignty and issues of jurisdiction emerge when investigating or prosecuting transnational criminal acts. The same can be said for addressing cyber terrorism. While Canadian security legislation, such as the *Anti-Terrorism Act* (ATA), addresses acts of terrorism against Canadian citizens abroad, it cannot take legal action against cyber terrorism without the consent of the foreign government from which the cyber terrorist act originated. National sovereignty remains enforced and universal jurisdiction is currently non-existent. As such, existing domestic legal mechanisms are insufficient.

BILATERAL AGREEMENTS

Bilateral agreements may not be feasible due to the mobility and deployability of cyber terrorism, as well as bureaucratic impracticability. First, cost-effectiveness, the global extension of computer technologies and lack of geographic restrictions suggests that cyber terrorist attacks can originate in almost any country. Second, with over 200 countries enjoying access to the Internet and related communications technologies, bilateral agreements are bureaucratically unfeasible. As such, governments must approach the issue at the international scale. Whereas Canada's *Securing an Open Society* is a national strategy, securing a network society requires approaching the issue transnationally.

International Agreements I: Combating Terrorism

Common international platforms are required to address the terrorist threat, and there are two components of international agreements worth considering: international law and policy harmonisation. International law originating within international, multilateral institutions can most successfully address cyber terrorism. While there has been disagreement over whether a universal definition of terrorism can be ascertained, the United Nations has successfully issued international legislation concerning weapons of terrorism, and regarding supporters of terrorism.

Multilateral institutions are particularly crucial because of the variegated definitions of terrorism and the legitimacy that comes from agreements among several states in an open and transparent forum. The legislating of any international law on cyber terrorism should consider three factors. First, a definition of what constitutes a cyber terrorist act should be established. Distinctions can and should be made between acts of cyber terrorism and acts of cyber dissent or hacktivism. Second, a designation of what actions are required for a legal response should be determined. This includes whether a target should be notified before retribution for a cyber terrorist act is executed, and under what circumstances. Third, the agreement should promote transnational cooperation. National interests should be compromised to the minimal extent possible when addressing the attribution of cyber terrorist attacks and subsequent potential retribution. Policy harmonisation is a consequence of common international platforms. International requirements for the legislating of domestic policies on cyber terrorism increase domestic and international security and transnational cooperation.

An instructive example, addressed specifically at terrorism, is *UN Security Council Resolution 1373*. A second example is the *Council of Europe Convention on Cyber -Crime*. Signed by Canada in 2001, this treaty is "the first-ever international treaty to address criminal law and procedural aspects of various types of criminal behaviour directed against computer systems, networks or data and other types of similar misuse". While not addressed specifically at cyber terrorism, the cyber crime treaty requires states to criminalise certain forms of abuse of computer systems and certain crimes when they are committed using computer systems. The treaty also supports international cooperation to detect, investigate and prosecute these criminal offences, as well as to collect electronic evidence of any criminal offence.

However, the *Convention on Cyber-Crime* does not include key elements of the terrorism definition. Specifically, it does not refer to political, ideological or religious motivations or objectives. Therefore, current international legal mechanisms are insufficient in addressing the cyber terrorist threat and new agreements must be established. The secondary danger is the collection of data by governments from commercial actors. This activity lacks transparency and accomplishes an "end-run around the checks otherwise applicable when government seeks personal information". Information-gathering requires governmental regulation, oversight and transparency, a feature not common in the commercial harvesting of personal data.

International Agreements II: Addressing the Causes of Terrorism

International agreements on combating terrorism necessarily require complementing initiatives on other issues that are perceived to be causes of individuals and groups turning to terrorist methods. The process of determining the causes of terrorism deserves much longer treatment than this chapter can provide. However, international policies directed at the alleviation of poverty, war, repression and other forms of social, political and economic exploitation should be a counterpart of any counter-terrorism campaign. Information and communications technologies can assist in this process by extending the ability of governments to understand which regions require aid and to the development of a transnationally scaled civil society that seeks to drive marginalised individuals away from destructive forms of political action.

COUNTER-TERRORISM II: TECHNOLOGY-DRIVEN SURVEILLANCE AND INTELLIGENCE

There are two methods of defending against cyber terrorism: passive defence and active defence. Passive defence is another name for target hardening, involving the use of technologies such as firewalls or cryptography to protect information technology assets and the data stored within. A considerable part of the problem is the combination of demands for large-scale connectivity and access, as well as the massive number of owners, operators and users of these systems and networks.

As Goodman argues, "the domain of actors in cyber space is much larger and more diversified than is the case with more traditional security issues." Analyses of private sector products and systems indicate that software quality assurance is problematic. Defective or poorly-designed products rushed to market without adequate concern for security raise many questions about whether regulation will be necessary. Additionally, in both the public and private sectors, the many legacy systems still in use were not designed with security in mind. Even presently, security is often perceived to be in conflict with design criteria focusing on accessibility and data throughput. Security is commonly identified with reduced efficiency and impaired functionality. Active defence seeks to determine the identity of the attacker and possibly initiate a counter-attack.

One form of active defence, discussed here, is computer-driven surveillance. An effective response to the threat of terrorism and cyber terrorism requires international cooperation, but such cooperation must be reinforced with transnational surveillance mechanisms. Technology-driven intelligence gathering methods can be more effective and less intrusive than traditional forms of surveillance and intervention. As such, while the following portion provides an analysis of the legal and political implications of new technology in counter-terrorism efforts. While there are currently no global surveillance systems with the full participation of all countries, two more limited types of systems are presently in operation: domestic systems and transnational systems.

Domestic systems, such as the FBI surveillance system known as Carnivore, are inward-looking. While domestic systems may be more comprehensive than transnational systems, the former does not infringe upon the national sovereignty rights of foreign countries, not does it violate the jurisdiction of foreign intelligence and security services. As such, neither bilateral nor international agreements are necessary for the legal functioning of domestic surveillance systems.

Transnational systems are a different breed altogether. These systems, such as ECHELON, are both inward-looking and outward-looking. Transnational systems are of a controversial nature due to a perceived lack of respect for national sovereignty rights and issues of jurisdiction. While transnational agreements or understandings are necessary for the functioning of transnational surveillance systems, such arrangements are often mired in secrecy. The features of transnational surveillance systems dictate that the types of transnational or international agreements are necessary for their legal operation.

ECHELON TRANSNATIONAL SURVEILLANCE SYSTEM

The ECHELON surveillance system began its current phase of development in 1971 as a component of the post-WWII UK/USA intelligence cooperation and information-sharing alliance. Using electronic-intercept stations and space satellites, the purpose of ECHELON is generally signals intelligence (SIGINT), and specifically communications intelligence (COMINT). The transnational surveillance system additionally has the capability to acquire other forms of intelligence and information. ECHELON captures military, political and diplomatic communications traffic from across the globe, though recent events have indicated that the system is also being used for economic purposes. ECHELON is not designed to eavesdrop on specific individuals. Instead, the surveillance system works on the basis of automated analysis. Messages and conversations are filtered though a computer system called Dictionary which detects keywords and phrases– a method of processing information is known as "data-mining." Five countries currently participate in the ECHELON system, providing global coverage through intercept ground stations and space-based satellites. Australia and its Defence Signals Directorate (DSD) monitors Indochina, Indonesia and Southern China.

The Government Communications Security Bureau (GCSB) of New Zealand covers the Western Pacific region. The United Kingdom's Government Communications Headquarters (GCHQ) monitors Europe, Africa and Russian territory west of the Urals. The National Security Agency (NSA) in the United States, possessing the most advanced and comprehensive surveillance infrastructure, covers Latin America, and Asia, as well as Asiatic Russia and northern China. Canada's Communications Security Establishment (CSE) monitors northern portions of the former Soviet Union, embassies around the world and central and southern parts of the Americas. Commentators argue that the nature of cyber terrorism demands that transnational surveillance systems be implemented to compliment international agreements, and that while legal issues and concerns over ECHELON in its current form will invariable arise, the basic transnational approach behind ECHELON is sound. The remainder of this chapter examines these legal dilemmas and explores some of the ways that surveillance systems such as ECHELON may gain increased or decreased legitimacy.

IMPLICATIONS OF TECHNOLOGICAL INTERVENTION IN THE AGE OF TERRORISM

Addressing matters of privacy and surveillance inevitably results in debates concerning oversight and the balancing of rights and security.

The following portion of this stage discusses these issues in five parts:

1. The proportionality test,
2. The existence of a right to privacy in the Canadian context,
3. The nature of automated surveillance; and an analytical section on "veil of ignorance",
4. The balancing act between the right to privacy and security; and
5. A proposal to remedy the problem of oversight.

THE PROPORTIONALITY TEST OR OAKES TEST

Derived from The Queen v. Oakes, the "Oakes test" considers S.1 of the Charter, which provides that:

- The *Canadian Charter of Rights and Freedoms* guarantees the rights and freedoms set out in it subject only to such *reasonable limits* prescribed by law as can be *demonstrably justified* in a free and democratic society.

In other words, the rights and freedoms under the *Charter* can be violated if the violation is reasonable and justifiable. The Supreme Court of Canada has defined a test for determining whether a violation is reasonable and justifiable. This test, referred to as the "*Oakes test*" or proportionality test, has two components: sufficient importance and proportionality. First, the government must demonstrate that its objective is sufficiently pressing and substantial to warrant the violation of a right or freedom. Second, the party invoking s.1 must show the means to be reasonable and demonstrably justified.

Proportionality itself has three requirements:

1. The measures must be fair and not arbitrary (the means chosen to limit rights and freedoms must be rationally connected to the objective);
2. There must be a minimal impairment of rights in achieving the objective; and
3. The detriments of the violation must not outweigh its benefits.

The *Oakes test* was further solidified in Canadian law after *Dagenais v. CBC*.

THE RIGHT TO PRIVACY

While not expressed explicitly in the Charter of Rights and Freedoms, the right to privacy has been interpreted through the Supreme Court of Canada's purposive approach to s.8 of the Charter, which provides that:

- Section 8. Everyone has the right to be secure against unreasonable search or seizure

Through precedence in case law, the right to a reasonable expectation of privacy has been demonstrated in Canadian law. As La Forest J. stated in *R. v. Dyment*, "the restraints imposed on government to pry into the lives of the citizen go to the essence of a democratic state". Historically, privacy was associated with private property, whose possession protected against intruders. "If the rights of private property were respected, and the curtains of the home were pulled, the King's agents could watch from a distance but would have no way of finding out what was going on inside". However, technological developments diminished the protections provided by property rights, and new interpretations of law or new legislation were required. As a result, the Supreme Court of Canada (SCC) has indicated that s.8 of the *Charter of Rights and Freedoms* provides for the right to a reasonable expectation of privacy.

Canadian case law has identified three different types of privacy:

1. Personal;
2. Territorial; and
3. Informational.

Personal privacy includes the protection of bodily integrity, as indicated in *R. v. Golden* and in *R. v. Stillman*. Territorial privacy includes the protection of privacy in the home, being the place where the most intimate and private activities are likely to take place. As per Cory J., in *R. v. Silveira*, "[t]here is no place on earth where persons can have a greater expectation of privacy than within their 'dwelling-house'". Other forms of territorial privacy include: in the perimeter space around the home, in commercial space, in private cars, in a school, and in prison. Territorial privacy is used as an analytical tool for evaluating the reasonableness of a person's expectation of privacy.

Much more controversial than personal privacy and territorial privacy is informational privacy, defined as "the claim of individuals, groups, or institutions to determine for themselves when, how, and to what extent information about them is communicated to others". The existence and lawfulness of a right to a reasonable expectation of informational privacy has been indicated in *R. v. S.A.B.* and in *R. v. Law*.

The "reasonable" nature of the expectation of privacy is derived from two factors:

1. The *Oakes test*; and
2. The "totality of the circumstances" test.

First, the expectation of privacy can be violated if the objective is reasonable and demonstrably justified. The *Oakes test* demands that two requirements be met before the violation of a right or freedom can occur: sufficient importance of the objective, and proportionality between the limiting measure and the objective.

Second the reasonable expectation of privacy is subject to the "totality of the circumstances" test set out by Cory J. in *R. v. Edwards*. Briefly, this test asks two questions: Did the respondent have a reasonable expectation of privacy? And if there was a reasonable expectation of privacy in this case, was it violated by police conduct? These questions must be specifically tailored, depending on facts of the case.

Thus the expectation of privacy can "reasonably" be violated:

- If the objective and means of the violation is in accordance with s.1 of the *Charter*; and
- If there is either no reasonable expectation of privacy, or if a reasonable expectation of privacy was violated by the lawful conduct of law enforcement.

A potential third factor affecting the "reasonable" nature of the expectation of privacy is s.33 of the *Charter*, though the relevance of the non-withstanding clause would depend on the nature of the violating legislation. Nonetheless, the development of case law suggests that Canada is either progressing towards or already situated at a position in which the right to privacy in constitutionally protected, but subject to the context of the crisis or emergency at hand.

AUTOMATED SURVEILLANCE AND THE "VEIL OF IGNORANCE"

The nature of ECHELON and other electronic surveillance systems is such that information is automatically filtered by computer systems. ECHELON is not designed to eavesdrop on specific individuals. Instead, the surveillance system works on the basis of automated analysis. Messages and conversations are filtered though a computer system called Dictionary which detects keywords and phrases.

This structure is analogous to John Rawls' conception of a "veil of ignorance." While those developing the surveillance system are not completely disinterested, automated analysis removes personal biases that pervade other forms of intelligence gathering. Automated systems, while not immune from subjectivity due to their construction by humans, are more capable of eliminating the discrimination often witnessed in human intelligence (HUMINT) or in law enforcement. The use of computer-based keyword and phrase analysis results in amplified complexities and increased difficulties in manipulating the system. Currently, electronic surveillance systems are the most objective components of the intelligence apparatus. However, the analysis of electronically-gathered information is the realm in which increased subjectivity and bias come into play. As such the issue concerns how the data is analysed rather than how information is collected.

BALANCING THE RIGHT TO PRIVACY AND SECURITY

Taking into consideration the threat of cyber terrorism, the preventative nature of law, the reasonable expectation of privacy and the automated nature of transnational surveillance, the "*Oakes test*" can be employed in analysing the balance between the privacy and security. When situating the risk in relation to national security, a tangible threat of cyber terrorism is non-existent, yet a potential threat remains. In the post-9/11 security environment, increasingly driven by information technology, preventative measures are necessary for the maintenance of security.

The potential number of casualties resulting from a cyber terrorist attack on critical infrastructure, or government systems is sufficient to warrant a limitation on the right to privacy. Therefore the first requirement of the "*Oakes test*" is satisfied. In the second component of the "*Oakes test*," the rational connection requirement is satisfied due to the transnational nature of cyber terrorism. Transnational surveillance is a prerequisite for any success derived from international agreements.

However the issue becomes more problematic when considering the final two requirements: proportionality between the effects of the violation and the objective; and the minimal impairment of rights. This complexity is the result of the secretive nature of the ECHELON system. To what extent does ECHELON eavesdrop on the global communication networks? Who has ultimate control over the intelligence acquired? What restrictions exist on access to and operationalisation of the intelligence collected? These questions are of significant importance in analysing the balance between rights and security. Without a deeper understanding on the functioning of the ECHELON surveillance system, the application of the "*Oakes test*" cannot be fully realised. However, a consideration of the automated nature of analysis in combination with an appreciation of the potential threat posed by terrorism and cyber terrorism may be sufficient to establish that a balance between rights and security in the utilisation of ECHELON can be achieved.

If further information on the functioning of ECHELON is unavailable for logistical or security reasons, oversight mechanisms will increase confidence in the stability, legality and efficiency of the ECHELON surveillance system. A potential issue, though outside the scope of this chapter, is the prospective balance required between transnational privacy and international security. While citizens may tolerate domestic surveillance within reasonable limits, it remains to be seen whether surveillance by a foreign government will be as acceptable.

Bibliography

Eric Maiwald: *Fundamentals of Network Security*, Tata McGraw-Hill, Delhi, 2010.

G Ram Kumar: *Cyber Crimes : A Primer on Internet Threats and Email Abuses*, Viva Books, Delhi, 2006.

G.S. Bajpai: *On Cyber Crime and Cyber Law*, Serials Publications, Delhi, 2011.

Gary Bahadur, Jason Inasi and Alex De Carvalho: *Securing the Clicks: Network Security in the Age of Social Media*, Tata McGraw Hill, Delhi, 2012.

Harish Goel: *Cyber Crime*, Rajat Publication, Delhi, 2007.

Jayant Malik: *Cyber Crime and Terrorism*, Swastik Publication, Delhi, 2011.

John Mallery: *Hardening Network Security*, Tata McGraw-Hill, Delhi, 2005.

Mohan Sen Gupta: *Cyber Crimes*, Centrum Press, Delhi, 2012.

Paul Grishman: *Cyber Terrorism: The Use Of The Internet For Terrorist Purposes*, Axis Publications, Delhi, 2010.

Paul T Augastine: *Combating Cyber Crime*, Crescent Publication, Delhi, 2007.

Paul T Augustine: *Cyber Crime and Legal Issues*, Crescent Publication, Delhi, 2007.

Pinkesh Anand: *Network Security*, Centrum Press, Delhi, 2011.

Pramod Kr. Singh: *Laws on Cyber Crimes : Alongwith IT Act and Relevant Rules*, Book Enclave, Delhi, 2007.

R K Suri and T N Chhabra: *Cyber Crime*, Pentagon Press, Delhi, 2002.

R.K. Pradhan: *Cyber Crime and Cyber Terrorism*, Manglam Publication, Delhi, 2010.

R.K. Pradhan: *Cyber Crime and Cyber Terrorism*, Manglam Publication, Delhi, 2010.

Rajan Nagia: *The Transnational Dimension of Cyber Crime and Terrorism*, Cyber Tech Publication, Delhi, 2010.

Randhir Pal: *Cyber Terrorism and Military Preparedness: An International Prospective*, Swastik Publication, Delhi, 2012.

Roberta Bragg: *Network Security: The Complete Reference*, Tata McGraw-Hill, Delhi, 2009.

S.K. Bansal: *Cyber Crime*, A P H Publication, Delhi, 2011.

S.R. Sharma: *Dimensions of Cyber Crime*, Anmol Publication, Delhi, 2004.

S.R. Sharma: *Indian Legislation on Cyber Crime*, Anmol Publication, Delhi, 2004.

Stuart McClure & Joel Scambray: *Hacking Exposed: Network Security Secrets and Solutions (With DVD)*, Tata McGraw-Hill, Delhi, 2008.

V.D. Dudeja: *Cyber Crimes and Law : Crimes in Cyber Space—Scams and Frauds (2 Vols-Set)*, Commonwealth Publication, Delhi, 2002.

V.D. Dudeja: *Cyber Crimes and Law Enforcement*, Commonwealth Publication, Delhi, 2003.

Vikram Singh Jaswal and Shweta Thakur Jaswal: *Cyber Crime and Information Technology Act, 2000*, Regal Publications, Delhi, 2014.

Y.K. Singh: *Cyber Crime and Law*, Shree Publication, Delhi, 2005.

Yogesh Barua and Denzyl P. Dayal: *Cyber Crimes : Notorious Aspects of the Humans and the Net (4 Vols-Set)*, Dominant Publication, Delhi, 2001.

Index